Gamified Approaches to Advertising and Marketing Communication

M. Nur Erdem
https://orcid.org/0000-0002-7034-201X
Ondokuz Mayıs University, Turkey

Cansu Mayadağlı
https://orcid.org/0000-0001-8919-0880
Ondokuz Mayıs University, Turkey

IGI Global
Scientific Publishing
Publishing Tomorrow's Research Today

Vice President of Editorial Melissa Wagner
Director of Acquisitions Mikaela Felty
Director of Book Development Jocelynn Hessler
Production Manager Mike Brehm
Cover Design Jose Rosado

Published in the United States of America by
IGI Global Scientific Publishing
701 East Chocolate Avenue
Hershey, PA, 17033, USA
Tel: 717-533-8845 | Fax: 717-533-7115
Website: https://www.igi-global.com E-mail: cust@igi-global.com

Library of Congress Cataloging-in-Publication Data

Names: Erdem, M. Nur, 1976- editor | Mayadağlı, Cansu, 1988- editor
Title: Gamified approaches to advertising and marketing communication / [edited by] M. Nur Erdem, Cansu Mayadağlı.
Description: Hershey, PA : IGI Global Scientific Publishing, [2026] | Includes bibliographical references and index. | Summary: "This book examines the role of games in the digitalization process, ofen with reference to their individual, social, and sectoral impacts, as well as how they are used in marketing communication and advertising"-- Provided by publisher.
Identifiers: LCCN 2025036611 (print) | LCCN 2025036612 (ebook) | ISBN 9798337363097 hardcover | ISBN 9798337363103 paperback | ISBN 9798337363110 ebook
Subjects: LCSH: Communication in marketing | Advertising | Gamification
Classification: LCC HF5415.123 .G36 2026 (print) | LCC HF5415.123 (ebook) | DDC 658.8/02--dc23/eng/20260126
LC record available at https://lccn.loc.gov/2025036611
LC ebook record available at https://lccn.loc.gov/2025036612

British Cataloguing in Publication Data
A Cataloguing in Publication record for this book is available from the British Library.

Editorial Advisory Board

Table of Contents

Detailed Table of Contents

One of the most significant trends in marketing communication strategies in recent years has been to consider digital games as advertising platforms and to support brand visibility efforts with in-game ad placements. This study will focus on the role of ads placed in digital games in marketing communications and examine the impact of in-game brand placements. The study utilizes a qualitative research approach, examining digital games such as Subway Surfers and Block Blast using content analysis. The analysis focuses on the type of in-game ad, its location and position, duration, potential relevance to the game, brand visibility, and its relationship to the user context. This analysis examines the awareness-raising potential of in-game advertising, its relationship with users and the game context, ethical responsibilities, and its contribution to brand visibility and sales strategies. The results of this study contribute to the field of research and offer important recommendations for brands, advertisers, and game developers, who are the primary focus of marketing communications.

Digital game advertising is one of the effective strategies advertisers use to create different experiences for younger generations. In this context, this study evaluates digital games as interactive narrative environments for brands. The study aims to examine digital game advertising within the context of brand identity, brand positioning, loyalty creating, and sustainable brand strategies from a theoretical and interpretive perspective. The study examines the theoretical aspects of digital game advertising and provides practical examples, focusing on brands' strategies within the digital ecosystem. In this context, practices such as in-game advertising,

With technological advancements, digital environments have become key spaces for entertainment, learning, and socialization. As individuals increasingly spend their free time online, brands have integrated advertising into these platforms, particularly through digital games, VR, AR, and mobile applications.These environments allow brands to reach audiences directly and deliver interactive, personalized, and engaging advertising experiences.Methods like in-game ads and advergames embed marketing messages naturally into user experiences, enhancing brand interaction, loyalty, and recall.Thus, digital recreation offers advertisers opportunities for targeted communication, creative engagement and data-driven strategy development across diverse digital touchpoints.

Gamification is changing how fashion interacts with consumers by leading them into new XR dimensions, challenging traditional marketing communication tools, resulting in heightened consumer engagement and improving marketing metrics like brand identification, enhanced favorability, and purchase intent. This research aims to analyze the application of Gamification in the fashion industry, identifying the benefits and challenges of gamification technologies powered by Augmented reality, Virtual Reality, and Mixed realities and their impact on consumers' fashion purchase experience. By analyzing secondary data and various fashion brand case studies, this research aspires to understand the marketing communication strategies of fashion brands employing Gamification to create immersive experiences by proposing three categories: Gamification in fashion, fashion games, and fashion in games.

As global beauty retail is evolving continuously due to rapid digital disruption and changing consumer expectations, Sephora has emerged as a global leader in leveraging gamification - game mechanics such as rewards, challenges, interactive content, and status 3-tiers loyalty program to create highly immersive, and data-driven hyper-personalised experiences that complement simultaneously and bridge in-store and online environments. This chapter investigates Sephora's strategic use of

Foreword

In the contemporary communication landscape, where attention has become fragmented and audiences increasingly resist traditional persuasive forms, gamification has emerged as a transformative paradigm in advertising and marketing communication. No longer confined to the logic of rewards and incentives, gamification operates as a deeper communicative architecture—one that reorganizes interaction, experience, and meaning within digital environments. *Gamified Approaches to Advertising and Marketing Communication*, edited by M. Nur Erdem and Cansu Mayadağlı, offers a comprehensive and theoretically grounded exploration of this transformation, situating gamified communication at the intersection of digital games, interactive media, and evolving brand strategies.

At its core, this book advances a crucial insight: gamification is not merely a technique for increasing engagement but a structural mechanism that translates engagement into persuasion. In interactive environments shaped by rules, feedback loops, challenges, and participation, communication shifts from message transmission to experiential construction. Users do not simply receive messages; they enact, inhabit, and internalize them through structured interaction. In this sense, gamification functions as a narrative architecture embedded in the human mind's interaction with its environment—organizing action, expectation, and meaning through rule-governed experiential frameworks.

This perspective aligns with a broader philosophical understanding of communication: meaning does not exist independently of use, but emerges through practice, interaction, and lived experience. Gamified environments create precisely such rule-based communicative spaces, where persuasion operates not as external imposition but as experiential formation. By mobilizing intrinsic motivation, curiosity, and exploratory behavior, gamified communication transforms participation into a narrative experience and that experience into persuasive influence.

The chapters in this book illuminate this transformation from multiple vantage points. The discussion of digital game advertising and brand strategies demonstrates how interactive environments reshape brand visibility, positioning, and identity formation. Concepts such as around-game advertising and hybrid communication arenas extend the communicative field beyond the game itself, revealing how marketing messages circulate across interconnected digital ecosystems. These contributions collectively show that gamified communication is not limited to in-game mechanics but constitutes a broader experiential architecture spanning platforms, contexts, and user journeys.

Technological developments further intensify this transformation. The integration of artificial intelligence, voice-assisted interaction, virtual and augmented reality, and data-driven personalization expands the adaptive and responsive capacity of gamified communication. These technologies do not merely enhance efficiency; they reorganize the communicative relationship between humans and mediated environments, enabling new forms of experiential immersion and interactive persuasion. In such contexts, advertising becomes less about delivering messages and more about designing participatory environments in which users co-construct meaning through interaction.

The book also highlights the expanding domain of gamified communication across industries and experiential spaces. From fashion and digital recreation to phygital consumer journeys and immersive brand experiences, gamification emerges as a unifying framework connecting engagement, interaction, and relational communication. The emphasis on experiential design reflects a broader shift within marketing communication—from exposure-based persuasion toward participatory meaning construction.

What makes this book particularly valuable is its capacity to integrate conceptual, strategic, and technological perspectives within a coherent communicative framework. Rather than treating gamification as a passing trend, the book positions it as a central paradigm in the evolution of advertising and marketing communication. By examining how interactive systems shape attention, motivation, and interpretation, the book reveals gamification as a fundamental restructuring of persuasive communication in the digital age.

Through its theoretical depth and interdisciplinary scope, *Gamified Approaches to Advertising and Marketing Communication* provides an essential reference for scholars, researchers, practitioners, and designers seeking to understand the future of communication in interactive, data-driven, and participatory environments. It demonstrates that gamification is not only reshaping marketing strategies but redefining how communication itself is organized—moving from transmission to interaction, from representation to experience, and from persuasion as influence to persuasion as lived meaning.

Recep Yılmaz
Ondokuz Mayıs University, Turkey

Preface

INTRODUCTION

Throughout human history, every technological advancement has reshaped social dynamics. While some have led to incremental changes, others have brought revolutionary transformations. Digitalization can also be evaluated in this context. The effects of digitalization are clearly observed across many areas, including social, cultural, economic, and political spheres. Marketing and advertising are also included in these areas.

It is clear that the dynamics of the digital age we live in have significantly changed the dimensions and scope of communication and interaction between brands and consumers. In an era where traditional media, even if they continue to exist, can only maintain their effectiveness when integrated into digital media, marketing and advertising strategies have also undergone significant changes. In this structure, where the consumer's/user's attention and focus span are extremely short and measured in seconds, it is certainly not enough for brands to simply make themselves visible. Consumers/users expect brands to create new areas of experience for them, and brands aim to meet this expectation. Moreover, consumers also expect to be reached in interesting, fun, and creative ways. In this context, concepts such as "infotainment" (entertaining information), 'advertainment' (entertaining advertising), and "merchantainment" (entertainment with commercial content) have emerged and become quite popular in recent decades. It is precisely at this point that gamification has emerged as an area where interaction and entertainment intersect, and it is clear that it will play an important role in advertising and marketing communications in the present and the future.

Our aim in assembling this book is to provide a rich, interdisciplinary reference source that addresses the scope and complexity of marketing communication and advertising through gamification. We aim to shed light on the mechanisms and frameworks that define this landscape: the conceptual and theoretical dimensions of gamification in marketing communication, new technologies and trends, and also critical, ethical and activist approaches to gamified advertising and marketing communication practices.

The chapters featured in this book offer a diversity of perspectives that collectively work to:

- Clarify the dynamics of the gamification in advertising and marketing communication,
- Introduce new concepts, models, and theories relevant to the field,
- Provide concrete insights into current technologies, applications, and practices, and
- Evaluate the issue in terms of its ethical and critical dimensions.

We envision this volume as a valuable resource for a broad readership, including researchers, students, and professionals in communication, marketing, advertising, game design, and digital media. By bringing together contributions from voices across disciplines and sectors, this book seeks to inform, challenge, and inspire ongoing discourse and innovation in advertising and marketing communication through gamification. We thank all contributors who have lent their expertise and vision to this endeavor, and we hope that *Gamified Approaches to Advertising and Marketing Communication* will serve as a foundational reference for both current inquiry and future research.

ORGANIZATION OF THE BOOK

In Chapter 1, titled "Advertising, Marketing Communication and Digital Games: A Research on the Transformation of Brand Placement," the authors focus on the role of advertisements placed in digital games in marketing communication and examine the impact of in-game brand placements. Using content analysis method, the study focuses on the type, position, location, duration, potential relevance to the game, brand visibility, and relationship with the user context of in-game advertisements. Thus, a fundamental conceptual framework is presented regarding the awareness-raising potential of in-game advertising, its relationship with users and the game context, ethical responsibilities, and its contribution to brand visibility and sales strategies.

In Chapter 2, "Digital Game Advertising and Brand Strategies", digital game advertising is examined from a theoretical and interpretive perspective in the context of brand identity, brand positioning, loyalty building, and sustainable brand strategies.

Chapter 3, "Around Game Advertising: A Conceptual Framework and Cases of Application", focuses on another application that receives less attention in the literature but is frequently encountered, referred to as "Around Game Advertising" (AGA) by Smith and colleagues (2014). In this chapter a conceptual framework is outlined through the concepts of banner ads, cross-promotion, sponsorship, and/or interstitial ads.

In Chapter 4, "Esports as a Hybrid Communication Arena: Evolving Marketing Communication in Digital Spaces", the authors position e-sports as a hybrid communication arena within contemporary digital culture and conduct a study on Generation Z's participatory and interactive engagement models.

Chapter 5, "Artificial Intelligence in Video Game Advertising Opportunities, Challenges and Academic Perspectives", examines the role of artificial intelligence in video game advertising, emphasizing opportunities, challenges, and academic perspectives.

In Chapter 6, "Voice Assistans and Gamified Advertising: A New Dimension in Artificial Intelligence Powered Brand Interactions", the author provides a perspective on voice assistants as interactive, user-centered, and experience-focused through a literature review, case studies, and future projections.

In Chapter 7, "The Power of Digital Recreation: The Rise of Gaming, Virtual Reality and Mobile Advertising," the authors focused on digital recreation as leisure activities conducted through digital platforms such as video games, VR and AR applications, online education, social media, and mobile applications. The concept is evaluated in terms of how brands reach their target audiences directly and deliver interactive, personalized, and engaging advertising experiences.

Chapter 8, "Enhancing Marketing Communication through Gamification in the Fashion Industry", analyzes gamification applications in the fashion industry. The author discusses the benefits and challenges of gamification technologies supported by augmented reality, virtual reality, and mixed reality, and how these can shape consumers' new purchasing experiences in fashion area.

In Chapter 9, "Personalizing the Customer Journey Across Phygital Touchpoints: Sephora's Gamification Strategies", The authors examine the strategic use of gamification to adapt customer-focused game designs to enhance retail innovation, using the example of Sephora.

CONCLUSION

All the chapters summarized briefly above were designed and written to explain the relationship between games, advertising, and marketing communication in both theoretical and practical contexts. And there is no doubt, each author made valuable contributions. However, another point that should be emphasized is that with this book, we experienced that it is possible to have fun while doing scientific work. The inherently fun nature of the game showed itself here too. Therefore, we would like to thank all our authors for sharing and accompanying us on this enjoyable journey while we produced this book.

Let's leave one final note for our readers... This book was created for anyone involved in games: those conducting academic research on games, those working in advertising and marketing, advertisers, and indeed anyone with an interest in games. We worked hard to create a kind of reference book, motivated by the fact that an area we frequently encounter in our work has not been sufficiently explored in publications. We hope it will be useful to those interested. Our aim is not only to document current trends, but also to trigger critical thinking and inspire responsible innovation in how advertising and marketing messages are created and experienced through digital games. As technology, the digital gaming ecosystem, and the areas it interacts with continue to evolve, our frameworks for analysis and action must also evolve. We invite our readers to take the insights presented in these pages forward.

Chapter 1
Advertising, Marketing Communication, and Digital Games:
A Research on the Transformation of Brand Placement

Esma Gökmen
http://orcid.org/0000-0002-9327-4558
Ondokuz Mayıs Üniversitesi, Turkey

Tuğçe Karaca Özdemir
http://orcid.org/0009-0009-2733-1284
Hacı Bayram Veli University, Turkey

ABSTRACT

One of the most significant trends in marketing communication strategies in recent years has been to consider digital games as advertising platforms and to support brand visibility efforts with in-game ad placements. This study will focus on the role of ads placed in digital games in marketing communications and examine the impact of in-game brand placements. The study utilizes a qualitative research approach, examining digital games such as Subway Surfers and Block Blast using content analysis. The analysis focuses on the type of in-game ad, its location and position, duration, potential relevance to the game, brand visibility, and its relationship to the user context. This analysis examines the awareness-raising potential of in-game advertising, its relationship with users and the game context, ethical responsibilities, and its contribution to brand visibility and sales strategies. The results of this

DOI: 10.4018/979-8-3373-6309-7.ch001

study contribute to the field of research and offer important recommendations for brands, advertisers, and game developers, who are the primary focus of marketing communications.

INTRODUCTION

Marketing is one of the fundamental areas that has gained importance and developed with the spread of consumer ideology and tools around the world. The capitalist economic system requires that all objects be treated as instruments of commercial exchange and operates on this basic motivation. Undoubtedly, one of the most fundamental tools in this process is advertising, which is considered to have significant value within marketing communication activities. Advertising defines the promotional environments and tools used by businesses to ensure that consumers purchase their products and services. The relationship between advertising and digital games, one of the most fundamental outcomes of the digitalization phenomenon in the media in recent years, is noteworthy. Digital games, which can be played on both computers and mobile technologies, are among the leading media platforms that have been used as an important advertising medium for many years.

Marketing is the name given to the process by which individuals fulfill their various needs and desires throughout their lives in the context of consumption demands. Companies use marketing techniques that involve strategic methods to respond to individuals' needs and desires and to ensure that they purchase their goods and services (Çelebi, 2021, p. 4). Marketing communication refers to the interaction process established between the brand and customers. Companies engage in marketing communication activities to make their products reach consumers, to enable brand recognition and awareness, to attract interest, to develop purchasing behavior, and to ensure brand integration (Çelebi, 2021, p. 7).

One of the most fundamental promotional tools used in marketing communication activities is advertising. All organizations that produce products and services, commercial enterprises, and advertisers outside of these allocate advertising budgets and carry out advertising activities in order to promote, direct consumers to sales, build brands, and compete in the international market (Ceran and Karaçor, 2013 p. 16). Digital advertising, which has become widespread in recent years, creates an interactive communication environment between organizations and customers, while social media and forums enable consumers to join brand communities and share their opinions with other consumers. Thus, consumers move away from their passive position in traditional advertising practices and gain an active position. In this context, it can be stated that digital advertisements provide customers with a degree of control (Başyazıcıoğlu, 2020, p. 211).

Based on this, this study examines the relationship between advertising, one of the marketing communication tools, and digital games, exploring how digital games, one of the most popular gaming platforms today, are used as an advertising medium. There are numerous types of digital games that can be played using mobile technologies, and these games appeal to different age groups and segments. The study examines the role of advertisements in these games in marketing communication and focuses on the effects of in-game brand placement practices. The study is conducted using a qualitative research approach and focuses on the type of in-game advertising, the location and position of the advertisement, its duration, its potential relevance to the game, brand visibility, and its relationship with the user context in the digital games Subway Surfers and Block Blast! using content analysis (). The analysis examines the function of advertisements in digital games, their potential to create awareness among users, the relationship between the advertisement and the user and game context, ethical responsibilities, and the contribution of advertising to brand visibility and sales strategies.

DIGITAL MARKETING AND ADVERTISING IN THE CONTEXT OF MARKETING COMMUNICATION

Marketing communication is considered the cornerstone of sustainable competitive advantage for businesses in the evolving consumer world of the 21st century (Kitchen and Schutz, 1997, cited in Hackley & Kitchen, 1998, p. 229). Which of the marketing communication activities—advertising, public relations, promotion, personal selling, etc.—are used may vary depending on the brand's marketing communication strategies and media visibility (Altınbaş, 2007, p. 97). Marketing communication is a management process through which a business creates an interactive environment with consumers. By understanding consumers' communication habits, businesses aim to create and share messages for specific stakeholder groups, analyze incoming responses to generate new moves, and influence the attitudes and behaviors of their target audiences by conveying specific messages that carry significance. Organizations that require marketing communication and need mutual interaction with customers include "companies, suppliers, retailers, wholesalers, value-added sellers, distributors, and other retailers," regardless of their size. It is extremely important for businesses to be able to communicate effectively with consumers, which is why they carry out a range of promotional activities. Advertising, sales promotion, public relations, direct marketing, personal selling, and sponsorship are among the most commonly used. Businesses use traditional media tools such as newspapers, radio, television, and cinema to convey their messages to their target audiences, but in recent years, the internet has been used intensively to interact with "customers, potential customers, suppliers, financiers, distributors, communities, employees, and others" (Fill and Turnbull, 2023, p. 2).

Marketing communication strategies include "traditional mass media advertising (TV, magazines, etc.), online advertising (websites, opt-in email messages, text messages, etc.), sales promotions (samples, coupons, discounts, premium products, etc.), store signs and point-of-sale communications, direct mailings, public relations and publicity releases, event and campaign sponsorships, presentations by sales representatives, and various auxiliary communication tools." Marketing communication tools and media are entirely within the promotion component of the traditional marketing mix (product, price, place, promotion) (Shimp, 2008, p. 7-8).

Marketing communication aims to persuade customers by sending messages. The aforementioned message delivery can be directed to a specific individual or individuals; this is personal communication. Prepared messages can also be sent to audiences whose individual members are unknown, via mass communication tools, in order to reach a wide audience. This situation defines mass communication. Personal communication forms are essentially direct and interactive marketing activities and personal selling. All other promotional tools constitute mass communication (Pelsmacker, Geuens & Bergh, 2013, p. 5).

Advertising and promotion are one of the basic media forms that support the sales process by informing consumers about a company's products and services and convincing them to meet their needs and demands (Belch and Belch, 2003, p. 6). Advertising is generally used synonymously with marketing communication because it is one of the most important tools in the communication mix. However, there are numerous communication tools with their own unique characteristics, strengths, and weaknesses that can be discussed alongside advertising. Advertising is a "non-personal communication activity that is clearly defined by a sender (company), paid for, and uses mass communication tools (TV, radio, newspapers, magazines, billboards, etc.)" (Pelsmacker, Geuens & Bergh, 2013, p. 4). Advertising is carried out through platforms such as "iPads, cell phones, television, newspapers, magazines, and even Facebook and MySpace." Advertising is done through a medium from any sender (or advertiser). In the online world, "promotional emails, mobile phone applications, social networks such as Facebook and Twitter, online advertising videos, search engine advertisements, and user-generated advertisements" are used as different advertising tools. Mobile phones, the internet, and e-readers are technologies used to publish advertisements (Thorson & Duffy, 2012, p.2-4).

Advertisements can be visual or verbal in nature. However, it can be said that visual advertisements may be more appealing than others and, in this context, may be more effective than traditional types of advertising. The live nature of a computer screen makes the advertisements viewed there more attention-grabbing than a printed advertisement in a magazine (Bezjian-Avery, Calder, & Iacobucci, 1998, pp. 24-25). Barnes explains the types of advertisements as follows (Barnes, 2002, p. 408):

Simple text advertisements. These are the most basic level of WAP advertising. As the name suggests, they do not contain graphics or interactive response mechanisms.

Rich ads. Based on simple text ads, rich ads are primarily defined by their graphical and interactive features and may include WAP-compatible graphics, pop-up menus, click or search response mechanisms, and other interactive displays of advertiser messages.

Transitional ads. These rich ads typically use graphics and interactive text across the entire screen of the device, often referred to as "splash" pages. These ads appear in the seconds between the user's request to view a site and the download of a WAP page. These types of ads are usually cached on the device and therefore do not extend the download time... Interstitial ads can also be timed to close automatically after a certain period of time.

Digital Games and In-Game Advertising Types

Games transported to virtual worlds through computer and mobile technologies are referred to as "digital games." The growth in the number of players and the amount of play in digital games today shows that interest in traditional games has declined and that digital games have become the most popular games (Özek, 2022, p. 1). Digital games emerged under the name of computer games in the late 1990s and began to be introduced to social networks in the 2000s. These networks, with their diversity that also includes digital games, have become the cornerstone that meets individuals' technology-based needs (Bayzan and Güneş, 2022, pp. 26-27).

Based on the assessments of Egenfeldt-Nielsen and colleagues, global digital game types are divided into three categories: "action games, strategy games, and process-based games" (Valkenburg and Piotrowski, 2017, p. 200). According to another classification, digital games are divided into "console games, PC games, and online games." It is also possible to play digital games on mobile devices such as cell phones and tablets (Aydemir, 2022, p. 41). Today, digital games can be played on "computers, consoles (e.g., Xbox 360, PlayStation, Wii), handheld consoles (e.g., Nintendo DS), computers, iPods, personal digital assistants, and mobile phones" (Anderson et al., 2010, p. 152).

The concept of digital games encompasses various and all types of "arcade (Atari) games, PC games, console games, and mobile games" (Binark and Bayrakturan, 2008, pp. 42-43). One aspect that distinguishes digital games from traditional games is the professional organization of the game construction process. Beyond the practice of playing games, digital games have their own intrinsic value and are a product of an industrial production process (Binark and Bayrakturan, 2008, p.

49). The digital game market represents an important area of economic production through its contributions to the local economy. This economy is connected to numerous sectors. The digital game market is located at the intersection of "technology, culture, and marketing" within a techno-cultural and capitalist structure. In recent years, the game market's efforts in terms of visuality have focused intensely on artificial intelligence-supported applications. The artificial intelligence techniques used in games are as follows: "Finite State Machines, Fuzzy State Machines, Genetic Algorithms, Artificial Life, Artificial Neural Networks" (Güneş, 2012, pp. 14-16).

In-game advertising (IGA) is a digital advertising application that involves integrating advertisements in image, video, or audio format into video games. This application is particularly common in iOS and Android mobile games, but it is also used in game consoles such as Xbox and PlayStation, as well as in computer games (Sweeney & Figas, 2024). In general terms, in-game advertising refers to the placement of marketing content within the game environment, ranging from product placements appropriate to the game scenario to advertisements appearing on loading screens or elements that become part of the game interface (Shalabi, 2024). Advergames and in-game advertising (IGA) are advertising strategies that promote brands and products through digital games, taking advantage of the interactive nature of games (Terlutter & Capella, 2013; Van Berlo et al., 2021, cited in Zagni, Baima, Nguyen, & Do, 2025, p. 4). While both methods provide opportunities to engage with consumers, they use different mechanisms to capture players' attention and influence brand perception; these differences, therefore, create various effects on consumer behavior and purchasing decisions.

In-game advertising types can be broadly categorized into three main categories: static ads, dynamic ads, and product placement/sponsored content.

Static in-game ads are defined as advertising formats integrated into the game during the design phase. These types of ads, which are usually encountered in the form of billboards or panel ads, are similar to product placement practices in the film industry. This method, which began to appear in football games in particular in the early 1990s, remains one of the most frequently used advertising formats today. It holds strategic importance for brands because it offers the opportunity for direct communication and can remain in the game for a long time. Static advertisements can be added to game menus, environmental elements, billboards, or characters' inventories, thereby conveying brand awareness to the player in a manner consistent with the game universe (Chaney, Lin, & Chaney, 2004, pp. 37-45). These types of ads are generally high-cost and priced on a flat-fee basis (Parkin, 2023). The most common examples of static ads include banner ads and native ads. Banner ads appear as small, fixed areas on the game screen, while native ads are integrated with the game's graphics and presented to the player without drawing attention (Shalabi, 2024). In the early days, in-game static ads were usually included in the programming during the game development process. However, today, these ads can be added to the game later, removed, or adapted to suit the brands' strategies through updates or additional content (DLC) (Acar, 2024, p. 49).

Dynamic in-game ads are ad formats that can be updated and changed when accessed via a computer, game console, or mobile device with an internet connection. These ads are targeted through the analysis of various information such as date, geographic location, game duration, time, and user demographic or behavioral data. Advertisers can optimize their ad content by leveraging this data, thereby offering players a more personalized experience. Thanks to these features, dynamic in-game ads stand out as an effective advertising format that allows brands to be promoted in a way that is integrated into the game when a video game is launched (Ghırvu, 2012, pp. 114-119).

Dynamic in-game ads refer to ad types that can be changed and updated by game designers as needed. This ad format is particularly prevalent in online video games. The difference from static ads is that they can be customized to suit specific demographics and target audiences after the game is released. This allows brands to analyze player behavior and deliver context-specific and personalized ad content (RapidFire In-Game Advertising, 2015; Shalabi, 2024). Furthermore, game developers can update the virtual advertising spaces placed in the game when needed, instantly publish ads according to the campaign calendar, and obtain the necessary data for performance evaluation after the campaign (RapidFire In-Game Advertising, 2015). This category includes interstitial ads and rewarded ads. Interstitial ads appear in full screen during pauses in gameplay, while rewarded ads give players in-game currency or special rewards in exchange for watching the ads. In addition, video ads are frequently used as a subtype of dynamic ads and are mostly viewed in exchange for rewards (Shalabi, 2024).

Product placement is a long-standing practice dating back to Charles Dickens' *Pickwick* Papers; its modern popularity began in the 1920s when cigarette companies used Hollywood actresses to promote specific brands. Since the 1980s, brands have begun to allocate significant budgets to showcase their products, and product placement has become increasingly widespread (Uslu & Kazaz, 2022, p. 66). Initially used heavily in traditional media platforms such as television and cinema, product placement has expanded its scope with the development of digital technologies and interactive platforms. Video games, in particular, offer a dynamic environment where players can interact directly with brands and form bonds through experience, making product placement strategies more effective and participatory.

In-game product placements play an important role in marketing by enriching digital gaming experiences. This practice involves the direct integration of brands into the game, offering players both visibility and direct experience through character clothing, vehicles, or in-game objects. For example, clothing worn by a character or vehicles used belonging to real brands can increase players' brand awareness. Research shows that players generally respond positively to such placements and that they do not negatively affect the experience; therefore, brands can strengthen brand loyalty by enriching the consumer experience (Lee, 2021, pp. 78–80). Examples of these practices include the inclusion of Mercedes-Benz vehicles in Mario Kart 8 (Parkin, 2023) or Chipotle's virtual restaurant in Roblox (Shalabi, 2024).

Initial research focused primarily on product placement applications in the context of in-game advertising (Terlutter & Capella, 2013; Van Berlo et al., 2021; Welden et al., 2022, cited in Zagni, Baima, Nguyen, & Do, 2025, p. 4). Today, however, in-game advertising strategies are not limited to product placement but also include more comprehensive applications such as content sponsorship. For example, in multiplayer games, character customization is often achieved through the purchase of in-game items or skins, while interstitial ads are presented to players as pop-ups between game sessions or levels (Terlutter & Capella, 2013; Van Berlo et al., 2021; cited in Zagni, Baima, Nguyen, & Do, 2025, p. 4). Sponsored game content allows brands to become part of the gaming experience, enabling stronger interaction with players . For example, KFC collaborated with Nintendo in the game *Animal Crossing: New Horizons* to design a KFC-themed virtual island and offered players the opportunity to win real-life chicken coupons (Parkin, 2023).

The Transformative Role of In-Game Advertising in Digital Games

In addition to being an advertising medium in the context of marketing communication, digital games can be said to be positioned as interactive digital environments that transform the ways in which advertising is produced, presented, and perceived. In traditional advertising, the messages created by brands are mostly designed as a one-way communication model; they are presented in structures that do not support the active participation of the audience, convey only positive features about the brand, and have limited interaction. Digital games, which have the largest share of advertising investment within digital media, break this structure and enable users to take an active role in the advertising process (Akcan & Kazaz, 2022, p. 53). Therefore, in-game advertising creates a foundation for advertising to go beyond being a displayed element and become an experienced form of communication.

In digital gaming environments, advertising is intertwined with narrative structure, game mechanics, and user interaction. In-game advertisements come in various forms, including static banner ads, ads integrated into the game flow, and video ads offered in exchange for rewards. This diversity of advertising formats causes advertising to take on different functions within the gaming context. As Oğuz (2021) emphasizes, interactive advertising formats, in particular, remove the user from a passive position and direct them to consciously interact with the advertising content. Consequently, advertisements become an integral part of the gaming experience.

This study examines the transformative role of in-game advertising in the context of interaction, experience, and ethical tension. The interaction dimension in in-game advertising refers to the evolution of the user-brand relationship from a one-way exposure to a process in which the user is active. In advergame applications, placing the advertisement within the entertainment and game structure ensures that the game user is exposed to the advertisement knowingly and willingly. Thus, the perceived push factor of the advertisement is transformed through entertainment elements. Users spending more time in the game, interacting with advertisements, and coming into direct contact with the brand ensures that the advertisement becomes a functional element of the experience (Altun, 2019, p. 75). Therefore, while in traditional advertising the user is merely exposed to the ad, in in-game advertising the user willingly watches the ad, receives in-game rewards in exchange for viewing it, and interacts with the ad to enhance their gaming performance. In other words, the ad is functionally integrated into the game's process, transforming the brand-user relationship into one based on active participation.

Secondly, in terms of experience, in-game advertisements encountered in digital games ensure that users experience the advertisement and cause in-game advertisements to become components that directly influence user perception, shaping the gaming experience, rather than merely conveying a brand message (Kılınç Özüölmez, 2019, pp. 1400-1401). Ad placements that are consistent with the game context create more positive brand attitudes than negative or neutral contexts, while ads that are disconnected from the context or intrusive negatively affect user satisfaction and perception (Yoo & Eastin, 2017, p. 614).

The third dimension, ethical tension, arguably constitutes the most controversial aspect of the transformative role of in-game advertising. Particularly in the digital gaming world, where children and young users are heavily represented, advertising content raises important ethical questions regarding age appropriateness, transparency, and the influence of targeting. The integration of advertisements into the gaming experience can cause users to remain focused on the game for longer periods of time in an environment centered on entertainment, leading to attention being directed indirectly toward the advertisement and blurring the line between advertising and entertainment (Öztürk & Coşkun, 2017, p. 49). While this increases the persuasive effect of advertising, it also brings ethical responsibilities. Therefore, in-game advertising represents a transformation process that must be addressed within the context of user-protective approaches.

A Brief Overview of Advergames and Gamification

Traditional advertising methods have begun to lose their effectiveness in today's communication environment and have been replaced by interaction-focused messages that are not limited to a specific target audience. The main reasons for this include consumers being exposed to countless advertising messages every day, communication shifting from a passive process to mutual interaction, postmodern individuals having different needs and desires, and many people, especially office workers, spending most of their time in front of computers. Furthermore, consumers' interest in experience-based, interactive, and personalized communication with brands is considered one of the most important indicators of the shift towards digital platforms (Buckner, Fang & Qiao, 2002; Jaffe, 2003; Russell, 2007, cited in Öztürk & Coşkun, 2017, p. 50).

Thanks to the rapid advancement of internet technologies, users encounter different advertisements every day in the virtual environment and also have the opportunity to have fun (Akyol, 2010, p. 94). The most striking and current of these media is advergames, which are computer games designed for advertising purposes that reach consumers through the internet or web-based applications (Yavuzyılmaz, 2017, p. 588). Advergames are defined as a contemporary marketing strategy that straddles the line between advertising and video games and aims to influence consumers' purchasing behavior (Ilgın, 2013, p. 26). Unlike in-game advertising (IGA), the direct integration of branded content into the game mechanics in advergames allows players to perceive the persuasive aspects of the game more clearly and enables the marketing objective to be presented transparently (Mallinckrodt & Mizerski, 2007; An & Stern, 2011, cited in Zagni, Baima, Nguyen, & Do, 2025, p. 14).

Advergames are defined as web-based games for advertising purposes, where messages supporting the brand image are integrated into the game design. Unlike traditional methods, they increase brand awareness by establishing an interactive connection with the consumer and offer the player a more powerful experience. Users' direct interaction with the brand ensures that they both have an enjoyable time and become part of the brand's story. This contributes to the development of emotional bonds and strengthens brand loyalty, while also enabling the collection of consumer data (Yamamoto, 2009). Finally, the impact of advergames on consumers is further enhanced by the seamless integration of the brand into the gaming experience. Tasks, collectible items, or sponsored content facilitate the cognitive processing of the advertisement, making the brand an integral part of the experience. This process affects players' cognitive processing, emotional attachment, and attention levels, creating a higher level of engagement compared to static advertisements. Increased perceptual fluency facilitates easier processing of the brand in a familiar context and enhances brand recall. The more prominent placement of the brand within the game is seen as an important feature that strengthens recall (Hanbazazah et al., 2022; Van Berlo & Chen, 2024; Kuo & Rice, 2015; Vashisht & Chauhan, 2017; Vashisht, 2017; Van Reijmersdal et al., 2012; cited in Zagni, Baima, Nguyen, & Do, 2025, p. 14).

Gamification is a strategy that aims to increase user motivation and guide specific behaviors by applying game design elements to non-game contexts (Deterding, Dixon, Khaled, & Nacke, 2011, pp. 9-15). The gamification approach can be defined as adapting and applying the philosophy of games and the elements that constitute this philosophy in non-game contexts, rather than treating the concept of games as a direct action (Bozkurt & Genç-Kumtepe, 2014, p. 148). The elements used in the design of gamification scenarios are divided into three main categories: dynamics, mechanics, and components (Werbach & Hunter, 2012, cited in Dichev & Dicheva, 2017, p. 36). Dynamics represent the highest conceptual level of a gamified system and encompass constraints, emotions, narrative, progression, and social relationships. Mechanics function as a set of rules that determine interactions within the system, and users' responses to these rules give rise to dynamics. Challenge, chance, competition, cooperation, feedback, resource acquisition, and rewards are among the game mechanics. Components, on the other hand, form the building blocks of gamification. Achievement badges, avatars, collections, content unlocking, leaderboards, levels, points, and virtual objects are evaluated in this group. For example, points (components) provide specific rewards (mechanics), and this process creates a sense of progress (dynamics) in the user (Dichev & Dicheva, 2017, p. 36).

Advertising Ethics in Digital Games and the Protection of Children

Digital games represent both entertainment and leisure activities for children and young users, as well as a digital environment where they are exposed to intense commercial messages. Therefore, in-game advertising practices must be evaluated within the framework of protective regulations, alongside marketing activities in the context of child users. In the examined examples of Subway Surfers (9+) and Block Blast!, the fact that a significant portion of in-game advertisements appear in games targeting children and young users makes this ethical dimension even more critical.

The findings obtained within the scope of this study reveal that advertisements for chat applications and similar content with a 17+ age restriction are present within a digital game aimed at the 9+ age group. Such advertising content raises significant ethical issues in the context of digital advertising, particularly in relation to children's cognitive and emotional development. The literature emphasizes that young people and children, whose critical thinking skills are not fully developed during adolescence, have limited ability to critically evaluate the target, intent, and persuasive aspects of advertising messages and are not protected from the influence of advertising (Packeret al., 2022, p. 1). Therefore, advertising content presented in digital gaming environments carries a high risk of influence and manipulability for children.

The literature on digital advertising targeting children highlights the need to protect children from advertising manipulation and treat them as a sensitive audience, as well as the importance of parents being aware to ensure children have a healthy digital gaming experience (Kasım & Can Tunç, 2024, p. 236). The integration of advertising messages into the context of games makes it difficult for children to realize that they are being exposed to advertising. Reward-based advertising, in particular, encourages child users to interact with advertisements by exploiting their desire to gain in-game advantages, thereby further increasing the persuasive effect of the advertisement.

In this context, three key elements stand out when considering the ethics of in-game advertising practices: age appropriateness, transparency, and protective mechanisms. The presence of advertisements for potentially risky applications, such as chat or dating apps aimed at adults, within digital games intended for children violates the principle of age appropriateness. Furthermore, the intertwining of advertisements with the in-game context violates the principle of transparency and makes it difficult for children to distinguish between advertisements and game content.

The data and algorithms used in digital advertising enable advertisers to access information about user behavior. However, regulatory bodies restrict this access on grounds of data ethics and algorithmic accuracy (Mete, 2021, p. 443). In this context, ethical violations must be prevented through preemptive regulations before they affect child users. As emphasized by Karpat Aktuğulu (2006, p. 9), advertisers, advertising agencies, media organizations, and all relevant institutions are key actors in sharing ethical responsibilities. Therefore, within this framework, it can be said that ethical responsibility in digital advertising targeting children lies with advertisers, digital platforms, and game developers.

The findings of this study show that the transformative role of in-game advertising in digital games is not limited to marketing communication strategies but also encompasses ethical, regulatory, and social dimensions. While in-game ads offer a powerful engagement space for brands, neglecting responsibilities in the context of protecting child users can lead to serious ethical issues. In this context, digital games should be treated as public spaces that require careful management in terms of advertising, children's rights, and digital ethics.

RESEARCH

This study contributes to the literature by examining the role of advertising formats in digital games within marketing communication and their effects on brand perception. While previous studies have generally addressed general user responses and motivations through advergame content, experiential marketing, or gamification, this study specifically examines in-game brand placements in popular mobile and console games such as Subway Surfers and Block Blast using qualitative content analysis. The type, frequency, location, and level of brand integration of advertisements, along with their impact on the player experience (whether they create interruptions or appear natural), are systematically evaluated, revealing the direct effects of in-game advertising on brand visibility and marketing strategies. Furthermore, the limited number of studies conducted in this field in the Turkish context increases the contribution of this study to the national literature and offers a unique perspective on marketing communication strategies related to in-game brand placements.

In this study, the relationship between advertising, one of the marketing communication tools, and digital games was conducted within the framework of a qualitative research approach, and the data were evaluated using content analysis. Content analysis is defined as a method that aims to examine visual images designed to be converted into written and verbal narratives () (Rose, 2023, p. 116). The sample in the study was determined using purposive sampling. In this method, the aim is to select samples that can provide information appropriate to the purpose of the research, and each sample has a typical feature (Akalın, 2018:103-104). In this context, two mobile games (Subway Surfers and Block Blast!) that are rich in advertising content, have high user interaction, and allow for the observation of different advertising formats were included in the scope of the study. The selection of these games was influenced by their potential to analyze how advertisements integrate with in-game dynamics, how they affect the user experience, and how brands in different sectors use this medium.

In this research, the digital games Subway Surfers and Block Blast! were examined for 3 hours each, and all advertisements seen on the screen were systematically recorded. The findings were examined in terms of the type of advertisement, sectoral area, location and position, duration, level of compatibility with the game, level of awareness creation in the player, and relationship with the user context.

Table 1. Content Analysis of Advertisements in Subway Surfers (9+ years)

Ad Name	Advertisement Area	Ad Type	Advertisement Location and Position	Ad Duration	Advertisement's Compatibility Potential with the Game	Brand Visibility in Advertising	The Potential of Advertising to Create Awareness in Players	The Relationship Between Advertising and User Context
Yalla Play-Game Voice Chat (12+)	Digital Game	Dynamic Advertising/ Interstitial Advertising/ Video Advertising	Full Screen	20 sec.	Low	Available	High	Low
Race Master 3D Car Racing (12+)	Digital Game	Dynamic Ads/ Interstitial Ads/Video Ads	Full Screen	30 sec.	Medium	Available	High	Medium
Snake io-Fun Online Snake (4+)	Digital Game	Static ad/Banner ad	Bottom of the screen	2 sec.	High	Yes	Medium	High
Yalla 101 Okey (12+)	Digital Game	/Interstitial Ad/Video Ad	Full Screen	20 sec.	Medium	Yes	High	Medium
Royal Kingdom (12+)	Digital Game	Static ad/Banner ad	Bottom section of the screen	10 sec.	Center	Yes	Center	Middle
Pokemon Go (9+)	Digital Game	Static ad/Banner ad	Bottom section of the screen	2 sec.	High	Yes	Medium	High
Seaside Escape (4+)	Digital Game	Static ad/Banner ad	Bottom section of the screen	10 sec.	High	Available	High	High
Yalla 101 Okey (12+)	Digital Game	Dynamic advertising/ Reward-based advertising/Video advertising	Full Screen	20 sec.	Medium	Available	High	Medium
Doomsday: Last Survivors (12+)	Digital Game	Static ad/Banner ad	Bottom section of the screen	2 sec.	Medium	Yes	Medium	Medium

continued on following page

Table 1. Continued

Ad Name	Advertisement Area	Ad Type	Advertisement Location and Position	Ad Duration	Advertisement's Compatibility Potential with the Game	Brand Visibility in Advertising	The Potential of Advertising to Create Awareness in Players	The Relationship Between Advertising and User Context
Race Master 3D: Car Racing (12+)	Digital Game	Dynamic Ads/ Interstitial Ads/Video Ads	Full Screen	20 sec.	Medium	Available	High	Medium
Petitecare Baby/ Kids	Baby Care Products	Static ad/Banner ad	Bottom section of the screen	2 sec.	Low	Available	Medium	Low
Turkey Education Academy	Education	Static ad/Banner ad	Bottom section of the screen	2 sec.	Low	Yes	Medium	Low
Meridian Therapy Training	Training	Static ad/Banner ad	Bottom section of the screen	10 sec.	Low	Available	Medium	Low
Mobile Legends: Bang Bang 12+	Digital Game	Static ad/Banner ad	Bottom of the screen	2 sec.	Center	Yes	Center	Middle
Yalla 101 Okey (12+)	Digital Game	Dynamic Ad/Interstitial Ad -in Ad/Video Ad	Full Screen	20 sec.	Medium	Yes	High	Medium
Candy Crush Saga (4+)	Digital Game	Dynamic Ads/ Interstitial Ads	Full Screen	10 sec.	High	Yes	High	High
Yalla Play Game-Voice Chat (12+)	Digital Game	Dynamic Ads/ Interstitial Ads/Video Ads	Full Screen	20 sec.	Low	Available	High	Low
Mustela	Mother and Baby Care Products	Static ad/Banner ad	Bottom section of the screen	2 sec.	Low	Available	Medium	Low

continued on following page

Table 1. Continued

Ad Name	Advertisement Area	Ad Type	Advertisement Location and Position	Ad Duration	Advertisement's Compatibility Potential with the Game	Brand Visibility in Advertising	The Potential of Advertising to Create Awareness in Players	The Relationship Between Advertising and User Context
Slayz	Investment Site	Static ad/Banner ad	Bottom section of the screen	10 sec.	Low	Yes	Moderate	Low
Borsa Istanbul	Investment Site	Static ad/Banner ad	Bottom section of the screen	2 sec.	Low	Available	Medium	Low
Hankook	Tire Sales	Static ad/Banner ad	Bottom section of the screen	10 sec.	Low	Available	Medium	Low
Block Crush (12+)	Digital Game	Dynamic Ads/ Interstitial Ads/Video Ads	Full Screen	20 sec.	High	Yes	High	High
Rhapsody Hotel	Hotel	Static ad/Banner ad	Bottom section of the screen	2 sec.	Low	Available	Medium	Low
Sugo-Online Chat Party (17+)	Online Chat	Static ad/Banner ad	Bottom section of the screen	10 sec.	Low	Available	Medium	Low
Ro Academics	Education (International exams and university preparation courses for)	Static ad/Banner ad	Bottom section of the screen	2 sec.	Low	Yes	Medium	Low
Brain Test: Tricky Puzzles (4+)	Digital Game	Dynamic Ads/ Interstitial Ads	Bottom of the screen	10 sec.	High	Yes	High	High

continued on following page

Table 1. Continued

Ad Name	Advertisement Area	Ad Type	Advertisement Location and Position	Ad Duration	Advertisement's Compatibility Potential with the Game	Brand Visibility in Advertising	The Potential of Advertising to Create Awareness in Players	The Relationship Between Advertising and User Context
Mico: Make Friends, Go Live (17+)	Online Chat	Static ad/Banner ad	Bottom of the screen	10 sec.	Low	Available	Medium	Low
QNB Mobile	Digital Banking	Static ad/Banner ad	Bottom section of the screen	2 sec.	Low	Available	Medium	Low
Doomsday: Last Survivors (12+)	Digital Game	Static ad/Banner ad	Bottom of the screen	10 sec.	Center	Yes	Center	Central
Chora Mykonos	Hotel	Static ad/Banner ad	Bottom section of the screen	2 sec	Low	Available	Medium	Low
Samsun Plumber	Plumbing Services	Static ad/Banner ad	Bottom section of the screen	2 sec.	Low	Yes	Medium	Low
Amazon.com.tr	Online Shopping Site	Dynamic advertising/ Reward-based advertising/Video advertising	Full Screen	20 sec.	Center	Available	High	Medium
Brawl Stars (9+)	Digital Game	Dynamic Ads/Reward-Based Ads/Video Ads	Full Screen	20 sec.	High	Available	High	High
BN Automation	Automation Systems	Static advertising/ Banner advertising	Bottom section of the screen	2 sec.	Low	Available	Medium	Low
Hüner Coal Holders	Industrial Product Sales	Static advertising/ Banner advertising	Bottom section of the screen	2 sec.	Low	Available	Medium	Low

continued on following page

Table 1. Continued

Ad Name	Advertisement Area	Ad Type	Advertisement Location and Position	Ad Duration	Advertisement's Compatibility Potential with the Game	Brand Visibility in Advertising	The Potential of Advertising to Create Awareness in Players	The Relationship Between Advertising and User Context
Vita Mahjong (4+)	Digital Game	Dynamic Ads/ Interstitial Ads/Video Ads	Full Screen	30 sec.	High	Available	High	High
Hidros Hydraulic Machinery	Industrial Product Sales	Static advertising/ Banner advertising	Bottom section of the screen	4 sec.	Low	Yes	Medium	Low
Alle Interior Design	Interior Design Services	Static ad/Banner ad	Bottom section of the screen	10 sec.	Low	Available	Medium	Low
Ergül	Furniture	Static ad/Banner ad	Bottom section of the screen	2 sec.	Low	Available	Medium	Low
Topdon	Technology Product Sales	Static advertising/ Banner advertising	Bottom section of the screen	10 sec.	Low	Available	Medium	Low
Bosh	White Goods	Static ad/Banner ad	Bottom section of the screen	2 sec.	Low	Available	Medium	Low
Misk Floral Cafe	Cafe/Restaurant	Static ad/Banner ad	Bottom section of the screen	10 sec.	Middle	Available	Center	Medium
Tomb of The Mask: Pixel Maze (4+)	Digital Game	Dynamic Ads/ Interstitial Ads/Video Ads	Full Screen	30 sec.	High	Available	High	High
Call Me: AI Friend (17+)	Online Chat	Static ad/Banner ad	Bottom of the screen	2 sec.	Low	Available	Medium	Low

continued on following page

Table 1. Continued

Ad Name	Advertisement Area	Ad Type	Advertisement Location and Position	Ad Duration	Advertisement's Compatibility Potential with the Game	Brand Visibility in Advertising	The Potential of Advertising to Create Awareness in Players	The Relationship Between Advertising and User Context
HBO Max	Digital Platform	Static ad/Banner ad	Bottom section of the screen	2 sec.	Center	Yes	Center	Middle
Bowmasters-Multiplayer Games (12+)	Digital Game	Dynamic Ads/Reward-Based Ads/Video Ads	Full Screen	30 sec.	High	Available	High	High
Sunwatershop	Water Purification Device Parts	Static ad/Banner ad	Bottom section of the screen	2 sec.	Low	Yes	Medium	Low
Aquateks Building Reinforcement	Building Chemicals and Insulation Systems	Static advertising/ Banner advertising	Bottom section of the screen	2 sec.	Low	Yes	Medium	Low
Dialog Turkey	Real Estate Education	Static ad/Banner ad	Bottom section of the screen	10 sec.	Low	Available	Medium	Low
Sole World	Sole Sales	Static ad/Banner ad	Bottom section of the screen	10 sec.	Low	Available	Medium	Low

Ad Types and Ad Display Duration

According to the data obtained, static ads (banner-style) are the most common type of ad encountered in the game. These types of ads appear intensively at the bottom of the screen for 2 to 10 seconds. Static ads constitute approximately two-thirds of all ads. Dynamic ads (video format) follow. These types of ads appear intensively during in-game transitions or with "reward-based" options. The duration of dynamic ads on the screen varies between 20 and 30 seconds. Reward-based ads are placed in the game using motivational strategies such as gaining new lives or extra time, which increases user engagement. According to Lee and Shin (2017), "offering free game items to mobile gamers through in-game 'reward ads' provides significant benefits to game producers by supporting game item sales. Indeed, by offering users free sample game items, they are given the opportunity to take their first steps in the game, and it is seen that this can initiate users' behavior to purchase game items. Thus, it becomes possible for users to experience game items and gain knowledge related to their value.

Advertising Positions

When examining ad placements in the study, it was observed that dynamic ads (video ads) covering the entire screen remain on the screen for 20-30 seconds, and that such ads temporarily interrupt the game flow. Static ads (banner ads) at the bottom of the screen remain on the screen for 2 to 10 seconds and are visible without interrupting the game flow. Thus, this application can be considered an advertising strategy aimed at creating awareness in a continuous manner without distracting users in the game.

Ad Content and Sector Distribution

When examining the advertising content in the game, it is seen that the most common category is digital game advertisements (Yalla 101 Okey, Candy Crush Saga, Brain Test: Tricky Puzzles, etc.). This indicates that a "cross-promotion" strategy has been developed in the digital gaming sector. In his work *"Self- and Cross-Promotion within Digital Games"* (2016), Mago defines "cross-promotion" on digital game platforms as "the usability of static in-game advertising in the areas of self-promotion and cross-promotion." According to the author, this definition refers to a strategy of directing players of any game to a different game or a separate title in a game portfolio through in-game elements. Thus, placing advertisements for different digital games within a digital game is approached based on this strategy.

In this sense, game developers or publishers ensure that a different game in their portfolio is brought to the screen through in-game advertising or promotion activities.

Other notable categories in the game include:

- Education (Turkey Education Academy, Meridian Therapy Education, Ro Academics, etc.),
- Personal care and baby products (Mustela, Petitecare),
- Online chat platforms (Mico, Sugo Chat Party),
- Industrial products and services (Hidros, Hüner Coal, BN Automation),
- Tourism and accommodation (Rhapsody Hotel, Chora Mykonos).

Level of Compatibility with the Game

When the game is analyzed, it is seen that the advertisements with the highest compatibility potential with the game are other digital game advertisements. Game advertisements appear to be compatible with the game under review and its target audience (children and young users) in terms of both theme and the dynamic structure of the game. Advertisements related to education, industrial products, or services have low compatibility potential with the game. Such advertisements are displayed in a way that is distant from the user experience and distracting.

Brand Visibility, Awareness, and User Context

Brand visibility is present in all advertisements examined. However, the potential of advertisements in the game to create awareness among users appears to be strongly related to the type of content. Dynamic video ads that remain on the screen for a long time, colorful and animated visuals, and digital games and shopping platforms (Candy Crush, Pokemon Go, Amazon, etc.) featuring familiar characters are seen to have a high potential for creating awareness. In this sense, it can be said that ads appropriate to the game context coincide with user motivation. However, it can be stated that sectoral advertisements such as care products, education, investment sites, tire sales, hotels, plumbing, automation systems, industrial product sales, interior design services, furniture, technological products, white goods, water purification device parts, construction chemicals, and insulation systems have low awareness-raising potential.

Advertisements associated with online chat applications such as Mico, Sugo Chat Party, and Beni Ara contain a 17+ age restriction. Considering that the game under review has a 9+ age restriction and its target audience consists mainly of children, it is problematic in terms of the risk of carrying inappropriate content such as sexual or dangerous content. This situation implies that a game whose target audience is predominantly children and young users is ethically problematic. It is a fundamental requirement that such platforms, which produce content aimed at children and young users, assume ethical responsibilities based on user protection.

Overall Assessment

When the Subway Surfers game is examined overall, it is seen that the game has a high volume of advertising content. The advertising strategy developed in the game is based on the goal of creating passive awareness with banner ads without disrupting continuity on the one hand, and ensuring active user participation with interstitial or reward-based video ads on the other. The game presents a rather mixed picture in terms of content diversity, suitability for the target audience, and ethics. While some of the ads appear to be appropriate in the context of the game, others disrupt the gaming experience.

Table 2. Content Analysis of Ads in Block Blast!

Ad Name	Advertisement Area	Ad Type	Ad Location and Position	Ad Duration	Advertisement's Potential Compatibility with the Game	Brand Visibility in the Advertisement	Advertisement's Potential to Create Awareness Among Players	The Relationship Between the Ad and the User Context
Binance Bitcoin & Crypto	Online Investment Application	Static ad/Banner ad	Bottom section of the screen	5 sec.	Center	Yes	Center	Middle
HBD Max: Watch TV and Movies	Entertainment	Static ad/Banner ad	Bottom of the screen	5 sec.	High	Yes	High	High
QNB Mobile & Digital Bridge	Bank	Static ad/Banner ad	Bottom section of the screen	5 sec.	Middle	Yes	Center	Middle
Gossip Harbor: Merge & Story	Digital Game	Dynamic Ads/ Interstitial Ads/Video Ads	Full Screen	15 sec.	High	Available	High	High
Gossip Harbor: Merge & Story	Digital Game	Static ad/Banner ad	Bottom section of the screen	5 sec.	High	Yes	High	High
OXX TR: Bitcoin Cryptocurrency	Online Investment Application	Static ad/Banner ad	Bottom section of the screen	5 sec.	Center	Yes	Center	Middle
Binance TR: Bitcoin and Crypto	Online Investment App	Static ad/Banner ad	Bottom section of the screen	5 sec.	Center	Yes	Center	Middle
MEXC: Buy Bitcoin BTC and Crypto	Online Investment App	Static ad/Banner ad	Bottom section of the screen	5 sec.	Middle	Yes	Middle	Middle

continued on following page

Table 2. Continued

Ad Name	Advertisement Area	Ad Type	Ad Location and Position	Ad Duration	Advertisement's Potential Compatibility with the Game	Brand Visibility in the Advertisement	Advertisement's Potential to Create Awareness Among Players	The Relationship Between the Ad and the User Context
MobileSea	Bank	Static ad/Banner ad	Bottom section of the screen	5 sec.	Middle	Yes	Center	Middle
XMEye Pro	Video Monitoring Software for IPC and DVR	Static advertising/ Banner advertising	Bottom section of the screen	5 sec.	High	Yes	High	High
MICO: Make Friends, Live Chat	Online Chat	Static ad/Banner ad	Bottom section of the screen	5 sec.	Middle	Available	Center	Middle
XM App: Confident Trading	Online Investment App	Static ad/Banner ad	Bottom section of the screen	5 sec.	Middle	Yes	Center	Middle
MatchPub - Video Chat	Online Chat	Static ad/Banner ad	Bottom section of the screen	5 sec.	Center	Available	Center	Middle
PokemonGO	Digital Game	Static ad/Banner ad	Bottom section of the screen	5 sec.	High	Yes	High	High
AMAZE!!!	Digital Game	Static ad/Banner ad	Bottom section of the screen	5 sec.	High	Yes	High	High

continued on following page

Table 2. Continued

Ad Name	Advertisement Area	Ad Type	Ad Location and Position	Ad Duration	Advertisement's Potential Compatibility with the Game	Brand Visibility in the Advertisement	Advertisement's Potential to Create Awareness Among Players	The Relationship Between the Ad and the User Context
Karaca Home & Living Shopping	Online Shopping Site	Static ad/Banner ad	Bottom section of the screen	5 sec	High	Yes	Medium	High
Koton: Clothing Shopping Site	Online Shopping Site	Static ad/Banner ad	Bottom of the screen	5 sec.	High	Yes	Medium	High
Seaside Escape: Merge & Story	Digital Game	Static ad/Banner ad	Bottom of the screen	5 sec.	High	Yes	High	High
Paycell - Digital Wallet	Fintech / Digital Payment Platform	Static ad/Banner ad	Bottom section of the screen	5 sec.	Middle	Available	Center	Middle
Fate War	Digital Game	Static ad/Banner ad	Bottom section of the screen	5 sec.	High	Yes	High	High
RAID: Shadow Legends	Digital Game	Static ad/Banner ad	Bottom section of the screen	5 sec.	High	Yes	High	High
Enpara Bank Mobile Branch	Bank / Digital Banking Application	Static ad/Banner ad	Bottom section of the screen	5 sec.	Middle	Yes	Center	Middle
Diablo Immortal	Digital Game	Static ad/Banner ad	Bottom section of the screen	5 sec.	High	Yes	High	High

continued on following page

Table 2. Continued

Ad Name	Advertisement Area	Ad Type	Ad Location and Position	Ad Duration	Advertisement's Potential Compatibility with the Game	Brand Visibility in the Advertisement	Advertisement's Potential to Create Awareness Among Players	The Relationship Between the Ad and the User Context
İşCep Banking & Finance	Bank	Static ad/Banner ad	Bottom section of the screen	5 sec.	Center	Yes	Center	Middle
Soho 101 Okey	Digital Game	Static ad/Banner ad	Bottom section of the screen	5 sec.	High	Yes	High	High
Beny - Find New Friends, Chat	Online Chat	Static ad/Banner ad	Bottom of the screen	5 sec.	Low	Available	Medium	Low
Gate - Bitcoin and Crypto	Online Investment Application	Static ad/Banner ad	Bottom section of the screen	5 sec.	Center	Available	Center	Middle
Painting Games with Numbers	Digital Game	Static ad/Banner ad	Bottom section of the screen	5 sec.	Low	Yes	Low	Low
Forge of Empires: Build a City	Digital Game	Static ad/Banner ad	Bottom section of the screen	5 sec.	High	Yes	High	High
Angry Birds	Digital Game	Static ad/Banner ad	Bottom section of the screen	5 sec.	Low	Available	Medium	Low
Mystery Town - Combine & Case	Digital Game	Static ad/Banner ad	Bottom of the screen	5 sec.	Low	Available	Medium	Low

continued on following page

Table 2. Continued

Ad Name	Advertisement Area	Ad Type	Ad Location and Position	Ad Duration	Advertisement's Potential Compatibility with the Game	Brand Visibility in the Advertisement	Advertisement's Potential to Create Awareness Among Players	The Relationship Between the Ad and the User Context
Age of Origins: Tower Defense	Digital Game	Static ad/Banner ad	Bottom section of the screen	5 sec.	High	Yes	High	High
Royal Match	Digital Game	Static ad/Banner ad	Bottom section of the screen	5 sec.	High	Yes	High	High
ReelShort - Stream Drama & TV	Entertainment	Static ad/Banner ad	Bottom section of the screen	5 sec.	High	Yes	High	High
BtcTurk/ Crypto: BTC/USD/XRP	Online Investment Application	Static ad/Banner ad	Bottom section of the screen	5 sec.	Middle	Yes	Center	Middle
eFootballTM	Digital Game	Static ad/Banner ad	Bottom section of the screen	5 sec.	High	Yes	Medium	High
Garanti BBVA Mobile	Bank	Static ad/Banner ad	Bottom section of the screen	5 sec.	Center	Yes	Center	Middle
Pop Us!	Digital Game	Dynamic Ad/ Interstitial Ad/Video Ad	Full Screen	15 sec	High	Yes	High	High

continued on following page

Table 2. Continued

Ad Name	Advertisement Area	Ad Type	Ad Location and Position	Ad Duration	Advertisement's Potential Compatibility with the Game	Brand Visibility in the Advertisement	Advertisement's Potential to Create Awareness Among Players	The Relationship Between the Ad and the User Context
Whiteout Survival	Digital Game	Dynamic advertising/ Reward-based advertising/Video advertising	Full Screen	15 sec.	High	Available	High	High
The Battle Cats	Digital Game	Static ad/Banner ad	Bottom section of the screen	5 sec.	Center	Yes	High	Medium
ING Mobile	Bank	Static ad/Ba nner ad	Bottom section of the screen	5 sec.	Middle	Yes	Middle	Middle
MySeaCard	Bank	Static ad/Banner ad	Bottom section of the screen	5 sec.	Middle	Yes	Center	Middle
Delta Store Voltage Regulator	Online Service/ Sales	Static advertising/ Banner advertising	Bottom section of the screen	5 sec.	Low	Available	Medium	Low
Boo- Flirt Friend. Chat.	Online Chat	Static ad/Banner ad	Bottom section of the screen	5 sec.	Center	Available	Center	Middle
GNÇ	Online Service/ Sales	Static ad/Banner ad	Bottom section of the screen	5 sec.	High	Available	High	High

continued on following page

Table 2. Continued

Ad Name	Advertisement Area	Ad Type	Ad Location and Position	Ad Duration	Advertisement's Potential Compatibility with the Game	Brand Visibility in the Advertisement	Advertisement's Potential to Create Awareness Among Players	The Relationship Between the Ad and the User Context
Car Jam: Escape: Traffic Puzzle	Digital Game	Static ad/Banner ad	Bottom section of the screen	5 sec.	Middle	Yes	Center	Middle
Goods Sorting Matching Game	Digital Game	Dynamic advertising/ Reward-based advertising/Video advertising	Full Screen	15 sec.	High	Yes	High	High
Getir: Market, food, and more - GetirYemek	Online Service/ Sales	Static ad/Banner ad	Bottom section of the screen	5 sec.	High	Yes	High	High
Car Jam: Escape: Traffic Puzzle	Digital Game	Dynamic Ads/ Interstitial Ads/Video Ads	Full Screen	15 sec.	High	Yes	High	High
101 Okey Yalla: Live and Audio	Digital Game	Dynamic advertising/ Reward-based advertising/Video advertising	Full Screen	15 sec.	High	Yes	High	High
Gossip Harbor: Merge & Story	Digital Game	Dynamic advertising/ Reward-based advertising/Video advertising	Full Screen	15 sec.	High	Available	High	High

continued on following page

Table 2. Continued

Ad Name	Advertisement Area	Ad Type	Ad Location and Position	Ad Duration	Advertisement's Potential Compatibility with the Game	Brand Visibility in the Advertisement	Advertisement's Potential to Create Awareness Among Players	The Relationship Between the Ad and the User Context
Kingshot	Digital Game	Dynamic advertising/ Reward-based advertising/Video advertising	Full Screen	15 sec.	High	Available	High	High
Color Block Jam	Digital Game	Static ad/Banner ad	Bottom section of the screen	5 sec.	High	Yes	High	High
Mackolik Live Results	Online Service/ Sales	Static ad/Banner ad	Bottom section of the screen	5 sec.	Middle	Available	Center	Middle
Etstur - Hotel Search, Flight Tickets	Online Service/ Sales	Static advertising/ Banner advertising	Bottom section of the screen	5 sec.	Middle	Available	Center	Low

Ad Types and Ad Duration

According to the data obtained, two main types of ads stand out in the Block Blast! game: static ads (banner ads) and dynamic ads. Static ads appear at the bottom of the screen every 5 seconds without interrupting the gaming experience. Static banner ads constitute approximately 80% of the distribution within the game. This distribution indicates that a sustainable revenue model has been adopted for the game, with ads that are constantly visible but not intrusive. Dynamic ads, on the other hand, are video ads that open across the entire screen and appear during in-game transitions or when earning rewards, such as . Dynamic video ads aim to increase user engagement and brand recall with a 15-second display duration.

Ad Placements

In Block Blast!, most of the ads are positioned at the bottom of the screen. This placement can be seen as a balanced strategy that maintains brand visibility without completely distracting the player. These ads, located in the bottom banner, create passive awareness through visuals that the player is constantly exposed to and ensure that the brand is mentally recognized. Dynamic video ads, on the other hand, are full-screen ads that briefly pause the game flow and bring the user face-to-face with the brand. Thus, it can be seen that a two-tiered advertising placement strategy based on different levels of attention is applied within the game: one is a passive approach that increases brand recall without disrupting the flow of the game, while the other is an active approach that creates high awareness with a brief interruption.

Ad Content and Sector Distribution

When examining advertising content in the game, the most common category is digital game advertisements (Gossip Harbor, Royal Match, RAID, Pokemon GO, Diablo Immortal, etc.) that align with the game's context.

Other notable categories in the game include:

- Finance and Crypto Applications (Binance, OXX, Btcturk, QNB, Enpara, Garanti BBVA, Paycell)
- Online Services/Shopping (Getir, Koton, Karaca, Etstur, Gnç)
- Social Chat Applications (MICO, Matchpub, Boo, Beeny)

Therefore, it is seen that the content is predominantly clustered around mobile lifestyle, digital finance, and entertainment.

Level of Relevance to the Game

When examining the Block Blast! game, it is seen that a large portion of the ads have a "medium" or "high" level of compatibility. In particular, other digital game ads, entertainment and fintech-themed ads overlap highly with the game context and show strong compatibility with the target audience of young mobile gamers. Game-based ads such as Gossip Harbor, Pop Us!, and Royal Match show a high level of compatibility, while banking, investment, and chat applications show a medium level of compatibility. In contrast, education or industrial product ads are far removed from the game context and weaken the user experience.

Brand Visibility, Awareness, and User Context

When examining the ads within the Block Blast! game, brand visibility is present in all ads. The potential to create awareness can be directly linked to the type of ad. Dynamic and reward-based video ads briefly pause the gaming experience, placing the brand at the center and creating a high level of awareness. Static banner ads, on the other hand, provide lower but continuous awareness. Therefore, they make the brand mentally visible without distracting the player. When evaluated in terms of user context, it can be said that entertainment and fintech-themed ads show a high level of compatibility with the game, and therefore are perceptually accepted without conflicting with the player's motivation to play the game. However, ads featuring non-game content such as chat applications, hardware, or hotel services may potentially cause disinterest or distraction in the player due to a disconnect from the context.

Overall Assessment

When examining the advertising structure of Block Blast!, it is seen that it is heavily based on the banner format, contains short-term and low-interference ads, has high brand visibility, is compatible with digital lifestyles in the sector, and has a content strategy that generally matches the user context. The game's advertising structure combines both passive awareness (banners) and active attention (videos) processes within the same game ecosystem.

FUTURE RESEARCH DIRECTIONS

This research examines the types of advertising found in digital games and the functions they serve in terms of brand visibility. The study systematically addresses the type, location, duration, and relationship of advertising with the game and user context, as well as its impact on the player experience (whether it creates interruptions, whether it appears natural). It focuses on the effects of in-game advertising on brand visibility. A review of the literature reveals that previous studies have largely focused on advergame content, experiential marketing, or gamification, examining general user responses and motivations. However, this study examines in-game brand placements in popular mobile games targeting children and young users. In this sense, future research examining games targeting other audiences will enable the identification of important findings regarding the functions of in-game advertising. Furthermore, it is important to examine in-game advertising in digital games not only from a formal perspective but also from a content perspective, enabling the analysis of advertisements in the context of narrative and message. Such research will make important contributions to the literature by revealing what kind of ideological meanings are produced by advertisements and their relationship with digital games.

CONCLUSION

The findings of this study demonstrate that digital games are not merely a form of entertainment, but also serve as a highly significant marketing communication and advertising tool. Both static (banner-style) and dynamic (video-style) advertisements placed in games such as Subway Surfers, and Block Blast! increase brand visibility on the one hand and enhance user awareness on the other, thereby significantly supporting sales strategies. In particular, "interstitial" or "reward-based" dynamic advertisements are displayed in full-screen format and have the potential to influence user awareness at a higher level. Some of these advertisements have a high potential for compatibility with the game, while others are considered to have low to medium compatibility. It was found that certain digital game advertisements are not suitable for the target audience of the game under review, posing a risk of containing dangerous content such as sexual or violent elements, and thus having low potential for compatibility with the game. Such advertisements also have certain limitations in terms of user satisfaction as they disrupt the continuity of the gaming experience.

The study found that static advertisements (banners) have a higher potential to be compatible with the game, but they are more limited in terms of user awareness and brand visibility because they remain on the screen for a short time. This finding supports studies suggesting that user engagement with the game and data surrounding the ad's position/importance are factors affecting ad awareness (Herrewijn & Poels, 2014; Lee & Faber, 2007) and experimental studies suggesting that moving/dynamic ads are more advantageous than static banner ads in terms of awareness (Huang & Yang, 2012; Hansson, 2017). On the other hand, reward-based advertisements voluntarily viewed by users create a more strengthening effect on the bond between the advertisement and the user. This is also consistent with Lee's (2017) view that reward-based advertisements viewed in games make the player's perception of the advertisement more positive.

The findings of the study reveal that the games examined predominantly feature advertisements targeting other digital games and online shopping, indicating that a strategy aligned with the game's target audience and the demographic characteristics of that audience has been developed. Considering that both games target a user base of children and young people, it can be said that other digital games and different mobile applications have gained an important opportunity to promote themselves to these segments. This points to Mago's (2016) concept of "cross-promotion" within the digital game ecosystem. Indeed, this concept refers to the strategy of placing advertisements for other digital games in the game portfolio within a digital game.

The findings of the study show that the games examined also feature advertisements for certain brands that are incompatible with the child and young user base and have low potential for compatibility with the game. The level of compatibility of advertisements related to areas such as care products, education, investment, hotels, plumbing, automation systems, industrial products, interior design services, furniture, technological products, white goods, water purification device parts, construction chemicals, and insulation systems, etc. have a very low level of compatibility with the game, and at the same time, the relationship of these types of advertisements with the user context appears weak. It cannot be said that these types of advertisements, which are mostly static (banner) and appear briefly at the bottom of the screen, have the potential to create a high level of awareness among users. For this reason, advertisers need to make a more detailed assessment and develop effective strategies regarding the placement of advertisements for brands that are incompatible with the game and user context in digital games.

According to the findings of the study, it can be said that in-game advertising generally plays a very important role in marketing communication. While brands have the opportunity to offer users interactive and personalized advertising through digital games, on the other hand, they can negatively affect users due to the abundance of advertisements and the inability to position the advertisement correctly, and an effective link between the game and the advertisement cannot be established. In this sense, it can be said that in-game advertising placement strategies vary according to the contextual relationship of the advertisement with the game and the user, the demographic characteristics and interests of the target user, and the advertisement's potential to create brand visibility.

The findings of the study revealed that in-game ads have different effects on brand visibility, user awareness, and gaming experience. Accordingly, when dynamic ads are displayed in full-screen and video formats, they create a significant level of awareness among users, but on the other hand, they have a negative impact on the player experience because they interrupt the flow of the game. Static ads (banners), on the other hand, appear more compatible with the natural flow of the game, but have a more limited impact in terms of user awareness. Reward-based ads encourage users to approach the ad with a sense of benefit, thereby positively supporting the user-game relationship. Developing advertising strategies tailored to user characteristics is a fundamental requirement for relevant brands in the process of identifying their target users. In this sense, advertising brands with high potential for alignment with the game and the user will create a functional advertising environment.

The findings of the study indicate that in-game advertising should also be considered in terms of ethical responsibility. In the games examined, digital game and mobile application advertisements with sexual or violent content that were not compatible with the demographic characteristics of the target audience were encountered, revealing a significant ethical issue. Considering that both games are aimed at children and young users, it can be stated that both these types of dangerous advertising content and industry advertisements that are incompatible with the user profile negatively affect the user experience and are problematic in terms of ethical responsibility. In this sense, when developing in-game advertising strategies, it is necessary to act in accordance with principles such as age and user suitability, transparency, ad distinguishability, and ethical responsibility. In conclusion, digital games constitute a very powerful and effective marketing communication arena, but designing this arena in a way that protects the user and gaming experience is one of the most fundamental requirements. In this context, future scientific studies that experimentally examine the different effects of advertisements placed in digital games on users and brand visibility will make significant contributions to the field.

REFERENCES

Acar, B. N. (2024). *The role of experiential marketing in in-game advertising* (Master's thesis, Istanbul Kultur University, Graduate School of Education). Istanbul Kultur University. https://openaccess.iku.edu.tr/entities/publication/38538e4d-cd23-4ec5-9f0e-7b5fe6d1b3c5

Akalın, M. (2018). *Research techniques in social sciences with sample explanations: Surveys* (2nd ed.). Seçkin Publishing.

Akyol, M. (2010). Game advertising as a brand communication tool: A study on its role in creating brand awareness. T.C. Selçuk University Institute of Social Sciences Department of Advertising and Promotion Public Relations and Promotion Division. Unpublished Doctoral Thesis https://tez.yok.gov.tr/UlusalTezMerkezi/tezDetay.jsp?id=rdrl-PfYM1STPpq62lPmBQ&no=zJ1UNQlaO-xvXUW5D1-ekw

Altınbaş, H. (2007). Marketing communication and city marketing: "Branding cities." *Selçuk Communication, 4*(4), 156–162. https://dergipark.org.tr/tr/pub/josc/article/200747?issue_id=19014

Altun, G. (2019). *Advergame Applications as a Marketing Communication Tool: A Study of Advergame Applications in Turkey* (Master's thesis, Sakarya University (Turkey)).

An, S., & Stern, S. (2011). Mitigating the effects of advergames on children. *Journal of Advertising*, *40*(1), 43–56. DOI: 10.2753/JOA0091-3367400103

Anderson, C. A., Shibuya, A., Ihori, N., Swing, E. L., Bushman, B. J., Sakamoto, A., . . . Saleem, M. (2010). Effects of violent video games on aggression, empathy, and prosocial behavior in Eastern and Western countries: A meta-analytic review. *Psychological Bulletin, 136(*2), 151–173. https://psycnet.apa.org/doiLanding?doi=10.1037%2Fa0018251

Aydemir, F. (2022). Digital games and their effects on children. *Adıyaman University Journal of Social Sciences Institute,* (41), 40–69. https://doi.org/DOI: 10.14520/adyusbd.1116868

Barnes, S. J. (2002). Wireless digital advertising: Nature and implications. *International Journal of Advertising*, *21*(3), 399–420. https://www.tandfonline.com/doi/pdf/10.1080/02650487.2002.11104939. DOI: 10.1080/02650487.2002.11104939

Başyazıcıoğlu, H. N. (2020). Interactive marketing communication and digital advertising. In Üzümlü, A. M. (Ed.), *Integrated marketing communication in all its aspects* (pp. 201–223). Nobel Yayınları.

Bayzan, Ş., & Güneş, A. (2022). History of digital games and Turkish gaming media. In Sağıroğlu, Ş., Bülbül, H. İ., Kılıç, A., Küçükali, M., Bayzan, Ş., & Samur, Y. (Eds.), *Digital games - 1: Tools, methodologies, applications, and recommendations* (pp. 25–83). Nobel Yayınları.

Belch, G. E., & Belch, M. A. (2003). *Advertising and promotion: An integrated marketing communications perspective* (6th ed.). McGraw-Hill., https://www.scribd.com/document/963071761

Bezjian-Avery, A., Calder, B., & Iacobucci, D. (1998). New media interactive advertising vs. traditional advertising. *Journal of Advertising Research, 38*(4), 23–32. DOI: 10.1080/00218499.1998.12466563

Binark, M., & Bayrakturan, G. (2008). *Digital games as a cultural industry*. Kalkedon Publications.

Bozkurt, A., & Genç-Kumtepe, E. (2014). *Gamification, game philosophy, and education: Gamification*. Academic Computing '14 - XVI. Academic Computing Conference Proceedings (pp. 147–156). Mersin University.

Buckner, K., Fang, H., & Qiao, S. (2002). Advergaming: A new genre in Internet advertising. *SoCbytes Journal, 2*(1), 1–5.

Çelebi, Ö. (2021). *The reflection of change in marketing communication on experiential marketing: An examination of brand applications from traditional to digital* (Master's thesis, Istanbul University, Institute of Social Sciences). Istanbul University. https://nek.istanbul.edu.tr/ekos/TEZ/ET002178.pdf?utm_source=chatgpt.com

Ceran, Y., & Karaçor, S. (2013). Advertising as a marketing communication tool: Advertising costs and accounting. *Niğde University Journal of Economics and Administrative Sciences, 6*(1), 9–22. https://dergipark.org.tr/tr/pub/niguiibfd/issue/19752/211410?utm_source=chatgpt.com

Chaney, I. M., Lin, K. H., & Chaney, J. (2004). The effect of billboards within the gaming environment. *Journal of Interactive Advertising, 5*(1), 37–45. https://www.researchgate.net/publication/228701546_The_Effect_of_Billboards_within_the_Gaming_Environment. DOI: 10.1080/15252019.2004.10722092

De Pelsmacker, P., Geuens, M., & Van den Bergh, J. (2013). *Marketing communications: A European perspective*. Pearson Education Limited.

Deterding, S., Dixon, D., Khaled, R., & Nacke, L. (2011). From game design elements to “gamefulness”: Defining “gamification.” *MindTrek '11* [Association for Computing Machinery.]. *Academic MindTrek, 2011*, 9–15. DOI: 10.1145/2181037.2181040

Dichev, C., & Dicheva, D. (2017). Gamifying education: What is known, what is believed and what remains uncertain: A critical review. *International Journal of Educational Technology in Higher Education, 14*(1), 9. DOI: 10.1186/s41239-017-0042-5

Fill, C., & Turnbull, D. S. (2023). *Marketing communications*. Pearson., https://www.iicseonline.org/marketing_communication_1.pdf

Ghirvu, A. (2012). In-game advertising: Advantages and limitations for advertisers. *The USV Annals of Economics and Public Administration, 12*(1 (15)), 114–119.

Güneş, A. H. (2012). *Legal and administrative regulation issues of digital games in the context of security* (Master's thesis, Police Academy Institute of Security Sciences, Department of Security Strategies and Management). Ankara. https://tez.yok.gov.tr/UlusalTezMerkezi/tezDetay.jsp?id=sqK-eB3NiJsEzLgOXs4l5A&no=F7dOig4g63YR7vXJ1RR6iA

Hackley, C., & Kitchen, P. (1998). IMC: A consumer psychological perspective. *Marketing Intelligence & Planning, 16*(3), 229–235. DOI: 10.1108/02634509810217345

Hanbazazah, A., Reeve, C., & Abuljadail, M. (2022). Influence of Advergames on brand outcomes and cross-cultural consumer behaviour. *International Business Reseach, 15*(8).

Hansson, L. (2017). *Dynamic in-game advertising: How important is it that ads are dynamic and capable of changing?* (Yüksek lisans tezi, Halmstad University). Halmstad University Open Access Repository. https://hh.diva-portal.org/smash/record.jsf?pid=diva2%3A1065214

Herrewijn, L., & Poels, K. (2014). Recall and recognition of in-game advertising: The role of game control. *Frontiers in Psychology, 5*, 1023. DOI: 10.3389/fpsyg.2013.01023

Huang, J. H., & Yang, T. K. (2012). The Effectiveness of In-Game Advertising: The Impacts of Ad Type and Game/Ad Relevance. *International Journal of Electronic Business Management, 10*(1).

Ilgın, H. Ö. (2013). Advergaming and brand relationship. The Turkish Online Journal of Design, Art and Communication – TOJDAC, 3(1), 24-33. https://dergipark.org.tr/tr/pub/tojdac/article/156783

Jaffe, J. (2003). *Advergaming Equals Attention. iMedia Connection, May 5.*

Kasım, M., & Tunç, P. C. (2024). AN EVALUATION ON THE RISKS AND ETHICAL ISSUES AWAITING CHILD USERS IN DIGITAL ADVERTISEMENTS. *Journal of Communication Studies*, *10*(2), 210–240.

Kuo, A., & Rice, D. H. (2015). Catch and shoot: The influence of advergame mechanics on preference formation. *Psychology and Marketing*, *32*(2), 162–172. DOI: 10.1002/mar.20770

Lee, J., & Shin, D.-H. (2017). Positive side effects of in-app reward advertising: Free items boost sales: A focus on sampling effects. *Journal of Advertising Research*, *57*(3), 272–282. DOI: 10.2501/JAR-2017-036

Lee, M., & Faber, R. J. (2007). Effects of product placement in online games on brand memory: A perspective of the limited-capacity model of attention. *Journal of Advertising*, *36*(4), 75–90. DOI: 10.2753/JOA0091-3367360406

Lee, S. (2021). *The impact of in-game product placement on consumer engagement*. Springer.

Mago, Z. (2016). Self- and cross-promotion within digital games. In Tănase, M. D. (Ed.), *Proceedings of the International Scientific Conference eLearning and Software for Education* (Vol. 1, pp. 335–340). Carol I National Defense University Publishing House., https://www.researchgate.net/publication/323192329_Self-_and_cross-promotion_within_digital_games

Mallinckrodt, V., & Mizerski, D. (2007). The effects of playing an advergame on young children's perceptions, preferences, and requests. *Journal of Advertising*, *36*(2), 87–100. DOI: 10.2753/JOA0091-3367360206

Mete, M. H. (2021). Programmatic advertising and ethical issues in digital media. *TRT Academy*, *6*(12), 426–449. DOI: 10.37679/trta.876044

Özek, B. M. (2022). Games from traditional to digital. In Sağıroğlu, Ş., Bülbül, H. İ., Kılıç, A., Küçükali, M., Bayzan, Ş., & Samur, Y. (Eds.), *Digital games - 1: Tools, methodologies, applications, and recommendations* (pp. 1–23). Nobel Publications.

Öztürk, M. C., & Coşkun, E. (2017). EVALUATION OF PLAYER MOTIVATIONS IN TERMS OF ADVERGAME APPLICATIONS. *Karadeniz Technical University Communication Research Journal*, *7*(1), 48–64.

Öztürk, M. C., & Coşkun, E. (2017). Evaluation of player motivations in terms of advergame applications. *Karaelmas Communication Faculty Electronic Journal*, *4*(13), 48–66. https://dergipark.org.tr/tr/pub/e-kiad/article/629600?issue_id=49304

Özüölmez, P. (2019). Yeni İletişim Ortamı Olarak Dijital Oyunlarda Deneyim İçerikli Yeni Bir Reklam Uygulaması: Skillful Finger Örneği. *Erciyes İletişim Dergisi, 6*(2), 1383–1404. DOI: 10.17680/erciyesiletisim.484759

Packer, J., Croker, H., Goddings, A. L., Boyland, E. J., Stansfield, C., Russell, S. J., & Viner, R. M. (2022). Advertising and young people's critical reasoning abilities: Systematic review and meta-analysis. *Pediatrics, 150*(6), e2022057780. DOI: 10.1542/peds.2022-057780

Parkin, T. (2023, March 10). *In-game advertising: A marketer's guide*. MarTech. Retrieved from https://martech.org/in-game-advertising-a-marketers-guide/ Accessed on August 31, 2025.

RapidFire In-Game Advertising. (2015, May 26). *RapidFire and Maxony Media partner to bring in-game advertising to Turkey*. RapidFire. https://web.archive.org/web/20160130150623/https://www.rapidfire.com/blog/dynamic-vs-staticin-game-advertising-a-comparison/ (Accessed: 08.09.2025)

Rose, G. (2023). *Visual methodology* (Akgülgil, G., Trans.). İnkılap Kitabevi. DOI: 10.4135/9781036231576

Shalabi, C. (2024, July 26). *Guide to video game advertising: Trends, tactics, and opportunities for marketers* [Original post March 11, 2024]. eMarketer. Retrieved August 31, 2025, from https://www.emarketer.com/learningcenter/guides/us-gaming-industry-ecosystem/

Shimp, A. T. (2008). *Advertising, promotion, and other aspects of integrated marketing communications* (7th ed.). Thomson Higher Education.

Sweeney, M., & Figas, N. (2024, May 15). *What is in-game advertising and how does it work?* Clearcode. Retrieved August 31, 2025, from https://clearcode.cc/blog/in-game-advertising/

Terlutter, R., & Capella, M. L. (2013). The Gamification of Advertising: Analysis and research Directions of In-Game advertising, Advergames, and advertising in social network games. *Journal of Advertising, 42*(2–3), 95–112. DOI: 10.1080/00913367.2013.774610

Thorson, E., & Duffy, M. (2012). *Advertising age: The principles of advertising and marketing communication at work*. Nelson Education Ltd., http://ndl.ethernet.edu.et/bitstream/123456789/49236/1/185.pdf

Uslu, E. G., & Kazaz, A. (2022). The reflection of the concept of consumption on the silver screen: Product placement in cinema, the example of the film *The Island*. In Kazaz, A. (Ed.), *New forms of consumption in the context of the individual, society, and digitalization* (p. 66). Education Publishing House.

Valkenburg, P. M., & Piotrowski, J. T. (2017). Digital games. In *Plugged In: How Media Attract and Affect Youth* (pp. 201–223). Yale University Press., DOI: 10.12987/yale/9780300218879.003.0012

van Berlo, Z., Reijmersdal, E., & Eisend, M. (2021). The gamification of branded content: A meta-analysis of advergame effects. *Journal of Advertising*, *50*(2), 179–196. DOI: 10.1080/00913367.2020.1858462

Van Reijmersdal, E. A., Rozendaal, E., & Buijzen, M. (2012). Effects of prominence, involvement, and persuasion knowledge on children's cognitive and affective responses to advergames. *Journal of Interactive Marketing*, *26*(1), 33–42. DOI: 10.1016/j.intmar.2011.04.005

Vashisht, D., & Chauhan, A. (2017). Effect of game-interactivity and congruence on presence and brand attitude. *Marketing Intelligence & Planning*, *35*(6), 789–804. DOI: 10.1108/MIP-01-2017-0018

Yamamoto, G. T. (2009). Games, Internet, Advergames, and Mobile Games. *PI Marketing and Communication Culture Journal*, *8*(29), 17–22.

Yavuzyılmaz, O. (2017). Advertising Games – Advergames. *Academic Social Research Journal*, *5*(62), 588–601. DOI: 10.16992/ASOS.13224

Yoo, S. C., & Eastin, M. S. (2017). Contextual advertising in games: Impacts of game context on a player's memory and evaluation of brands in video games. *Journal of Marketing Communications*, *23*(6), 614–631. DOI: 10.1080/13527266.2016.1155074

Zagni, L. M., Baima, G., Nguyen, L. D. X., & Do, B. (2025). Convergence and divergence in digital game-based advertising: A systematic review of advergames and in-game advertising. *Review of Managerial Science*. Advance online publication. https://link.springer.com/article/10.1007/s11846-025-00876-z

ADDITIONAL READING

Balasubraman, S., Peterson, R. A., & Jarvenpaa, S. L. (2002). Exploring the implications of m-commerce for markets and marketing. *Journal of the Academy of Marketing Science, 30*(4), 348–361. https://www.researchgate.net/publication/226035725. DOI: 10.1177/009207002236910

Bryce, J., & Rutter, J. (2006). *Understanding digital games*. Sage Publications. DOI: 10.4135/9781446211397.n1

Cauberghe, V., & De Pelsmacker, P. (2010). Advergames: The impact of brand prominence and game repetition on brand responses. *Journal of Advertising, 39*(1), 5–18. DOI: 10.2753/JOA0091-3367390101

Ekelund, R. B., & Saurman, D. S. (1999). *Advertising and the market process* (Savaş, V., Trans.). Liberte Publications.

Keller, K. L. (2001). Mastering the marketing communications mix: Micro and macro perspectives in integrated marketing communications programs. *Journal of Marketing Management, 17*, 823–851.

Mazur, L., & Miles, L. (2007). *Marketing lessons from 12 marketing masters* (Kökkaya Çalar, Z., Trans.). MediaCat Publications.

Mihart, C. (2012, April 1). Impact of integrated marketing communication on consumer behavior: Effects on consumer decision-making process. *Academy of Economic Studies*, 122–133. https://www.researchgate.net/publication/267422434

Parsons, A., Zeisser, M., & Waitman, R. (1998). Organizing today for the digital marketing of tomorrow. *Journal of Interactive Marketing, 12*(1), 31–46. DOI: 10.1002/(SICI)1520-6653(199824)12:1<31::AID-DIR4>3.0.CO;2-X

Yasmin, A., Tasneem, S., & Fatema, K. (2015). Effectiveness of digital marketing in the challenging age: An empirical study. *International Journal of Management Science and Business Administration, 1*(5), 69–80. https://www.researchgate.net/publication/314550609. DOI: 10.18775/ijmsba.1849-5664-5419.2014.15.1006

Youn, S., & Lee, M. (2019). *Advertising theory*. Routledge.

KEY TERMS AND DEFINITIONS

Advergame: A digital game created to promote a brand or product.

Brand Awareness: The level at which a brand is recognized and noticed by its target audience.

Digital Advertising: Promotion of a business's brand, products, or services through digital media platforms

Digital Game: An interactive game that can be played on digital devices such as computers, tablets, consoles, or smartphones.

Dynamic Ad: An advertisement in digital environments that contains moving images (video format) and whose design and features can change depending on the user and environment.

In-Game Advertising: Advertising placed within a digital game.

Static Ad: An ad that contains a static (fixed) visual in a digital environment and does not include any changes.

Chapter 2
Digital Game Advertising and Brand Strategies

Tuğçe Şen
http://orcid.org/0000-0002-4307-5622
İstanbul Beykent University, Turkey

Emel Karayel Bilbil
http://orcid.org/0000-0001-6932-8096
Marmara University, Turkey

ABSTRACT

Digital game advertising is one of the effective strategies advertisers use to create different experiences for younger generations. In this context, this study evaluates digital games as interactive narrative environments for brands. The study aims to examine digital game advertising within the context of brand identity, brand positioning, loyalty creating, and sustainable brand strategies from a theoretical and interpretive perspective. The study examines the theoretical aspects of digital game advertising and provides practical examples, focusing on brands' strategies within the digital ecosystem. In this context, practices such as in-game advertising, around-game advertising, and advergaming have been identified in the literature as redefining brand-consumer interaction. Of course, to use this potential effectively, brands need to ensure perfect harmony between their strategic goals and the unique dynamics of the digital gaming world.

INTRODUCTION

The profound transformation that communication practices have undergone, both in terms of content and form, is widely recognized. Digital games are just one of

DOI: 10.4018/979-8-3373-6309-7.ch002

the areas undergoing this transformation. In the digital age, games are much more than just entertainment or a leisure activity. Technology-focused communication centers on digital games, interaction, storytelling, and user experience, bringing together a few components. The evolving nature of games over time has become a field of research and practices for communicators and marketers. Digital games offer a multifaceted communication environment between institutions, brands, and consumers through their defining features such as participation, narrative structure, and immersive experience. In line with this trend, digital games are now regarded both as a platform for cultural expression and as an economic strategy tool.

One of the areas that has undergone fundamental change with the digitalization process is advertising. One of the most prominent examples of the transformation the field has undergone is the shift in the relationship brands establish with their target audience from passive recipients to active participants. Meanwhile, the digital gaming industry, which has reached a market volume of billions of dollars globally, has become a rapidly growing sector. Parallel to the transformation in advertising, users in digital games are no longer just recipients of messages. Users have become actors who participate in the production of content in games and shape the gaming experience. Users, who are part of the gaming experience, are building a new area of interaction. Thanks to this dynamic interaction, digital games provide unique opportunities in processes such as influencing consumer behavior, strengthening brand value and positioning, and creating cultural meaning. As a result of this structure, digital game advertising has become one of the most innovative application areas of marketing communication.

In the literature, digital game advertising is examined through the approaches of in-game advertising, around-game advertising, and advergaming. The definitions of these approaches will be provided in the following sections of this study, along with current practice examples. Today, brands and institutions integrate their brand identity, value system, and narrative forms into the dynamics of the gaming world. This creates the potential to establish a new emotional bond with the target audience through digital game advertising. At this point, players' attention levels, focus capacity, interaction experience throughout the game, and even in-game reward systems are among the decisive factors in the relationship brands establish with their target audience. In this context, digital games have become one of the fundamental elements that transform advertising from its traditional understanding into an interaction-based structure.

The interactive transformation of advertising has reached a new level with the integration of new digital technologies into communication and marketing. In particular, the inclusion of artificial intelligence, virtual reality, metaverse, blockchain, and NFT (Non-Fungible Token)-based practices in marketing communications has transformed digital gaming advertising into a multi-layered structure. Virtual brands and identities built in the metaverse, NFT-supported in-game assets, and AI-powered predictive personalized ads are redefining the boundary between consumers and brands. This innovative transformation between consumers and brands brings with it opportunities as well as significant debates. One of the most notable debates in this regard is that children are becoming an easily targetable audience through digital games. Children who become vulnerable to manipulation through digital games can be guided through their gaming experiences, primarily through in-game reward systems. Throughout the game, branded content and various behavioral incentives can unknowingly steer children toward consumption. Issues such as data privacy violations, user surveillance, algorithmic steering, manipulation, and addiction that accompany the digital interaction environment blur the ethical boundaries of digital game advertising.

This study is grounded in a deeper understanding of the digital gaming world within the context of game advertising and brand strategies. The strategies adopted by brands in digital gaming environments are examined using current examples. Approaches such as in-game advertising, around game advertising, and advergaming increase brand-consumer interaction. The aim of the study is to reveal how brand identity, brand positioning, brand loyalty, and brand sustainability strategies are integrated in the context of game advertising. First, the concepts of gaming and gamification are examined historically. Then, the relationship between digital games and advertising is explained. The digitization of games and their development as an advertising medium are conveyed. In this context, the different types of digital game advertising are explained in detail. Finally, how digital games integrate with brand strategies is evaluated through examples.

THEORETICAL FRAMEWORK

The Concept of Games and Gamification

Throughout history, many thinkers have attempted to define the concept of "game". However, the multi-layered and dynamic structure of the concept has made it difficult to come up with a single, agreed-upon definition. The discussion on the concept of "game" put forward by Wittgenstein in his work *Philosophical Investigations* (1953) can be given as an example of this situation. Wittgenstein argued that "game" cannot be reduced to a single common feature. According to the author, although different examples such as chess, football or children's games have certain common aspects, it is impossible to make a universal definition that covers them all (Wittgenstein, 1953). This approach reveals the difficulty of clearly defining the boundaries of the game. Philosophy professor Bernard Suits, on the other hand, argued that games can be defined, contrary to Wittgenstein. In his book Suits, *The Grasshopper: Games, Life and Utopia* (1978), he defines the game as an activity that involves voluntarily overcoming obstacles in accordance with rules that the individual has willingly adopted. According to the author, playing games involves consciously rejecting the most efficient path to a goal and choosing a more challenging path that the rules permit. In this respect, the game is seen as both a rational and ethical act of will (Suits, 1978).

Dutch historian Johan Huizinga developed a comprehensive definition centered on play in his work Homo Ludens (1938). According to the author, play is one of the fundamental building blocks of culture. He argued that the concept of play existed before culture. In fact, humanity evolved through play. According to the author, play, while being non-serious, stands far outside of ordinary life, is also a free activity that completely centers the player. It takes place within a specific time and place and proceeds according to specific rules. Play differs from the reality of everyday life and creates an alternative space for the player. The Latin word "ludus" means play, sport, and school, and forms the basis of many play-related concepts in Western languages (Huizinga, 1970). This meaning suggests that play is a space of learning, competition, and order.

Following Huizinga's fundamental approach, Roger Caillois both defined and classified games in his book *Man, Play and Games.* Caillois expanded Huizinga's approach, which treated play as a cultural founder, establishing play as a systematic framework explaining different aspects of human behavior. Caillois classified games as *agon* (competition), *alea* (chance), *mimicry* (simulation), and *ilinx* (vertigo), revealing the different aspects of gaming experiences on human behavior. *Agon (competition)* refers to games based on competition. Sports matches, chess, or e-sports competitions are examples of agon. The goal here is for individuals competing under equal conditions to demonstrate superiority in terms of skill, strategy, or performance. *Alea (chance),* games of chance fall into this category. Lottery or roulette can be given as examples. In these games, the players control is limited, and the outcome is entirely dependent on chance. *Mimicry (simulation)* refers to games where players assume another identity or take on a role in a fictional universe. Role-playing games or online avatar-based games are examples of this category. *Ilinx (vertigo),* on the other hand, refers to games that shake the player's perception, disrupt their sense of balance, or evoke excitement. Speed-focused digital games such as skateboarding are examples of this category (Caillois, 2001, pp. 12-13).

On the other hand, Caillois argues that games are positioned on a spectrum between *paidia* and *ludus. Paidia* are spontaneous and unstructured games. Games that children play freely fall into this category. *Ludus* are games based on strict rules, regular structured, and goals. Modern sports or strategy games can be examples of this category (Caillois, 2001, p. 13). These fundamental distinctions are crucial for understanding how brands design their gamification strategies today. Because today, many brands are leveraging game dynamics to build stronger engagement with their target audience. For example, while the point systems used in brands loyalty programs operate on a ludus logic, campaigns that highlight players creativity reflect elements of paidia.

Based on these theoretical foundations of games, gamification in the modern sense first gained visibility in the literature in the early 2000s. Gamification is defined as the use of game mechanics, dynamics, and fiction to encourage desired behaviors (Lee & Hammer, 2011, p. 1). Deterding et al. (2011, p. 10) defined gamification as *"the use of game design elements in non-game contexts."* This definition has become a reference point in subsequent research. Huotari and Hamari expand this definition, defining gamification as *"the process of enhancing a service with game-like experiences to support users' overall value creation"* (2017, p. 25). In this context, gamification is not only an element that enhances entertainment but also stands out as a communication strategy that strengthens interaction with the user and creates value. Brands connect with their target audiences through game-based platforms that appeal to basic human motivations, using the psychological mechanisms described below.

The development of the concept of gamification is evaluated within the framework of its close relationship with psychology and behavioral sciences. The theoretical basis for this relationship is provided by Self-Determination Theory (SDT), developed by Ryan and Deci. This theory provides a significant framework for explaining the motivational dynamics of gamification. According to self-determination theory, people are driven by three fundamental psychological needs. These are autonomy, competence, and relatedness. These needs appear necessary to facilitate constructive social development and personal well-being, in addition to natural tendencies toward growth and integration (Ryan & Deci, 2000, p. 68). Gamification practices aim to meet these three needs with elements such as point systems, badges, leveling up, and social leaderboards. Gamification elements such as points, badges, and leaderboards are not random game mechanics, but tools designed to satisfy these three fundamental psychological needs. When a brand strategically implements these tools, it has the potential to transform its interaction with consumers from a simple shopping dynamic into a deeper, psychological, and emotional connection. McGonigal presents an argument that supports this potential. McGonigal argues that the motivation, resilience, and collaboration skills players develop through games can contribute to solving real-life social and political problems through gamified processes (McGonigal, 2011). Thus, gamification is now used in a wide variety of fields, from education to healthcare, finance, and public services (Deterding et al., 2011, p. 12). The importance of gamification becomes even more apparent when it comes to advertising and brand strategies. After all, gamification is one of the most effective ways to build a strong bond between the consumer and the brand, creating an interactive and sustainable platform for communication.

Gamification positively influences consumers' perceptions and behaviors towards brands, especially in the digital age. Companies that integrate gamification into their brand strategy shape their brand image. For customers seeking innovative and engaging experiences, gamification makes the brand more appealing and ensures brand differentiation (Li et al., 2025).

The Relation between Digital Games and Advertising

Advances in information and communication technologies and the spread of the internet have created differences in games and gaming environments. Traditional game formats based on physical interaction, which require players to be in the same environment, have been replaced by digital games that can be played independently of time and place with the support of information and communication technologies (Yılmaz, 2015). Digital games have become one of the most interactive media environments since the mid-20th century, when information and communication technologies gained momentum. When examining the history of digital games, it is seen that the first examples emerged in the 1950s. Early productions such as *"Tennis for Two"* (1958) and *"Spacewar!"* (1962) are important digital games. These two digital games are considered pioneers in the application of computer technology to the gaming experience. The 1970s marked the birth of the commercial video game industry. Atari's game *"Pong"* (1972) transformed digital games into a mass entertainment form (Kent, 2001). The evolution of games from the analog to the digital world has triggered a fundamental transformation in cultural production (Wolf, 2008).

In the 1980s, arcades experienced the golden age of gaming culture, influenced by iconic titles like *Pac-Man* and *Donkey Kong* that defined the era. However, this period gradually came to an end with the spread of home consoles and personal computers. Following this period, digital games have become part of home culture on a global scale. Since the 1990s, game consoles developed by Sony *(PlayStation)*, Nintendo, Microsoft *(Xbox)*, and Sega have been introduced to players with hardware that is updated at regular intervals and games featuring higher resolution graphics. During this period, as the digital gaming industry rapidly diversified, the game *Majestic*, developed by EA Games, played a significant role in introducing the concept of *"immersion"* into digital gaming literature. Because this game blurs the boundaries between the virtual and the real by offering a form of interaction that, for the first time, allows the player to influence reality outside the game through their in-game actions (Sepetçi, 2022, p.113).

With the widespread adoption of the internet in the 2000s, desktop games, online games, multiplayer virtual worlds, and mobile games have expanded the digital gaming ecosystem. Digital games can be described as a central arena for social interaction, identity construction, and economic circulation. In other words, the digital gaming environment has become an interactive space where players express themselves, establish a sense of belonging, and develop new social roles (Taylor, 2006). Digital games are interactive environments that incorporate fundamental characteristics specific to the communication media of the digital age, such as "digitality, interactivity, virtuality, variability, and modularity." By integrating these characteristics with the act of playing games, they create a new form of communication between individuals (Yengin, 2012, p. 111). According to Rose (2012, p. 41), digital games are built within a software framework called a game engine as a new communication medium. This system integrates fundamental components such as physics (object collisions and movement), artificial intelligence (character behaviors), sound, animation, and graphics. The author emphasizes that this technical structure is not merely a visual process, but rather a narrative infrastructure that enables the player's active participation in the story. According to Lieberman et al., a digital game is an interactive system in which the player progresses within a set of rules to achieve a specific goal, receiving continuous feedback on their performance throughout the process (2009, p. 300). According to another definition, a digital game is an interactive simulation system that offers the user the opportunity to experience the rules governing a story rather than simply watching it unfold (Frasca, 2001). In the literature on digital games, there are many definitions that approach the concept from different angles. While some researchers consider digital games to be an interactive form of media, others define them as rule-based systems or simulation models. This diversity stems from the fact that digital games are not merely a form of entertainment, but rather a multi-layered structure that touches upon technology, culture, and communication. This multifaceted structure has led to the continuous evolution of digital games, both formally and technologically, throughout history.

With the advancement of digital technologies and the emergence of new hardware they bring, millions of different types and forms of games have been produced from the very beginning of gaming to the present day. These games can now be played on a wide variety of platforms, including computers, game consoles, smartphones, and tablets. By the 21st century, digital games have reached billions of users globally and continue to develop as a powerful industry in cultural, economic, and communicative terms. According to Newzoo's 2025 *Global Games Market Report* (2025) data, the global market value of the digital games industry has reached $188.8 billion. The same report states that this value is projected to reach $206.5 billion by 2028 (Newzoo, 2025). The strategic importance of such a massive industry in terms of advertising is clear. Digital games can be described as one of the most effective advertising channels due to their high potential for user interaction and their ability to reach different demographic groups on a global scale. In this regard, it is relevant to explain the concept of digital game advertising, which also forms the focus of this study.

Digital game advertising is a strategy that interactively integrates brands into the content of the gaming world. Digital games possess unique elements in terms of establishing a relationship with consumers, strengthening brand appeal, and increasing memorability. Digital game ads, which come into play when players show a high level of attention and engagement, convey brands to the target audience through a fun, dynamic, and engaging experience. Consumers can easily internalize the advertising message (Akan, 2022, p. 218). Digital game advertising creates an interactive and entertaining experience for consumers and integrates advertising messages within and around digital games. This form of advertising is one of the most effective strategies advertisers use to create different experiences for children, teenagers, and young adults. Recent studies have shown that some brands use multiple advertising strategies to reach consumers through digital games (Cicchirillo & Mabry, 2016, p. 588).

The use of advertising in games can take various forms. Various classifications have been made in the literature on this subject. This study is based on the game advertising classification developed by Smith and colleagues. This classification examines advertising in games under three main categories: in-game advertising, around-games advertising, and advergaming (Smith et al., 2014).

In-Game Advertising: In-game advertising is a type of advertising that involves incorporating products or brands into a digital game. The primary goal of these types of games is to provide the player with an enjoyable experience while making the brand a natural part of the gaming world. Just like in cinema product placement applications, game developers also offer advertisers areas where they can place their brands and products within game content (Terlutter & Capella, 2013). In recent years, in-game advertising has become one of the fastest-growing types of advertising in terms of both annual spending volume and projected growth rate. The main reason for this rise is the increasing popularity of digital games and the potential for brands to reach a broad and diverse target audience directly through these environments (Herrewijn & Poels, 2013). In these types of games, ad placements are designed to preserve the integrity of the gaming experience. In-game advertising can be integrated into the game in hidden (implicit) or obvious (explicit) ways, or it can be presented during game downloads. Advertisers interact with players by placing their ads in these areas in static or dynamic formats. Static in-game advertising refers to fixed ad placements determined during the game's development phase that cannot be changed after release. The most important advantage of this type of advertising is that no online connection is required to display the visuals in the game. However, the disadvantage of this situation is that no changes can be made to the content after the game is released. In contrast, dynamic in-game advertising is more flexible and can be filled instantly by different advertisers. For this system to work, the player must have a reliable internet connection (Terlutter & Capella, 2013). Dynamic in-game advertising offers brands the opportunity to run real-time campaigns while also providing the advantage of keeping the gaming experience up to date.

Around Game Advertising: These types of ads do not contain direct messages within the gaming environment. Instead, they consist of different application forms positioned around the game. Around games advertising encompasses four key elements: banner ads, cross-promotion, interstitial ads, and sponsorship. First, banner ads can be seen as visual, or video ads placed around the game. These ads are typically supplementary ads shown before the game starts, after the game is completed, or between game levels. Banner ads typically contain links that direct users to websites promoting products or services related to the game's theme or target audience.

Secondly, cross-promotion can be described as a form of marketing where the customers of one product or service are targeted for the promotion of another product or service. In other words, it is a collaboration-based marketing tactic in which two or more businesses come together to reach a broader shared target audience. Cross-promotion aims to create mutual benefit for both parties by providing access to a shared customer base. Thirdly, when evaluated in the context of gaming, interstitial ads are advertisements displayed before the game starts, after the game is completed, or during the loading phase (Smith et al., 2014). Interstitial ads completely cover the screen, intensely drawing the user's attention (Yörük, 2024, p. 21). Finally, sponsorship is a traditional advertising method where the advertiser finances a specific part of the game environment. Such sponsorships may take the form of providing free access to the game, supporting a specific game level, or customizing a part of the game's design area for the brand using the "game skinning" method. In the "game skinning" application, the advertiser customizes the entire virtual environment where the game is located, or a portion of it, with sponsored content, or acquires a dedicated sponsorship area on the game portal. These three methods are frequently used in advergames found on certain gaming portals (Smith et al., 2014).

Advergaming: The term is derived from the combination of "adver," the abbreviated form of the English word "advertisement," and "game". In today's rapidly digitizing world, advergaming stands out as an advertising method conducted through computer games. It offers brands the opportunity to interact with their target audiences and promote their products in an experiential way (Sucu, 2011, p. 36). The first attempts at advergaming applications can be seen in the online multiplayer games of the 1980s. This application may take the form of brand or product placement within the game. In later periods, brands began collecting consumer data through advergaming applications that reached their target audiences through specific gaming sites (Elden, 2013, p. 551). Advergaming utilizes interactive game technologies to deliver advertising messages to consumers by integrating them into the game (Chen & Ringel, 2001). According to another definition, advergaming involves entertainment-focused games that feature game and brand pairing, as well as the placement of businesses, products, or brands and related advertising messages within the game. In doing so, it sometimes creates and develops the brand's own games and sometimes brings the brand and the consumer together on a common platform by placing the brand or product within a game. Thus, it facilitates the achievement of advertising objectives (Tosun, 2010, p. 413). Advergaming can be described as advertising messages that are fully gamified. It is a type of advertising that utilizes game concepts and mechanics to increase brand engagement and ultimately achieve a commercial goal (van Berlo et al., 2021, p. 179). According to another definition, advergaming refers to interactive games developed around a brand, product, or character associated with that brand. Elements belonging to the brand or product are incorporated into the structure of the game using associative or demonstrative methods. In other words, games can be designed to demonstrate the use of a product or to associate the product with a specific activity or lifestyle (Gurau, 2008, p. 106). The primary purpose of advergaming applications is to strengthen the image of the advertised brand and attract more users to the brand's website (Akan, 2022, p. 223).

In her study, Nelson (2002) concluded that even if players play a game for the first time and for a limited period, they can easily remember the brands placed in the games in both the short and long term. Mallinckrodt and Mizerski (2007) found that children's attitudes toward brands change when they are exposed to advergaming, and that this effect is reflected in their purchasing demands. These results indicate that digital games have the potential to shape consumer attitudes and influence behavior.

Digital games, due to their interactive nature, turn the consumer into an active subject. In this context, games enable advertising to move beyond being merely a message and instead be designed as an experiential process. As Henry Jenkins (2006, p. 3) puts it, it is a space for producing a "participatory culture." While interacting with brands, players also create their own content, becoming an active part of the gaming world.

The advantages that digital games offer to advertising are quite diverse. First, thanks to the *high level of interaction* in digital games, players are in direct contact with the brand. In-game processes such as completing tasks, making choices, and customizing characters facilitate the establishment of an emotional connection with the brand. The second advantage of digital games in advertising is the *long-term attention* they provide. This sustained attention helps advertisements gain a more permanent place in brand memory through repeated exposure (Lee & Faber, 2007). Furthermore, it can be said that the immersive experience offered by the nature of games contributes to brands establishing stronger emotional bonds with players.

Immersion describes the state in which the player is completely involved in the game world on an emotional, perceptual, and cognitive level. As the player interacts with the environment, sounds, story, and tasks offered by the game, they disconnect from the outside world and experience a holistic experience within the game world (Jennett et al., 2008, p. 642). The player, represented by a digital avatar, accesses the sounds and images within the game through wearable devices. Thus, immersive technologies place the player right in the middle of the story. These technologies provide players with the feeling of being in a real place (Çakır, 2023). This allows players' state of psychological concentration to enable brands to convey their messages not only on a cognitive level but also on an emotional level. In other words, as the time spent in the game world increases, players begin to perceive brands not as external elements, but as natural parts of the gaming experience. In this way, the brand becomes an emotional component of the story experienced by the player.

Thirdly, one of its most notable advantages is its *measurability and targeting capacity* with advanced analytics tools. While measuring the effectiveness of advertising in traditional advertising channels is often done using limited methods, digital games offer the ability to track user behavior in real time. Due to the nature of the games, the amount of time players spends interacting with the brand, their task completion rates, which objects they select, and their in-game spending behavior are continuously recorded. These data provide brands with real-time feedback, offering a unique advantage in measuring advertising effectiveness (Hamari & Lehdonvirta, 2010). In this regard, games contribute to the development of data-driven strategies in advertising. Finally, digital games have the potential to create a strong *cultural context* for brands because they are shaped around shared symbols, values, and communities on a global scale. Douglas Holt's (2004) cultural branding approach provides a powerful framework for understanding the strategic use of brands from the perspective of digital games. According to Holt, brands are symbolic representatives of social identities and cultural values (Holt, 2004). In this respect, iconic brands create cultural myths that fulfill consumers' identity quests. Marlboro's “masculinity” myth or Harley Davidson's “freedom” myth represent the cultural codes of brands. Digital games offer opportunities for brands to realize this process. Games are considered not only entertainment tools but also spaces for identity construction, belonging, and cultural experience. Players don't just see brands in games; they also experience the values, narratives, and social symbols represented by the brands. This situation allows brands to build cultural meaning through games. For example, a brand that stands out with its sustainability-focused products appearing in an environmentally themed game serves as a cultural message that supports ecological values in addition to promoting its products. Similarly, brands targeting youth culture gaining visibility through esports events or online gaming communities demonstrates that they play a significant role in brand identity and belonging. Therefore, digital games go beyond economic benefit in the context of advertising and encompass a cultural dimension.

When all these dimensions are considered together and viewed from today's perspective, digital games constitute one of the most innovative, interaction-focused, and culturally rich platforms for advertising. The role of this field in advertising is to capture users' high engagement and sustained attention, provide measurability through advanced data analytics, and create cultural context. In addition to various advantages, the ethical dimension of digital games and advertising is an important topic of discussion. In particular, children's greater susceptibility to persuasive messages, the collection of personal data, and the extent to which advertisements should be integrated into the gaming experience are frequently discussed topics in the literature (van Reijmersdal et al., 2012). Therefore, the role of digital games in advertising is defined more by responsibilities than by opportunities.

Brand Strategies in Digital Games

Intense competition in the globalizing market has forced brands to explore new channels. Digital games stand out as the most innovative and effective platforms in this context. Today, digital games have transformed into a communication ecosystem where brands generate strategic value and support their long-term positioning. In this intensely competitive environment, organizations and brands must deliver effective communication messages at the right time and place to reach consumers. Brands can only stand out from the multitude of messages by developing a common and holistic communication strategy (Karayel Bilbil, 2004). As Erdem and Urfalı (2022, p. 23) point out, brands are turning to the digital gaming arena to adapt to the changing consumer profile. The player base is defined as an important part of the new audience. The storytelling, experience-focused interaction, and emotional connection opportunities provided by games have become an important strategic investment area for brands.

A brand strategy is a comprehensive management approach that aims to give the brand a sustainable competitive advantage, correctly define the target audience, and effectively communicate the benefits the brand offers to consumers. Brand strategy is primarily addressed in line with the organization's overall strategic direction, considering the value propositions offered by the brand and the target consumer group. The brand position desired in the target consumer is shaped because of integrating corporate strategy decisions in harmony with the basic elements of the marketing mix (product, price, place, and promotion). After this stage, it is necessary to evaluate other details related to the brand strategy, determine the promise that best represents the brand, and support this promise with appropriate promotional strategies (Aktuğlu, 2022, p. 116).

Brand strategies have a multidimensional structure that determines the brand's identity, positioning, value, and the nature of its relationship with its target audience. These strategies have been addressed in various dimensions in different studies in the literature. In general, brand identity strategy, positioning strategy, loyalty creating strategy, cultural brand strategy, emotional brand strategy, experiential brand strategy, sustainable brand strategy, and storytelling strategy are discussed in depth under these headings (Aaker, 2020; Aktuğlu, 2022; Ar, 2007; Holt, 2012; Holt & Cameron, 2012; Morrison & Crane, 2007; Rosenbaum-Elliott et al., 2015; Schmitt, 2009; Kotler & Keller, 2016; Scozzese & Gelli, 2023; Grubor & Milovanov, 2017; Fog et al., 2005). The scope of these strategies is quite broad. As this study is a book chapter, the aim is to highlight the dimensions of brand identity strategy, brand positioning strategy, loyalty creation strategy, and sustainable brand strategy. This study evaluates how brands implement these strategies in digital game-based interactions.

Brand Identity Strategy

According to Aaker, brand identity is the totality of associations related to the brand that brand strategists strive to create and manage in a sustainable manner. In this context, brand identity is not limited to visual elements. It is a holistic structure that encompasses the values promised by the brand, its personality, its cultural positioning, and the emotional responses it evokes in the consumer's mind. Brand identity provides direction, purpose, and meaning for the brand. Identity is based on what the brand is, what it represents, and how it wants to be perceived by consumers (Aaker, 2020, p. 84). Aaker's brand identity model defines brands not as a product or service, but through personality, symbolic values, vision, and cultural context. Digital games are unique platforms that enable the direct experience of this identity. Digital game advertising not only makes brand identity visible but also integrates it into the player's experience through game tasks, reward systems, and interactive mechanics. The applications included in the game create a simulation environment that allows players to experience specific brand values.

Schmitt (1999) argues that brands must create holistic experiences at the emotional, sensory, and cognitive levels. In other words, it means experiencing the brand with all five senses and behaving accordingly. In digital game advertising, this strategy works by allowing the player to physically and emotionally experience the brand's values through game elements such as tasks, points, or achievements. For example, Fortnite is a shooter game designed by Epic Games. In this game, players can build buildings, shelters, and islands, while elements such as in-game appearances can only be designed by the platform (Wang et al., 2023, p. 326). Fortnite, which has millions of active players globally, has become more than just a battle royale game; it has transformed into an experiential platform for brands. With constantly updated events, brand collaborations, movie promotions, and an in-game community culture, Fortnite offers an interactive environment where brands can connect with young audiences. Holmes (2019) emphasizes that Fortnite is not just a game but also functions as a social network and cultural meeting point.

According to Aaker's brand identity model, a strong brand is defined by the integrity of its values, personality, symbols, and vision (Aaker, 2020). The Air Jordan collaboration between Fortnite and Nike is an effective example of conveying these identity components to the target audience through a digital gaming experience. Nike has built its brand identity strategy for many years on values such as "athletic spirit," "freedom," "determination," and "youthful energy." Nike has designed this identity not only through visual symbols (shoes, brand logo) but also in a way that can be experienced through the player's actions. Players experienced the brand's athletic energy by completing Air Jordan-themed "Downtown Drop" challenges, identifying with the Nike identity, in-game performance, and sense of achievement throughout the process (Rooney, 2022). Here, Nike's "Just Do It" philosophy was lived out not as a slogan, but as an in-game action. As the player jumps, speeds up, or completes tasks, they become integrated with the brand's identity. This example concretely embodies the concept of "beyond-product values" in Aaker's brand identity model. The brand is no longer just a shoe, it's an experience.

The image of a brand is based on people's knowledge and experiences (Karayel Bilbil, 2004). As a result of the experiential process, the consumer's experience of the brand identity lays the groundwork for the consolidation of perceptions about the brand at a mental level. In other words, consumers do not merely interact with a brand; they also reproduce in their minds the value judgments, symbolic meanings, and emotional associations related to that brand. Thus, digital games have become areas where brands are also built through consumer perception and experience.

The Air Jordan collaboration between Fortnite and Nike successfully reflects the three levels of brand identity strategy. First, on a symbolic level, the Nike logo and Air Jordan products are positioned in the game as indicators of status and success. Thus, the brand's symbolic value has been transferred to the game. Secondly, at an experiential level, players did not merely observe the brand; they interacted with it, directly experiencing its energetic, bold, and dynamic personality. Culturally speaking, considering Fortnite's global player base, this collaboration has transformed Nike from a sports brand into a representative of youth culture and digital lifestyle. When a positive image can be reflected with a strong identity, the brand will be differentiated from its peers by individuals, and this will carry the brand to a positive place in the minds of individuals (Karayel Bilbil & Şen, 2023).

Brand Positioning Strategy

Brand positioning is a strategic process aimed at determining how a brand will be perceived in the minds of consumers. This perception is shaped by the values the brand represents, its personality traits, and the way it interacts with its target audience (Keller, 2013). Similarly, positioning strategy is a planned process aimed at consumers recognizing products or brands and establishing a specific place in the consumer's mind relative to competitors. Positioning strategies are extremely important in terms of brand management. After all, the fundamental element that differentiates a brand is how it is perceived in the consumer's mind, continuously supported by communication strategies (Aktuğlu, 2022). In this context, the Fortnite and LEGO collaboration is one of the most striking examples of brand positioning in the digital gaming environment. LEGO Fortnite is a new survival crafting game developed through a partnership between the LEGO Group and Epic Games. Designed for people of all ages to enjoy together, the game encourages creativity, experimentation, and collaboration through play (LEGO, 2025). Thus, LEGO's creativity and building experience combined with Fortnite's interactive game world has positioned the brand not only as a toy manufacturer, but also as a pioneer of digital creativity and collaborative production culture. LEGO-themed elements integrated into Fortnite have given players the opportunity to build virtual worlds made entirely of LEGO bricks, design their own spaces, and interact with other users. This experience has brought LEGO's core brand value of "building with imagination" into the digital realm, making the brand's creativity and productivity-focused philosophy interactive and tangible. Thus, LEGO has shed its identity as a physical toy manufacturer and repositioned itself as a global digital experience brand that appeals to all age groups.

The Fortnite and LEGO collaboration clearly demonstrates the core objectives of the brand positioning strategy. First, it has integrated the brand with the lifestyle of its target audience. Second, it has redefined the brand's meaning in line with the digital values of the era. Finally, it has differentiated the brand in a competitive digital culture. LEGO's strategic partnership with Fortnite demonstrates that the brand has adapted to the digital transformation process and effectively implemented its experience-based positioning strategy centered on user engagement.

Brand Loyalty Creation Strategy

Brand loyalty is defined not only as consumers repeatedly purchasing a specific brand, but also as developing an emotional, cognitive, and behavioral attachment to that brand (Tosun, 2020). In traditional marketing, brand loyalty is often associated with measurable variables such as product performance, price advantage, satisfaction, or appeal. However, in today's digital world, this loyalty has become more experienced, identity, and community focused. Digital games play a significant role in this transformation. Digital games are platforms where users engage with brands over the long term, based on interaction and voluntary participation, and are one of the most powerful areas for rebuilding brand loyalty.

Digital games enable players to have continuous and meaningful experiences with specific brands. Thus, digital games make it possible to establish loyalty on an emotional basis. In this context, brands contribute to users internalizing their perception of the brand, identifying the brand with their own gaming identity, and developing long-term loyalty by using the in-game experience as a strategic communication tool. One of the most well-known examples of this situation is the Adidas brand's constant presence in the FIFA game series. FIFA's long-standing gaming universe presents soccer as more than just a sport, but as a cultural experience. Players are constantly seeing Adidas products in the game with each new release. This repeated visual exposure ensures that the brand is perceived as a natural part of football culture. In this way, Adidas establishes an emotional connection with users by associating itself with the matches they win, the teams they create, or their moments of success in career mode. The player experiences the sense of achievement they feel in the game together with the brand. Therefore, loyalty is built on the feeling created by experience.

A similar strategy has also been implemented by Nike for many years through the NBA 2K game series. Characters in the game can be customized with shoes and designs worn by real-world athletes. As players achieve success wearing Nike shoes in "MyPlayer" modes, they see the brand as a symbol of their personal performance. Thus, Nike has become not just a brand in the eyes of athletes, but the embodiment of the idea of "pushing oneself beyond limits and achieving success." Such examples clearly demonstrate the power of in-game advertising in building loyalty. In digital games, the brand is a meaningful part of the player's experience.

Digital games are social platforms that bring communities together as well as providing individual experiences. Digital game advertising has the potential to create a collective sense of belonging to the brand by leveraging this community structure. At this point, brand loyalty is reinforced through community identity. Players embrace the brand as part of the digital community they belong to. For example, the international esports tournaments organized by Riot Games in the League of Legends game demonstrate how brands can engage with these communities. Brands that sponsor tournaments gain traction not by attracting players' attention through advertising, but by contributing to the gaming ecosystem. This strengthens the bond established with the brand and lays the foundations for sustainable loyalty.

Brand loyalty is strengthened in the physical world as well as in virtual environments through digital games. This situation has become particularly evident with the proliferation of "phygital" brand experiences. The Pokémon Go and Starbucks partnership is a successful example of this hybrid loyalty model. The conversion of Starbucks stores into "PokéStop" locations in the game has enabled players to interact with the brand in physical spaces. Users have interacted with the brand both in the game and in the real world. This recurring interaction process has transformed loyalty into a behavioral habit. The Pokémon Go and Starbucks collaboration has transformed the concepts of sustainability and multi-channel experience into behavioral habits in the process of creating brand loyalty through digital games. In-game rewards, promotions, or special missions have transformed brand interaction into a routine part of daily life by ensuring players constantly encounter the brand. Brand loyalty in digital gaming communities evolves into brand advocacy over time. Loyal users become voluntary ambassadors who support the brand and make it part of their identity. In summary, digital game advertising is redefining the concept of brand loyalty. Brand loyalty is a factor that influences consumers' repeat purchases of a brand. Strong brand loyalty increases the success of brands and provides them with an advantage in intense competition (Karayel Bilbil & Güngör, 2024). Today, loyalty is based on a long-term, meaningful relationship with a brand. Digital games stand out as one of the most effective communication channels through which this relationship can be built sustainably.

Sustainable Brand Strategy

Today, individuals expect companies not only to generate economic benefits but also to take responsibility in areas such as the environment, human rights, and social justice. The decline in trust in institutions today requires consumers to demand greater transparency, ethics, and sensitivity from brands. In this context, brands can play a transformative role in solving social and environmental issues. From a corporate strategy perspective, brands that can inspire and create long-term loyalty become reference points that build trust and generate value in society. Today, brands do not merely offer a product or lifestyle; they also present a value system and a social stance. Brands with high symbolic value and a strong emotional connection to their target audience create significant awareness by developing concrete actions to protect the environment. This ensures consumer satisfaction during the purchasing process and creates a real opportunity to build a sustainable brand (Karayel Bilbil & Güngör, 2024; Scozzese & Gelli, 2023).

Loyal consumers are a driving force for brands. For this reason, loyal consumers are eager to embrace and defend the philosophy of their favorite brands. Thus, it also serves as a catalyst for the expansion of an environmentally conscious consumer group. When the majority embraces an idea, it becomes an unstoppable force. The attitudes and behaviors that develop with the adoption of sustainable brands have the potential to lead to deeper changes in people's lives. This approach also enables a balance to be struck between the interests of consumers, companies, and society (Grubor & Milovanov, 2017; Schultz & Block, 2015). Conscious consumers value brands that prioritize sustainability as well as quality products and are even willing to spend additional money for these brands if necessary (Karayel Bilbil & Güngör, 2024).

Play, games and gamification have the potential to support sustainability-focused transformations by engaging various stakeholders and encouraging psychological and behavioral changes (Fernández Galeote et al., 2025). Brand collaborations centered on sustainability themes in digital games have become an important aspect of game-based advertising in recent years. In this context, brands are creating environmental awareness and strengthening their brand image by presenting their environmentally conscious messages in interactive formats within gaming environments. For example, the sustainability-focused projects run by Microsoft in the Minecraft game provide a concrete example of this approach. The company encourages players to build environmentally friendly structures, use renewable energy sources, and develop ecological city models through games such as "Build a Better World" and "Sustainability City" (Minecraft, 2025). These games have enabled players not only to experience a virtual environment but also to learn environmentally conscious behaviors within the game setting. Thus, Microsoft has moved beyond being merely a technology company to embrace the image of a responsible global actor that promotes environmental awareness. These digital experiences, aligned with sustainable development goals, establish a value-driven connection between the brand and the consumer, serving as an effective tool that transforms game-based learning into social benefit.

Similarly, PUBG Mobile, which is recognized worldwide and has millions of players, has partnered with Tesla, one of the most innovative automotive brands. In this collaboration, electric car manufacturer Tesla presented the theme of "mobility of the future" in a way that players could directly experience (Çakır, 2021). Players have become aware of electric vehicle technologies and sustainable mobility by assembling Tesla Model Y vehicles at the virtual production facility called "Gigafactory." The importance of electric vehicle production and the transition to renewable energy have been emphasized, and the concept of eco-friendly mobility has been made visible through the in-game experience. The PUBG Mobile and Tesla collaboration creates a mutual interaction between "eco-awareness" and brand image by representing eco-friendly technologies in a fun way within the gaming environment, thereby strengthening the brand's environmentally friendly image within digital culture. Another example of this type of game-vertising is Gucci, one of the global fashion brands, which has developed a special collaboration focused on sustainable fashion in The Sims 4 game by combining its understanding of environmental sustainability with digital culture. As part of this collaboration, the brand has launched Gucci Off the Grid, the first digital reimagining of a sustainable fashion series, for the virtual world. When players use Gucci Off the Grid pieces in the game, they earn a green ecological footprint and 10 environmental points. When they enter rooms containing Gucci Off the Grid items, the moods of the Sim characters improve (Gucci, 2025). Gucci has drawn attention to sustainable fashion through virtual products made from recycled materials. In this way, environmental awareness has been brought into the gaming world through an aesthetic value. This example demonstrates that luxury fashion brands are moving towards strengthening their eco-friendly identities in the digital gaming arena.

Based on these examples focusing on sustainability themes in digital games, it can be said that games have transformed into cultural spaces with high potential for raising awareness and conveying social values, beyond being mere entertainment tools.

From a brand perspective, these environments are becoming powerful communication tools for making sustainability themes visible. Sustainability practices offer great potential for businesses to increase brand loyalty (Karayel Bilbil & Güngör, 2024). Furthermore, bringing environmentally sensitive gaming practices into the gaming world strengthens brands' ethical identities and creates a new interactive space where players engage with environmental awareness. In this context, digital games can be considered areas with the potential to influence individuals' environmental awareness and understanding of social responsibility.

FUTURE RESEARCH DIRECTIONS

Future research should focus on the relationship between brands and consumers as emerging technologies such as artificial intelligence, augmented reality, and the metaverse are integrated into digital game advertising formats. AI-powered systems can dynamically adjust the placement and content of ads based on the player's real-time behavioral data. Thus, future research can include in-depth studies measuring the effects of dynamic in-game advertising experienced by players on brand awareness, brand attitude, and brand loyalty. Another important area of research is examining the effects of cultural differences in the context of digital game advertising. Comparative analyses of data obtained by reaching different cultural audiences on a global scale can be conducted. This research could result in a comprehensive understanding of digital game advertising. Finally, brands can convey sustainability messages to their target audiences in digital games. However, it is important to examine the long-term effects of this not only in terms of brand perception but also in terms of creating behavioral change in players.

CONCLUSION

We can say that we are experiencing a process of social change as new technological and scientific developments affect our lives every day. As our world transforms with the advancement of technology, particularly with the spread of digital capabilities, the gaming and advertising sectors are inevitably affected by this transformation. Digital games stand out as one of the most effective advertising channels due to their high level of interactivity and ability to reach different demographic groups on a global scale. Digital game advertising integrates brands into the content of games. In digital games, players have transitioned from being passive receivers of brands to becoming active participants in the meaning worlds of brands. Thus, the one-way narrative structure of traditional advertising is transforming into a participatory and multi-layered communication process.

As examined in this study, digital games do not merely increase brand visibility. Digital games are an area where brands convey their values, stories, and social stances to their target audiences through user experience. This space serves as a strategic ground where brand identity, positioning, and loyalty are rebuilt in digital gaming environments. The strategies brands implement through in-game advertising, around-game advertising, and advergaming strengthen the bond consumers form with the brand. On the other hand, the development of digital game advertising should be carefully examined in terms of ethical and legal dimensions. Particularly, issues such as children being exposed to a significant amount of advertising content in digital gaming environments, data privacy violations, user surveillance, algorithmic steering, and the regulation of AI-powered personalized advertising should be reconsidered and addressed. For this reason, digital game advertising should be approached as a comprehensive communication process that includes ethical responsibilities.

The study examines the theoretical dimension of digital game advertising and focuses on brands' strategies in the digital ecosystem through current, application-based examples. The gaming environment ensures that the brand identity is experienced on a symbolic, cultural, and experiential level. At the same time, the gaming environment strengthens the brand's positioning. Digital games enable players to build meaningful experiences with brands. Brands use the in-game experience as a strategic communication tool. This ensures that players develop long-term loyalty to the brand. In the context of a sustainable brand strategy, socially beneficial approaches are reflected. Games centered around themes such as social values and environmental awareness enable brands to establish themselves as socially responsible actors. Thus, digital games make a significant contribution to brands' value-focused and sustainable brand perception. Digital games offer brands opportunities to develop a sustainable and ethically grounded identity that aligns with social values. Environmental awareness and sustainability themes enable game-based advertising to serve a normative and cultural function. Thus, it is evident that digital games have the potential to both increase social awareness and develop environmental consciousness. Digital games are also effective in creating a sustainable brand image with ethical and social values.

This study emerged as an effort to better understand the ever-growing world of digital gaming in the context of game advertising and brand strategies. As is well known, technology has always made significant contributions to the gaming and advertising sectors. Today's digital technology has provided brands with new opportunities for expression and meaning creation. The effectiveness of digital game advertising depends on the extent to which brands integrate their strategic goals with the unique dynamics of the gaming world. A properly implemented digital gaming advertising strategy contributes to establishing a strong connection with the target audience by integrating the brand's values into the gaming universe. Although in-game advertising, around-game advertising, and advergaming are clearly distinct in theory, practitioners need information on how to implement these advertising types in practice. First, platform selection is of particular importance. Different game types have distinct player cultures and interaction styles. Therefore, it is crucial for practitioners to ensure platform compatibility by jointly evaluating the target audience demographics, the dynamics of the game type, and the brand's communication objectives. A mismatch between the platform and the brand can reduce the effectiveness of the advertisement and may also lead to a negative perception of the brand. Determining the right type of advertisement to use is a critical strategic decision. Practitioners need to decide which type of advertisement is appropriate, considering the balance between their strategic goals and player expectations.

One of the most important managerial responsibilities in digital game advertising is preventing player alienation. Advertising applications that are poorly timed or interrupt the flow of the game can create negative feelings among players. Therefore, the appropriateness of the advertisement to the context, balanced intensity, and the preservation of the gaming experience are important criteria. Consequently, digital games are not only a space for visibility but also a communication space where brand values, cultural stance, and sustainability narratives are reproduced. Therefore, practitioners must consider players as long-term stakeholders. The participatory structures offered by games present significant opportunities for brands to develop strategies. However, for these opportunities to translate into effective communication, it is essential to select the right advertising formats that align with the brand's objectives.

REFERENCES

Aaker, D. (2020). Güçlü markalar yaratmak. (Çev: E. Demir). İstanbul: Mediacat Yayınları.

Akan, N. A. (2022). Dijital oyunlarda reklam ve etkileri. Ş. Sağıroğlu, Hİ Bülbül, A. Kılıç, M. Küçükali, Ş. Bayzan & Y. Samur (Ed.*), Dijital Oyunlar-2: Araçlar, Metodolojiler, Uygulamalar ve Öneriler* içinde (pp. 215-245). Ankara: Nobel Yayınevi.

Aktuğlu, I. K. (2022). *Marka yönetimi: Güçlü ve başarılı markalar için temel ilkeler*. İletişim Yayınları.

Ar, A. A. (2007). *Marka ve marka stratejileri*. Nobel Yayın Dağıtım.

Caillois, R. (2001). *Man, play, and games*. University of Illinois press.

Çakır, E. (2023). Metaverse evreninde dijital mimarilerin haber üretimindeki konumsallıkları. E. Güven & İ. Kılınç (Ed.), Yeni çağda dönüşen gazetecilik: Gazetecilikte yeni yaklaşımlar içinde (pp. 263-283). İstanbul: Eğitim Yayınevi.

Çakır, O. (2021, July 19). PUBG Mobile'dan Tesla hayranlarını sevindiren iş birliği. https://shiftdelete.net/pubg-mobiledan-tesla-hayranlarini-sevindiren-isbirligi

Chen, J., & Ringel, M. (2001). Can advergaming be the future of interactive advertising. *Fast Forward. Available online:* http://www.kpe.com

Cicchirillo, V., & Mabry, A. (2016). Advergaming and healthy eating involvement: How healthy eating inclinations impact processing of advergame content. *Internet Research, 26*(3), 587–603. DOI: 10.1108/IntR-04-2014-0091

Deterding, S., Dixon, D., Khaled, R., & Nacke, L. (2011). From game design elements to gamefulness: Defining "gamification." *Proceedings of the 15th International Academic MindTrek Conference: Envisioning Future Media Environments, MindTrek 2011,* pp. 9–15. DOI: 10.1145/2181037.2181040

Elden, M. (2013). *Reklam ve reklamcılık*. Say Yayınları.

Erdem, M. N., & Urfalı, M. M. (2022). Neden game-vertising? Gelenekselden dijitale oyun ve reklam ilişkisi. M. Nur Erdem (Ed.), *Game-vertising dijital çağda oyunlaştırma ve Reklam* içinde (pp. 12-25). İstanbul: Eğitim Yayınevi.

Fernández Galeote, D., Gabrielaitis, L., Guillén, G., & Hamari, J. (2025). Play, games, and gamification to support sustainability transitions: A scoping review and research agenda. *Environmental Innovation and Societal Transitions, 57,* 101025. Advance online publication. DOI: 10.1016/j.eist.2025.101025

Fog, K., Budtz, C., Munch, P., & Blanchette, S. (2005). *Storytelling: Branding in practice*. Springer.

Frasca, G. (2001). Rethinking agency and immersion: Video games as a means of consciousness-raising. *Digital Creativity (Exeter)*, *12*(3), 167–174. DOI: 10.1076/digc.12.3.167.3225

Grubor, A., & Milovanov, O. (2017). Brand strategies in the era of sustainability. *Interdisciplinary description of complex systems, 15*(1), 78-88.

Gucci (2025). Gucci off the grid X The Sims 4 Community. https://www.gucci.com/us/en/st/stories/article/gucci-off-the-grid-x-the-sims shoppable?srsltid=AfmBOooSSs0BQjPpb-Ttnf_CTjsYvprCU92vjbdp7rXoNEiupzgdFjjV

Gurau, C. (2008). The influence of advergames on players behaviour: An experimental study. *Electronic Markets*, *18*(2), 106–116. DOI: 10.1080/10196780802044859

Hamari, J., & Lehdonvirta, V. (2010). Game design as marketing: How game mechanics create demand for virtual goods. *International Journal of Business Science and Applied Management*, *5*(1), 14–29. DOI: 10.69864/ijbsam.5-1.48

Herrewijn, L., & Poels, K. (2013). Putting brands into play: How game difficulty and player experiences influence the effectiveness of in-game advertising. *International Journal of Advertising*, *32*(1), 17–44. DOI: 10.2501/IJA-32-1-017-044

Holmes, R. (2019, March 6). *More than a game, Fortnite is emerging as the best new social network.* Fast Company. https://www.fastcompany.com/90315238/the-best-new-social-network-may-surprise-you

Holt, D. B. (2004). *How brands become icons: The principles of cultural branding*. Harvard Business School Press.

Holt, D. B. (2012). Cultural brand strategy. In Shankar, V., & Carpenter, G. S. (Eds.), *Handbook of Marketing Strategy* (pp. 306–317). Edward Elgar. DOI: 10.4337/9781781005224.00029

Holt, Douglas B., & Cameron, D. (2012). *Cultural strategy: Using innovative ideologies to build breakthrough brands*. New York: Oxford University Press.

Huizinga, J. (1970). *Homo Ludens: A study of the play element in culture*. Maurice Temple Smith Ltd.

Huotari, K., & Hamari, J. (2017). A definition for gamification: Anchoring gamification in the service marketing literature. *Electronic Markets*, *27*(1), 21–31. DOI: 10.1007/s12525-015-0212-z

Jenkins, H. (2006). *Convergence culture: Where old and new media collide.* New York University Press.

Jennett, C., Cox, A. L., Cairns, P., Dhoparee, S., Epps, A., Tijs, T., & Walton, A. (2008). Measuring and defining the experience of immersion in games. *International Journal of Human-Computer Studies, 66*(9), 641–661. DOI: 10.1016/j.ijhcs.2008.04.004

Karayel Bilbil, E. (2004). Bütünleşik pazarlama iletişimi içerisinde marka kavramı ve bu kavramın halkla ilişkiler boyutu. *İstanbul Üniversitesi İletişim Fakültesi Dergisi, 20, pp.* 197-206.

Karayel Bilbil, E., & Güngör, S. S. (2024). The Impact of Corporate Sustainability Practices on Consumers' Brand Loyalty. *Academıc social resources journal, 8*(51), pp. 2931-2941.

Karayel Bilbil, E., & Şen, T. (2023). Türkiye'de çevreci STK'ların kurumsal kimlik ve imaj bileşenlerinin analizi. *Selçuk İletişim, 16*(1), 166–201.

Keller, K. L. (2013). *Strategic brand management: Building measuring, and managing brand equity* (Global Edition). Pearson Education.

Kent, S. L. (2001). *The ultimate history of video games: From Pong to Pokémon and beyond.* Three Rivers Press.

Kotler, P., & Keller, K. L. (2016). *Marketing Management.* Pearson Prentice Hall.

Lee, J., & Hammer, J. (2011). Gamification in education: What, how, why bother? *Academic Exchange Quarterly, 15*(2), 1–5.

Lee, M., & Faber, R. J. (2007). Effects of product placement in online games on brand memory: A perspective of the limited-capacity model of attention. *Journal of Advertising, 36*(4), 75–90. DOI: 10.2753/JOA0091-3367360406

LEGO. (2025). *All about LEGO Fortnite.* https://www.lego.com/en-us/service/help-topics/article/all-about-lego-fortnite

Li, W., Corral de Zubielqui, G., & Rao Hill, S. (2025). Gamification Impact on Brand Strategies: A Systematic Review. *Journal of Computer Information Systems,* •••, 1–19. DOI: 10.1080/08874417.2025.2503954

Lieberman, D. A., Fisk, M. C., & Biely, E. (2009). Digital games for young children ages three to six: From research to design. *Computers in the Schools, 26*(4), 299–313. DOI: 10.1080/07380560903360178

Mallinckrodt, V., & Mizerski, D. (2007). The effects of playing an advergame on young children's perceptions, preferences, and requests. *Journal of Advertising, 36*(2), 87–100. DOI: 10.2753/JOA0091-3367360206

McGonigal, J. (2011). *Reality is broken: Why games make us better and how they can change the world.* The Penguin Press.

Minecraft (2025). https://www.minecraft.net/tr-tr

Morrison, S., & Crane, F. (2007). Building the service brand by creating and managing an emotional brand experience. *Journal of Brand Management, 14*(5), 410–421. DOI: 10.1057/palgrave.bm.2550080

Nelson, M. R. (2002). Recall of brand placements in computer/video games. *Journal of Advertising Research, 42*(2), 80–92. DOI: 10.2501/jar-42-2-80-92

Newzoo. (2025). *Newzoo's global games market report 2025.* Newzoo. https://newzoo.com/resources/trend-reports/newzoo-global-games-market-report-2025

Rooney, K. (2022, September 26). *Fortnite x Jordan brand unveil new downtown drop LTM.* https://www.hotnewhiphop.com/219751-fortnite-x-jordan-brand-unveil-new-downtown-drop-ltm-news#google_vignette

Rose, F. (2012). *The art of immersion: How the digital generation is remarking Hollywood, Madison avenue, and the way we tell stories.* W. W. Norton & Company.

Rosenbaum-Elliott, R., Percy, L., & Pervan, S. (2015). *Strategic brand management.* Oxford University Press.

Ryan, R. M., & Deci, E. L. (2000). Self-determination theory and the facilitation of intrinsic motivation, social development, and well-being. *The American Psychologist, 55*(1), 68–78. DOI: 10.1037/0003-066X.55.1.68 PMID: 11392867

Schmitt, B. (1999). *Experiential marketing: How to get customers to sence, feel, think, act, and relate to your company and brands.* The Free Press.

Schmitt, B. (2009). The concept of brand experience. *Journal of Brand Management, 16*(7), 417–419. DOI: 10.1057/bm.2009.5

Schultz, D. E., & Block, M. P. (2015). Beyond brand loyalty: Brand sustainability. *Journal of Marketing Communications, 21*(5), 340–355. DOI: 10.1080/13527266.2013.821227

Scozzese, G., & Gelli, M. (2023). Lifestyle as a Branding Strategy for the Sustainable Brand. *European Scientific Journal, 19*(22), 1–26. DOI: 10.19044/esj.2023.v19n22p1

Sepetçi, T. (2022). Dijital oyun kültürü ve sosyal etkileşim. Ş. Sağıroğlu, Hİ Bülbül, A. Kılıç, M. Küçükali, Ş. Bayzan & Y. Samur (Ed.), *Dijital Oyunlar-1: Araçlar, Metodolojiler, Uygulamalar ve Öneriler* içinde (pp. 111-150). Ankara: Nobel Yayınevi.

Smith, M. W., Sun, W., Sutherland, J. ve Mackie, B. (2014). Game advertising: A conceptual framework and exploration of advertising prevalence. *The computer games joumal, 3*(1), pp. 95-124.

Sucu, A. (2011). Global Markaların Advergame Tasarımı ve Kültür İlişkisi. *ABMYO dergisi*, 24, pp. 32-41.

Suits, B. (1978). *The grasshopper: Games, life and utopia*. Broadview Press. DOI: 10.3138/9781487574338

Taylor, T. L. (2006). *Play between worlds: Exploring online game culture*. MIT Press. DOI: 10.7551/mitpress/5418.001.0001

Terlutter, R., & Capella, M. L. (2013). The gamification of advertising: Analysis and research directions of in-game advertising, advergames, and advertising in social network games. *Journal of Advertising, 42*(2–3), 95–112. DOI: 10.1080/00913367.2013.774610

Tosun, N. (2020). *Marka yönetimi* (4. Baskı). İstanbul: Beta Yayıncılık.

Tosun, N. B. (2010). *İletişim temelli marka yönetimi*. Beta Basım Yayım Dağıtım.

van Berlo, Z. M. C., Van Reijmersdal, E. A., & Eisend, M. (2021). The Gamification of Branded Content: A Meta-Analysis of Advergame Effects. *Journal ofAdvertising, 50*(2), 179–196. DOI: 10.1080/00913367.2020.1858462

van Reijmersdal, E. A., Rozendaal, E., & Buijzen, M. (2012). Effects of prominence, involvement, and persuasion knowledge on children's cognitive and affective responses to advergames. *Journal of Interactive Marketing, 26*(1), 33–42. DOI: 10.1016/j.intmar.2011.04.005

Wang, Y., Su, Z., Zhang, N., Xing, R., Liu, D., Luan, T. H., & Shen, X. (2023). A Survey on Metaverse: Fundamentals, Security, and Privacy. *IEEE Communications Surveys and Tutorials, 25*(1), 319–352. DOI: 10.1109/COMST.2022.3202047

Wittgenstein, L. (1953). *Philosophical investigations*. Blackwell Publishing.

Wolf, M. J. P. (2008). *The video game explosion: A history from PONG to PlayStation and beyond*. Bloomsbury Publishing USA.

Yengin, D. (2012). *Dijital oyunlarda şiddet*. Beta Yayınları.

Yılmaz, E. A. (2015). *Oyunlaştırma*. Abaküs.

Yörük, E. (2024). *Reklamın yeni dünyaları*. İstanbul: Eğitim yayınevi.

ADDITIONAL READING

Angelides, M., & Agius, H. (2014). *Handbook of digital games*. IEEE Press., DOI: 10.1002/9781118796443

Bogost, I. (2007). *Persuasive games: The expressive power of videogames*. MIT Press. DOI: 10.7551/mitpress/5334.001.0001

Calin, G. (2010). Advergames: Characteristics, limitations and potential. *Annals of the University of Oradea, Economic Science Series*, *19*(1), 726–730.

Cauberghe, V., & De Pelsmacker, P. (2010). Advergames. *Journal of Advertising*, *39*(1), 5–18. DOI: 10.2753/JOA0091-3367390101

Chaney, I., Hosany, S., Wu, M. S. S., Chen, C. H. S., & Nguyen, B. (2018). Size does matter: Effects of in-game advertising stimuli on brand recall and brand recognition. *Computers in Human Behavior*, *86*, 311–318. DOI: 10.1016/j.chb.2018.05.007

Ingendahl, M., Vogel, T., Maedche, A., & Wänke, M. (2023). Brand placements in video games: How local in-game experiences influence brand attitudes. *Psychology and Marketing*, *40*(2), 274–287. DOI: 10.1002/mar.21770

Mackay, T., Ewing, M., Newton, F., & Windisch, L. (2009). The effect of product placement in computer games on brand attitude and recall. *International Journal of Advertising*, *28*(3), 423–438. DOI: 10.2501/S0265048709200680

Nelson, M. R., & Waiguny, M. K. J. (2012). Psychological processing of in-game advertising and advergaming: Branded entertainment or entertaining persuasion. In Shrum, L. J. (Ed.), *The psychology of entertainment media: Blurring the lines between entertainment and persuasion* (2nd ed., pp. 93–146). Routledge.

Wise, K., Bolls, P. D., Kim, H., Venkataraman, A., & Meyer, R. (2008). Enjoyment of advergames and brand attitudes. *Journal of Interactive Advertising*, *9*(1), 27–36. DOI: 10.1080/15252019.2008.10722145

Zagni, L. M., Baima, G., Do, B., & Nguyen, L. D. (2025). Convergence and divergence in digital game-based advertising: A systematic review of advergames and in-game advertising. *Review of Managerial Science*. Advance online publication. DOI: 10.1007/s11846-025-00876-z

KEY TERMS AND DEFINITIONS

Advergaming: These are practices that integrate advertising messages with the game experience to promote a brand's product or service.

Around-Game Advertising: These are advertising formats that are not directly included in the game content but are displayed on platforms around the game.

Brand Strategies: Brand strategies are a set of planned, long-term approaches that guide how a brand will position itself in the market, create value, differentiate itself from competitors, and build sustainable relationships with its target audience.

Digital Game Advertising: Digital game advertising is a form of advertising based on games, where brands utilize the interactive structure offered by digital games to promote their products and services.

Digital Game: A digital game is an interactive system played through digital technologies, in which the player progresses by adhering to certain rules to achieve a specific goal.

Gamification: Gamification is an approach that aims to increase participation, learning, or interaction by using game mechanics, dynamics, and motivational elements in non-game contexts.

In-Game Advertising: In-game advertising is the direct placement of a brand's product or message within the game content.

Chapter 3
Around Game Advertising:
A Conceptual Framework and Cases of Application

M. Nur Erdem
http://orcid.org/0000-0002-7034-201X
Ondokuz Mayıs University, Turkey

Meryem Aldağ
Ondokuz Mayıs University, Turkey

ABSTRACT

In a highly competitive environment, digital games offer alternative worlds that serve as ideal platforms for marketing communication and advertising for brands seeking new avenues. In-game advertising or advergames are applications that cannot be overlooked at this stage. On the other hand, another application that receives less attention in the literature but is frequently encountered is what Smith et al. (2014) refer to as "Around-Games Advertising" (AGA). This concept refers to applications where advertising messages are not directly present in the game environment but are conveyed through applications such as banner ads, cross-promotion, sponsorship, and/or interstitial ads. In this context, this chapter discusses the relationship between games and advertising in terms of around game advertising.

INTRODUCTION

The concepts of games and gamification are among the most discussed topics in recent years. This situation is indicative of the rapidly expanding gaming market.

DOI: 10.4018/979-8-3373-6309-7.ch003

The gaming industry has evolved into a vast ecosystem that encompasses software and hardware manufacturers, developers, designers, publishers, and advertisers. According to Newzoo's data, the gaming market was valued at approximately $189 billion as of September 2025 (Buijsman, 2025). Additionally, there are approximately 3.32 billion active players worldwide (Duarte, 2025). These market dynamics clearly demonstrate why gaming is such a popular topic. On the other hand, this situation can also be viewed as a consequence of an ongoing debate—one whose roots extend back to ancient times—now resurfacing amid digitalization.

Indeed, even in the Ancient Era, Plato discussed games and play, which have an irresistible charm despite lacking concrete benefits and having no connection to truth or reality (Tleubayev et al., 2017). The scientific, philosophical, and theoretical foundations of the game in the West were established by notable figures such as Friedrich Schiller (18th century), Johan Huizinga (1938), Roger Caillois (1961), and Hilde Hein (1968). They produced important writings that define the game, explain its connection to culture, and establish its role in daily life and its relationship to aesthetics.

Today, gaming is a topic discussed in a much broader context. Like almost everything else affected by digitalization, it has changed as well. Gaming no longer exists just for entertainment or education; it has become industrialized, creating its own institutions, employment opportunities, and, in a sense, its own economy. Moreover, it has also attracted a significant revenue stream that greatly influences this industrialization process: Advertising.

The development of production and transportation technologies has created an environment of intense competition among brands because many similar products are available in the market. The same applies to communication technologies. In such an environment, brands are constantly exploring new platforms, media, and methods to deliver their marketing and advertising messages to consumers. This is where digital games emerge as ideal advertising environments, offering alternative worlds. Frequently, product and brand placement within existing games and designing or publishing games specifically for brands are practices that cannot be overlooked at this stage. Additionally, aside from in-game advertising or advergaming, there is another practice that is less covered in the literature but often encountered. As defined by Smith et al. (2014), Around-Games Advertising (AGA) is a concept designed to comprehensively address these types of applications. This concept refers to applications in which advertising messages are not directly embedded within the game environment but delivered through methods such as banner ads, cross-promotions, sponsorships, and interstitial ads.

In this context, this chapter examines the relationship between games and advertising, with a focus on Around-Games Advertising. First, a conceptual framework is established, followed by an examination of examples of practices that can be addressed under this concept.

CONCEPTUAL FRAMEWORK

It is a well-known fact that advertising is one of the fields most sensitive to technological developments in the field of communication and one of the fastest to adapt to them. Each technological advancement offers a new method or medium for brands to interact with consumers from an advertising perspective. Digital games are one of the most important examples of this. However, when examining the relevant literature, the combination of games and advertising is often approached by placing products and brands within the game and by creating an experience environment for the player/consumer. However, the scope of applications that could be considered game-vertising is much broader than this. The abundance and variety of game types, their adaptability, and the fact that games often involve the use of materials make them an extremely attractive medium for conveying advertising and marketing messages. Moreover, these features allow the game to be considered more than just a simple product/brand placement medium. The Around Game Advertising (AGA) category should also be evaluated in this context.

AGA differs from the typical practices that come to mind when we think of combining games and advertising. The issue here is not direct interaction with a brand or product within the game. Smith et al. (2014, p. 99) state that this type of advertising involves associating marketing messages with the game without entering the game environment, through combinations of four basic components: banners, cross-promotion, interstitials, and sponsorship. Therefore, before explaining the AGA in more detail, it seems appropriate to explain these four components. At this point, the first concept to address is banner ads.

Banners are one of the most fundamental forms of advertising, defined as display advertising. Digital advertising investments, totaling approximately $800 billion (Kemp, 2025), include display ads, which account for a significant share—particularly with the rise of programmatic advertising. Display ads have been among the most heavily invested in and most readily recognized applications in digital advertising since the internet began to be used as an advertising medium. Hoi (2020, p. 2) defines this type as the most popular form of digital advertising, noting that messages are conveyed through text, logos, animations, videos, images, or other graphic media. It targets consumers with unique characteristics to increase advertising effectiveness and enables advertisers to serve ads based on geographic location. It targets consumers with unique characteristics to increase advertising effectiveness and enables advertisers to serve ads based on location. Banner ads are one of the most important practices in display advertising. First appearing in 1994, banner ads were among the most popular types of online applications before they were caught in the filter of ad blockers. Wang et al. (2017, p. 3) note that this advertisement, published by HotWired for AT&T in the years when the number of web users was only 30 million, was the first. This first example, with the slogan "Have you ever clicked right here? You will," can be said to have marked the beginning of an era (McCambley, 2013). He states in his article in The Guardian that this first banner ad, which he created, emerged as one of the most effective forms of advertising—even though it has lost its impact today. According to him, this first example had three important advantages over modern digital advertising: it was part of an integrated marketing campaign, it provided a great experience, and it was created with good intentions toward consumers. First and foremost, it contained the phrase "You will," which had been used consistently in a campaign launched by AT&T two years prior to the broadcast of the banner ad, thus providing integration and consistency. In addition to being just an advertising message or simply a link directing users to the advertiser's website, this banner ad enabled users to virtually visit major museums, thereby providing them with a new and incredible experience. Another point is that the purpose was not purely advertising, but rather to enable a relationship between the brand and the consumer that, in a sense, involved a sharing of control between the parties, as the consumer evolved from being exposed to the advertising message to choosing to view the message through the act of clicking.

This first example subsequently created an advertising investment area worth billions of dollars. These ads, which can be placed in any suitable section of web pages, come in various sizes and are typically rectangular. They are used to attract the user's attention through striking designs with graphic animations and to direct the user to the address associated with the banner ad (Mestçi, 2013, p. 66). In this sense, banner ads can also be defined as visuals that promote a website's name and identity with a brief description. On the other hand, as technology has advanced over time, the structure of banner ads has also evolved and can now include audio or video (Innovationpei, 2012, p. 2). Today, there are many types and formats of banner ads. These types can be listed as follows (Tuyan, 2005):

- Standard Banner Ads: These are ads that are usually displayed in a 468*60 pixel ad space. Although there is no requirement, they are generally preferred to be placed in the upper right corner of the web page.
- Vertical Banner Ads: These have almost all the same features as standard banner ads. Again, most often added to the right corner of the page, these applications feature a banner ad placed vertically in dimensions of 120*600 pixels.

- Floating Banner Ads: These are banner ads that move around a web page for about 10 seconds and then disappear or shrink, remaining in a corner of the page..
- Rollover Banner Ads: This type appears as a standard banner ad when the page opens but expands when the mouse hovers over it, allowing for a more detailed presentation of the message. This provides details without redirecting to the website.

At this point, it is possible to say that the ways in which banner ads are implemented have evolved and diversified in parallel with technological developments. On the other hand, the spirit that was attempted to be created with the banner ad published for AT&T in 1994 is not found in modern versions of traditional or digital advertising, especially in display ads. And especially this type of digital advertising has evolved in a way that will greatly overwhelm the user and lead to advertising clutter on a monotonous axis. In the best-case scenario, banner ads can be ignored by users. Benway and Lane (1998) refer to a trend they call "banner blindness" in this context. The findings from their research, conducted through a website they created to investigate whether banner blindness actually exists, corroborate previous studies in this field. Accordingly, people searching for specific information on the web tend to clearly ignore large, colorful elements that stand out from other elements on the page. However, when there was no other way to access the desired information, they discovered banner ads. Although banner ads have advantages such as ensuring the efficient use of the advertising budget, directing the message to the right target audience, selecting the right timing, and measuring advertising effectiveness (Vural and Öz, 2007, p. 228), the large number of advertisers who prefer to use them causes more ads than the content the user is looking for to appear. As a result, users sometimes find themselves unable to even discover advertising messages that are genuinely targeted to them. The advertisements—sometimes dozens of them—on a page they open overwhelm users in a sense and cause them to resist advertising. This has raised some questions about the effectiveness of banner ads and necessitated the development of a strategic perspective on this practice. Booth and Koberg (2012, p. 14) state that when advertisements are placed on websites, the job of advertisers and/or advertising agencies is not only to attract the attention of the right type of potential consumer but also to divert the user's attention from the content they are currently consuming and direct it toward the advertisement. They emphasize that to achieve this, it is necessary to connect with users on a cognitive level, identify their problems, and then show how brands can help them solve those problems.

This perspective can certainly increase the effectiveness of banner ads, but consumers are also discovering new ways to increase their resistance to advertising at this stage and protect themselves from commercial information bombardment.

Adblockers are at the forefront of these methods. The use of these tools, which appear to be the most effective way to avoid advertising in the digital space, has increased significantly in recent times.

In 2024, the adblocker usage rate is 42.7% and continues to rise. Approximately 40% of internet users aged 18-24 and approximately 36% of internet users aged 25-34 use ad blockers. 63.2% of users block ads because there are too many, while 53.4% say ads get in the way. 40.3% block ads to protect their privacy. Mobile users block ads to save mobile data. 30.6% block ads to improve device performance, while 30% do it to avoid malware risks (Opena, 2025). Although the main issue today is the violation of privacy and confidentiality for the purpose of data collection, the fact that the main reason for using ad blockers is to avoid ads essentially confirms the above. Another way to avoid ads is to choose ad-free versions of the platforms or applications used. Consequently, banner ads appear to have lost their popularity. However, they are still in use. They are particularly important from a strategic perspective in relation to digital games, as will be discussed in the examples of practices.

The scope of cross-promotion (including cross-media promotion) is much more complex than banner ads. This is because it involves not just the transmission of a message but also a multimedia experience. However, before addressing this topic, it seems appropriate to briefly explain the concept of cross-media.

As a concept, cross-media is used to describe integrated applications that involve two or more media platforms (Erdal, 2007, p. 52). The concept is also defined as "an interactive system that is not limited to a single medium." Although the theme and narrative are singular, a cross-media system emerges through its application to many different narrative fields. The components within this different system have specific roles, and each of these components is designed to support a different aspect of a specific human activity. Cross-media reaches more users in different ways as narrative and viewing applications in different narrative environments" (Bolat, 2019, p. 518). Davidson et al. (2010) state that cross-media refers to integrated experiences across multiple media, including the internet, video and films, broadcast and cable TV, mobile devices, DVDs, print, and radio. The new media aspect of this experience inherently involves a high level of interaction and means that the user reads a kind of story through different actions across different media. This experience is connected across the various media involved through the story and viewer interaction.

According to Bechmann (2007), the field of cross-media is related to many similar or competing concepts such as transmedia, multi-platforms, hybrid media, intermedia, and divergence. This lack of homogeneity in both concepts and meanings necessitates a clarification of cross-media. The concept can be used to describe the communication of a general story, production, or event through a coordinated combination of platforms. Cross-media can be conceptualized from both an internal and an external perspective. Externality refers to practices directed toward users, while internality refers to practices within media organizations themselves. User-oriented cross-media (external perspective) focuses on creating cross-promotion and cross-media storylines. Cross-media productions use various media platforms, each of which is included in a communicative division of labor, with an expected added value or increased user interest (shares) and a retention strategy for users.

Narratives created through cross-media are not fundamentally new. They are frequently seen in traditional media as well. Over time, this type of content formation has shifted toward new media, contributing to the enrichment and diversification of narrative content (Bolat, 2020, p. 122). However, it should be emphasized that the change is not only formal but also interactive. New media, with Web 2.0, has transformed the audience from passive viewers into active participants, bringing many opportunities with it.

Cross-promotion or cross-media promotion is an important part of the process described by Bechmann (2007) and can be said to have emerged in response to a perceived gap, particularly in the fields of advertising and marketing, in the early 2000s. With the widespread adoption of the internet, websites have become essential. In the early stages, advertisements were published with the expectation that they would attract users to visit websites; however, they were not very effective on consumers. This is because, during this period, the general approach was simply to publish advertisements and wait for users to visit through these ads. This approach, largely a reflection of the traditional media mindset of *publish an ad + ensure it is seen + wait for a purchase*, was, according to Edwards and La Ferle (2000), extremely inadequate. There was a need for research that focused on both cross-media promotion methods that encouraged consumers to visit websites and the reasons that prompted consumers to take action when they encountered a direct-response advertisement. Referring to research conducted in the late 1990s, the authors emphasized that URLs displayed in TV commercials were effective at eliciting positive responses from consumers. With follow-up research, cross-promotion began to be implemented effectively. Hardy (2010) states that the concept is used by marketers and advertisers to describe any promotional campaign that uses multiple channels. Essentially, there is nothing new about using multiple channels to drive retention in a campaign. What is new is that marketers and advertisers use the concept to refer to a planned promotional strategy that uses multiple media to promote a product or service. Hardy (2010) emphasizes that he uses the term to refer to promotion carried out by allied media. This state of being allied essentially involves a strategic or structural partnership. In other words, the concept is used by him to describe a situation in which media that are related to each other in some way carry out promotional cooperation around a common goal, which is also how those working in marketing and advertising approach the concept. Global and large-scale brands frequently engage in this type of collaboration. Such collaborations, often described as "unexpected" and "sensational," can also occur between competing brands in the same sector. Examples include the "Hacker Project" campaign, carried out in collaboration with Balenciaga and Gucci; the Uber and Spotify car music playlist partnership; the Crocs and Haribo collaboration; the Nestle KitKat and Google Android 4.4 collaboration; and many others. The number of these examples can certainly be increased. It is clear that such collaborations involve a win-win relationship. Brands directly or indirectly influence each other's awareness levels and, naturally, their profitability. Therefore, one of the most fundamental elements to emphasize is that cross-promotion is a strategic process. Setting goals, choosing the right partner, and selecting the right tools are vital in this context. Collaboration and promotion through cross-promotion increase brands' competitive potential and provide a strategic advantage (Song and Tang, 2015). Increased brand awareness, attracting new potential consumers, higher sales, lower advertising costs, and enhanced reputation are among the advantages offered by cross-promotion (SendPulse).

Interstitial ads are another type of application that should be considered in this context. Transitional ads, which have become widespread with the development of mobile technologies, can be defined as intrusive applications that are loaded without the user's request (Kaya and Bayat, 2022, p. 763). It is a full-screen advertising application that covers the entire interface of a specific application, usually a game. In this form, "it has a more obvious advertising purpose and a higher degree of forced exposure and perceived annoyance or intrusiveness due to the overlay of a full-screen ad rather than placing a small rectangular ad during the game session or integrating the ad into the game" (Wang and Chou, 2019, p. 229). The reason it is defined as a transition ad is that it appears at pause or transition points between specific levels, events, or pages within the application. In this way, it is possible to state that transition ads are a type of in-app advertising.

> *"In-app ads are campaigns displayed through mobile applications. Common ad formats include overlay banner ads displayed alongside screen content, interstitial ads shown before or after an activity within the app, click-to-expand ads, and app ads" (Bhave et al., 2013, p. 64). Grewal, Bart, Spann, and Zubcsek (2016) mention four different types of ads within the scope of in-app advertising: static, dynamic, interactive, and video ads (as cited in Truong et al., 2019, p. 25).*

The main feature of interstitial ads is that they can be easily applied to any game without changing the original design of the game or placing advertising products within the game. They generally cover the interface of the main computer application without interfering with the main game content or design, allowing players to clearly distinguish ads from the game (Wang and Chou, 2019, p. 230). Of course, at this point, a situation may arise in which the advertisement is compatible or incompatible with the game. When compatibility is achieved, no problems occur, and in a sense, the image of the advertised brand is reinforced in a positive way through the game content. However, when incompatibility arises, the cognitive processes underlying the target consumer's perception of the brand may be negatively affected. For example, placing a game of chance alongside a healthcare institution or a financial services brand on the same page could create different connotations. This issue of harmony or disharmony can undoubtedly be considered in the context of other types of advertising as well. Therefore, technology is again being used to solve this problem, with programmatic advertising largely providing the desired answer.

"Programmatic advertising can be defined as a technology that brings together data provided by publishers and advertisers on digital commerce platforms, enabling parties to buy and sell online advertising automatically, faster, and much more effectively" (Zeren and Keşlikli, 2019, p. 315). At the heart of programmatic advertising lies the principle of ensuring cost-effective advertising. In other words, the idea of connecting advertising with the consumer group with the highest purchasing potential is effective. Advances in data acquisition and processing technologies have made this possible. The traceability of consumers'/ users' digital footprints on the internet and the ability to map their behavior in this regard enables them to encounter personalized advertising messages. Traces of this approach can also be seen in recent applications for interstitial ads.

Given these features, interstitial ads are among the most effective ad formats for mobile devices. They enable broader ad campaigns, deliver more effective impressions, and drive greater user engagement, while also helping to overcome issues such as ad viewability problems or banner ad blindness in the smartphone environment (Munro, 2026).

The IAB (Internet Advertising Bureau) (2017) has outlined a framework for interstitial ads, specifying which elements this type of advertising should or should not include. According to this (IAB, 2017, pp. 18-19):

- Ads that cover or obscure content after the user has started viewing it are not interstitial ads. They are considered pop-up ads.
- • There must be an interruption in the content experience to serve interstitial ads.
- • All interstitial ads must have a prominent close button.
- • Ads should not feature a mandatory countdown before allowing the user to close an interstitial ad.
- • If the interstitial ad is presented as a video, the autoplay duration should be no more than 15 seconds (although videos in the 6-8-second range are more effective, even though their effectiveness cannot be fully measured).

Of course, this framework provided by the IAB is presented at a general scope. However, interstitial ads can also be evaluated in two different groups: rewarded and non-rewarded. Non-rewarded interstitial ads are the type that usually appear suddenly to the user and must be viewed to continue using the application. It is highly likely that users will develop a negative reaction to this type of advertising. When attempting to download any application from app stores and reviewing comments from other users, it is frequently observed that there are complaints about excessive advertising. This situation not only reduces advertising effectiveness but also harms the application itself. This type of ad, which causes weariness in users, can result in the app being deleted and even, due to the influence of comments, not being downloaded at all. Therefore, it must be used in a highly strategic manner. For example, it should be designed to appear only during transitions between levels and for very short periods of time.

Rewarded interstitial ads should be considered in a different context because they incentivize the user to watch the ad. This approach, which provides users with additional lives, energy, and/or in-game currency/gems in games, informs the user about the reward and, more importantly, gives them the option to choose whether or not they want to watch the ad. Google explains how these types of ads work as follows: "Rewarded interstitial ads can be displayed without requiring the user to enable viewing. At any point during the experience, the user can decide to skip the ad or stop viewing it. You can set the reward values associated with the ad units in your app and set different rewards for different ad units. Users will receive rewards in exchange for interacting with the ad without having to download anything" (Google). Rewarded interstitial ads, which largely leave control to the user, provide much more effective and efficient results when implemented in conjunction with programmatic advertising, as they also increase the likelihood of user acceptance.

There are also different implementation formats for award-winning interstitial ads. These are (Google):

- Video Ad Type:.

Closable Video Ads: When the X icon is clicked, a prompt is created asking the user if they want to close the ad. The user is warned that they will lose the reward if the ad is closed.

Countdown: Lets the user know how long they have left to receive the reward.

Delayed Setup: The user is taken to the appropriate app store upon completion of the view.

End: The user receives a reward for viewing the video ad (no download required).

When the video is complete, the download button becomes prominent. Clicking the button takes the user directly to the appropriate app store.

- Interactive Ad Type:

Playable Ads: These are click-and-download ads that allow the user to try out a game during the ad duration. Afterwards, the user is offered the opportunity to download the app.

Survey Ads: The user is asked a question. A reward is given after the response action is completed.

Interstitial ads are commonly seen in games played on smartphones and tablets. Similarly, they can be implemented in any type of application that is free and/or offers in-app purchases. They are typically encountered in applications that offer similar features to those that have been downloaded and used. Additionally, ads for applications that the user has previously downloaded and/or has a high potential to use are displayed.

The final concept discussed under this heading is sponsorship. This type of advertising operates under the traditional sponsorship model. The gaming industry, which is growing and developing at an incredible pace and reached a value of approximately $197 billion in the last quarter of 2022, has also become one of the most important areas for sponsorship investments. Brands that sponsor many events of varying scales have also entered into competition to support digital games. According to Smith et al. (2014, p. 100), sponsorship in games occurs in three ways:

- An advertiser sponsoring a part of a gaming environment that allows access to free games,
- An advertiser sponsoring a specific level of a game,
- Sponsoring a game through "Game Skinning". In this type of application, the advertiser sponsors the gaming environment where the game is placed or is given a sponsored area on the game portal. According to Michaud, this application can also be defined as the advertiser making its brand colors visible throughout the game or in part of it, or promoting a specific product within the game environment. In this type of sponsorship, the advertising format is fixed. It works particularly well in MMO games (massively multiplayer online role-playing games) because the duration of these games is much longer than that of others, and therefore exposure to advertising is also correspondingly high (2009, p. 27).

The power of sponsorship applications in traditional contexts also applies to digital games. Michaud (2009, p. 80) states that sponsorship allows advertisers to add virtual objects to a third-party universe developed for them or unrelated to them, while also providing a complete gaming experience. According to him, the main advantage of this application is that it provides the advertiser with a privilege and the ability to convey a message to a universe that has no connection with the brand other than viewer characteristics.

Furthermore, sponsorship can also be implemented through in-game advertising or integrated into advertising games. Characters in the game wearing clothes belonging to a specific brand or using accessories, or reflecting the brand name in specific locations, etc. Therefore, these reflect what the game consumer expects to see in the real world onto the game world (Smith, et al., 2014, p. 108). Clavio et al. (2009) refer to the results of a striking study on the outcomes of sponsorship applications carried out in the context of digital games. According to this study conducted by Nelson in 2002, even in what could be defined as the relatively early days of digital games, players could remember 25-30% of brands in the short term and approximately 10-15% of brands in the long term. For brands associated with a large part of the game or brands already relevant to the consumer, a much higher recall rate could be achieved.

The main areas of application for AGA are evaluated within the scope of these four headings conveyed so far, and these applications originate from traditional applications. In other words, they are not applications that can be evaluated solely within the context of the relationship between games and advertising. However, just like traditional applications, it is possible to achieve extremely effective and powerful results.

EXAMPLES OF AROUND GAME ADVERTISING

This section presents examples and brief analyses of AGA, whose conceptual framework was presented under this heading. However, before moving on to these examples, it seems appropriate to discuss where and how AGA are positioned within game-vertising. Smith et al. (2014), in their detailed and comprehensive study of the relationship between games and advertising, positioned AGA applications between advergames and in-game advertising applications. The fundamental logic here is not to create a randomly organized scheme, but to highlight AGA's central position. Although it has been stated that this type of advertising involves implementing an application without directly integrating marketing and advertising messages into the game, it is clear that AGA intersects with both advergames and in-game advertising at certain points.

Advertisements surrounding the game are structured within a framework that can essentially be expanded to "include advertising and promotional aspects that enable game developers to enter into licensing agreements as an additional source of revenue" (Smith et al., 2014, p. 100). Therefore, they can appear in many different forms and applications.

In this context, the first example discussed under this heading is the collaboration between Pepsi and Nintendo. This example demonstrates that there was a connection between advertising and games even before digital games and mobile devices became widespread. During this period, advertising examples surrounding games mainly took the form of distributing promotional products. In 2005, Pepsi launched its Pepsi Twist product in Japan. In a joint promotion with Nintendo, users were sent metallic blue accessories with "Pepsi Twist" written on them (Erdem, 2018). (Visuals and details related to the example can be accessed from the website of Handheld Museum). There is no connection or direct relationship between the brand and the game in this application. Therefore, it cannot be considered a direct marketing or advertising message. In this example, it is seen more as a gesture by Pepsi towards gamers. This is effective in creating a positive attitude towards Pepsi.

A similar example at this point also belongs to the Coca-Cola brand. In this study conducted in Japan in 1994, a red device specially produced for the Sega Game Gear, a type of game console similar to (and competing with) Nintendo, was distributed with the Coca-Cola logo. The Coca-Cola Kid mascot, created within an adventure game, directly referenced the brand and also constituted one of the first examples of the integration of games and advertising. (Visuals and details related to the example can be accessed from the article of Machkovech, 2022).

As previously stated, one of the primary applications of in-game advertising is banner ads. Banner ads frequently appear on both mobile applications and websites. In mobile applications, they are more likely to be displayed continuously on the screen at one or more levels of a specific brand game. On websites, banner ads for a brand can appear in various formats. However, ads for multiple brands can also be found on a web page. As mentioned earlier, banner ads are often perceived as annoying by users. This is why ad blockers are used. To prevent this, especially on gaming sites, ad blockers must be disabled in order to play games. These applications can be in the form of standard, vertical, rollover, and floating banner ads.

As previously stated, one of AGA's most important applications is cross-media, which also includes cross-media promotions. Smith et al. (2014, p. 100) state that cross-promotion is a form of marketing promotion in which the customers of a product or service are targeted with the promotion of a related product (or service). It is also a specific marketing tactic in which two or more businesses come together to reach a broader common target audience. Accordingly, cross-promotion is not a direct marketing or sales tactic or a strategy to quickly increase revenue. It involves a strategic or structural partnership that benefits both parties.

In recent years, games have become suitable platforms for cross-promotion to emerge in more effective forms, as increasingly creative and impressive campaigns have been observed in the field of advertising. The first example that can be given at this point is the collaboration between Mountain Dew, Game Fuel, and Doritos with the game Call of Duty: Black Ops Cold War. The brands, all owned by PepsiCo, announced an event with Activision, the publisher of Call of Duty, between October 2020 and January 2021 that would earn players double experience points.

One of the more recent examples is the collaboration between Coca-Cola and Twitch. In an announcement made during an online event held by Coca-Cola on September 29, 2021, Real Magic, a global brand platform, was introduced. The platform is designed to support Coca-Cola's brand promises to date (bringing people together and making the world a better place). It is based on the philosophy of being able to live in harmony in a new generation of virtual and fragmented world; this duality is associated with the characteristics of the Coca-Cola brand: "modest but iconic, authentic but mysterious, real but magical..." As Manolo Arroyo, Chief Marketing Officer of The Coca-Cola Company, said: "The roots of the Real Magic philosophy are based on the belief that dualities can make the world a more interesting place—a world of extraordinary people, unexpected opportunities, and wonderful moments. It also captures the essence of Coca-Cola: an indescribable, unique, real taste with a touch of real magic" (Web16). Along with this philosophy, which was announced during the event, the collaboration with Twitch was also announced, and the launch film was released.

The film depicts an e-sports event. The event can be watched both in the venue where it takes place and on other digital platforms (referring to Twitch). The character controlled by the player is suddenly injured while fighting on the battlefield. At this point, the player takes a Coca-Cola from the nearby cabinet, drinks it, and boosts both their own and their character's energy. The character first remembers his wife and child. He then stands up and sees how much the others on the battlefield are suffering. At this point, it is also seen that the player has lost control over the character. Right at this moment, the image shown in Figure 15 is displayed to the viewer, and then the character throws down the axe in his hand, indicating that he will not fight. At this point, where complete silence reigns among the audience watching the game, people question in astonishment what they have witnessed. The character lifts his enemy from the ground, and together they raise their arms as a sign of friendship and victory. Immediately afterwards, the dark and gloomy atmosphere within the game disappears, the sun comes out, and the slogan "We are one Coke away" appears on the screen. Then the player raises the Coca-Cola bottle in their hand towards the screen, and the player and the character they control smile at each other. The campaign was also announced by Coca-Cola on social media. This was done with the aim of increasing viewership. While Coca-Cola's brand may be considered to be emphasized more in this striking example of cross-promotion, the launch film's demonstration of how widely Twitch is used highlights the mutual benefit aspect of this type of advertising. In the launch film, Twitch usage prevalence is featured in many segments. At this point, as much as the prevalence of usage, the fact that users are representatives of Generation Z aligns with Coca-Cola's target audience. This situation also refers to what was previously stated, that the new generation can live in harmony in a virtual and fragmented world. Of course, both the analysis of the Coca-Cola campaign and other cross-promotion examples could be expanded. However, the main concern of this study is to provide examples of applications. Therefore, a more detailed explanation has not been provided within the limitations of this study.

The final type of application to be discussed in this section on AGA is sponsorship. The coexistence of a game and a brand within a sponsorship relationship on the same platform, and more importantly, the sponsorship of a game, a level of the game, and/or the environment in which it is placed, creates an advantageous situation for both parties.

The sponsorship activity between the Angry Birds 2 game and the Honey Nut Cheerios brand can be cited as an example of this type of application. In this example, the Angry Birds 2 game provided users with the opportunity to use a new spell in the form of Honey Nut Cheerios to defeat the pigs. This feature was promoted through the famous Honey Nut Cheerios "Spokesbee" and lasted for two weeks. At the same time, a discount was offered for a limited time. The limited duration increased the frequency of interaction between the brand and users.

The second example occurred within Zynga's Farmville game, which was quite popular at the time. This collaboration in 2010 can also be described as an in-game advertising-like application. In this farming game, McDonald's is featured as a neighboring farm, and users are given gifts that help them progress faster in the game in exchange for visiting their neighbors (Erdem, 2018, p. 247).

Another sponsorship activity within the Farmville: Harvest Swap game, also published by Zynga, is another important example in this regard. An application was designed within the game that requires users to interact with the Hidden Valley Ranch brand in order to complete their tasks. The fact that the users of this game are predominantly women aged 25-55 has significantly increased the success of the target audience and brand interaction (Crook, 2015).

FUTURE RESEARCH DIRECTIONS

Around Game Advertising is one of the most common practices in reality, yet it is often overlooked in the literature. This study aims to establish a general theoretical framework for this type of advertising and to make it more understandable through examples. In this context, the fundamental issues and recommendations for future studies can be listed as follows:

- Effectiveness: The impact of AGA applications on the target audience in terms of driving purchases, the level of efficiency in terms of interaction with the advertised brand/product, etc.
- Ethical violations: Uncertainty regarding the use of data collected through AGA, privacy and confidentiality violations. In addition, potential negative effects on the target audience (such as violent and pornographic images)
- Adaptation of new research methods and tools to AGA: Measuring AGA effectiveness through research using neuromarketing tools such as eye tracking, EEG, and fMRI.

CONCLUSION

Over the past few decades, the digital gaming industry has grown significantly in both quality and quantity, becoming an important industrial structure for all areas related to it. It also presents an extremely suitable field for marketing and advertising applications. Essentially, the combination of advertising and gaming, whose origins can be traced back to the pinball machine designed for the Ford Mustang in the 1960s, has further developed over the following decades with the improvement of visual and audio graphics in games, as well as the proliferation of computer technology and, soon after, mobile devices. Today, we encounter many different types and formats of advertising and gaming integration. While in-game advertising and advergames are frequently discussed in the literature, there are also applications that fall outside these types, and the AGA application area should also be considered at this point. Although examples are almost as numerous as the others, and sometimes even more so, there is a lack of academic research in this area. This section attempts to present theoretical information and case studies on this largely unexplored field.

AGA refers to activities conducted without the concern of directly conveying a marketing or advertising message within the game. This type, which can be categorized into four main categories—banner ads, cross-promotion, interstitial ads, and sponsorship—is currently evolving, particularly in the context of the rise of mobile applications and the emergence of new revenue models in this direction.

Surrounding ads, whose basic logic is to increase brand and user interaction without being directly present in the game but in absolute harmony with it, are also increasing their share in digital advertising investments day by day. Even though they may still create annoying ad clutter for users due to misapplication, efforts that are consistent and aligned with brands' marketing strategies increase the effectiveness of this type of advertising. Moreover, as brands' perspectives change with the advancement of technology, this type of advertising holds great potential for the advertising industry.

REFERENCES

Bechmann, P. A. (2007). "Realizing Cross-media". In Ambivalence towards Convergence: Digitalisation and media change, (Eds.) Storsul, T. and Stuedahl, D., Nordicom, pp. 57-72.

Benway, J. P., & Lane, D. M. (1998). "Banner Blindness: The Irony of Attention Grabbing on the World Wide Web", *Proceedings of the Human Factors and Ergonomics Society 42nd Annual Meeting*, 1, pp. 463-467. DOI: 10.1177/154193129804200504

Bhave, K., et al. (2013). "Understanding the Orientatıon of Gen Y Toward Mobile Applications and In-App Advertısıng in India", IJMM Summer, 8(1), pp. 62-74.

Bolat, N. (2019). "Geleneksel Mecralarda Çapraz Medya ve Transmedya Anlatıları Üzerine Bir İnceleme: Ağır Roman Örneği" (An Examination of Cross-Media and Transmedia Narratives in Traditional Media: The Case of Ağır Roman) [Journal of Selçuk Communication]. *Selçuk İletişim Dergisi, 12*(2), 503–531.

Bolat, N. (2020). "Televizyonun Teknik Dönüşümünün İçeriğe Etkisi" (The Impact of the Technical Transformation of Television on Content). In Yeni, İ. Y. İ. (Ed.), *Sirer, E* (pp. 111–130). LiteraTürk Publications.

Booth, D., & Koberg, C. (2012). *Display Advertising*. John Wiley & Sons.

Buijsman, M. (2025). "Global games market to hit $189 billion in 2025 as growth shifts to console". Retrieved from: https://newzoo.com/resources/blog/global-games-market-to-hit-189-billion-in-2025), Date of Access: 12th of September 2025.

Clavio, G., Kraft, P. M., & Pedersen, P. M. (2009). Communicating with Consumers through Video Games: An Analysis of Brand Development within the Video Gaming Segment of the Sports Industry. *International Journal of Sports Marketing & Sponsorship, 10*(2), 39–52. DOI: 10.1108/IJSMS-10-02-2009-B005

Crook, A. (2015, October 28). *A fresh look at in-game sponsorships*. Adrian Crook. https://adriancrook.com/a-fresh-look-at-in-game-sponsorships/

Davidson, D.. (2010). *Cross-Media Communications: an Introduction to the Art of Creating Integrated Media Experiences*. ETC Press.

Duarte, F. (2025). "How Many Gamers Are There? (New 2025 Statistics)". Retrieved from: https://explodingtopics.com/blog/number-of-gamers, Date of Access: 12th of September 2025.

Edwards, S., & La Ferle, C. (2000). Cross Media Promotion of the Internet in Television Commercials. *Journal of Current Issues and Research in Advertising*, *22*(1), 1–12. DOI: 10.1080/10641734.2000.10505098

Erdal, I. J. (2007). Researching Media Convergence and Crossmedia News Production. *Nordicom Review*, *28*(2), 51–61. DOI: 10.1515/nor-2017-0209

Erdem, M. N. (2018). "Markalar Oyunda! Dijitalde Bir Ürün / Marka Yerleştirme Alanı Olarak Game-Vertising" (Brands are in the Game! Game-vertising as a field of Product / Brand Placement in Digital. In Bolat, N. (Ed.), *Ürün Yerleştirme Uygulamaları (Product Placement Practices)* (pp. 215–266). LiteraTürk Publications.

Google. (n.d.). *Overview of rewarded interstitial ad units (Beta)*. Google AdMob Help Center. https://support.google.com/admob/answer/9884467?hl=en

Handheld Museum. (n.d.). *Nintendo DS Pepsi Limited Edition*. Handheld Museum. http://devkits.handheldmuseum.com/NintendoDSPepsi/index.htm

Hardy, J. (2010). *Cross-Media Promotion*. Peter Lang. DOI: 10.3726/978-1-4539-0001-7

Hoi, H. T. (2020). "Attractiveness of Online Marketing in the Age of Industry 4.0", in Proceedings of the 2020 The 6th International Conference on E-Business and Applications, Malaysia, Published: ICEBA 2020. pp. 1-4. DOI: 10.1145/3387263.3387264

IAB. (2017). IAB New Standard Ad Unit Portfolio. IAB Technology Laboratory. Retirieved from: www.iab.com/newadportfolio

Innovationpei (2012). Successful Online Display Advertising. Retrieved from: http://www.gov.pe.ca/photos/original/IPEI_ebiz_ads

Kaya, R., & Bayat, M. (2022). Çevrimiçi Dünyada Yükselen Bir Trend: Display (Görüntülü) Reklamlar. *Elektronik Sosyal Bilimler Dergisi*, *21*(82), 759–770. DOI: 10.17755/esosder.1031584

Kemp, S. (2025, January). *Digital 2025: Global Advertising Trends*. Data Reportal. https://datareportal.com/reports/digital-2025-sub-section-global-advertising-trends

Machkovech, S. (2022, April 30). *Tasting Coca-Cola's first "gamer" flavor—and the history of game-and-soda tie-ins. Ars Technica*. https://arstechnica.com/gaming/2022/04/coca-colas-first-gamer-flavor-and-the-history-of-game-and-soda-tie-ins/

McCambley, J. (2013, December). *The First ever banner ad: Why did it work so well?* https://www.theguardian.com/media-network/media-network-blog/2013/dec/12/first-ever-bann er-ad-advertising

Mestçi, A. (2013). *İnternette Reklamcılık (Internet Advertising)*. Pusula Publications.

Michaud, L. (2009). In-Game Advertising: Advertising and Video Game, 2009-2013, IDate Consulting and Research. Retrieved from: www.idate-research.com

Munro, B. (2026, January 15). *Interstitial ads: Best practices and examples for publishers*. Publift. https://www.publift.com/blog/interstitial-ads-a-best-practice-guide-for-publishers#Why-Use-an-Interstitial-Ad

Opena, A. (2025). "Ad Blockers Usage Statistics [2025]: Who's Blocking Ads & Why?". Retrieved from: https://cropink.com/ad-blockers-usage-statistics

SendPulse. (n.d.). Cross-promotion – Support glossary. SendPulse. https://sendpulse.com/support/glossary/cross-promotion

Smith, M. W.. (2014). Game Advertising: A Conceptual Framework and Exploration of Advertising Prevalence. *The Computer Games Journal*, *3*(1), 94–123.

Song, T., & Tang, Q. (2015). "Cross-Promotion in Social Media: Choosing the Right Allies", PACIS 2015 Proceedings. Research Collection School Of Information Systems, Retrieved from: https://ink.library.smu.edu.sg/sis_research/2945

Tleubayev, S. S.. (2017). The game as the essence of culture. *Revista Espacios*, *38*(54), 29–41.

Truong, V., Nkhoma, M., & Pansuwong, W. (2019). An Integrated Effectiveness Framework of Mobile In-App Advertising. *AJIS. Australasian Journal of Information Systems*, *23*, 1–25. DOI: 10.3127/ajis.v23i0.1971

Tuyan, B. (2005). İnternette Reklam (Internet Advertising). Retrieved from: https://www.chip.com.tr/haber/internette-reklam_1365.html

Vural, İ., & Öz, M. (2007). "Bir Reklam Mecrası Olarak İnternet" (Internet as a Medium of Advertising) [Journal of Erciyes University Institute of Social Sciences]. *Erciyes Üniversitesi Sosyal Bilimler Enstitüsü Dergisi*, *23*(2), 221–240.

Wang, S. S., & Chou, H. Y. (2019). Effects of Game-Product Congruity on İn-App Interstitial Advertising and the Moderation of Media-Context Factors. *Psychology and Marketing*, *36*(3), 229–246. DOI: 10.1002/mar.21174

Zeren, D., & Keşlikli, İ. (2019). "Programatik Reklamcılık: Kavram, İşleyiş ve Potansiyeli Açısından Değerlendirmesi", Ç.Ü. *Sosyal Bilimler Enstitüsü Dergisi*, *28*(2), 312–326.

ADDITIONAL READING

Bogost, I. (2007). *Persuasive Games: The Expressive Power of Videogames*. MIT Press. DOI: 10.7551/mitpress/5334.001.0001

Borawska, A., Biercewicz, K., Borawski, M., & Duda, J. (2021). The Impact of Advertisements Placement in the Computer Game on the Effectiveness of Social Campaign Messages. *European Research Studies*, *XXIV*(2B, 2B), 515–537. DOI: 10.35808/ersj/2249

Candy, L., & Ferguson, S. (Eds.). (2014). *Interactive Experience in the Digital Age*. Springer. DOI: 10.1007/978-3-319-04510-8

De la Hera, T. (2019). *Digital Gaming and the Advertising Landscape*. Amsterdam University Press. DOI: 10.2307/j.ctvnp0j4g

De Pelsmacker, P.. (2019). How Ad Congruity and Interactivity Affect Fantasy Game Players' Attitude toward In-Game Advertising. *Journal of Electronic Commerce Research*, *20*(1), 55–74.

Fromme, J., & Unger, A. (2012). *Computer Games and New Media Cultures: A Handbook of Digital Games Studies*. Springer. DOI: 10.1007/978-94-007-2777-9

Ghosh, T.. (2021). *Brands in a Game or a Game for Brands? Comparing the Persuasive Effectiveness of In-game Advertising and Advergames*. Psychology & Marketing., DOI: 10.1002/mar.21752

Zeman, N. B. (2017). *Storytelling for Interactive Digital Media and Video Games*. CRC Press. DOI: 10.1201/9781315382098

KEY TERMS AND DEFINITIONS

Around Game Advertising: This type of advertising includes applications that do not directly involve brand or product placement within the game. These advertisements appear as banners on websites where the game is hosted, sponsorship activities carried out within the game, cross-promotional campaigns conducted by partner brands—sometimes using transmedia storytelling—and interstitial ads.

Cross-Promotion: Cross-promotion campaigns refer to the mutual support between two or more brands. Within the scope of AGA, this practice is generally an integral part of advertising campaigns.

Game-Vertising: An umbrella term encompassing the relationship between advertising and games. Any type of advertising application within the game or on the platform where the game is published is considered under this concept.

Interstital Ads: These are full-screen ads that appear at regular intervals in mobile applications. In mobile games, the goal is to interact with a brand, download an application, or be directed to a specific website, particularly through rewarded and interactive ads via interstitals.

Sponsorship: Sponsorship practices under the AGA involve the target audience accessing a specific game or a specific part of a game free of charge with the support of a brand.

Chapter 4
Esports as a Hybrid Communication Arena:
Evolving Marketing Communication in Digital Spaces

Maryam El Oraiby
http://orcid.org/0000-0003-0485-9325
Kadir Has University, Turkey

Meltem Kiygi-Calli
http://orcid.org/0000-0002-2979-9309
Kadir Has University, Turkey

ABSTRACT

The chapter positions esports as a hybrid communication arena within contemporary digital culture, reflecting Generation Z's participatory and interactive engagement patterns. It presents esports as an evolving ecosystem where diverse stakeholders co-create value across competitive, community, and communicative dimensions, generating new forms of engagement, content creation, and brand interaction. Engagement, driven by motivation, immersion, and parasocial connection, turns audiences into active participants who generate eWOM and experiential consumption. Esports games function as experiential products that foster identity, belonging, and emotional investment. Ethical, cultural, and gender-related dynamics further frame the inclusivity, sustainability, and practices of marketing communication within this participatory environment.

DOI: 10.4018/979-8-3373-6309-7.ch004

INTRODUCTION

The global esports industry has evolved into one of the fastest-growing segments of the digital economy, gaining unprecedented significance in both popularity and revenue. Within this ecosystem, sectors such as gaming, streaming, and digital advertising have expanded rapidly, with esports at their intersection, blending entertainment, technology, and marketing innovation. The global esports market is projected to reach approximately $16.7 billion by 2033 (Market.us, 2024), reflecting the industry's rapid growth as a professionalized form of digital entertainment and its increasing relevance as a marketing medium (Lehnert et al., 2022). More and more, marketers are directing attention to the emerging communication and engagement opportunities within esports. Many global brands are investing in sponsorships, in-game integrations, and live-stream collaborations to connect with the digitally native audiences who constitute the largest segment of the esports environment.

It is worth noting that the rapid advances in digital technology, streaming infrastructure, and immersive media such as virtual and augmented reality are reshaping the nature of media consumption and audience engagement. As esports continues to evolve, understanding its structure and dynamics is essential for analyzing how it functions as a complex communication arena. The following section present an overview of the components that define this environment, namely the definition of esports, main genres and platforms, the positioning of esports games as experiential products, the stakeholders who shape its ecosystem, and the role of Generation Z audiences whose interactive and participatory media habits play an important role in driving its growth.

THEORETICAL FOUNDATIONS

Esports: Definition, Genres, and Platforms

Esports (short for electronic sports) refers to the organised, rule-governed video game competitions conducted through electronic systems (Pedraza-Ramirez et al., 2020; Jenny et al., 2017; Hamari & Sjöblom, 2017). While competitive gaming has existed for decades, its consolidation into a global industry marks a distinct cultural and communicative formation. In contrast to gaming in its general form, esports operates within institutional frameworks that include governing bodies, professional leagues, sponsorship systems, and audience measurement metrics comparable to those of traditional sport (Funk et al., 2018). Unlike casual gaming which is a leisure activity, esports is a mediated social system that generates economic value and symbolic capital through viewership and participation.

Scholarly definitions of esports vary in emphasis. For instance, Wagner (2006) conceptualises it as an area of sport where people develop and train their mental or physical abilities through the use of communication technologies. Pedraza-Ramirez et al. (2020) expands the definition of esports by framing it as a structured digital competition that not only relies on electronic systems and formal ranking mechanisms but also supports players' personal and professional growth through the cultivation of cognitive, perceptual, and social skills within a community-oriented environment. While there is no single consensus on what constitutes esports, we define it as the structured and competitive playing of video games, often organised through official leagues and ranking systems (El Oraiby & Kiygi-Calli, 2026).

Esports include different game genres, each requiring distinct cognitive, strategic, and mechanical skills. This diversity in the game genre parallels the diversity in traditional sports, demanding specialized training and performance metrics. Although there are many different classifications of games by genre, the most popular games belong to the following categories: Multiplayer Online Battle Arenas (MOBA), First-Person Shooters (FPS), Battle Royale, and Real-Time Strategy (RTS). Jang and Byon (2020) developed a three-category framework for eSports games classification based on the complexity and common aspects of games: imagination, physical enactment, and sports simulation. First, imagination-genre games, such as MOBA (e.g., League of Legends) and RTS (e.g., StarCraft II), have intricate rule systems, fictional worlds, and high strategic complexity. These games demand mastery of abstract mechanics (e.g., resource management, team coordination). Physical enactment-genre games, including FPS (e.g., Valorant) and fighting games (e.g., Street Fighter), prioritize real-time reflexes, vigilant monitoring, and precise mechanical execution. Unlike imagination games, they emphasize intuitive, fast-paced interactions where split-second decisions can determine the game outplay. Sports simulation games replicate real-world sports rules and structures (e.g., FIFA, NBA 2K), which emulate real-world sports rules, teams, and gameplay. These genre distinctions are not merely taxonomic: they shape communicative affordances, production formats, and audience expectations, influencing how marketing, commentary, and fan participation unfold within each ecosystem. In addition to these classifications, it is important to note that games can be played on different devices, such as PC, console, and mobile. Particularly, mobile gaming has witnessed significant growth, driven by its accessibility, advances in smartphone technology, and game publishers' investment in this type of competitive ecosystem. As interactive technologies continue to evolve, we can expect emerging technologies such as virtual reality and cloud-based gaming to further reshape the esports industry's structure as we know it today.

Esports' digital media intermediaries, or digital platforms, constitute the infrastructure that facilitates the complex ecosystem of gaming. These include service, tournament, communication, broadcast, and analytics platforms that together support the organisation and circulation of competitive play. Service platforms, such as Steam and the Epic Games Store, provide access to games and manage updates, while competitive integrity is primarily sustained by specialized anti-cheat systems and dedicated matchmaking services, most often developed by the game publishers themselves. Tournament and ranking platforms like FACEIT, Challengermode, and Battlefy organise structured competition by hosting leagues and tournaments, maintaining ranking systems, and linking amateur play with professional circuits.

Regarding community and communication platforms, they are diverse, and their popularity varies by region. However, the most notable ones are Discord, Reddit, and TeamSpeak, which enable coordination, fan conversations, and socialization within and across games. Most importantly, they allow direct dissemination of news and meta-strategies between players, teams, and fans. Broadcast and live-streaming platforms, including Twitch and YouTube Gaming, transform gameplay into a participatory media form through real-time commentary, interactive chat, and integrated monetisation. These platforms contribute to the growth of esports by merging broadcast and social-network functions, enabling synchronous viewing, commentary, and microtransactions. Chat interactions, emotes, digital tipping, and meme circulation transform consumption into co-production, which is why Turtiainen et al. (2020) describe esports as a form of "media sport." That is because esports depend on digital mediation and live streaming. Rather than being ancillary to play, these mediated exchanges constitute an essential component of esports' experiential and economic value, situating the industry within the broader transformation of digital media toward participatory ecosystems.

Additionally, there are analytics and performance platforms, such as Esports Charts and Insights.gg, which collect and interpret data to provide viewership metrics for the industry and performance statistics for teams. All together, these platforms operate as interdependent intermediaries that link production, competition, participation, and spectatorship, defining the communicative and economic architecture of the esports ecosystem.

Esports Games as Experiential Products

Esports games are best described as experiential products. That is because they are interactive systems designed to generate immersive, gamified, and emotionally engaging experiences (Duan & Jeong, 2025; Hollebeek et al., 2022), in contrast to material products that depend on a tangible commodity. The value of esports games derives from the experiences they create for both players and audiences. Earlier research on video gaming highlights that enjoyment, immersion, and engagement form the foundation of the gaming experience (Brown & Cairns, 2004; Abbasi et al., 2019). In esports, these experiential dimensions are intensified through real-time competition, skill display, and social interaction, transforming play into a shared experience. Esports consumption aligns with research on hedonic and playful consumption (Hirschman & Holbrook, 1982; Holbrook et al., 1984), where sensory pleasure, emotion, and fantasy shape consumer value. Empirical studies further show that people engage with esports to fulfil enjoyment, escapism, social connection, and self-expression needs (Rehman et al., 2022; Abbasi et al., 2023).

As experiential products, esports titles capitalize on user engagement. While the access to esports games is free, the enhanced experiences are sold through continually refreshed seasonal events, ranked modes, and global tournaments. The commercial value arises from in-game purchasable digital items, such as champions to unlock, skins, emotes, and battle passes, which enhance and personalize the user's interaction with the game and various aspects of the overall gaming experience. These virtual products enable identity expression, signal status, and reinforce emotional investment (Gul & Yurtsizoglu, 2025). For spectators, the experiential value extends to the emotional intensity of viewing, live interaction in chat, and community participation, which often includes tangible forms of support such as donating to streamers out of emotional attachment or appreciation (Wohn & Freeman, 2020).

Stakeholders and Audience Dynamics in the Esports Ecosystem

The esports ecosystem functions as a multilayered network of interdependent stakeholders who interact in a way that transforms digital games into professionalized and socially embedded forms of mediated competition. These actors collectively create value by developing, governing, distributing, and consuming competitive play. In this ecosystem, primary stakeholders (developers, players, teams, tournament organizers) and secondary stakeholders (sponsors, media, and fan communities) depend on one another for value creation and legitimacy. Each stakeholder fulfils a distinct yet interconnected role that collectively sustains esports as a business and a cultural practice (Scholz, 2020).

At the core of the ecosystem are game publishers and developers, who create and control the intellectual property of the titles that enable competition. We consider them the core stakeholders because they exercise structural dominance. They design and maintain the games and define competitive rule systems (Peng et al., 2020). Their authority extends beyond production to governance; in fact, they can modify competitive balance (the meta), restrict event sponsors, or even discontinue a title's esports support, thereby determining the survival of the entire game titles.

Through this combination of direct authority and indirect influence, publishers shape the esports ecosystem as regulators, marketers, and commercial gatekeepers, exerting a form of control that extends beyond game design. Next, the tournament and league organizers, who convert digital games into structured sporting events. They operationalize rules, ensure compliance, and distribute prizes and media rights. Some operate independently (e.g., ESL, DreamHack), while others are integrated with publishers (e.g., Riot's League Championship Series). Organizers serve as the institutional bridges, linking developers, teams, sponsors, and audiences. Their rulebooks and conduct standards (e.g., eligibility, gaming behavior), form a secondary governance layer.

The professional teams and players are primary stakeholders that constitute the human foundation of the ecosystem (Hong, 2025). Players provide the skill, personality, and talent that attract and drive spectatorship, shaping not only competition but also community identity. Esports teams mainly assemble talented players, offer comprehensive support, including training and coaching, and secure sponsorships and event participation opportunities. However, despite their visibility and cultural influence, players and teams remain structurally dependent on publisher-controlled platforms, continuous game updates, and competition regulations, which limit their institutional power and autonomy within the ecosystem.

Around these primary stakeholders, we find a broader network of audiences and intermediaries. Sponsors and commercial brands provide economic resources, they fund tournaments and teams, and broadcast events with the goal of strengthening fan attachment to the brand. When fans strongly identify with an esports event, that attachment also extends to its sponsors; they tend to view sponsor brands more favorably and are more willing to support or purchase from sponsoring brands (Calapez et al., 2024). Media and broadcasting partners translate competitive play into consumable content, mediating the relationship between events and global audiences. Their platforms enable live viewing and real-time interaction, turning gaming into a participatory form of entertainment that blends play, community, and spectatorship (Welden et al., 2025).

Fans and online communities represent the largest secondary stakeholder groups in size. Their attention, emotional commitment, and participatory practices transform esports from a contest into a shared participatory experience (Welden et al., 2025). Fan identification with players, teams, and events sustains engagement and stimulates online participation, reinforcing the social momentum that surrounds tournaments (Calapez et al., 2024). In parallel, associations, federations, and integrity bodies seek to institutionalize governance by promoting fair play, player welfare, and event standards. These organizations mark a gradual move toward formalized oversight and professional legitimacy within the esports field (Peng et al., 2020).

The esports ecosystem is thus defined by a dynamic tension between its stakeholders: the foundational control of publishers, the commercial and promotional roles of sponsors and media partners, the professionalizing efforts of organizers and institutions, and the vital, co-creative energy of player and fan communities. Within this ecosystem, audiences play an influential role, as participation and engagement largely reflect dominant communicative practices associated with digital-native media use. The audience dynamics of esports are fundamentally shaped by the attributes of its core demographic, Generation Z. Gen Z are digital natives, technology-oriented and actively engaged in gaming experiences (Jasrotia et al., 2022). Their early immersion in networked media has cultivated expectations of interactivity, continuous connectivity, and personalization (Rue, 2018). Esports aligns naturally with these expectations: its multi-platform structure allows spectators to engage in playing, viewing, and commenting, creating overlapping roles of participant, critic, and fan. eMarketer projects that by 2027 nearly three-quarters of US Gen Zers will engage in some form of digital gaming (Flores-Marquez, 2025). For this reason, Gen Z exhibits exceptionally high participation in gaming and digital environments, establishing a natural predisposition toward esports, as players and as spectators.

Empirical research indicates that audiences engage with esports for various reasons, including cognitive and experiential motivations. For instance, they watch to acquire tactical knowledge and improve their own skills (Tang et al., 2023; Jenny et al., 2018), to experience novelty and escapism (Hamari & Sjöblom, 2017), and to appreciate mastery and competitive excellence (Qian et al., 2020). Esports audiences also demonstrate a uniquely immersive orientation where spectators psychologically inhabit the perspective of players (Pu et al., 2022).

Regarding the gender composition of this audience, it is gradually becoming more diverse. While male segment remains the dominant one in esports, female participation is growing (Darvin et al. 2021). Nonetheless, women continue to encounter structural and interpersonal barriers, including limited access to competitive networks and persistent gendered stereotypes, that restrict their visibility and professional advancement (Tang et al., 2025). The persistence of such gendered dynamics underscores that the participatory culture of Generation Z in esports is not uniformly inclusive but continually negotiated within broader social and cultural boundaries.

Gaming Culture in the Context of Integrated Marketing Communication

Integrated Marketing Communication (IMC) is defined as "a strategic business process used to plan, develop, execute and evaluate coordinated, measurable, persuasive brand communication programmes over time with consumers, customers, prospects and other targeted, relevant external and internal audiences" (Schultz

& Schultz, 1998). This early definition marked a turning point in conceptualizing IMC as a strategic business process that integrates multiple stakeholders and time horizons. IMC has then evolved from a coordination mechanism for promotional activities into a strategic approach guiding how brands communicate and build relationships with their audiences.

Previous studies emphasized the importance of message consistency, cross-channel coordination, and the management of brand meaning across diverse communication touchpoints (Kitchen & Burgmann, 2010; Schultz & Patti, 2009; Keller, 2001). As digital platforms and consumer-generated content became central to marketing, IMC expanded from message control to relationship-building and audience engagement. Studies highlight that coordinated communication enhances synergy and overall brand effectiveness, reducing fragmentation and reinforcing consumer perceptions of brand coherence (Porcu et al., 2017). Because the effects of individual communication channels are difficult to isolate within integrated systems (Kliatchko & Schultz, 2014), IMC emphasizes the interdependence of channels, where coordinated activities across platforms produce stronger and more coherent outcomes than separate efforts (Reinold & Tropp, 2012). This interdependence is particularly evident in esports, where marketing communication unfolds simultaneously across live streams, social media, in-game elements, and sponsorship activations, creating a consistent and immersive communication environment.

Within this ongoing evolution, the principles of IMC have become particularly relevant in digital and interactive environments, with esports providing a perfect representative example of integrated and participatory communication practices. Although academic research explicitly linking IMC to esports remains limited, Esiri (2022) proposes an IMC framework tailored to the esports industry, illustrating how digital marketing, sponsorship, event management, and community engagement operate together to strengthen brand growth and audience interaction. The framework reflects IMC's modern orientation toward integration, engagement, and experiential communication, showing that in esports, brand messages are embedded within entertainment experiences through live streaming, influencer collaborations, and participatory fan cultures. This integration exemplifies how IMC has progressed from a one-way, brand-centered communication model to a dialogic, consumer-inclusive framework (Rehman et al., 2022), where audiences engage with and reinterpret brand messages social media participation and community-driven content in the esports environment (Esiri, 2022).

Esports emerges from broader gaming culture, where community norms, digital interaction, and shared practices shape how players engage with content and participate in virtual environments (Sjöblom et al., 2019). Gaming culture represents the shared practices, meanings, and social structures that have developed around digital games. It encompasses the ways people interact, communicate, and attribute significance to games as cultural artifacts and social experiences (Orme, 2022). From a cultural perspective, gaming is not considered as a simple form of play or recreational activity, but is considered a social and symbolic practice shaped by power, participation, and representation (Shaw, 2010). Gaming culture operates as a communicative environment in which players and viewers co-construct shared codes of behaviour, humour, and sense of belonging. Within this digital environment, meaning circulates continuously through interaction, voice and text chat, memes, emotes, reaction GIFs, and commentary, so that communication becomes as central as play itself. In this sense, gaming culture embodies the dialogic, participatory logic that contemporary Integrated Marketing Communication (IMC) also seeks to capture: value and attention emerge through reciprocal engagement rather than top-down message delivery.

Early analyses of gaming culture highlighted how the industry's discourse produced the image of the authentic gamer, representing technologically skilled individuals, usually males, where competitiveness and mastery are considered valued attributes (Kirkpatrick, 2012). This construction contributed to enduring boundaries within gaming communities, dividing "hard-core" and "casual" players, a hierarchy that became gendered as masculine versus feminine (Vanderhoef, 2013; Orme, 2022). Such distinctions sustain symbolic power within gaming spaces, privileging certain players as legitimate members of the culture while marginalizing others. Studies show that women and minoritized players frequently face exclusion or harassment that affects their participation and representation (Darvin et al., 2020). These dynamics reveal that gaming culture is a contested social field in which inclusion, legitimacy, and identity are continually negotiated.

Concurrently, gaming culture embodies participatory dynamics in which players and fans co-create content (Kunz et al., 2022). Platforms such as Twitch and YouTube Gaming have transformed play into an ongoing performance in which spectators' real-time chat, donations, and emotes become part of the esports event itself (Wohn & Freeman, 2020). Discord servers or Reddit communities act as hubs of coordination, humour, and peer support, showing how networked communication sustains identity and loyalty beyond the game interface. These examples illustrate how cultural participation and mediated communication have fused what once separated play from media consumption is now a single, convergent system, where individuals interact and communicate, construct identity and develop unique social bonds (Zervas & Maronitis, 2025).

Moreover, gaming culture has extended beyond entertainment into institutional and educational settings. The integration of virtual reality and serious games into museums and heritage projects demonstrates its recognition as a legitimate medium for education and storytelling (Theodoropoulos & Antoniou, 2022). Additionally, various universities offer esports education as a field of study, highlighting an increasing interest in competitive video gaming both academically and professionally. Examples of universities offering esports programs include the University of California-Irvine, Staffordshire University, and Maryville University.

Overall, gaming culture can be characterized a domain that enables creativity, collaboration, and connection while also reproducing hierarchies of gender, skill, and legitimacy. Understanding these dynamics is essential for examining communication in esports, where interaction both arises from and magnifies the same social and symbolic tensions that define gaming culture.

Motivation, Engagement, and Immersion in Esports

Investigating the motivations for engagement will allow a better understanding of the needs and interests of the esports community. The literature distinguishes between diverse intrinsic and extrinsic motivations underlying esports participation, such as competition, achievement, social interaction, and escapism (Bányai et al., 2020; Giakoni-Ramírez et al., 2022). These factors reflect both psychological needs and social gratifications that influence the intensity and form of engagement in gaming environments.

Motivations in esports are commonly classified into three broad categories: achievement, social, and immersion (Yee, 2006; Penezoğlu Yıldırım & Ulukol, 2022). According to Yee et al. (2012), achievement motivation refers to the pursuit of advancement, mastery, and recognition; social motivation involves maintaining relationships and collaboration within gaming communities; and immersion motivation centers on escaping real-world pressures and becoming absorbed in the virtual environment. These motivational orientations shape distinct patterns of participation. For instance, achievement-oriented players engage more competitively and seek measurable performance outcomes, while socially motivated participants prioritize cooperation and belonging. Immersion-driven individuals emphasize the experiential and escapist dimensions of gaming (Snodgrass et al., 2013). Understanding these motives provides valuable insights into how and why individuals sustain long-term involvement in esports, both as active players and as part of broader communities.

The Uses and Gratifications Theory (UGT) provides a valuable lens for understanding these dynamics, explaining how individuals use games and esports to fulfill cognitive, affective, and social needs (Rehman et al., 2022; Settle, 2018). Within this framework, hedonic and playful-consumption experiences, including escapism, enjoyment, fantasy, role-projection, emotional involvement, arousal, and sensory stimulation, illustrate how esports function as immersive, pleasure-oriented environments that foster psychological engagement and sustained participation (Abbasi et al., 2023; Hollebeek et al., 2022; Wu & Holsapple, 2014). These hedonic gratifications help explain why esports operate not only as competitive and skill-based activities but also as emotionally charged, identity-forming experiences for participants.

Recent research by Hussain et al. (2025) extends this motivational understanding by adopting a self-determination theory (SDT) framework to conceptualize in-game customer purchase motivations (IGCPMs). Their work advances prior SDT studies by revealing that autonomy, competence, and relatedness are multifaceted motivational domains, each comprising unique sub-facets that differently shape players' engagement, immersion, and competition. Specifically, autonomy consists of creativity, choice, and uniqueness, which foster freedom and flow; competence encompasses achievement, skillfulness, and dominance, which enhance mastery and self-efficacy; and relatedness includes social interaction and social affiliation, which strengthen social connection and belonging. This multidimensional view clarifies how distinct motivational facets contribute to different experiential outcomes: autonomy and competence facets often intensify flow and immersive engagement, while relatedness facets promote social presence and community attachment. Such differentiation enriches traditional SDT applications in esports by demonstrating that specific motivational sub-dimensions drive different aspects of players' sustained participation. Motivational drivers therefore, act as precursors to engagement, shaping how individuals allocate cognitive, emotional, and behavioral resources during gameplay or spectating (Qian et al., 2020). High levels of achievement or social motivation, for instance, may intensify players' attention, enthusiasm, and participation, leading to deeper and more sustained engagement within esports environments.

Previous studies linking engagement to well-being find that increased engagement with esports may reduce players' capacity for a healthy and active lifestyle, as gaming involves extended periods of sedentary behavior (Chan et al., 2022). Engagement can be defined as "a dynamic and iterative process, reflecting actors' dispositions to invest resources in their interactions with other connected actors in a service system" (Brodie et al., 2011). It is a multidimensional construct comprising cognitive, emotional, and behavioral dimensions (Pansari & Kumar, 2017). Cognitive engagement reflects the level of cognitive processing and attention directed toward a specific goal or activity and includes absorption and concentration during play. Emotional engagement refers to affective investment (enthusiasm, passion, and dedication) while behavioral engagement represents observable actions such as in-game interaction, community participation, and content creation, through which players or viewers demonstrate their involvement (Abbasi et al., 2021; Brodie et al., 2011). Although some studies highlight the negative consequences of excessive engagement, such as anxiety or reduced physical activity, it is important to recognize that esports share several characteristics with traditional sports. Both domains involve long hours of training and performance demands that can entail physical or psychological strain (Bányai et al., 2020). This perspective underscores the need to examine engagement not only in terms of risks but also as a potential source of positive psychological outcomes.

Immersion represents the experiential culmination of motivation and engagement; the state in which players or viewers feel completely absorbed within a digital environment. Immersion is closely linked to sensory and emotional intensity, as well as to the audiovisual design and interactivity of esports platforms. For spectators, immersive experiences emerge vicariously through identification with players, suspense, and real-time communication on streaming platforms such as Twitch, where chat functions and live commentary heighten social co-presence and emotional resonance (Taylor, 2018). Playful-consumption experiences, such as enjoyment, fantasy, emotional involvement, and sensory stimulation enhance player immersion and reinforce ongoing participation (Abbasi et al., 2023; Rehman et al., 2022). The affective and sensory dimensions of play intensify emotional attachment and contribute to sustained engagement behaviors such as continuous play, content sharing, and community interaction. As Hollebeek et al. (2022) note, esports offer a synthetic yet emotionally resonant environment that can generate deep and enduring consumer relationships.

Overall, motivation, engagement, and immersion form a mutually reinforcing triad that underpins esports participation and consumption. Motivational drivers initiate involvement, engagement sustains ongoing interaction, and immersion deepens experiential intensity.

Parasocial Interaction and Audience Affiliation

Affiliation in esports develops through communicative situations that make spectators feel socially connected to streamers and professional players. In early media research, parasocial interaction was defined as the illusion of face-to-face contact produced when audiences perceive performers as personally addressing them through familiar conversational styles and gestures (Horton & Wohl, 1956; Leith, 2021).

This perception of mutual awareness is noticeable in live-streaming environments. For instance, on live-streaming platforms such as Twitch, chat functions, emotes, and verbal acknowledgments allow spectators to experience this connection (Taylor, 2018). One way to experience this intimacy between spectators and streamers is through language. To illustrate, streamer-directed chat messages include more personal pronouns, direct forms of address, and emotional expressions than those exchanged among viewers, indicating a deliberate performance of relational proximity (Leith, 2021). When a streamer responds to a viewer's message or highlights a donation during a match, spectators perceive this as a direct acknowledgment, reinforcing emotional connection and loyalty.

Parasocial relationships develop when these momentary interactions accumulate into stable emotional attachments (Giles, 2002). Viewers who admire a streamer's competence or persona often wish to emulate them, and this wishful identification, combined with shared emotional engagement in the chat, can predict continued loyalty to the channel (Lim et al., 2020). Social connectedness, entertainment, escapism, and tension release as core drivers of viewing, and interactive features such as chat, donations, and direct communication amplify these motives (Rietz & Hallmann, 2023). This provides audiences with repeated opportunities to express attention, support, and shared emotions. Through these communicative exchanges, spectators sustain a sense of inclusion in the streamer's community and, by extension, in the wider esports culture. Parasocial interaction therefore, offers a framework for understanding how mediated communication produces affiliation in esports. It links micro-level interactions with enduring participation, forming the emotional basis for community engagement and for behaviors such as subscriptions, donations, and advocacy within gaming networks.

Co-Creation and Hybrid Communication Practices

Co-creation in esports refers to the collaborative generation of communicative, experiential, and economic value among players, audiences, organizers, sponsors, and digital platforms within a service ecosystem (Welden et al., 2025). Within this system, communication becomes a shared productive process through which meanings, relationships, and market value emerge. The service-dominant logic explains this configuration by emphasizing that value is created through the integration of resources by multiple participants who operate under shared institutional arrangements and norms (Vargo & Lusch, 2017; Roth et al., 2023).

In this ecosystem, what is co-created extends across several interdependent dimensions. Participants collectively produce experiential value as players and commentators. Spectators and fans construct the atmosphere and emotional intensity of competition through live chat, reactions, and social exchange. They generate cultural value by developing shared narratives, humor, and rituals that define community identity in esports. Interactions produce economic and brand value, as engagement metrics and community creativity feed into sponsorship, merchandising, and promotional strategies (Welden et al., 2025). Co-creation also generates institutional and technological value, as tournaments, leagues, and streaming platforms establish norms, interfaces, and algorithms that coordinate and amplify these exchanges. Together, these processes transform participation into continuous value creation that sustains the esports ecosystem.

A clear example of institutional co-creation can be seen in League of Legends. Riot Games regularly performs balance adjustments, modifying champions' abilities or statistics when community feedback and gameplay data indicate that a champion (character) is too powerful or too weak. This iterative process, often described by players as "nerfing" or "buffing," reflects an ongoing dialogue between developers, professional players, and audiences. Through these interactions, design decisions become a shared outcome of collective communication, transforming feedback into concrete changes in the competitive environment. Riot also collaborates with championship-winning teams to design commemorative in-game skins that incorporate each player's preferred champion and aesthetic choices, integrating fan interest and professional identity into commercial game content. These practices illustrate how game design, governance, and community engagement operate as continuous forms of co-creation.

An illustration of cultural co-creation is Arcane, the animated series produced by Riot Games in collaboration with Fortiche Productions and released on Netflix in 2021 (Riot Games, 2022). The series extends the League of Legends universe beyond gameplay, transforming its narrative and visual identity into an independent cultural text. Riot connected the show to in-game missions and cosmetic rewards, encouraging players to engage across both media. This transmedia collaboration demonstrates how esports organizations and creative industries co-produce content that circulates across entertainment platforms, deepening emotional attachment and cultural legitimacy for the game.

Commercial actors are equally embedded in this co-creative structure. Partnerships between brands, Epic Games, Twitch, and major esports tournaments demonstrate how cross-platform coordination generates simultaneous entertainment, engagement, and marketing value. For instance, in 2023, Coca-Cola Ultimate Zero Sugar was launched as a limited-edition product inspired by League of Legends. Players unlocked themed "Ultimate Emotes" and interacted with augmented-reality features through QR-coded packaging, linking gameplay with branded storytelling. This collaboration illustrates how co-creation extends beyond sponsorship to the joint design of hybrid physical-digital experiences that merge consumption, participation, and cultural meaning (The Coca-Cola Company, 2023).

Co-creation sustains the continuity and legitimacy of the industry by aligning cultural expression, institutional coordination, and commercial value. The result is an environment in which meaning, community, and economic performance are produced through interconnected communicative processes that define the esports ecosystem.

MAPPING THE ESPORTS ECOSYSTEM

Professional Elite and Aspiring Amateur Players

Building on the discussion in section 1.3, developers and publishers exercise structural dominance (Peng et al., 2020), yet the visibility and cultural vitality of esports depend on the agency and communicative performance of players themselves. They produce the skill, emotion, and personality that give competitive gaming legitimacy and entertainment value (Scholz, 2020; Hong, 2025). Through their public presence, players connect the commercial, technological, and cultural layers of esports, mediating between publisher governance, team infrastructures, sponsor interests, and fan communities (Calapez et al., 2024; Welden et al., 2025). Players form the human foundation of this system. Esports encompasses both amateur and professional participation, providing opportunities for skill development, community engagement, and mastery in perceptual-cognitive and fine-motor abilities (Pedraza-Ramirez et al., 2020).

Professional elite players occupy the most visible and institutionalized layer. They compete in organized teams supported by sponsors, coaches, analysts, and performance staff, within structures that resemble traditional sport organizations (Bubna et al., 2023; Hong, 2023), but remain dependent on publisher-controlled platforms and continuous game updates. Their careers involve contractual, promotional, and emotional labour, positioning them as both athletes and media figures central to the global expansion of esports (Scholz, 2020; Welden et al., 2025).

Nonetheless, it is important to highlight that elite players constitute only a small fraction of the esports population. While they are celebrated as icons and often achieve considerable income and fame, their professional careers tend to be short and unstable (Funk et al., 2018). Intense competition, rapid shifts in game balance, and high physical and cognitive demands frequently lead to early retirement or transitions into coaching, content creation, or management roles. In fact, the majority of competitions in esports remain at amateur or semi-professional levels, where earnings are limited and long-term careers are insecure.

Amateur players, on the other hand, are a large subset of gamers, existing at developmental base of the esports career hierarchy. Amateur players are defined as "those who play to climb ranks and actively compete in tournaments, with the intention of transitioning to the professional scene, but who do not yet earn a living through esports; they are primarily focused on the pursuit of game expertise and excellence" (El Oraiby & Kiygi-Calli, 2026). Their focus lies in developing expertise and achieving mastery (Montag et al., 2022; Wechsler et al., 2021; Poulus et al., 2024). These players operate within a system of aspiration and informal professionalism, where self-training, peer recognition, and exposure through online tournaments serve as informal routes to advancement.

The definition of amateur players is important, because there is confusion in the existing literature on the notion of "amateur" players. In scholarship, especially for scholars who are not familiar with the esports world, tend to use non-professional, amateur, and recreational players interchangeably. In fact, within esports culture, amateur players are usually players actively compete and want to pursue excellence (Poulus et al., 2024). Whether the category is defined by income, competitive level, or expertise continues to be debated. Some authors were conscious about this distinction and highlighted the difference, by describing them as "non-professional players with a plan," that is, competitors intending to become professional in the near future (Montag et al., 2022), and others define them as players who "compete in tournaments but do not earn money as a main income," in contrast to professionals who do (Wechsler et al., 2021). Pedraza-Ramirez et al. (2020) underline that this level is a crucial part of the wider esports community and its talent-development system. In the esports world, even talented players affiliated with clubs or receiving small rewards till identify themselves as amateurs (not professionals) when esports is not yet their primary occupation and they have not reached (yet) the elite status.

The relationship between elite and amateur players illustrates how esports institutionalizes pathways of progression. Professionals act as cultural symbols and commercial assets; amateurs sustain the ecosystem by providing a continuous flow of emerging talent and audience engagement. Together, professional and aspiring amateur players' participation generates both the spectacle and the meaning of competition, connecting technical performance with cultural expression and community formation.

Creative Core: Content Creators and Streamers

The creative core transforms competitive play into continuous, audience-oriented media. Content creators produce edited materials such as match highlights, analysis, tutorials, or narrative features, and streamers perform live broadcasts that merge gameplay with commentary and real-time interaction. Together, they constitute the communicative interface between competition, spectatorship, and commerce, making the digital play a cultural experience (Taylor, 2018; Scholz, 2020). Unlike pre-produced influencer content, live streaming is immediate and enables ongoing dialogue through chat, voice, and visual feedback. This interactivity fosters parasocial connection, as viewers feel socially engaged with the streamer, and emotional attachment becomes the engine of community cohesion. The credibility and consistency of a streamer, especially when grounded in skill and authenticity, amplify this bond and strengthen brand attitudes among viewers through mechanisms of trust and loyalty (Xu et al., 2022). These dynamics make streamers highly effective communicators for brands and teams seeking to translate fan identification into purchase or participation intentions.

Content creation also drives how esports events are mediated and narrated. Advances in broadcast technology enable data-driven storytelling, where gameplay statistics and highlights are visualized to enhance commentary and deepen the understanding of the gameplay. At major tournaments, production tools such as Echo have demonstrated that integrating live data into visual storytelling enhances narrative coherence, emotional intensity, and audience immersion (Block et al., 2018). This integration illustrates how content creators and broadcasters co-produce meaning through gameplay data, expert narration, and creative visualization to render complex play both legible and engaging. Despite the diversity of creators, only a small number of prominent figures dominate audience attention and influence the creative economy. The departure of a high-profile streamer can trigger measurable declines in both viewership and content supply, demonstrating the dependence of streaming markets on a limited set of star creators (Qian & Xie, 2026).

Streaming channels run by professional organizations and teams such as G2 Esports exemplify how competition, entertainment and marketing converge. These team channels are less about raw, high-level practice and more about building personality-driven narratives that foster fan loyalty, attract sponsors, and create a cohesive brand identity across platforms. Thus, content creators and streamers contribute to the mediated visibility and emotional engagement that characterize contemporary esports spectatorship.

Fans, Community, and Recreational Mass

Esports fans often occupy overlapping roles in the cosystem, as players, viewers, and content contributors, using streaming and social platforms to co-create meaning (Taylor, 2018; Hamilton et al., 2014). With an estimated global audience of over 640 million in 2023 and the number of users is expected to reach 896 million users by 2029 (Statista, 2025). esports represents one of the largest fandoms in digital culture. Millions of viewers engage regularly with live events, while hundreds of millions more participate through streaming platforms and social media. The active player base in competitive titles illustrates how play and spectatorship are clearly intertwined. Unlike traditional sport fandoms anchored in geography, esports communities are networked and transnational, linked by platforms such as Twitch, YouTube Gaming, and Discord that enable synchronous global participation. Community platforms such as Discord and Reddit host participatory cultures that extend competition into everyday life. Fans contribute commentary, feedback, fan art, and moderation, co-producing both meaning and value (Welden et al., 2025). Within the esports ecosystem, socialization, knowledge exchange, and emotional engagement structure new forms of digital participation (Huettermann & Pizzo, 2022).

The recreational mass, composed of players who engage in esports primarily for enjoyment and social connection differ significantly from players. In fact, unlike amateur or professional athletes, the involvement of recreational players is guided by intrinsic motivations rather than career aspiration. Empirical work shows that recreational gameplay often predicts engagement with streaming content and later professional event viewership, creating behavioral continuity between casual play and organized esports (Jang et al., 2020; Jenny et al., 2017). Their activity sustains player populations, audience flow, and the cultural relevance of esports titles across regions and genres.

Supportive and Developmental Actors

The supportive and developmental actors are often a neglected segment in the esports ecosystem. Yet, they are important, as they cultivate talent, regulate activity, and provide the technological and educational infrastructure necessary for competition.

Training and educational institutions play a central role in transforming play into structured expertise. Professional teams maintain academies to nurture emerging talent, while universities and private programs increasingly integrate esports coaching, analytics, and business management into their curricula (Jenny et al., 2017). Within these environments, pedagogical approaches that emphasize autonomy support, positive feedback, and learner-centred instruction have been shown to enhance motivation (Iwatsuki, et al., 2022). Coaches, in particular, serve as crucial developmental actors, evaluating amateur player progress, structuring training routines, and adapting strategies to continuously evolving game mechanics and competitive metas (McCormack et al., 2022; Thaicharoen et al., 2023; Watson et al., 2022). Their role extends beyond technical preparation to include psychological guidance and emotional support, helping players maintain motivation and well-being throughout the demanding transition from amateur to professional competition (El Oraiby & Kiygi-Calli, 2026). The reliance of players on coaches and mentors underscores how human guidance complements technological expertise within the esports training ecosystem.

Global and national organizations such as the Global Esports Federation (GEF) coordinate event standards, athlete representation, and policy advocacy (Witkowski & Harkin, 2025). Hardware manufacturers and analytics firms, such as Intel and Razer, and performance-tracking platforms invest in research and sponsorships that connect technological innovation with performance. Educational and community initiatives complement these structures by promoting digital literacy, inclusion, and mental-health awareness.

Recent studies underscore that welfare and psychological care are essential to sustainable performance (Kim & Ahn, 2025; Hong, 2025). Professional players face overlapping stressors that can result in exhaustion and burnout (Poulus et al., 2024). Comprehensive support systems, including psychological counselling, emotional-labor training, and structured communication with families and fan communities, are critical developmental resources for maintaining player well-being and long-term career stability (Kim & Ahn, 2025).

Event Organizers and Publishers

As discussed in Section 1.3, publishers (e.g., Riot Games) constitute the structural core of the esports ecosystem. Publishers exercise institutional sovereignty through their ownership of game IP, determining not only the technical design of titles but also the legal and economic conditions under which competition occurs (Peng et al., 2020; Holden et al., 2017). In esports, publishers act to a certain extent as regulators, marketers, and rights holders. This convergence is a defining feature of the esports ecosystem; publishers set competitive balance, licensing conditions, and sponsorship eligibility, while retaining the power to withdraw official support, technically determining the survival of entire titles and their professional circuits.

The economic center of publisher-organizer collaboration is sponsorship and media distribution. Industry reports consistently identify sponsorships and broadcast/streaming rights as the largest revenue streams in esports' commercial mix, with distribution agreements on platforms such as Twitch, YouTube, or regional streamers structuring audience access and value creation. Industry reports consistently identify sponsorships and broadcast/streaming rights as the largest revenue streams in esports' commercial mix (Statista, 2025). Because sanctioning, licensing, and brand use ultimately rest with IP owners, effective authority concentrates with publishers.

Although regulatory bodies such as the International Esports Federation and Global Esports Federation attempt to standardize rules, effective authority remains concentrated in publisher-organizer alliances. The same entities that create symbolic value through play also capture the economic and communicative flows that sustain the industry. Event organizers, including ESL FACEIT and BLAST, operate within these licensed boundaries, translating publisher frameworks into competitive events and live productions that connect teams, sponsors, and audiences. Consequently, publishers and event organizers not only manage competitive infrastructure but the narratives, timing, and emotional engagement that make global competitions relevant and meaningful.

MARKETING COMMUNICATION STRATEGIES IN ESPORTS

Sponsorship Effectiveness: Congruence, Authenticity, and Brand Equity

Sponsorship has long been considered a strategic instrument within marketing communication. Within sport and entertainment industries, it allows brands to enhance visibility, foster consumer relationships, and build symbolic associations that strengthen brand equity (Cornwell et al., 2024). In esports, this function is amplified by the industry's digital structure and participatory culture. Sponsorship represents the principal source of sectoral revenue, which illustrates both its financial weight and communicative significance (Noh et al., 2025). Unlike traditional sports audiences, esports communities are highly interactive, global, and digitally native. Esports audiences tend to respond more positively when sponsors provide relevant added value and esports-specific content that integrates with community practices, which enhances perceived authenticity (Freitas et al., 2021).

The effectiveness of a sponsorship depends primarily on perceived congruence, which refers to the cognitive and affective fit between sponsor and sponsored property (Speed & Thompson, 2000). Functional congruence occurs when a sponsor's product category naturally supports gameplay or performance, as in the case of hardware or peripheral brands such as Logitech or Intel. Image-based congruence occurs when non-endemic sponsors share symbolic meanings with esports culture, such as Red Bull's association with energy, competition, and youthful innovation (Noh et al., 2025). Spectators who attend live tournaments or follow streamed matches transfer the positive emotions of those experiences to brands they perceive as fitting the scene.

Likewise, value congruence, which refers to alignment between brand and consumer values, fosters higher media engagement and long-term brand sustainability (Kordyaka et al., 2023). When audiences perceive shared purpose or ethos, they infer authenticity and respond with greater loyalty and advocacy. In esports, traditional visibility or naming rights rarely suffice because audiences reward brands that contribute meaningful value to the ecosystem. Freitas et al. (2021) describe this as "relevant added value," the process through which sponsors integrate themselves by supporting tournaments, producing esports-related content, or facilitating fan participation. Such initiatives move sponsorships beyond transactional exposure toward genuine community partnership (e.g., Coca-Cola's co-created amateur tournaments). This illustrate how brands demonstrate commitment rather than opportunistic presence. Authenticity emerges when fans perceive that the brand understands the culture and adds tangible benefits, which can transform non-endemic companies into quasi-endemic participants (Freitas et al., 2021). In contrast, incongruent or performative sponsorships often provoke resistance, as digitally literate audiences quickly identify insincere gestures.

The communicative effectiveness of sponsorship ultimately manifests in brand-equity outcomes. Esports sponsorship strengthens awareness through repeated visual and verbal exposure across tournaments and streams. It enhances brand image when the sponsored property's attributes, such as innovation, skill, or competitiveness, become linked to the sponsor's identity through associative learning. Ultimately, it fosters loyalty when fans perceive the sponsor as a facilitator of their enjoyment and sense of community belonging (Noh et al., 2025). Kordyaka et al. (2023) demonstrate that sustained media engagement rooted in value congruence supports brand sustainability and extends equity from short-term attention to enduring relevance. This evidence suggests that effective esports sponsorship is less about reach and more about relational resonance, as brands succeed when they authentically share the cultural space of gaming.

All in all, congruence provides cognitive legitimacy, authenticity secures affective legitimacy, and together they generate brand equity that can evolve into sustainable cultural capital. Brands that invest in understanding esports norms, narratives, and participatory structures are more likely to achieve credible and long-term positioning in esports.

In-Game Advertising, Advergaming, and Gamified Immersive Experiences

In esports, it is common to find commercial messages part of the competitive and experiential flow of the games. In-game advertising refers to the inclusion of brands or products inside existing games whose main purpose is entertainment (Terlutter & Capella, 2013). The format formats include static or dynamic billboards, branded textures, or sponsor signage placed within the virtual environment (Chang et al., 2024). In esports contexts, this can be seen in tournament versions of Counter-Strike 2 or Rocket League, where sponsor logos such as Intel or Red Bull appear on in-game arenas and broadcast overlays. This visibility mirrors the spatial branding of traditional sports and maintains continuity with the aesthetics of digital competition.

Advergaming, on the other hand, describes digital games or game modes created specifically for a brand, using gameplay itself to communicate brand values or product meanings (Cauberghe & De Pelsmacker, 2010; Terlutter & Capella, 2013). Instead of inserting a logo into an existing title, the brand becomes the core of the play experience. In esports-related marketing, advergaming frequently appears through branded side events or casual activations that extend tournament engagement. For instance, KFC Gaming mini-games supporting its sponsorship of professional teams.

Such initiatives transform advertising into interactive storytelling, where the brand narrative unfolds through the player's performance rather than explicit messaging.

A third layer involves gamified immersive experiences, which merge the logics of play, narrative, and technology to produce a heightened sense of presence. Immersion refers to the state of psychological absorption in a mediated environment where sensory, cognitive, and emotional boundaries are dissolved (Jung et al., 2024). Gamified immersive experiences extend this concept beyond the game itself by integrating virtual interaction with live or social contexts. To illustrate, Louis Vuitton's partnership with League of Legends combined a physical fashion line with in-game skins and trophy-case design, creating a hybrid experience that spanned the digital and material arenas.

From a marketing communication perspective, these strategies demonstrate how persuasion in esports is driven by engagement, authenticity, and the creative use of emerging technologies. When brand integration aligns with the logic of play and community culture, the experience produces emotional attachment and co-created meaning. In-game advertising provides continuous symbolic presence, advergaming generates interactive storytelling, and gamified immersive experiences construct participatory ecosystems that connect brands, players, and audiences within a unified narrative. Together they demonstrate how esports transforms advertising into an experiential component of integrated marketing communication.

Influencers, Streamers, and Community Engagement

Within the esports ecosystem discussed in Section 3, influencers and streamers constitute the primary communicative link between professional play, audiences, and brands. Their visibility and interaction transform competitive gaming into an ongoing cultural experience. Influence in esports extends beyond the traditional celebrity model. Streamers represent the live, high-frequency end of this spectrum, as they broadcast matches or personal play sessions, interact with viewers in real-time, and cultivate stable communities (Jang et al., 2024).

Engagement develops through relational immersion. Audiences experience familiarity and reciprocity through chat, emotes, and direct address, forming parasocial relationships that evolve into loyalty and repeated viewing (Leith, 2021). When this loyalty aligns with sponsorship, it enhances attitudes toward promoted brands by transferring affective trust from the streamer to the commercial partner (Xu et al., 2022). In other words, persuasion in esports marketing operates through social connection, not exposure; audiences support brands that appear embedded in the communities they value. Viewers create highlight clips, memes, and commentary on Twitch, Discord, and Reddit, circulating content that extends both cultural and commercial visibility. During major tournaments such as the League of Legends

World Championship, influencers function as communication nodes that sustain dialogue, convert spectators into advocates, and prolong campaign life cycles through ongoing interaction (Elareshi et al., 2025).

For integrated marketing communication, influencers exemplify the contemporary logic of integrated communication: a continuous, participatory and relational model. Brand success depends on cultural fit and transparency, as the esports community can quickly identify inauthentic sponsorships. Influencers and streamers embody the participatory shift in esports communication. They transform marketing into dialogue and audiences into co-creators of meaning, marking a decisive move from exposure-driven campaigns to networked, culturally embedded relationships.

eWOM, Purchase Intentions, and Consumption Behaviors

Electronic word-of-mouth (eWOM) in esports refers to consumer-generated communication about games, events, and brands that circulates through live and asynchronous digital channels. It includes live chat interactions on streaming platforms, such as community discussions on Discord or Reddit, and commentaries or reviews on video-on-demand content. These exchanges derive persuasive power from social proximity and authenticity, shaping how audiences evaluate games, teams, and sponsors (Hennig-Thurau et al., 2004). In esports, eWOM is embedded within continuous spectating and community participation, creating a feedback loop between what audiences watch, how they play, and what they choose to purchase.

Understanding purchase intention and consumption in this context requires a broader definition compared to traditional media models. Consumption in esports are of both digital and material nature. It encompasses in-game spending on cosmetic items, virtual currency, or battle passes; monetary support for streamers and teams through subscriptions and donations; purchases of licensed merchandise and peripherals; attendance at live or virtual tournaments; and the consumption of sponsor products featured within esports content. Each of these activities reflects both functional and symbolic value, as they express belonging to the esports field and the communities that define it.

Empirical research shows that spectating is a central pathway linking communication and consumption. Motivations to watch esports directly influence watching intention, which then predicts gaming intention, and subsequently purchase intention (Macey et al., 2022) The more people engage in spectating, the more likely they are to play the related game and to make in-game purchases. This relationship is particularly strong in free-to-play and live-service games, where ongoing updates, microtransactions, and community events sustain both engagement and spending. Beyond behavioral mechanisms, esports consumption also involves identity work. Seo (2016) conceptualized esports from a professionalized consumption perspective, where participants invest symbolic capital in skills, recognition, and authenticity. Purchasing in-game items or sponsor products signals participation in the culture's norms and values. Consequently, the responsiveness to eWOM increases as identity centrality within the esports community intensifies. Players and fans who define themselves through the esports field are more likely to act on persuasive cues shared by peers and influencers, perceiving such acts as both social validation and personal expression.

Taken together, these dynamics reveal that eWOM in esports is best understood as an outcome of participatory engagement and consumption (Abbasi et al., 2023). Spectating, playing, and purchasing behaviors generate communicative activity as participants share opinions, recommendations, and experiences across platforms. The decision to engage with a game, buy digital items, or support a team often leads to further interaction, reinforcing community visibility and sustaining the cycle of engagement. Watching intention drives gaming and purchasing intentions, and these consumption acts in turn stimulate new waves of eWOM that influence audiences.

Case Studies

Through these discussions, the chapter identifies areas where marketing communication strategies must adapt to the unique characteristics of esports as a hybrid communication arena. Below, we present selected case studies on brands' successful applications of esports marketing strategies and their contributions to marketing outcomes and audience engagement. These case studies illustrate three different examples of how global brands have transformed the theoretical principles into practical strategies within esports.

First case, the collaboration between Mercedes-Benz and ESL demonstrates sponsorship congruence and sustained brand equity building. The partnership, first announced in 2017 and renewed in subsequent years (Mercedes-Benz, n.d.), positioned Mercedes-Benz as an embedded stakeholder in professional esports. The company's message of high-performance engineering aligns naturally with ESL's focus on performance and competitive excellence, creating a coherent symbolic relationship that reinforces authenticity. This authenticity emerged through contribution: Mercedes-Benz enhanced the competitive ecosystem by introducing the Mercedes-Benz Most Valuable Player (MVP) award, which became a recognized element of tournament broadcasts. The collaboration prioritized cultural longevity and associated Mercedes-Benz with esports based on shared values.

Second, the partnership between Mastercard and Riot Games for League of Legends illustrates how a global non-endemic brand adapts the logic of immersive communication to esports contexts. Since 2018, Mastercard has integrated its "Priceless experiences" campaign into the live viewing ecosystem and sponsoring flagship tournaments such as the World Championship through experiential activations that offered backstage access, fan engagement, premium event experiences (Mastercard, n.d., Riot Games, 2023). Mastercard stands as a strong example of a global brand strategically aligning with the participatory culture of esports to create emotionally resonant communication. Rather than attempting in-game integration, Mastercard presented its sponsorship in a form of cultural participation, considering fans' passion and engagement as forms of shared value. In the context of esports, this strand of Mastercard's marketing communication strategy helps cultivate an image of the brand as a facilitator of value and inclusive participation, extending its identity beyond that of a traditional financial institution.

Third, the collaboration between Gucci and Fnatic highlights the extension of esports communication into lifestyle and luxury domains. Announced in 2020 (Fnatic, 2020), it featured a limited-edition Gucci Dive watch and a visual campaign that included Fnatic players. Rather than focusing on mass-market reach, the initiative pursued aspirational congruence, aligning Gucci's emphasis on craftsmanship and exclusivity with the creativity and prestige associated with professional esports. Limited to one hundred pieces, the watch became a symbol of rarity and cultural fusion, generating wide attention across fashion and gaming media. This strategy enhanced the relevance of Gucci among younger digital audiences and illustrated how luxury aesthetics can intersect with the participatory culture of esports.

Taken together, these cases demonstrate how marketing communication in esports progresses from visibility to participation and then to cultural integration. Mercedes-Benz achieved authenticity through sustained contribution to competition narratives. Mastercard transformed audience engagement by extending interactivity beyond viewing, embedding experiential and emotional participation across the esports environment. Gucci connected digital and material consumption by turning competitive performance into a form of cultural expression. Collectively, these partnerships illustrate that effective brand communication in esports relies on congruence, value creation, and cultural resonance rather than on exposure alone.

CHALLENGES AND ETHICAL CONSIDERATIONS

Gender Disparity and Inclusivity Challenges

Gender disparity remains one of the most persistent structural and ethical challenges in esports. Despite an increase in female gaming participation, professional esports continues to be overwhelmingly male-dominated, with men the majority (up to 95%of professional players are male, Tang et al., 2021). While gender disparity is most visible in professional esports competition, casual gaming and esports spectatorship show a more balanced gender composition, with women comprising 46%, which is nearly half of global gamers (ESA, 2024) indicating that exclusion is largely structural rather than interest-based.

Therefore, this imbalance in professional play cannot be explained by differences in skill or motivation. That is because female players display equal or higher levels of achievement motivation and valence compared with their male counterparts (Kordyaka et al., 2023). However, Female esports enthusiasts face cultural and dispositional barriers, including hostile in-game environments, biased community norms, and skepticism toward their competence, that restrict advancement into professional tiers (Darvin et al., 2021; Madden, 2021). This suggest that gender disparities are less the result of individual capability and more the product of enduring structural and cultural exclusions.

Gender bias further manifests in representation and discourse. Games and broadcasts often perpetuate hyper-sexualized portrayals of women and associate gaming competence with masculine identity, reinforcing exclusionary stereotypes. Within esports ecosystems, all-female teams are often perceived as less credible, making the expectations lower for their skill and legitimacy (Madden, 2021). Female gamers frequently encounter violence-coded or objectifying content, contributing to negative body image and social anxiety, while some mask gender through avatars to avoid harassment (Lopez-Fernandez et al., 2019). Gender biases in esports are sustained by community discourses that discourage women's identification with gaming and limit their pursuit of professional careers, while male players continue to dominate visible and legitimized pathways (Madden, 2021). In addition, esports environment is known for continuous incivility and harassment, forming what is called hostile environment (Darvin et al., 2021). Toxic behaviors and hostility operates across multiple layers, which is common and even normalized in the gaming community.

From a marketing communication perspective, inequalities translate into underrepresentation in sponsorships, influencer contracts, and branded storytelling, narrowing the pool of visible role models and limiting brands' resonance with diverse audiences (Darvin et al., 2021; Kordyaka et al., 2023). Recent initiatives such as the Women in Esports program by the British Esports Association illustrate growing institutional efforts to improve representation and safety within the competitive scene. Such programs signal a shift in industry norms, where inclusivity is increasingly recognized as both a moral responsibility and a pathway to audience diversification and community trust.

Player Well-Being and Support Systems

The hypercompetitive structure of esports requires from players sustained focus, high coordination, and constant adaptation, often under intense psychological pressure. These conditions expose players to risks such as physical strain, stress, and burnout (Poulus et al., 2024). For instance, long hours of training and insufficient sleep can diminish reaction time and impair decision-making, while repetitive hand and arm movements lead to musculoskeletal discomfort. Recognizing how these domains interact is vital for maintaining both player health and consistent performance outcomes (Hong, 2025).

Esports players well-being is shaped by the broader social and organizational systems surrounding them. Esports competitors often depend on informal social networks, such as teammates, coaches, and family, for emotional and motivational support (Trotter et al., 2021). However, such informal structures are not sufficient without institutional mechanisms that address mental-health management, workload regulation, and recovery routines (Poulus & Sharpe, 2025). Kim and Ahn (2025) highlight that mental health challenges among esports athletes stem not only from individual stressors but also from performance-driven structures and social relationships within the competitive environment. Their study finds that social support networks, comprising teammates, managers, families, and online communities, can provide both relief and added pressure, highlighting the complex role of social interactions in shaping player well-being. Thus, supportive communication from the players' social can help them navigate the stressful and demanding world of competitions. Additionally, well-being promotion mechanisms, such as physical training programs, nutrition education, and psychological counseling, can help players sustain both health and motivation. Educational workshops and mentoring programs that address tactical strategy, time management, and career planning can support the transition from amateur gaming to professional esports (Salo, 2021).

Establishing a structured support system for esports players at all levels is therefore crucial to ensure their long-term health and enhance performance (Hong, 2023). While elite players increasingly benefit from organizational support, such as access to professional coaching and mental health resources, amateur players often lack these provisions (Hong, 2024; Salo, 2021). This disparity represents a critical developmental gap: since esports careers are typically short, fostering the next generation of players through early-stage support is essential for the sustainable growth of the esports industry.

As esports continues to mature, embedding structured, inclusive, and evidence-based support systems will be critical for transforming short-lived careers into sustainable professional pathways.

Regulatory and Cultural Considerations

The communicative power of esports and its capacity to mobilize audiences generate risks that require institutional and cultural mediation. To illustrate, research shows a strong correlation between intensive esports spectating and gambling-like participation, such as loot boxes and skin betting (Macey & Hamari, 2019). This underscores that the experiential design of esports can elicit powerful forms of consumer investment, making regulation and cultural context central to how the field should be governed.

A useful way to frame why and how regulation takes shape is through Windholz's (2020) synthesis of regulatory theory. Public-interest accounts justify intervention to correct market failures (e.g., youth protection, integrity, and consumer safeguards) or to capture positive externalities (e.g., health, cohesion). Private-interest accounts emphasise capture, public choice, and interest-group pressures: powerful actors seek rules that serve their own ends, and governments sometimes accommodate them. Institutional accounts explain the durability of traditional sport's "pyramid" structures that mediate among stakeholders, and ideational accounts show how norms of autonomy and self-regulation confer legitimacy on sporting bodies. Esports may seem to overlap with sport on the surface (leagues, teams, fans); however, it differs in an important aspect, as we highlighted in previous sections: publishers own the core intellectual property and operate for profit. Blindly integrating traditional sport's governance template risks policy failure, that is because esports' hybrid nature (IP-owned, platformised, and globally distributed) calls for a different body of law and self-regulation.

Labor relations remain sensitive, as most professionals sign team agreements, which offer limited job security, restrict access to collective bargaining, and provide limited statutory labor protection (Holden et al., 2020). Minimum age thresholds have become a basic safeguard in recent years, typically 17 or 18 (e.g., the League of Legends Championship Series); however, contract standards for working hours, benefits, and education are often underspecified in most jurisdictions. Integrity governance in esports remains largely self-regulatory. Industry bodies such as the Esports Integrity Commission (ESIC) coordinate investigations into match-fixing, doping, and cheating, while publishers apply their own platform-level sanctions. However, without statutory harmonization or international legal oversight, enforcement remains inconsistent, and legal recourse is limited (Holden et al., 2017). Gambling-adjacent monetisation intensifies regulatory risk: "skin betting" markets and random-reward loot boxes have prompted intervention in parts of Europe (e.g., Belgian regulators treating certain loot boxes as gambling), while other jurisdictions rely on self-regulation, heightening youth-exposure concerns (King & Delfabbro, 2019). Transnational mobility adds further frictions: few states recognise "esports athlete" as an occupation, complicating visas and taxation, with occasional accommodations (e.g., US P-1A visas) but no universal pathway (Holden et al., 2020).

Cultural factors deeply influence how esports is organised and experienced. Age limits and youth policies reveal distinct moral and policy logics: South Korea's former "Shutdown Law" which restricted minors' late-night gaming, illustrates a welfare-oriented approach to digital play. Western systems on the other hand may rely more on parental consent and self-regulation. Persistent gender disparity and online harassment continue to challenge inclusivity, prompting diversity initiatives and women-only circuits (Kim & Ahn, 2025). Overall, these regulatory and cultural dynamics explain why esports cannot be governed effectively by copying sports' frameworks nor by leaving everything to platforms. Public-interest justifications (youth protection, integrity, consumer safeguards) are real, and private-interest pressures (publisher control, lobbying by teams, betting operators) are powerful. Unlike traditional sports with entrenched governance systems, esports lacks strong institutional path dependencies. Because publishers hold both intellectual property and regulatory authority, autonomy in the ecosystem is structurally limited. This dual control impacts and shapes the communicative and marketing boundaries of the field; what can be said, shown, sponsored, or measured depends as much on platform policies and national laws as on local moral and cultural norms that define legitimacy. Thus, an effective strategy demands glocal compliance (across IP, labour, gambling, data, and age regulation) and cultural legibility (attuned to norms of inclusion, risk, and identity politics), recognizing that the same experiential intensity driving engagement can also produce harm without careful governance.

KEY IMPLICATIONS AND TAKEAWAYS

The conceptualization of esports as a hybrid communication arena advances existing marketing and communication theory by demonstrating that audience participation, technological affordances, and regulatory asymmetries co-produce meaning within a convergent media economy. In this digital environment, persuasion is achieved through participation and performance rather than message repetition. Communication value emerges from the interaction between gameplay, spectatorship, and brand presence, each shaping the experiential texture of consumption. Engagement depends on how players, streamers, and audiences co-create meaning through emotional intensity and shared rituals of competition. This interdependence extends marketing communication theory by emphasizing value co-creation and coordination among multiple actors to produce symbolic and commercial outcomes.

For marketing and advertising, the digital world of esports highlights the need to design communication that blends experience and interaction. Sponsorship, branded content, and in-game advertising are most effective when they enhance rather than interrupt the game experience. Brands must invest in the experiential alignment, embedding themselves in the competitive and affective flow of events. Campaigns that use collaborative storytelling with creators and fans, or community challenges that reward creativity foster stronger emotional bonds and sustained engagement. These strategies are especially effective for Generation Z, whose media behavior is shaped by co-creation and immediacy.

From a managerial perspective, the esports arena demands adaptive coordination among brands, publishers, and event organizers. Publishers' ownership of intellectual property defines the boundaries of what can be sponsored or modified, while organizers manage the experiential frame in which audiences encounter brands. Effective management involves building long-term partnerships that respect creative rights but, at the same time, allow flexibility in brand integration and audience engagement. Supporting amateur players is also strategically important; these future esports athletes are talented young individuals who often lack stable organizational or financial support. Their performances contribute to audience growth, content diversity, and the fostering of emerging talent that sustains the competitive scene. Providing structured opportunities and visibility through brand partnerships or co-sponsored events strengthens both competitive continuity and community engagement. In doing so, brands and organizers can align commercial objectives with the developmental and social sustainability of the esports ecosystem.

Ethical and social considerations are equally central to communication outcomes. Gender inequality, online toxicity, and mental-health risks persist as barriers to inclusive participation. Particular attention should be given to non-male players, whose participation remains underrepresented despite proven skill and audience appeal. Ensuring equitable access, safeguarding against harassment, and featuring diverse competitors in branded content and event narratives are essential for achieving inclusivity across the ecosystem. Addressing these issues through deliberate representation, safe-community initiatives, and inclusive sponsorships is a social obligation and a strategic imperative.

Overall, esports repositions marketing communication as an experiential and relational practice that relies on continuous negotiation among technological systems, cultural communities, and commercial objectives. The takeaways are clear: effectiveness depends on cultural resonance rather than exposure; managerial success depends on cooperation across institutional layers; and ethical commitment is a determinant of both brand and industry sustainability. Esports thus provides a blueprint for understanding how marketing communication evolves in participatory, data-driven, and socially contested digital environments.

CONCLUSION

This chapter traced how esports, as a multidimensional phenomenon, reshapes the principles and practices of marketing communication. Beginning with its technological and cultural foundations, esports was presented as an experiential and participatory medium that combines play, media production, and spectatorship. The examination of its stakeholders, including players, streamers, fans, organizers, publishers, and brands, revealed a communicative ecosystem sustained by interdependence. Within this environment, Generation Z audiences expect interaction, authenticity and immediacy, redefining what engagement and value creation.

The theoretical discussion positioned esports within the evolution of Integrated Marketing Communication, highlighting how its principles are reinterpreted through co-creative and dialogic practices that reflect the realities of digital convergence. Motivation, immersion, and parasocial affiliation emerged as the psychological mechanisms that transform gameplay and viewing into meaningful consumption experiences. Co-creation was shown to be the communicative link that connects the diverse actors of the ecosystem. Through streaming, commentary, modification, and fan content, audiences participate directly in producing both symbolic and economic value.

Mapping the ecosystem clarified that communication is embedded in every layer of esports. Professional players and amateurs together drive narrative continuity. Content creators translate competition into community. Fans convert attention and affect into consumption, while publishers and event organizers determine how these relationships are monetized and presented. Drawing on existing research, the discussion of marketing strategies in esports reveals that sponsorship, advertising, and influencer collaborations achieve impact when they align with the logic of play and the emotional rhythm of competition. In-game advertising and gamified experiences show how persuasion can merge with enjoyment when designed around user experience. At the same time, electronic word-of-mouth and experiential consumption reveal that affective and social engagement drive behavioral outcomes.

FUTURE RESEARCH DIRECTIONS

The dynamics examined in this chapter reveal a set of ethical, social, and governance-related issues that call for further scholarly investigation. In particular, the challenges outlined in the final sections remind us that the promise of participation also produces new responsibilities. Persistent gender disparity, online toxicity, and mental health pressures require deliberate governance and ethical sensitivity from both brands and organizers. Sustainable growth will depend on inclusive representation, support for amateur competitors, and transparent partnership models that distribute visibility and value more equitably across the ecosystem. Taken together, these insights suggest that esports is not a temporary marketing trend but a durable communicative form that exemplifies the direction of contemporary media.

It blurs the boundaries between producer and consumer, between entertainment and promotion, and between local identity and global connectivity. For marketing and communication scholarship, esports provides a laboratory for studying how engagement, legitimacy, and cultural meaning are generated in participatory digital environments.

Future inquiry should build on these foundations to understand how evolving technologies, especially artificial intelligence and extended reality, will transform participation, personalization, and governance in esports communication. Comparative research across cultures and gendered experiences will be crucial for capturing how inclusivity and representation evolve as the field matures. Ultimately, the study of esports points toward a broader redefinition of marketing communication as a practice grounded in interaction and shared experience in contemporary digital environments.

REFERENCES

Abbasi, A. Z., Alqahtani, N., Tsiotsou, R. H., Rehman, U., & Ting, D. H. (2023). Esports as playful consumption experiences: Examining the antecedents and consequences of game engagement. *Telematics and Informatics*, *77*, 101937.

Abbasi, A. Z., Asif, M., Hollebeek, L. D., Islam, J. U., Ting, D. H., & Rehman, U. (2021). The effects of consumer esports videogame engagement on consumption behaviors. *Journal of Product and Brand Management*, *30*(8), 1194–1211.

Abbasi, A. Z., Ting, D. H., Hlavacs, H., Costa, L. V., & Veloso, A. I. (2019). An empirical validation of consumer video game engagement: A playful-consumption experience approach. *Entertainment Computing*, *29*, 43–55.

Bányai, F., Zsila, Á., Griffiths, M. D., Demetrovics, Z., & Király, O. (2020). Career as a professional gamer: Gaming motives as predictors of career plans to become a professional esport player. *Frontiers in Psychology*, *11*, 1866. PMID: 32903792

Block, F., Hodge, V., Hobson, S., Sephton, N., Devlin, S., Ursu, M. F., & Cowling, P. I. (2018, June). Narrative bytes: Data-driven content production in esports. In *Proceedings of the 2018 ACM international conference on interactive experiences for TV and online video* (pp. 29-41).

Brodie, R. J., Hollebeek, L. D., Jurić, B., & Ilić, A. (2011). Customer engagement: Conceptual domain, fundamental propositions, and implications for research. *Journal of Service Research*, *14*(3), 252–271.

Brown, E., & Cairns, P. (2004, April). A grounded investigation of game immersion. In *CHI'04 extended abstracts on Human factors in computing systems* (pp. 1297-1300).

Bubna, K., Trotter, M. G., Watson, M., & Polman, R. (2023). Coaching and talent development in esports: A theoretical framework and suggestions for future research. *Frontiers in Psychology*, *14*, 1191801. PMID: 37235101

Calapez, A., Ribeiro, T., Almeida, V., & Pedragosa, V. (2024). Esports fan identity toward sponsor–sponsee relationship: An understanding of the role-based identity. *International Journal of Sports Marketing & Sponsorship*, *25*(1), 42–66.

Cauberghe, V., & De Pelsmacker, P. (2010). Advergames. *Journal of Advertising*, *39*(1), 5–18.

Chan, G., Huo, Y., Kelly, S., Leung, J., Tisdale, C., & Gullo, M. (2022). The impact of eSports and online video gaming on lifestyle behaviours in youth: A systematic review. *Computers in Human Behavior*, *126*, 106974.

Chang, Y. K., Chen, K., & Li, Z. (2024). Systematic Framework for Esports Training: Informing eSports Training with the Learning Sciences. *Simulation & Gaming*, *55*(1), 82–108.

Cornwell, T. B., Frank, A., & Miller-Moudgil, R. (2024). A research agenda at the intersection of sport sponsorship and service. *Journal of Service Management*, *35*(1), 108–126.

Darvin, L., Holden, J., Wells, J., & Baker, T. (2021). Breaking the glass monitor: Examining the underrepresentation of women in esports environments. *Sport Management Review*, *24*(3), 475–499.

Darvin, L., Vooris, R., & Mahoney, T. (2020). The playing experiences of esport participants: An analysis of treatment discrimination and hostility in esport environments. *Journal of Athlete Development and Experience*, *2*(1), 3.

Duan, Z., & Jeong, G. (2025). What Drives Continuance Usage Intention Toward Virtual Reality Games? Gamer-Avatar Identification and Experiential Consumption Perspectives. *International Journal of Human-Computer Interaction*, *41*(14), 8581–8592.

El Oraiby, M., & Kiygi-Calli, M. (2026). Rethinking performance measurement in esports: How games shape coaching priorities for amateur player development. *International Journal of Sports Science & Coaching*, *21*(1), 97-108.

Elareshi, M., Ahmed, W., Das, R., Hardey, M., Fenton, A., Chadwick, S., & Alaawad, H. (2025). Esports Interaction and Influencer Impact: Insights from the League of Legends World Championship. In *Tech Fusion in Business and Society: Harnessing Big Data, IoT, and Sustainability in Business* (Vol. 2, pp. 291–300). Springer Nature Switzerland.

ESA - Entertainment Software Association. (2024, July 16). *Annual ESA study reveals video games' universal appeal across generations.* https://www.theesa.com/annual-esa-study-reveals-video-games-universal-appeal-across-generations

Esiri, S. (2022). Integrated marketing communication framework for esports brand growth and audience expansion. *Journal of Advance Multidisciplinary Research*, *1*(2), 39–47.

Flores-Marquez, P. (2025, February 12). *Gen Zers have the highest rate of digital gaming adoption.* eMarketer. Retrieved from https://www.emarketer.com/content/gen-zers-have-highest-rate-digital-gaming-adoption

Fnatic (2020, June 2020). https://fnatic.com/news/fnatic-x-gucci

Freitas, B. D. A., Contreras-Espinosa, R. S., & Correia, P. Á. P. (2021). The importance of incorporating relevant-added value into esports sponsorships. *Journal of contemporary marketing science, 4*(3), 397-423.

Funk, D. C., Pizzo, A. D., & Baker, B. J. (2018). eSport management: Embracing eSport education and research opportunities. *Sport Management Review, 21*(1), 7–13.

Riot Games. (2022, March 14). *Riot Games announces new equity investment in Arcane animation studio Fortiche Production* [Press release]. https://www.riotgames.com/en/news/riot-games-announces-new-equity-investment-in-arcane-animation-studio-fortiche-production

Riot Games. (2023, June 20). *Mastercard expands global partnership to VALORANT esports.* https://www.riotgames.com/en/news/mastercard-riot-games-global-valorant

Ghosh, T. S. S., & Dwivedi, Y. K. (2022). Brands in a game or a game for brands? Comparing the persuasive effectiveness of in-game advertising and advergames. *Psychology and Marketing, 39*(12), 2328–2348.

Giakoni-Ramírez, F., Merellano-Navarro, E., & Duclos-Bastías, D. (2022). Professional esports players: Motivation and physical activity levels. *International Journal of Environmental Research and Public Health, 19*(4), 2256. PMID: 35206445

Giles, D. C. (2002). Parasocial interaction: A review of the literature and a model for future research. *Media Psychology, 4*(3), 279–305.

Gul, O., & Yurtsizoglu, Z. (2025). Development and Validation of the Scale for Analysing the Consumption Behaviours of E-Sports Players Using a Mixed-Methods Approach. *SAGE Open, 15*(3), 21582440251357721.

Hamari, J., & Sjöblom, M. (2017). What is eSports and why do people watch it? *Internet Research, 27*(2), 211–232.

Hamilton, W. A., Garretson, O., & Kerne, A. (2014, April). Streaming on twitch: fostering participatory communities of play within live mixed media. In *Proceedings of the SIGCHI conference on human factors in computing systems* (pp. 1315-1324).

Hennig-Thurau, T., Gwinner, K. P., Walsh, G., & Gremler, D. D. (2004). Electronic word-of-mouth via consumer-opinion platforms: What motivates consumers to articulate themselves on the internet? *Journal of Interactive Marketing, 18*(1), 38–52.

Hirschman, E. C., & Holbrook, M. B. (1982). Hedonic consumption: Emerging concepts, methods and propositions. *Journal of Marketing, 46*(3), 92–101.

Holbrook, M. B., Chestnut, R. W., Oliva, T. A., & Greenleaf, E. A. (1984). Play as a consumption experience: The roles of emotions, performance, and personality in the enjoyment of games. *The Journal of Consumer Research*, *11*(2), 728–739.

Holden, J. T., Edelman, M., & Baker III, T. A. (2020). A short treatise on esports and the law: How America regulates its next national pastime. *U. Ill. L. Rev.*, 509.

Holden, J. T., Kaburakis, A., & Rodenberg, R. (2017). The future is now: Esports policy considerations and potential litigation. *Journal of Legal Aspects of Sport*, *27*(1), 46–78.

Hollebeek, L. D., Abbasi, A. Z., Schultz, C. D., Ting, D. H., & Sigurdsson, V. (2022). Hedonic consumption experience in videogaming: A multidimensional perspective. *Journal of Retailing and Consumer Services*, *65*, 102892.

Hong, H. J. (2023). eSports: The need for a structured support system for players. *European Sport Management Quarterly*, *23*(5), 1430–1453.

Hong, H. J. (2024). Duty of Care in Esports: Organizational Support for Esports Players' Mental Wellbeing and Physical Health. In *Proceedings of the 57th Hawaii International Conference on System Sciences 2024* (pp. 4443- 4452).

Hong, H. J. (2025). Exploring stakeholders' perspectives on esports players' well-being and career prospects. *Computers in Human Behavior Reports*, *17*, 100589.

Horton, D., & Wohl, R. R. (1956). Mass communication and para-social interaction. *Psychiatry*, *19*(3), 215–229. PMID: 13359569

Huettermann, M., & Pizzo, A. D. (2022). Esports fan engagement: A comparison of PC and console esports team fans. *Frontiers in Sports and Active Living*, *4*, 880294. PMID: 35571745

Hussain, A., Hollebeek, L. D., Marder, B., & Ting, D. H. (2025). In-game content purchase motivations (IGCPMs): Conceptualization, scale development, and validation. *Information & Management*, *62*(7), 104207.

Iwatsuki, T., Hagiwara, G., & Dugan, M. E. (2022). Effectively optimizing esports performance through movement science principles. *International Journal of Sports Science & Coaching*, *17*(1), 202–207.

Jang, W., & Byon, K. K. (2020). Antecedents and consequence associated with esports gameplay. *International Journal of Sports Marketing & Sponsorship*, *21*(1), 1–22.

Jang, W., Byon, K. K., Baker, T. A., & Tsuji, Y. (2020). Mediating effect of esports content live streaming in the relationship between esports recreational gameplay and esports event broadcast. *Sport, Business and Management*, *11*(1), 90–106.

Jang, W., Choi, W., Kim, M. J., Song, H., & Byon, K. K. (2024). What makes esports consumers watch streamers' esports live-streaming contents? Extending the theory of planned behavior. *International Journal of Sports Marketing & Sponsorship, 25*(2), 288–309.

Jasrotia, S. S., Kamila, M. K., Chib, S., & Mishra, H. G. (2022). Role of engagement in online gaming: A study of generation Z customers. *Digital Creativity, 33*(1), 64–76.

Jenny, S. E., Keiper, M. C., Taylor, B. J., Williams, D. P., Gawrysiak, J., Manning, R. D., & Tutka, P. M. (2018). eSports venues: A new sport business opportunity. *Journal of Applied Sport Management, 10*(1), 8.

Jenny, S. E., Manning, R. D., Keiper, M. C., & Olrich, T. W. (2017). Virtual (ly) athletes: Where eSports fit within the definition of "Sport". *Quest, 69*(1), 1–18.

Jung, S., Chen, J., & Cai, L. A. (2024). Beyond video game competition: Novel dimensions of live esports event experiences through co-creation. *Journal of Hospitality & Tourism Research (Washington, D.C.), 48*(8), 1453–1466.

Keller, K. L. (2001). Mastering the Marketing Communications Mix: Micro and Macro Perspectives on Integrated Marketing Communication Programs. *Journal of Marketing Management, 17*(7–8), 819–847.

Kim, Y. V., & Ahn, H. (2025). Protecting the Mental Health of Esports Players: A Qualitative Case Study on Their Stress, Coping Strategies, and Social Support Systems. *International Journal of Mental Health Promotion, 27*(9).

King, D. L., & Delfabbro, P. H. (2019). Video game monetization (eg, 'loot boxes'): A blueprint for practical social responsibility measures. *International Journal of Mental Health and Addiction, 17*(1), 166–179.

Kirkpatrick, G. (2012). Constitutive tensions of gaming's field: UK gaming magazines and the formation of gaming culture 1981–1995. *Game Studies, 12*(1), 3.

Kitchen, P. J., & Burgmann, I. (2010). Integrated marketing communication. *Wiley international encyclopedia of marketing*.

Kliatchko, J. G., & Schultz, D. E. (2014). Twenty years of IMC: A study of CEO and CMO perspectives in the Asia-Pacific region. *International Journal of Advertising, 33*(2), 373–390.

Kordyaka, B., Pumplun, L., Brunnhofer, M., Kruse, B., & Laato, S. (2023). Gender disparities in esports–An explanatory mixed-methods approach. *Computers in Human Behavior, 149*, 107956.

Kunz, R. E., Roth, A., & Santomier, J. P. (2022). A perspective on value co-creation processes in eSports service ecosystems. *Sport, Business and Management, 12*(1), 29–53.

Lehnert, K., Walz, A., & Christianson, R. (2022). The booming eSports market: A field day for fans. *The Journal of Business Strategy, 43*(2), 122–128.

Leith, A. P. (2021). Parasocial cues: The ubiquity of parasocial relationships on Twitch. *Communication Monographs, 88*(1), 111–129.

Lim, J. S., Choe, M. J., Zhang, J., & Noh, G. Y. (2020). The role of wishful identification, emotional engagement, and parasocial relationships in repeated viewing of live-streaming games: A social cognitive theory perspective. *Computers in Human Behavior, 108*, 106327.

Liu, Y., Yu, H., Sonbudak, M. F., Troiano, G. M., & Harteveld, C. (2021, May). "Why are you playing games? You are a girl!": Exploring gender biases in Esports. In *Proceedings of the 2021 CHI conference on human factors in computing systems* (pp. 1-15).

Macey, J., & Hamari, J. (2019). eSports, skins and loot boxes: Participants, practices and problematic behaviour associated with emergent forms of gambling. *New Media & Society, 21*(1), 20–41.

Macey, J., Tyrväinen, V., Pirkkalainen, H., & Hamari, J. (2022). Does esports spectating influence game consumption? *Behaviour & Information Technology, 41*(1), 181–197.

Market.us. (2024). *eSports market size worldwide from 2023 to 2033 (in billion U.S. dollars)*. Statista. Accessed 7 March 2025. https://www.statista.com/statistics/1256162/global-esports-market-size/

Mastercard. (2018, September 18). *Mastercard and League of Legends announce multi-year global partnership* [Press release]. Mastercard Newsroom. https://www.mastercard.com/news/press/digital-press-kits/2018/mastercard-league-of-legends-esports-partnership

Mastercard. (n.d.). *League of Legends e-sports*. Priceless. https://www.priceless.com/celebrity/19286/league-of-legends-e-sports

McCormack, S., Jones, B., & Elliott, D. (2022). Coaches' assessment of players' physical performance: Subjective and objective measures are needed when profiling players. *European Journal of Sport Science, 22*(8), 1177–1187. PMID: 34304720

Mercedes-Benz. (n.d.). *Esports*. Mercedes-Benz. https://www.mercedes-benz.com/en/art-and-culture/zeitgeist/sports/esports/

Montag, C., Schivinski, B., Kannen, C., & Pontes, H. M. (2022). Investigating gaming disorder and individual differences in gaming motives among professional and non-professional gamers: An empirical study. *Addictive Behaviors*, *134*, 107416. PMID: 35901542

Noh, Y., Ryu, Y., & Kim, K. (2025). eSport Consumption and Sponsor Brand Equity: The Mediating Role of Congruence. *Frontiers in Psychology*, *16*, 1594068. PMID: 40678431

Orme, S. (2022). "Just watching": A qualitative analysis of non-players' motivations for video game spectatorship. *New Media & Society*, *24*(10), 2252–2269.

Pansari, A., & Kumar, V. (2017). Customer engagement: The construct, antecedents, and consequences. *Journal of the Academy of Marketing Science*, *45*, 294–311.

Pedraza-Ramirez, I., Musculus, L., Raab, M., & Laborde, S. (2020). Setting the scientific stage for esports psychology: A systematic review. *International Review of Sport and Exercise Psychology*, *13*(1), 319–352.

Penezoğlu Yıldırım, D. N., & Ulukol, B. (2022). Dijital Oyunlar ve Şiddet. *TRT Akademi*, *7*(16), 1162–1171.

Peng, Q., Dickson, G., Scelles, N., Grix, J., & Brannagan, P. M. (2020). Esports governance: Exploring stakeholder dynamics. *Sustainability*, *12*(19), 8270.

Porcu, L., Del Barrio-Garcia, S., & Kitchen, P. J. (2017). Measuring integrated marketing communication by taking a broad organisational approach: The firm-wide IMC scale. *European Journal of Marketing*, *51*(3), 692–718.

Poulus, D. R., Sargeant, J., Zarate, D., Griffiths, M. D., & Stavropoulos, V. (2024). Burnout, resilience, and coping among esports players: A network analysis approach. *Computers in Human Behavior*, *153*, 108139.

Poulus, D. R., Sharpe, B. T., Jackman, P. C., Swann, C., & Bennett, K. J. (2024). Defining elite esports athletes: A scoping review. *International Review of Sport and Exercise Psychology*, 1–36.

Pu, H., Xiao, S., & Kota, R. W. (2022). Virtual games meet physical playground: Exploring and measuring motivations for live esports event attendance. *Sport in Society*, *25*(10), 1886–1908.

Qian, K., & Xie, Y. (2026). The Power of Star Creators: Evidence from the Live Streaming Industry. *Journal of Marketing Research*, *63*(1), 149-166.

Qian, T. Y., Wang, J. J., Zhang, J. J., & Lu, L. Z. (2020). It is in the game: Dimensions of esports online spectator motivation and development of a scale. *European Sport Management Quarterly*, *20*(4), 458–479.

Rehman, S. U., Gulzar, R., & Aslam, W. (2022). Developing the integrated marketing communication (imc) through social media (sm): The modern marketing communication approach. *SAGE Open*, *12*(2), 21582440221099936.

Rehman, U., Shah, M. U., Abbasi, A. Z., Hlavacs, H., & Iftikhar, R. (2022). Investigating male gamers' behavioral intention to play PUBG: Insights from playful-consumption experiences. *Frontiers in Psychology*, *13*, 909875. PMID: 36059783

Reinold, T., & Tropp, J. (2012). Integrated marketing communications: How can we measure its effectiveness? *Journal of Marketing Communications*, *18*(2), 113–132.

Rietz, J., & Hallmann, K. (2023). A systematic review on spectator behavior in esports: Why do people watch? *International Journal of Sports Marketing & Sponsorship*, *24*(1), 38–55.

Roth, A., Kunz, R. E., & Kolo, C. (2023). The players' perspective of value co-creation in esports service ecosystems. *Journal of Media Business Studies*, 1–25.

Rue, P. (2018). Make way, millennials, here comes Gen Z. *About Campus: Enriching the Student Learning Experience*, *23*(3), 5–12.

Salo, M. (2021). Career transitions of eSports athletes: A proposal for a research framework. In *Research anthology on business strategies, health factors, and ethical Implications in sports and eSports* (pp. 478–490). IGI Global.

Scholz, T. M. (2020). Deciphering the World of eSports. *International Journal on Media Management*, *22*(1), 1–12.

Schultz, D. E., & Patti, C. H. (2009). The evolution of IMC: IMC in a customer-driven marketplace. *Journal of Marketing Communications*, *15*(2–3), 75–84.

Schultz, D. E., & Schultz, H. F. (1998). Transitioning marketing communication into the twenty-first century. *Journal of Marketing Communications*, *4*(1), 9–26.

Seo, Y. (2016). Professionalized consumption and identity transformations in the field of eSports. *Journal of Business Research*, *69*(1), 264–272.

Settle, Q. (2018). Introducing communication theory: Analysis and application. *Journal of Applied Communications*, *102*(3), 7.

Shaw, A. (2010). What is video game culture? Cultural studies and game studies. *Games and Culture*, *5*(4), 403–424.

Sjöblom, M., Törhönen, M., Hamari, J., & Macey, J. (2019). The ingredients of Twitch streaming: Affordances of game streams. *Computers in Human Behavior*, *92*, 20–28.

Snodgrass, J. G., Dengah, H. F., Lacy, M. G., & Fagan, J. (2013). A formal anthropological view of motivation models of problematic MMO play: Achievement, social, and immersion factors in the context of culture. *Transcultural Psychiatry*, *50*(2), 235–262. PMID: 23690445

Speed, R., & Thompson, P. (2000). Determinants of sports sponsorship response. *Journal of the Academy of Marketing Science*, *28*(2), 226–238.

Statista. (2025). *eSports – worldwide: Market outlook 2025*. Statista Market Insights. https://www.statista.com/outlook/amo/esports/worldwide

Tang, D., Peng, B., Ma, R., & Sum, K. W. R. (2025). Dispelling stigma and enduring bias: Exploring the perception of esports participation among young women. *Humanities & Social Sciences Communications*, *12*(1), 1–13.

Tang, D., Sum, R. K. W., Li, M., Ma, R., Chung, P., & Ho, R. W. K. (2023). What is esports? A systematic scoping review and concept analysis of esports. *Heliyon*, *9*(12). PMID: 38149186

Tang, T., Cooper, R., & Kucek, J. (2021). Gendered Esports: Predicting why men and women play and watch esports games. *Journal of Broadcasting & Electronic Media*, *65*(3), 336–356.

Taylor, T. L. (2018). *Watch Me Play: Twitch and the Rise of Game Live-Streaming*. Princeton University Press.

Terlutter, R., & Capella, M. L. (2013). The gamification of advertising: Analysis and research directions of in-game advertising, advergames, and advertising in social network games. *Journal of Advertising*, *42*(2-3), 95–112.

Thaicharoen, S., Gow, J., & Drachen, A. (2023). An ecosystem framework for the meta in esport games. *Journal of Electronic Gaming and Esports*, *1*(1), 1–14.

The Coca-Cola Company. (2023, June 7). *Coca-Cola Ultimate Zero Sugar launches in collaboration with Riot Games' League of Legends* [Press release]. https://www.coca-colacompany.com/media-center/game-on-coca-cola-riot-games-team-up-ultimate-flavor-and-experiences

Theodoropoulos, A., & Antoniou, A. (2022). VR games in cultural heritage: A systematic review of the emerging fields of virtual reality and culture games. *Applied Sciences (Basel, Switzerland)*, *12*(17), 8476.

Trotter, M. G., Coulter, T. J., Davis, P. A., Poulus, D. R., & Polman, R. (2021). Social support, self-regulation, and psychological skill use in e-athletes. *Frontiers in Psychology*, *12*, 722030. PMID: 34858261

Turtiainen, R., Friman, U., & Ruotsalainen, M. (2020). "Not only for a celebration of competitive overwatch but also for national pride": Sportificating the Overwatch World Cup 2016. *Games and Culture*, *15*(4), 351–371.

Vanderhoef, J. (2013). Casual threats: The feminization of casual video games. *Ada: A Journal of Gender. New Media, and Technology*, *2*(2), 1–28.

Vargo, S. L., & Lusch, R. F. (2017). Service-dominant logic 2025. *International Journal of Research in Marketing*, *34*(1), 46–67.

Wagner, M. G. (2006, June). On the scientific relevance of eSports. In *International conference on internet computing* (Vol. 6, pp. 437-442).

Watson, M., Smith, D., & Fenton, J. (2022). Introducing esports coaching to sport coaching (not as sport coaching). *Sports Coaching Review*, *14*(1), 1–20.

Wechsler, K., Bickmann, P., Rudolf, K., Tholl, C., Froböse, I., & Grieben, C. (2021). Comparison of multiple object-tracking performance between professional and amateur esports players as well as traditional sportsmen. *International Journal of eSports Research*, *1*(1), 1–17.

Welden, R., Hewett, K., Yoo, K., Haenlein, M., Smith, K. M., Pauwels, K., & Hulland, J. (2025). Leveling up retail: How retailers and brands thrive in the video game ecosystem. *Journal of Retailing*.

Windholz, E. (2020). Governing esports: Public policy, regulation and the law. *Sports Law eJournal*, *1*(1).

Witkowski, E., & Harkin, S. (2025). Esports under sports mega-event conventions: Associational values, inclusivity, and national representation at the Commonwealth Games. *Sport in Society*, *28*(3), 452–472.

Wohn, D. Y., & Freeman, G. (2020). Live streaming, playing, and money spending behaviors in eSports. *Games and Culture*, *15*(1), 73–88.

Wu, J., & Holsapple, C. (2014). Imaginal and emotional experiences in pleasure-oriented IT usage: A hedonic consumption perspective. *Information & Management*, *51*(1), 80–92.

Xu, Q., Kim, H., & Billings, A. C. (2022). Let's watch live streaming: How streamer credibility influences brand attitude in esports streamer marketing. *Communication & Sport*, *10*(2), 271–290.

Yee, N. (2006). Motivations for play in online games. *Cyberpsychology & Behavior*, *9*(6), 772–775. PMID: 17201605

Yee, N., Ducheneaut, N., & Nelson, L. (2012, May). Online gaming motivations scale: development and validation. In *Proceedings of the SIGCHI conference on human factors in computing systems* (pp. 2803-2806).

Zervas, K., & Maronitis, K. (2025). Digital bonds: A gamers' perspective on the role of online gaming communities in fostering social interaction and identity. *International Review for the Sociology of Sport*, 1-18.

ADDITIONAL READINGS

Friman, U., Ruotsalainen, M., & Ståhl, M. (2023). Communicating and practicing diversity, equity, and inclusion in Finnish esports organizations: Challenges and opportunities. *Journal of Electronic Gaming and Esports*, *1*(1).

Jang, W. W., Yim, B. H., & Byon, K. K. (2024). Communication in Esports: An Overview of Esports Consumption. *Communication in Sport Management*, 49-58.

Jenny, S. E., Besombes, N., Brock, T., Cote, A. C., & Scholz, T. M. (Eds.). (2024). *Routledge handbook of esports*. Taylor & Francis.

Lee, M., & Chung, P. (Eds.). (2021). *Media technologies for work and play in east Asia: Critical perspectives on Japan and the Two Koreas*. Policy Press.

Maier, T. (2024). Talking to win: The impact of communication on performance in esports. *Journal of Electronic Gaming and Esports*, *2*(1).

McCauley, B., Berndt, A., Helmefalk, M., & Hedlund, D. (2025). Innovation in the esports servicescape: A media business research agenda. *Journal of Media Business Studies*, *22*(2), 87–117.

Ozenc, O. E. (2020). User experience and motivation of professional video game players: A case study of esports in Turkey. *Game User Experience And Player-Centered Design*, 77-120.

Pluss, M. A., Bennett, K. J., Novak, A. R., Panchuk, D., Coutts, A. J., & Fransen, J. (2019). Esports: The chess of the 21st century. *Frontiers in Psychology*, *10*, 156. PMID: 30761055

Scholz, T. M. (2019). *eSports is business: Management in the world of competitive gaming*. Cham, Switzerland: Palgrave Macmillan.

Sharpe, B. T., Nicholson, M., Leis, O., Poulus, D., Birch, P. D., & McNulty, C. (2026). Indexing league of legends performance: A systematic review and focus group study. *International Journal of Sports Science & Coaching*, *21*(1), 625-637.

Wang, X., You, X., Xu, Y., & Zheng, J. (2024). Online posting intention: Do the social communication and brand equity of esports matter? *International Journal of Sports Marketing & Sponsorship*, *25*(1), 161–187.

Wong, D., & Meng-Lewis, Y. (2023). Esports: An exploration of the advancing esports landscape, actors and interorganisational relationships. *Sport in Society*, *26*(6), 943–969.

KEY TERMS AND DEFINITIONS

Amateur esports players: Amateur players actively participate in competitive or ranked play with the goal of advancing toward the professional scene, but esports is not yet their primary source of income. They focus on developing their skills and expertise while operating without the financial stability or institutional support typically available to elite players. Unlike recreational players, who play primarily for leisure, amateurs train and compete as part of an aspirational pathway toward professionalization.

Consumption in esports: Consumption in esports reflects the diverse ways audiences engage with competitive gaming, through viewing matches and streams, interacting with players and communities, and purchasing digital items or material goods. This includes in-game spending, subscriptions, donations, event attendance, merchandise purchases, and the consumption of products associated with esports sponsorships. These activities generate both functional and symbolic value, as consumption expresses belonging, participation, and identity within the esports community.

Electronic word-of-mouth (eWOM) in esports: In esports, electronic word-of-mouth refers to audience-driven communication that unfolds across streaming chats, community platforms, forums, and social media discussions surrounding games, players, events, and sponsors. It occurs within participatory environments where spectators comment, review, react, and co-create meaning as part of ongoing interaction. These exchanges derive persuasive force from immediacy, visibility, and perceived authenticity, forming a communicative loop between viewing, playing, and consumption.

Elite esports players: Elite players represent the professional tier of competitive gaming, distinguished by contractual affiliation, income generation, and visibility within major leagues or tournaments. Their activity combines athletic performance, digital skill, and media presence, making them both competitors and communicative figures within the esports field. While they embody the highest level of expertise and recognition, elite players also navigate a demanding environment marked by intense competition, short career spans, and constant performance pressure.

Esports as a hybrid communication arena: esports functions as a hybrid communication arena in which competition, media production, audience interaction, and brand activity coexist within digitally networked platforms. Communication flows are dialogic and iterative, shaped by both user participation and institutional governance, transforming play, viewing, and promotion into interconnected forms of cultural expression and economic exchange.

Esports audience: The esports audience refers to the spectators, fans, and participants who follow competitive gaming across digital and physical environments. Through streaming, social media, and event participation, audiences actively shape how matches are experienced and represented. The audience includes participants of different ages, though it is strongly shaped by the digitally fluent habits of Generation Z. They assume the roles of spectator, learner, and contributor, driven by tactical learning, entertainment, and a sense of social belonging.

Esports ecosystem: the esports ecosystem encompasses the interdependent network of actors, institutions, and platforms that produce, distribute, and regulate the flow of content, meaning, and value in competitive gaming. It includes players, teams, streamers, fans, publishers, organizers, and sponsors, whose interactions generate both symbolic and commercial value. Each actor contributes to how communication, visibility, and engagement unfold, making the ecosystem a dynamic environment of interdependence and co-creation.

Esports games as experiential products: Esports games are interactive systems designed to generate immersive and emotionally engaging experiences within communicative and participatory environments. Their value emerges from real-time competition, social interaction, and the continuous personalization of play through in-game purchases and events. As experiential products, they transform entertainment into participation, enabling players and spectators to express their identity, emotions, and sense of belonging through digital engagement.

Esports: esports refers to the organized, competitive playing of video games structured through official leagues, ranking systems, and publisher governance. It operates as a participatory and co-creative domain within digitally mediated environments, where multiple actors, including players, audiences, and brands collaboratively produce entertainment, cultural meaning, and economic value.

Gaming culture: gaming culture encompasses the shared practices, meanings, and modes of interaction that emerge around digital games. It involves how players, creators, and audiences engage with games, generate meaning, and build communities through participation, performance, and communication. Beyond gameplay, it extends into streaming, fan production, and social media, where play becomes a medium of cultural expression and identity formation. Gaming culture fosters creativity, collaboration, and belonging while also reflecting hierarchies of skill, gender, and legitimacy, shaping how communication and community evolve within esports.

Immersion in esports: Immersion refers to the experiential state in which players or spectators become fully absorbed in the gaming environment. In esports, it arises through audiovisual design, interactivity, and emotional intensity, reinforced by real-time communication and identification with players or in-game elements such as game characters and virtual identities. Immersion reflects the convergence of sensory stimulation and emotional investment, transforming gameplay and viewing into experiences of presence, attachment, and sustained participation.

Chapter 5
Artificial Intelligence in Video Game Advertising:
Opportunities, Challenges, and Academic Perspectives

Burak Çeber
http://orcid.org/0000-0002-3760-3177
Üsküdar University, Turkey

Şükrü Yanmaz
İstanbul Üniversitesi, Turkey

ABSTRACT

This chapter examines the role of artificial intelligence in video game advertising, emphasizing opportunities, challenges, and academic perspectives. AI enhances personalization, programmatic advertising, and in-game brand integration while generative AI introduces creative possibilities. Despite these advantages, ethical concerns such as privacy, transparency, and data security remain. Literature reveals limited research on AI in this field; therefore, this chapter aims to provide a comprehensive overview for both scholars and industry professionals on how AI reshapes video game advertising.

INTRODUCTION

Since the Industrial Revolution, technological advancements have transformed many tasks and processes that were once carried out manually. This transformation has laid the groundwork for the widespread use of artificial intelligence (AI) technologies in advertising (Yu, 2021, p. 190). As technology advances, the frameworks

DOI: 10.4018/979-8-3373-6309-7.ch005

surrounding AI advertising and its impact on the sector continue to evolve (Rodgers, 2021, p. 6). AI is projected to add 15 trillion dollars to the global economy by 2030. This influence extends beyond individual enterprises and shows that AI has become a significant trend, especially in marketing and advertising. By redefining interactions between consumers and brands, AI has started a new era. Advertising professionals now need to adapt to changes in consumer behaviors (Murugan & Kumar, 2024, p. 1072).

Today, consumers are fatigued by constant exposure to advertisements. Many either do not notice most ads or choose to ignore them. Advertisers now seek new methods to reach target audiences without disrupting user experience. One such method is video game advertising (Kadry, 2024, p. 163). As AI technologies advance, brands' approaches to video game advertising are also transforming (Disrupted, 2024).

Artificial intelligence (AI) technologies are effectively employed both in in-game advertising and in game advertising positioned outside but connected to the gameplay experience. From the perspective of in-game advertising, AI enables the personalization and seamless integration of advertisements placed within video games (Palfreyman, 2025). In addition, AI technologies play a significant role in the effective promotion of games themselves to target audiences. Programmatic advertising, which has recently become widespread and has emerged as a major marketing channel, automates advertising purchasing processes and optimization through the use of data and algorithms, thus enhancing advertising effectiveness (Changmai, 2024, p. 445). Artificial intelligence (AI), whose influence in the creative industries has been steadily expanding, has begun to offer various contributions to the field of video game advertising with the integration of generative AI technologies into the process. Trained on large datasets, these systems are capable of processing diverse forms of content such as text, images, audio, and video, and with their capacity to generate realistic outputs, they are introducing a new dimension to video game advertising (Epstein et al., 2023; Morandini et al., 2023, p. 42).

Despite the considerable advantages AI technologies offer to the digital advertising sector, they also bring forth a range of challenges that must be carefully managed by developers and advertising professionals (Yu, 2021, p. 192). Whether in in-game advertising or in promotional campaigns for games, companies must adopt proactive approaches and implement effective data protection mechanisms to address ethically critical concerns such as data security, privacy, transparency, and intellectual property.

A review of the existing literature reveals that while numerous studies address video game advertising in general, research specifically focusing on the use of AI in video game advertising remains limited. This study aims to provide a comprehensive examination of the role of AI systems in video game advertising and to identify the areas in which these technologies are applied. At the same time, the research is of importance to both scholars and industry representatives, as it explains the use of AI in video game advertising through the perspectives, knowledge, and experiences of academics.

THE EVOLUTION OF VIDEO GAME ADVERTISING

One of the most significant obstacles marketers face in their efforts to establish long-term communication with consumers and draw them toward brand messages is the prevalence of advertising clutter and intense competition. In particular, when it comes to advertisements disseminated through traditional media channels such as television, radio, and print publications, consumers often display a tendency to avoid exposure to advertisements. In this context, consumers may engage in behaviors such as changing channels to avoid commercials (Dix & Phau, 2017), skipping newspaper and magazine pages containing advertisements (Prendergast et al., 2010), and avoiding radio advertisements (Speck & Elliott, 1997).

The challenges encountered in persuading consumers have prompted marketers to explore new approaches. One such approach is the gamification of advertising (Peters & Leshner, 2013). With the growing interest of individuals in games, including video games, advertisers have increasingly turned to this medium as a strategic communication tool (Bozkurt, 2019, p.1342). In the related literature, various studies have examined games from the perspectives of advertising, advertisers, brands, and users (Acar, 2007; Glass, 2007; Lee & Faber, 2007; Winkler & Buckner, 2006).

The video game industry stands out as one of the most prominent global sectors, bringing together players who can be considered potential consumers. For many years, companies and brands have conducted advertising activities through digital games, thereby reaching their target audiences more effectively and efficiently. Today, in-game advertising has emerged as one of the most impactful and efficient methods of promotion in this sector (Baltezarević & Baltezarević, 2024, p.650).

In-game advertising can be defined as the integration of advertisements or promotional content into games or the placement of a brand's products within a commercial gaming environment for promotional purposes. In this regard, it is crucial that in-game advertising takes into account the characteristics of the gaming environment (Sreejesh et al., 2021; Zagni & Pera, 2024; Smith et al., 2020). Within the scope of in-game advertising, two main classifications can be identified: static and dynamic in-game advertising. Static in-game advertisements refer to ads that are strongly coded into the game and placed in fixed spaces such as banners or billboards. In this form of advertising, users can interact with integrated objects in the game to access information and details related to the storyline. In contrast, dynamic in-game advertisements can be updated each time the game is accessed through a console or an internet-connected computer. Dynamic advertising utilizes information such as gameplay duration, date, location, and data collected about the player. Moreover, the ability of advertisers to access data on the duration of ad exposure and thereby optimize performance constitutes a key feature of dynamic in-game advertising (Ghirvu, 2012, pp.115-116). In this context, the literature includes various studies examining in-game advertising with a focus on efficiency and performance optimization (Sebastian et al., 2016).

On the other hand, it has been argued that in-game advertising may offer a lower level of interaction compared to advergames (Zagni & Pera, 2024). Unlike in-game advertising, advergames are video games that transform entertainment content into a conventional game format while serving a promotional function for the brand (Kretchmer, 2005, p.7). Advergames employ branded elements to facilitate consumers' understanding of the purpose of the game, thereby making the promotional aim more transparent (Mallinckrodt & Mizerski, 2007; An & Stern, 2011). By incorporating game design elements such as missions or collectibles into the process, advergames integrate the brand as an inseparable component of the player experience. This, in turn, engages users on multiple levels—emotional closeness, cognitive processing, and activation—resulting in higher overall interaction compared to static advertisements (Hanbazazah et al., 2022; Van Berlo & Chen, 2024).

In addition to advertisements embedded within games, the promotion of the games themselves also plays a significant role. The numerical growth and qualitative development observed in the gaming industry have intensified competition, making it increasingly difficult for gaming companies to find effective ways to market their products. Within this framework, game trailers or promotional videos stand out as one of the most important methods of introducing games, as they directly showcase the visual imagery of the product (Kwon, 2015). From the perspective of programmatic advertising, it can be argued that all advertising formats can be programmatically implemented, serving as a solution that enables personalized, localized, and real-time advertising through automation and data (Mete, 2021; Li, 2019). Based on this, programmatic advertising is considered to facilitate the promotion of games by allowing more personalized, localized, and real-time communication through data and automation (White & ve Samuel, 2019).

Considering that global revenues from gaming are projected to exceed $300 billion within the next decade, and that individuals in the United States alone play video games between one and five hours per week, this sector clearly offers substantial advertising opportunities (Ahmad, 2024). Factors such as global population growth, strengthened collaborations between gaming companies and marketers, increasing demand for immersive experiences, and the rising popularity of mobile games contribute to the expansion of this market. In this respect, the in-game advertising market is expected to reach USD 6.07 billion between 2025 and 2029, with a compound annual growth rate of 15% (Technavio, 2025). Moreover, given that in-game advertising has been shown to increase brand awareness by 64%, commercial awareness by 69%, purchase intention by 37%, and brand rating by 37% (Ghirvu, 2012, p.117), the contributions of this sectoral growth to brands, both current and future, are noteworthy.

From this perspective, it can be stated that the commercial popularity of games is particularly striking. The commercial relevance of games is also evident in other domains. The literature includes research examining games holistically alongside advancing technologies, in relation to video games, television, computer use, and media education (Rohr-Sendlmeier et al., 2008). Studies on gaming have also extended into the field of education. Within this framework, research has investigated the readiness of students, classrooms, and teachers for the influence of games in education; the role of games in foreign language teaching; and the ways in which games can be integrated into learning and instruction (Annetta, 2008; Connolly, 2008; Jong et al., 2008).

Initially, research on video games, including computer games, and video game advertising has predominantly focused on the benefits these games may provide when used for educational purposes, as well as on audience behaviors regarding video game advertisements (Hilton, 2006; Thomas, 2005; Bogost, 2005; Consalvo, 2005; Jayakanthan, 2002). Additionally, studies have examined the potential effects of in-game violence on users in real-world contexts (Peng et al., 2008; Ferguson et al., 2008; Wei, 2007; Gentile et al., 2004). Regarding the field of game advertising, the literature includes various studies (Yang et al., 2006; Nicovich, 2005; Grigorovici & Constantin, 2004; Nelson et al., 2004). In contrast to general game advertising, comprehensive research specifically on in-game advertising is also available in the literature (Chaney et al., 2004; Ghirvu, 2012; Baltezarević & Baltezarević, 2024; Zagni et al., 2025).

The concept of games has evolved, particularly since the 2000s, in line with technological advancements, reaching its current form. As artificial intelligence technologies have become increasingly integrated into human life, the understanding of games has also undergone a significant transformation (Sancaklı & Sarı, 2025, p.88). These developments have, in turn, directly impacted the field of advertising. Prior to discussing the use of artificial intelligence in video game advertising, it is important to consider AI applications from an advertising perspective.

OVERVIEW OF ARTIFICIAL INTELLIGENCE IN ADVERTISING

In today's rapidly changing world, vast amounts of information are entering our lives at an unprecedented pace, and artificial intelligence (AI) technology is profoundly transforming our way of life under the influence of this information flow. Defining this technology, which impacts our daily lives, not only aids in understanding its effects on individuals but also helps to comprehend its transformative role across various industries. Artificial intelligence is a technology that simulates functions of human intelligence such as reasoning, learning, and self-correction (Singhal, 2024, p.437). Broadly speaking, AI is the science of transferring the cognitive activities of all natural systems, including organic systems, to artificial systems (Say, 2024, p.83), and even enabling machines to perform cognitive tasks that humans can accomplish in more advanced forms (Penrose, 2023, p.35). In this context, it can be stated that this technology has a significant impact on human life. AI not only integrates into our daily routines but also enters the advertising industry, reshaping it and generating novel solutions (Xu, 2025, p.51).

One of the earliest examples of AI use in advertising is target audience segmentation. The impact of AI technologies in this domain is considerable, as AI can predict consumers' future behavioral patterns based on historical data, thereby laying the groundwork for optimized product recommendations and more personalized advertising campaigns (Moore et al., 2022). Another key application of AI in advertising is personalization. Tailoring advertising messages to individual consumers enables brands to redefine their communication and interaction with target audiences. In this regard, technologies such as machine learning and data analytics allow advertising content to be adapted to consumers' needs and preferences, thereby enhancing the relevance and effectiveness of advertising campaigns (Ioni ă et al., 2025, p.40; Wang, 2020, pp.1287-1322).

In this process, the analysis of individual and behavioral data aimed at understanding consumer preferences by artificial intelligence (AI) is of paramount importance (Kietzmann et al., 2018). AI technology can analyze users' expressed preferences and past behaviors on online platforms and media using collaborative filtering algorithms. This in-depth analysis is employed to provide personalized recommendations based on users' histories and to deliver advertising content tailored to these recommendations. Considering that AI technology can also be integrated into the personalization of advertising messages through facial feature analysis and facial recognition systems, it can be argued that AI plays a significant role in the evolution of recommendation systems and provides new extensions and supportive mechanisms for personalized recommendation systems (Duan et al., 2019; Adomavicius & Tuzhilin, 2005; Wang & Kosinski, 2018).

One of the applications and benefits of AI in advertising is the automation of advertising processes. The use of predictive analytics models and machine learning algorithms within AI frameworks offers significant opportunities to save time, increase efficiency, and optimize ad placement and distribution. In AI-driven personalization and adaptation processes in advertising, optimized machine learning methods such as the Adam method for stochastic optimization are among the recommended techniques (Kumar et al., 2024; Kingma & Ba, 2014; Ioni ă et al., 2025). Beyond automation and personalization, AI technology can also be effective in competitor analysis, providing deep insights into competitors' advertising expenditures, strategies, and ad elements. Moreover, AI is reported to have the capability to generate both text-based and visual advertising content (Chen, 2024, p.33). Within the scope of content production activities in advertising, generative AI technology has emerged as a prominent tool.

Considering features such as automation, targeting, speed, and real-time strategy development, it can be argued that generative artificial intelligence (AI) has transformed advertising campaigns (Barsha & Munshi, 2023; Rane et al., 2024; Moor et al., 2023). Unlike traditional advertising, where processes from ideation to production are conducted manually, generative AI technologies automate content creation according to principles of creativity and audience relevance, thereby making the process more efficient. Today, slogans and video advertisements generated by AI can deliver brand messages directly to consumers. In addition, AI tools can rapidly create different ad variations for A/B testing to determine the most effective approach, thus enhancing the overall effectiveness of advertising campaigns. This speed and efficiency provided by generative AI can significantly increase advertisers' return on investment.

From a strategic perspective, programmatic advertising is also noteworthy (Li, 2019). AI-based systems enable advertising content to be adapted in real-time according to customer mood, weather conditions, and geographic location, making programmatic advertising a prominent approach within the advertising industry (McStay, 2017). This method has the potential to maintain high relevance with target audiences and increase engagement. Moreover, generative AI is not only effective in traditional advertising but also in influencer marketing. AI technologies that can analyze target audience preferences and digital trends on platforms such as YouTube, Instagram, and TikTok enable the design of viral campaigns, playing a significant role in helping marketers reach broader audiences (Abdulwahid et al., 2023; Patil et al., 2024; Fitria, 2023; Patil, 2024).

AI technologies, with their diverse applications including automation, personalization, audience analysis, content and idea generation, segmentation, and measurement, have undoubtedly created a profound transformation in the advertising industry. Examining this transformation from the perspective of AI within the context of advertising in video games holds particular significance.

APPLICATIONS OF AI IN VIDEO GAME ADVERTISING: APPLICATIONS, CHALLENGES, AND ACADEMIC PERSPECTIVES

Artificial intelligence promises to transform the very nature of advertising, influencing all aspects of the advertising process (Qin & Jiang, 2019; Li, 2024, p.439). As technology continues to advance, the impact of artificial intelligence technologies on advertising has also manifested in various ways (Rodgers, 2021, p.6). In this regard, artificial intelligence (AI) has significantly altered the way organizations reach and interact with potential consumers (Kietzmann et al., 2018, p.264; Rodgers & Nguyen, 2022, p.1046). One of the most influential methods in recent years has been video game advertising (citation needed?). With advancements in AI technologies, brands' approaches to advertising within video games have also undergone a profound transformation (Disrupted, 2024).

To comprehend the transformative power of AI technologies on video game advertising, it is crucial to first address the effects these systems have on video games themselves. Game artificial intelligence refers to the application of AI technologies in all areas related to games (Tian, 2024, pp.161–162). AI primarily changes the way video games are created and played. Today, through the use of systems such as machine learning, artificial neural networks, and deep learning, games are able to respond to players in more personalized and intelligent ways (Agrawal & Raikwar, 2025, p.1). These AI techniques enable developers to create content that adapts to each player's behavior and preferences (Zhou & Li, 2020; Agrawal & Raikwar, 2025, p.1). This method employed in game development is also applied in in-game advertising, as well as in advertising that exists outside of but remains connected to the game (game advertising).

From the perspective of in-game advertising, artificial intelligence is employed to personalize the placement of advertisements within video game environments (Palfreyman, 2025). In this context, ideas and concepts related to product placement are considered useful for understanding and defining in-game advertising, as well as for enhancing brand management (Louro & Cunha, 2001). Through big data and intelligent algorithms, AI can customize advertising content according to users' preferences, interests, and behaviors. This personalized form of advertising supported by AI contributes to strengthening the connection between brands and users while also enhancing the overall user experience (Li, 2024, p.439). Moreover, AI technologies analyze in-game contexts, user behavior, and interaction patterns to deliver advertisements at the most appropriate moments, thereby increasing the effectiveness of advertising efforts within game environments (Brand Safety Institute, 2023).

Traditional in-game advertising typically involved static displays such as billboards, posters, or branded objects placed within a game environment. For example, in a racing game, a player might drive past a virtual advertising billboard with their selected car. With the integration of AI into this process, such advertisements have been replaced by real-time, contextual ads tailored to individual players and their unique playing styles (Palfreyman, 2025). In contemporary racing games, for instance, billboards can now change according to the player's interests and are placed at natural, non-intrusive moments. Accordingly, it can be argued that the defining feature of AI-driven in-game advertising lies in its capacity to deliver personalized advertisements to players (Disrupted, 2024).

From Traditional to Digital: In-Game Advertising can be described as follows:

- Traditional Banner Advertisements: It has now been replaced by localized in-game placements, such as digital billboards in sports and racing games.
- Interstitial Advertisements: It has transformed into dynamic ad placements that are adjusted in real time according to player activity.
- Product Placement: It has evolved into interactive brand experiences in which players directly engage with the advertisements.

Personalization in in-game advertising can be realized in three main ways: content customization, contextual placement, and dynamic difficulty adjustment. Content customization refers to tailoring products according to the player's interests; contextual placement involves embedding advertisements in natural and meaningful locations within the game; and dynamic difficulty adjustment refers to adapting the advertising content displayed to players based on their in-game skill levels (Disrupted, 2024). Examples of in-game advertising include digital billboards in NBA 2K, FIFA, and racing games, sports brands sponsoring in-game uniforms, and fast-food companies offering rewards within the game upon level completion (Viant, 2025). In-Game Advertising Example on the Anzu Platform also constitutes a strong example of this approach (https://www.anzu.io/blog/ubisoft-in-game-advertising).

AI technology processes vast datasets to uncover patterns in user behavior and preferences, thereby providing advertisers with deeper and more comprehensive user insights. Artificial intelligence not only conducts a more precise analysis of users' past data but also predicts future behavioral trends (Li, 2024, p.440). At the stage of embedding advertisements into the gaming environment, user profiles generated through such insights play a critical role. These profiles are constructed by AI through an analysis of player demographics, in-game behavioral preferences, and decision-making patterns. Through these profiles, AI determines which types of advertisements are likely to resonate with which players (Disrupted, 2024).

Artificial intelligence technologies are employed not only in in-game advertising but also in the effective promotion of the games themselves to target audiences. Programmatic advertising, which has recently become widespread and emerged as an efficient marketing channel, automates the purchase and optimization of advertisements by utilizing data and algorithms (Changmai, 2024, p.445).

Programmatic advertising refers to advertising practices that develop purchasing and selling processes based on automation systems (Martinez-Martinez et al., 2017). While manual ad purchases relied on analyses conducted with static, predetermined data, programmatic advertising has enabled advertisers to access detailed and transparent information regarding the campaigns they purchase (White & ve Samuel, 2019). It has both facilitated real-time tracking of consumer preferences through continuous updates and allowed advertisers to easily determine how their budgets are being spent (Stevens et al., 2016). Particularly in 2024, with the continuous development of big data and artificial intelligence, programmatic ad-buying technology has gained increasing significance in game marketing. The precise targeting feature used for game promotion enhances click-through and conversion rates, thereby improving both the visibility of games and user acquisition. Accordingly, advertising strategies and budgets can be adjusted in real time based on data-driven insights, maximizing the effectiveness of advertisements. As a result, game companies gain access to effective promotional opportunities with accurate targeting (Changmai, 2024, p.445).

As artificial intelligence technologies continue to influence the creative industries, the integration of generative AI into the process has further diversified and expanded AI's contributions to the domain of video game advertising. Previously trained on large datasets, these systems are capable of processing various types of content—including text, images, audio, and video—and of generating realistic outputs (Epstein et al., 2023; Morandini et al., 2023, p.42). Fundamentally, generative AI analyzes large datasets, learns patterns, and produces new content aligned with specific parameters or objectives (Gujar, Paliwal, & Panyam, 2024, p.4). Some generative AI applications used in video game advertising include ChatGPT, Jasper, Midjourney, GPT for Sheets, Copy.ai, Gigapixel AI, WatermarkRemover.io, Revoicer, Descript, Otter.ai, D-ID, Synthesia, LEX, Stable Diffusion, Artbreeder, and DALL·E 2 (appagent.com).

For instance, ChatGPT, with its capacity for data analysis and narrative construction, can generate ideas and propose new concepts for products or services to be advertised. Moreover, by analyzing target audiences in line with advertising objectives, it can offer recommendations for the development of effective advertising strategies (Zhang & Kim, 2023, p.207). Through generative AI, compelling narratives for advertisements can be created, effectively conveying the unique story and appeal of each game to potential players. As a result, multiple advertising scenarios can be produced in a fraction of the time traditionally required by advertising professionals (Joygame, 2024).

Beyond text generation, generative AI is also widely applied in visual production (Tian, 2024, pp.166–167). Image-generation tools such as MidJourney create visuals from textual input by leveraging large datasets. These AI applications stand out for their various advantages, including generating novel advertising concepts, enhancing designers' creativity, producing design drafts that can be further refined with graphic software, and addressing complex advertising themes (El-aasy, 2023). For example, in games such as *Deck Dash* and *Borderland Defender*, AI technologies have been employed to design striking visuals that reflect the spirit of each game. Whether depicting stylized helmets in *Deck Dash* or visualizing the intense border scenes in *Borderland Defender*, AI provides the capability to produce visually compelling imagery (Joygame, 2024).

On the other hand, voice-based artificial intelligence technologies have also advanced significantly. These technologies employ diffusion models in the field of speech synthesis to generate natural-sounding voice outputs (Zhang et al., 2023). For instance, in games such as *Perfect Beauty Salon* and *Desert Warrior*, AI-powered voiceover technologies are used to bring advertising characters to life. The ability to rapidly produce high-quality voiceovers allows campaigns to adapt in real time to different demographic groups and regions (Joygame, 2024).

In addition to this, generative AI also assists in producing and optimizing complex videos (Gujar, Paliwal, & Panyam, 2024, p.5). These applications contribute to various stages of the advertising process. For example, during video production, they can enhance efficiency by converting text into video format at high speed and by generating animated content. Moreover, they can optimize video content for specific platforms and make adjustments based on user feedback, thereby rendering the process more flexible and agile (Çeber, 2025, pp.177–178). These advancements have also positively impacted video advertisements created for games. For instance, in the game *Patrol Officer*, AI-based tools were employed to produce dynamic and compelling video advertisements that reflect the action-packed gameplay. Taken together, these developments demonstrate that AI applications not only enhance the quality of advertisements but also enable games to reach the right players with the right message at the right time (Joygame, 2024).

Despite the numerous benefits AI technologies bring to the digital advertising sector, they also introduce several challenges that must be carefully managed by developers and advertising professionals (Yu, 2021, p.192). Among these challenges are issues of privacy, security, transparency, bias, and the displacement of professions (Çeber, 2024, p.67). For instance, the transfer of human biases into artificial intelligence systems may lead to ethical concerns. These issues arise from two distinct sources of bias. The first stems from biases inherent in the data used to train the systems. The second emerges from biases related to the manner in which algorithms are developed for implementation (Rodgers & Nguyen, 2022, p. 1054). Another significant concern is algorithmic transparency. Algorithms whose development processes lack transparency may, by design, exhibit tendencies toward bias and discrimination (Valin & Gregory, 2020, p. 7).

Algorithmic transparency, an emerging area within computer science, is an interdisciplinary subfield focused on understanding the decisions made by algorithms. It has been observed that many social science scholars, including advertising researchers, operate under the assumption that artificial intelligence algorithms are value-neutral in nature, a perspective that is believed to give rise to numerous problems in the future (Rodgers, 2021, p. 8). In the context of in-game advertising, however, concerns regarding privacy, transparency, and security are particularly prominent.

Artificial intelligence collects and analyzes player data to create a personalized gaming experience. This raises concerns regarding how such data are stored, who has access to them, and whether players are aware that their actions are being tracked through content analytics (Agrawal & Raikwar, 2025, p.7; Culnan & Clark, 2009). When consumers are not sufficiently informed about how their data is being used, issues of transparency arise (Du & Xie, 2021, p.961). The U.S. Federal Trade Commission (FTC) emphasizes that AI-powered advertisements must not mislead consumers and expects companies to be accountable for claims made through such content. In this regard, on September 25, 2024, the FTC launched "Operation AI Comply" (Palfreyman, 2025).

At the same time, the use of AI in the production of in-game advertising raises questions of intellectual property, since traditional legal frameworks are based on human authorship, while the ownership of AI-generated content remains ambiguous. Consequently, intellectual property considerations should be addressed with particular care in all contracts related to AI services (Palfreyman, 2025).

In both in-game advertising and the promotion of games themselves, companies must act proactively on ethically critical issues such as data security, privacy, transparency, and intellectual property, and must adopt the necessary data protection measures. Once these concerns are effectively addressed, AI is expected to play a pivotal role at the intersection of gaming and advertising, enabling the delivery of innovative advertising experiences.

METHOD

The purpose of this study is to examine academics' perspectives and experiences regarding video game advertising and artificial intelligence, thereby revealing how AI applications are utilized in video game advertising. This research is significant for both scholars and industry practitioners, as it explains the use of AI in video game advertising through the knowledge and experiences of academics.

Accordingly, the research questions developed based on the relevant literature are as follows:

- In which areas and in what ways are AI applications utilized in video game advertising?
- What are the limitations and challenges arising from the use of AI applications in video game advertising?
- What are the experiences, perspectives, and recommendations of academics regarding the use of AI in video game advertising?

To address these questions, the study will employ a qualitative research design and the interview technique.

The population of the study consists of academics in the field of communication in Türkiye. Due to limited access to the entire population, criterion purposive sampling—one of the non-probability sampling methods—was used to select a sample group that could best represent the population. A subgroup within the population that most accurately reflects its characteristics is determined as the sample. The purpose of employing purposive sampling is to identify information-rich cases and thereby contribute to solving the research problem. Among purposive sampling techniques, criterion sampling is selected. The criterion established for academics included in the sample is having conducted scholarly research in the field of "artificial intelligence and game advertising."

In this study, a semi-structured interview technique was employed for data collection. The interview technique allows meaning to be examined within its social context and enables reality to be interpreted through multiple perspectives rather than a single viewpoint. Moreover, through interviews, it is possible to develop a research method built upon the systematic organization of participants' statements and to reach well-grounded conclusions accordingly (Türnüklü, 2000, p. 544). Within this scope, the study seeks to understand, explain, and systematically present the use of AI applications in video game advertising, relying on the knowledge and experiences of academics who have conducted research in this area. Accordingly, in-depth interviews will be conducted with academics specializing in game advertising and artificial intelligence. In order to ensure the validity and reliability of the study, the criteria of internal validity, external validity, internal reliability, and external reliability were fulfilled. In studies employing qualitative research methods, it is expected that one or more validity and reliability criteria be met in order to test the accuracy and trustworthiness of the findings (Creswell, 2003, p. 176). Accordingly, internal validity in this study was ensured through data triangulation by conducting interviews with different participants. The interview questions were developed after being reviewed by one academic expert and one industry professional, and necessary revisions were made in line with the feedback received. In this respect, internal validity was supported through expert review prior to the interviews.

Conducting the study solely with academics selected through a purposive sampling method constitutes the primary limitation of the research. Another limitation of the study is that interviews were conducted only with academics. In future studies, conducting interviews with advertising professionals is considered important for directly revealing practical experiences.

FINDINGS

A descriptive analysis method was employed to analyze the data collected in the study. During the descriptive analysis process, concepts, observations, or interviews are utilized to construct a thematic framework. The themes according to which the data will be organized are determined, and the data are processed and evaluated accordingly. Once the processed data are described in line with the thematic framework, they are supported with direct quotations. Subsequently, the described and quotation-supported data are interpreted and related to one another to provide meaning (Yıldırım & Şimşek, 2011, p. 256).

The data obtained in the findings section of the study were presented in accordance with a descriptive analysis approach. Participant codes were used in the presentation of the data.

Table 1. Interview and Code Information Regarding Academics Participating in the In-Depth Interviews

Participant Title	Interview Duration	Code Name
Associate Professor, PhD	40 dk.	P - 1
Professor, PhD	1.18 dk.	P - 2
Assistant Professor, PhD	38 dk	P - 3
Associate Professor, PhD	40. dk	P - 4

*The order has been arranged according to the interview date.

Advantages of Video Games in Advertising

The participants highlighted the advantages offered by video games in the field of advertising, including increased attention and engagement, naturalness, realism, and a sense of belonging, as well as targeting and personalization. These concepts were derived from the participants' statements.

Table 2. Advantages of Video Games in Advertising

Advantages and Disadvantages	Participant Codes
High Attention and Engagement	P1- P3
Authenticity	P1- P4
Realism and Sense of Belonging	P1
Advantages of Targeting and Personalization	P4

High Attention and Engagement

One participant expressed the advantage of high attention and engagement provided by video games in advertising as follows:

"An activity where all attention is focused on the game provides a significant advantage for the attention economy, particularly for advertisers. In-game advertisements do not somehow divert the viewer's attention; rather, the viewer becomes part of it, meaning they cannot skip the ad. Games serve as an effective tool for adding realism to the scene." (P1)

Another participant shared their thoughts on the topic as follows:

"Video games are a powerful medium for advertising because they are complex, and this complexity is precisely the kind that can capture the interest of the new generation. Unlike other platforms, the user is no longer just a passive viewer; they become a participant, an experiencer, and part of the content. This significantly impacts attention levels while playing. Attention is at a much higher and more intense level than in ads on Instagram or YouTube. This creates opportunities for brands, allowing for deeper and longer-lasting engagement with players." (P3)

Authenticity

One participant described the advantage provided by the level of authenticity in in-game advertisements as follows:

"The sensitive point here, of course, is that this should be done without causing discomfort. On the other hand, its visibility—perhaps how it is placed within the scene and how authentic it appears—can serve as a criterion." (P1)

Another participant emphasized the advantage of authenticity in video game advertising in terms of delivering the right message to the right target audience as follows:

"It is as if we are following the flow of natural life; the same logic applies while playing the game, where everything appears to proceed authentically within the game's flow. However, the advertisements and brands we encounter during

gameplay may actually allow us to deliver the right message to a more accurate target audience." (P4)

Realism and Sense of Belonging

One participant shared their perspective on the topic as follows:

"Adding realism to the scene is an incredible advantage. At one point, I conducted a study on the game Zula, which children played very intensively. The presence of familiar brands was appreciated, and when giving directions on the map—for example, on the Trabzon map—they would say, 'turn from the Algida fridge.' In other words, the player is either unaware that the brand is part of the environment or is aware and enjoys it. Of course, I cannot be certain. The duration of engagement with the target audience is crucial here. Being present and noticeable in an environment that receives such intense attention is extremely valuable for the brand." (P1)

Advantages of Targeting and Personalization

One participant described the advantage provided by video games in advertising in terms of targeting and personalization as follows:

"If we know who the game's user is and understand the characteristics of the target audience, it becomes much easier for us to craft our message according to those characteristics. Because we know what the target audience needs, their expectations, lifestyle, and interests, and how to spark their curiosity, positioning any advertising message within the game becomes much more accurate when we have this knowledge." (P4)

The Use of Artificial Intelligence in Digital Advertising and the Gaming Industry

The participants highlighted several concepts regarding the use of artificial intelligence (AI) in digital advertising and the gaming industry, including data collection and insights, the transformation of in-game experiences, and variations in the level of AI utilization. These concepts were conveyed based on the statements of the relevant participants.

Table 3. The Use of Artificial Intelligence in Digital Advertising and the Gaming Industry

The Use of Artificial Intelligence in Digital Advertising and Games	Participant Codes
Data Collection and Insights	P2
Personalization and Targeting	P1 - P3 - P4

Data Collection and Insights

AI applications are transforming traditional processes used in digital platforms, such as monitoring, tracking, managing, and reporting. Consumers express their desires, needs, attitudes, or opinions in digital environments through various forms, including likes, comments, and tweets. These data are collected in datasets and transformed into insights that contribute to the organization by leveraging artificial intelligence (Çeber, 2024, p. 594).

One participant shared their perspective on this topic as follows:

"Currently, with digital games, we have started to be captured by AI in its most natural form. While we may not even remember what we ate yesterday, AI knows what we ate 3–5 years ago, how we felt in that moment, how we reacted, how many times we repeated it, and in which situations we would respond in a certain way. It stores all of this in what is called big data. Therefore, one of AI's most important features is the ability to retrieve and utilize this information when needed. At present, we cannot use games independently of AI." (P2)

Another participant emphasized the contribution of AI in processing data effectively to promote the game and guide users to more appropriate games as follows:

"AI processes user data very effectively; it can combine pieces that the human mind cannot perceive and establish relationships between them. Therefore, it functions as an excellent tool both for promoting the game and for guiding users to other games." (P1)

Personalization and Targeting

Artificial intelligence (AI) can generate customized advertisements in real-time based on collected data, and the combination of targeting and personalization enhances the effectiveness of these advertisements (Gao et al., 2023, p. 10).

One participant shared their perspective on this topic as follows:

"As in all media, personalized content is very important. Although advertising is generally a mass communication, AI allows us to reach audiences and individuals with more specific content. With AI tools and programmatic advertising support, especially in the case of mobile games, personalized targeting can be implemented." (P1)

Another participant expressed their views as follows:

"In the past, advertising was largely mass-oriented, meaning the same content was presented to everyone. Nowadays, with AI and highly targeted, personalized algorithms, individuals encounter hyper-personalized advertisements. This represents a more advanced stage in the gaming industry." (P3)

A third participant emphasized the effectiveness of AI in personalization and targeting as follows:

"As with all digital platforms, the same applies to digital games. If we are to conduct targeting there, AI makes our work easier. Instead of collecting data on our target audience—such as which sites they visit, which games they play, and

what they pay attention to during gameplay—over long periods, the information provided by AI facilitates our work. (P4)

Applications of Artificial Intelligence in Video Game Advertising

The participants interpreted the applications of artificial intelligence (AI) in video game advertising primarily through in-game advertisement placements.

Table 4. Applications of Artificial Intelligence in Video Game Advertising

Applications of Artificial Intelligence in Video Game Advertising	Participant Codes
In-Game Advertising Placements	P1 – P2 – P3

In-Game Advertising Placements

Artificial intelligence enables the personalization and integration of advertisements within video games (Palfreyman, 2025).

One participant described the topic as follows:

"Elements can be integrated into the scene in in-game advertising, either explicitly or implicitly. Normally, when we are exposed to content on television and encounter product placement, there is usually a question of whether it is truly there to add realism to the scene or if it is a form of advertising communication. We cannot fully distinguish this, but in games, since nothing appears randomly with branding, everything present is necessarily the product of a commercial communication activity." (P1)

Another participant expressed their views on the matter as follows:

"When we talk about product placement here, it does not merely mean that a product exists in a medium. Product placement involves integrating a product into the advertisement or the game in such a way that it is not simply 'we placed the product, and that's it.' It requires predicting the emotional state of the player at that moment and creating the conditions that will elicit that emotional response before placing the product." (P2)

A third participant contributed to the discussion in the following way:

"Let's start with in-game advertising. These advertisements are no longer fixed; they can vary according to location, environment, player behavior, and even past interactions. This is, in a sense, programmatic advertising. Additionally, there are advertisements presented outside the game but in the format of the game itself, which are more common in mobile games. These function like small demos of the game. For example, players may need to play until a certain time elapses. This increases engagement and can occupy users by triggering impatience. In this context, artificial intelligence actively plays a role in determining which

game or advertisement is shown to which user and in optimizing the dynamic structure of the advertisement." (P3)

Artificial Intelligence in Ad Placement and User Experience

Participants indicated that the natural integration of artificial intelligence in ad placement and user experience enhances the overall user experience. They highlighted that AI provides advantages such as personalization and programmatic targeting, while also increasing both the duration of gameplay and user engagement. The role of artificial intelligence in user experience was conveyed through the participants' statements.

Table 5. Artificial Intelligence in User Experience

Artificial Intelligence in User Experience	Participant Codes
Strengthening User Experience via Natural Integration	P1 – P3
The Benefits of Personalization and Programmatic Targeting	P2 – P3 – P4
Enhancing User Playtime and Engagement	P1 – P4

Enhancing User Experience through Seamless Integration

Nowadays, consumers often fail to notice most advertisements or consciously ignore them. In this context, advertisers have sought new and innovative methods to reach their target audiences without disrupting the user experience. One such method is video game advertising (Kadry, 2024, p. 163).

One participant expressed their perspective as follows:

"The closer it is to being natural, the better it will be for the user experience. Resistance will not develop, and it may even provide the advantage of forming a connection with the brand." (P1)

Another participant elaborated on the topic:

"The key difference created by artificial intelligence lies in its ability to place advertisements both temporally and spatially in a smart manner. AI not only determines where to place the advertisement but also decides in what context it should appear and which user should see it and when. For example, if a player is playing a racing game, which is very exciting, AI selects a brand that appeals to energetic young audiences—say, Red Bull. However, in an exploratory game with a narrative segment, it prefers softer, contextually harmonious content. Since this does not disrupt the player's experience, it makes the advertisement noticeable and provides an advantage." (P3)

Advantages of Personalization and Programmatic Targeting

Programmatic advertising, which has recently become increasingly widespread and an important marketing channel, automates the processes of ad purchasing and optimization through data and algorithms, thereby enhancing advertising effectiveness (Changmai, 2024, p. 445).

One participant described the role of artificial intelligence in personalization and programmatic targeting as follows:

"The prominent role of AI in media usage, especially on the programmatic side, is pushing us toward a new point in the gaming sector. Therefore, we do not show the same advertisement to every individual; within games, different ads are displayed to each user independently. For example, there are studies where, if you prefer pastel tones, you are shown the same ad in pastel tones. I might see it in different tones, or while you see a visual in blue tones, I might see it in red tones. (P2)

Another participant expressed their perspective:

When advertisements are integrated into the game's own universe, such as consuming a beverage in an open-world game, they appear as a natural part of that world. This prevents players from judging the advertisements. Moreover, when the game collaborates with brands that players encounter in daily life, it becomes highly relevant due to accurate targeting." (P3)

A third participant elaborated on the matter as follows:

"When presenting a visual on a billboard, a music clip, or a moving animation to the target audience, AI likely considers the characteristics of that audience. It is instructed to 'create an advertisement,' and AI assists in determining where and how to place it within the game. The gaming universe is vast and varies by genre. One can tell AI, 'I want to reach this type of user; which game genres should I target?' AI makes it easier and faster to identify which games and consumer segments are most appropriate, guiding us toward more accurate targeting." (P4)

Enhancing User Playtime and Engagement

One participant shared their perspective on the topic as follows:

"An advertisement with a native appearance that operates in line with the game's narrative will be more appreciated by the player because it does not disrupt the gaming experience." (P1)

Another participant elaborated:

"From the perspective of user experience, our primary concern is sustaining gameplay behavior. To maintain continuity, elements that enhance the gaming experience must inevitably be incorporated. In this context, games are continuously updated, with numerous additional features that are suitable for the current day, conditions, or technology. Similarly, the gaming instruments themselves are updated, which can also be considered within the scope of AI or technology." (P4)

Advantages of Artificial Intelligence in Game Promotion

Artificial intelligence technologies are utilized not only in in-game advertising but also in effectively promoting the game itself to the target audience.

Participants identified the advantages of AI in game promotion as speed and ease of production, efficiency and cost savings, and game-hardware integration. The participants' perspectives on the topic are presented through their own statements.

Table 6. Advantages of Artificial Intelligence in Game Promotion

Advantages of Artificial Intelligence in Game Promotion	**Participant Codes**
Speed and Ease of Production	P1 – P2 – P3
Efficiency and Cost Savings	P2 – P3
Game and Hardware Integration	P4

Speed and Ease of Production

One participant expressed their views on speed and ease of production as follows:

"Thanks to artificial intelligence and behavioral data, it is now possible to produce content that includes multiple scenes of a game." (P1)

Another participant explained the factor of speed in terms of avoiding wasted effort on irrelevant individuals, stating:

"It must be acknowledged that when you use artificial intelligence, you know exactly whom to target; therefore, you do not waste unnecessary energy on irrelevant people." (P2)

A further participant shared the following perspective:

"I would say the greatest advantages are speed and personalization. In this sense, in the past, promoting a game could take weeks, but now, thanks to artificial intelligence, this process can be completed in a much shorter time with far less human effort." (P3)

Efficiency and Cost Savings

One participant expressed their perspective as follows:

"We can say that it directly convinces the individual in financial terms and increases the efficiency of budgets." (P2)

Game and Hardware Integration

A participant described the issue in the following way:

"The gaming industry cannot advance without computers, consoles, or mobile phones. Established studio games promote themselves and ensure continuity, forming the first category. The second includes newer games with their own players and fans. Like the Star Wars franchise with its audience and merchandise, games also build communities. However, gamers are demanding and do

not overlook flaws, especially visual ones. Therefore, advertising support is essential. Here, artificial intelligence plays a role in shaping marketing strategies, communication, and meeting player expectations." (P4)

The Impact of Generative Artificial Intelligence on the Industry

Participants highlighted several key concepts regarding the impact of generative artificial intelligence on the video game advertising industry. These included democratization and accessibility, challenges of quality and originality, the transformation of the perception of reality, and the continuing importance of creativity and the human touch. The impact of AI technology on the sector was conveyed through the participants' statements.

Table 7. The Impact of Generative Artificial Intelligence on the Industry

The Impact of Generative Artificial Intelligence on the Industry	Participant Codes
Democratization and Accessibility	P1 – P3
Issues of Quality and Originality	P1
Changes in the Perception of Reality	P2
The Importance of Creativity and the Human Touch	P3

Democratization and Accessibility

One participant expressed their views on the topic as follows:

"With generative artificial intelligence, much higher-quality visuals are now available, and the process is somewhat democratized. You may not have a large design team, but you have a strong business idea or a well-prepared game technically. Previously, if you did not have a good team or studio for the game's presentation, it was not possible, but today, you do not even need a studio. In this regard, I can say that AI is revolutionary." (P1)

Another participant conveyed their perspective as follows:

"We can say it has literally transformed the industry. In the past, creating a video or an advertisement required a large team—designers, copywriters, voice actors, video editors—but this was both time-consuming and costly. Now, with generative AI, part of this process can be completed much faster, with far fewer people and at a much lower cost." (P3)

Issues of Quality and Originality

One participant expressed their views as follows:

"It has now extended far beyond capital ownership. Someone with a good idea can now produce highly qualified work thanks to AI. However, we are now exposed to so much that we can distinguish AI-generated content from content created

by a designer. This inevitably reduces quality in works generated with poorly prepared prompts and results in a careless or low-quality appearance." (P1)

Changes in the Perception of Reality

A participant described the topic as follows:

"Visual hyperrealism is emerging here. People are starting to dislike reality because it is flawed. In real life, there are no perfect people or objects. However, with generative AI, almost perfect visuals can be created. This allows people, especially in advertising and games, to exist as themselves in artificial spaces. As a result, people may begin to devalue reality and no longer desire it. Generative AI is starting to replace reality.." (P2)

The Importance of Creativity and the Human Touch

One participant highlighted:

"There is also the creative dimension. Generative AI accelerates content production, true. However, the content often ends up being very similar, using the same tone or phrasing repeatedly. At this point, it depends on the skill of the team. If they can work effectively with AI and train it as a true assistant, and if the human advertiser performs the real artistic production, the result is a much more effective, faster, and cost-efficient advertisement." (P3)

Contribution of Generative AI-Based Game Advertising Content to Advertising

Participants identified the contributions of generative AI-produced text, visual, video, and audio content to advertising in terms of speed and efficiency, Cost Efficiency, personalization and targeting, as well as diversity and format richness. The participants' perspectives on the topic are presented through their own statements.

Table 8. Contribution of Generative AI-Based Game Advertising Content to Advertising

Contribution of Generative AI-Based Game Advertising Content to Advertising	Participant Codes
Speed and Efficiency	P1 – P3
Cost Efficiency	P1 – P3
Personalization and Audience Targeting	P1
Diversity and Format Richness	P3

Speed and Efficiency

One participant shared their perspective as follows:

"Beyond optimization, it is something that enhances communication success before publication and increases efficiency." (P1)

Another participant added:
"It provides an excellent opportunity, especially for A/B testing. We can quickly test which aspects of an advertisement or which features receive more clicks, which players engage more, and then highlight the more effective option or correct any errors. This process is much faster, and being data-driven and less costly is also advantageous for advertisers. Another contribution is the diversity of formats." (P3)
Cost Advantage
One participant noted:
"First and foremost, it reduces labor requirements. A task that five people could do can now be handled by one person, automatically lowering costs." (P1)
Another participant stated:
"The ability to adapt an advertisement's text or visuals to different target audiences very quickly, at minimal or even no cost, naturally provides greater speed and diversity." (P3)
Personalization and Targeting
A participant highlighted:
"The ability to perform real-time optimization is one of the best aspects. There may be points about the advertisement that we cannot detect before it is published, but if performance is low, we can intervene immediately to correct errors. Traditionally, we would conduct pre-tests and post-tests, even during publication, but all of these were limited by human capacity. Now, we have a tool that works with data beyond human perception and calculation, showing us errors that we otherwise could not detect." (P1)
Diversity and Format Richness
A participant explained:
"Another contribution is the diversity of formats. With generative AI, it is possible to produce visuals, videos, and even audio content alongside text. For example, in promoting a game character, AI could generate a short text introducing the character, draw its face, give it a voice, and create a mini promotional record. This makes campaigns more dynamic and richer." (P3)

Limits and Challenges of AI in Video Game Advertising

Participants identified the limits and challenges of AI in video game advertising as ethical and privacy issues, transparency and trust, and technical and industry-specific constraints. The participants' statements were used to convey this framework.

Table 9. Limits and Challenges of AI in Video Game Advertising

Limits and Challenges of AI in Video Game Advertising	Participant Codes
Ethical and Privacy Issues	P1 – P2 – P3
Transparency and Trust Issues	P1
Technical and Industry-Specific Constraints	P1 – P3

Ethical and Privacy Issues

The involvement of AI systems in advertising-related tasks, work, and communication processes has emerged as a topic that warrants examination within an ethical framework (Rodgers & Nguyen, 2022, p. 1043).

One participant expressed their views on ethical and privacy issues as follows:

"Starting with the ethical aspect, there is an issue here regarding privacy. Regardless of which tool we use, it points to a problematic area. Of course, one could consider this a problem in a different context, but the main issue is the use of data for which the user has not given consent, or whether such data is truly readable. More than the extent to which 'I read and agreed' contracts are processed, what matters is the extent to which the data explicitly permitted in these agreements is being used." (P1)

Another participant stated:

"When we consider the triangle of games, AI, and advertising, we see a clear ethical issue. Another ethical problem is misleading or deceptive advertising; there is hardly any advertising today that is not potentially misleading. Brands face a challenging process and experience significant problems in this regard." (P2)

A third participant added:

"One of the limitations is data privacy. These systems require an enormous amount of user data, which raises privacy concerns. Players often do not know to what extent they are being tracked, which data is collected, or how it is used, and this creates issues regarding the transparency of the technologies." (P3)

Transparency and Trust Issues

When consumers lack adequate information regarding the use of their personal data, a lack of transparency emerges, which in turn leads to a perceived loss of personal control. This situation gives rise to profound ethical concerns related to artificial intelligence (Du & Xie, 2021, p. 961). Addressing these concerns requires meeting consumer expectations, which is of critical importance.

One participant shared their perspective as follows:

In the game Zula, a razor brand gives a "razor case" to players who complete a survey. However, most players are between 11 and 17 years old. This age group is a period when appearance becomes more important. The data collected in the survey is obtained from individuals under 18 without parental consent. Al-

though players are asked to state that they are over 18, both the developers and the player data show that they are not. Since both sides benefit, this situation is often ignored. Ethically, this is problematic. In-game rewards may cause players to form an unnecessary attachment to the brand. More ethical and responsible practices should be encouraged.. (P1)

Technical and Industry-Specific Constraints

One participant commented:

"Technically, it may not be possible to show different content to every player in every game, and how accurately it works is important. For example, if I am an avatar entering a game, I may only be identified by my username, and the account might be used by more than just me. Therefore, the targeted individual may not always match the profile, which is a limitation." (P1)

Another participant added:

"For small and independent studios, implementing, using, or testing these systems can be technically challenging and costly. Large companies can integrate these systems easily, but smaller businesses have more difficulty accessing these technologies, which creates another imbalance in the industry." (P3)

The Impact of AI on the Future of Video Game Advertising

Participants explained the transformations that AI is expected to bring to video game advertising in the next five to ten years through the lenses of personalization and targeting development, game narrative, emotional and cognitive state analysis, and the integration of virtual and real worlds. These anticipated future transformations were conveyed through the participants' statements.

Table 10. The Impact of Artificial Intelligence on the Future of Video Game Advertising

The Impact of Artificial Intelligence on the Future of Video Game Advertising	Participant Codes
Advancements in Personalization and Targeting	P1 – P3
Game Narrative	P1 – P3
Emotional and Cognitive State Analysis	P3
Integration of Virtual and Real Worlds	P2 – P4

Advancements in Personalization and Targeting

One participant stated:

"It may enable much more detailed player profiling. Instead of the 5–6 player categories we currently define, I believe it will build more specialized categories and provide different tools for targeting them." (P1)

Another participant added:

"In the next 5–10 years, I think personalization will reach a completely new level, as many people also anticipate. Personalization is already quite advanced, but in the future, it will go beyond interests. I believe it will evolve according to mental and emotional states as well. So, we could imagine that two players on the same map in the same game will encounter different advertisements, different content, different characters, and different character reactions. We can already see this to some extent, but we will witness a more advanced version." (P3)

Game Narrative

One participant commented:

"Within the game, it might involve something highly futuristic, but it could transform the game narrative, including the storyline, areas, and environments." (P1)

Another participant noted:

"The Meta versus phenomenon, which was popular for a period of time, sparked discussions about avatars and how individuals relate to them. It highlighted how personal identities are extended into virtual worlds through avatars. As games and avatars continue to evolve, they are transforming into entirely new forms. People now purchase products for their avatars as part of gamification, creating opportunities for monetization in advertising. As virtual experiences become more advanced and realistic, they integrate more deeply into daily life, and the advertising industry quickly adapts to and capitalizes on this transformation." (P3)

Emotional and Cognitive State Analysis

One participant explained:

"In the next 5–10 years, the role of AI in digital video advertising will undoubtedly expand significantly. Especially with the emergence of emotional AI systems, which can analyze tone of voice, facial expressions, and in-game behaviors to interpret mood, this could evolve into something entirely new." (P3)

Integration of Virtual and Real Worlds

One participant stated:

"It seems that people will gravitate toward games where they can move their bodies and maximize physical efficiency during daily life. We will be able to play games in the physical spaces we occupy. We will witness the integration of the virtual and real worlds, and as soon as this integration is achieved, games will consist of a blend of half-real and half-virtual worlds. There are various studies related to this." (P2)

Academic and Industry Recommendations

Participants highlighted the gaps in existing academic studies on the topic and provided various recommendations for industry professionals and researchers. The participants' perspectives are presented through their own statements.

Table 11. Academic and Industry Recommendations

Academic and Industry Recommendations	Participant Codes
Lack of User Experience and Engagement	P3
Insufficient Local and Cultural Context	P4
Academia–Industry Collaboration	P2

Lack of User Experience and Engagement

One participant commented on the gaps in academic studies as follows:

"We see more focus on topics such as how AI works with various systems, which algorithms are most efficient, and how optimizations are implemented. However, the human aspect is the most important and has received insufficient attention. I believe players' experiences, perceptions, and reactions have not yet been adequately examined." (P3)

Insufficient Local and Cultural Context

One participant stated:

"Regarding game developers in Turkey, for example, topics such as what they pay attention to when creating a game, how they adapt the local cultural context, and the similarities or differences between games made in Turkey and games worldwide have not been sufficiently studied so far." (P4)

Academia–Industry Collaboration

One participant expressed:

"I believe scientific research should be conducted in collaboration with the industry. My recommendation to the industry is to engage more closely with academia and work together more extensively." (P2)

FUTURE RESEARCH DIRECTIONS

This study is limited to the perspectives and experiences of academics. Future research may obtain up-to-date and comprehensive data from industry professionals. Moreover, the effects of video game advertising on consumer attitudes and behaviors can also be further investigated.

CONCLUSION

One of the most profound transformations of the 21st century is the emergence of artificial intelligence (AI) technologies from laboratory settings into everyday life. AI plays a transformative role in nearly every domain with which humans interact. The pace of this transformation is influenced not only by advances in AI technologies but also by the extent to which individuals, societies, institutions, and even states adapt to and integrate these technologies into their processes.

The field of advertising, which has gained momentum through digitalization, is also being affected by AI technologies and is undergoing a process of restructuring (Türksoy, 2022, p. 399). One of the processes currently experiencing transformation in advertising is video game advertising. In particular, with the development of AI technologies, the approach of brands toward in-game advertisements is undergoing a profound change (Disrupted, 2024).

The study aims to examine academics' perspectives and experiences regarding video game advertising and artificial intelligence (AI), and to elucidate how AI applications are utilized in video game advertising, as well as their advantages, limitations, and challenges. This research makes a significant contribution to both researchers and industry practitioners by explaining the use of AI in video game advertising through the knowledge and experiences of academics.

The findings of the study indicate that video game advertisements, compared to traditional advertising channels, enhance advertising effectiveness by capturing more attention, facilitating longer engagement, and providing a higher level of realism. The use of AI technologies in video game advertising further increases this effectiveness. Consistent with the findings of Gao et al. (2023), participants emphasized that AI's effectiveness in data collection, user behavior analysis, and the generation of meaningful insights enables advertisements to become more targeted and personalized. When this finding is evaluated within the framework of the Uses and Gratifications Theory, it suggests that the use of artificial intelligence in video game advertising indirectly serves the types of gratifications that players seek from media use. This is because the Uses and Gratifications Theory posits that individuals actively select media content in order to satisfy specific cognitive and emotional needs (Özdemir, 2022, p. 141). In this context, the highly interactive nature of video games, when combined with AI technologies, increases the visibility and memorability of advertisements, aligning with the theory's emphasis on active media use and audience engagement.

Another finding of the study indicates that AI applications can dynamically transform in-game characters, scenes, and storylines, allowing advertising messages to be naturally integrated into the gaming experience. In particular, with the inclusion of generative AI technologies, the contributions of AI have become more tangible through the production of text, visuals, video, and audio. Participants highlighted that AI technologies facilitate and accelerate content production processes in video game advertising and significantly enhance efficiency. AI technologies also provide notable cost advantages by reducing labor and production expenses. This finding indicates that the ability of AI applications to dynamically modify in-game characters, scenes, and narratives enables advertising messages to be seamlessly integrated into the game world. This situation can be associated with the concepts of immersion and experiential gratification emphasized in Uses and Gratifications Theory. According to the participants' views, particularly generative AI technologies provide more realistic and fluid advertising experiences, thereby enhancing player gratification.

Studies in the literature addressing the use of generative AI in video game advertising are very limited. In this context, academics have approached the topic within a limited scope, mainly emphasizing speed, efficiency, and cost advantages.

Although AI technologies offer numerous benefits to the digital advertising sector, they also bring certain challenges (Yu, 2021, p. 192). The findings reveal that ethical and privacy concerns, lack of transparency and trust, and technical and industry-specific limitations are among the most significant challenges. From the perspective of Uses and Gratifications Theory, such ethical concerns have the potential to undermine users' need for trust, thereby reducing their motivation to engage with media content. In particular, data privacy and ethical usage are considered critical discussion points for the sustainability of AI-based advertising.

In terms of future perspectives, the findings suggest that AI will transform game advertising by enabling personalization, targeting, and the dynamic shaping of game narratives. Additionally, the integration of virtual and real-world experiences through emotional and cognitive state analysis is expected to provide significant gains for the advertising sector.

In conclusion, AI applications have a widespread role in video game advertising and hold the potential to shape the future of video advertising. In the future, strong collaborations between industry and academia may ensure that technological innovations are balanced with ethical responsibilities, thereby contributing to a more sustainable approach to advertising.

REFERENCES

Abdulwahid, A., Pattnaik, M., Palav, M. R., Babu, S. T., Manoharan, G., & Selvi, G. P. (2023). Library management system using artificial intelligence. In *2023 Eighth International Conference on Science Technology Engineering and Mathematics (ICONSTEM)* (ss. 1-7). IEEE.

Acar, A. (2007). Testing the effects of incidental advertising exposure in on-line gaming environment. *Journal of Interactive Advertising*, *8*(1), 45–56. DOI: 10.1080/15252019.2007.10722136

Adomavicius, G., & Tuzhilin, A. (2005). Toward the next generation of recommender systems: A survey of the state-of-the-art and possible extension. *IEEE Transactions on Knowledge and Data Engineering*, *17*(6), 734–749. DOI: 10.1109/TKDE.2005.99

Agrawal, S., & Raikwar, Y. (2025, May). *AI-driven content creation in gaming: Opportunities, challenges, and monetization*. Gyan Ganga College of Technology, Yash Raikwar's Lab. DOI: 10.13140/RG.2.2.31586.24007

Ahmad, M. (2024, March 5). *Exploring the Booming Landscape of In-Game Advertising*. ExchangeWire. https://www.exchangewire.com/blog/2024/03/05/exploring-the-booming-landscape-of-in-game-advertising/

An, S., & Stern, S. (2011). Mitigating the effects of advergames on children: Do advertising breaks work? *Journal of Advertising*, *40*(1), 43–56. DOI: 10.2753/JOA0091-3367400103

Annetta, L. A. (2008). Video games in education: Why they should be used and how they are being used. *Theory into Practice*, *47*(3), 229–239. DOI: 10.1080/00405840802153940

Baltezarević, R., & Baltezarević, I. (2024). Effects of in-game advertısıng on the world economy. *4th Internatıonal Cankaya Scıentıfic Studıes Congress*, September 7-9, 2024, Ankara-TÜRKİYE.

Barsha, S., & Munshi, S. A. (2023). Implementing artificial intelligence in library services: A review of current prospects and challenges of developing countries. *Library Hi Tech News*, *41*(1), 7–10. DOI: 10.1108/LHTN-07-2023-0126

Bogost, I. (2005). Videogames and the future of education. *On the Horizon*, *13*(2), 119–125. DOI: 10.1108/10748120510608151

Bozkurt, Y. (2019). Tutum ve davranış niyeti üzerinde oyun reklam algısının rolü. *Gümüşhane Üniversitesi İletişim Fakültesi Elektronik Dergisi*, *7*(2), 1341–1371.

Brand Safety Institute. (2023, May 25). *AI trends in digital advertising for gaming*. https://www.brandsafetyinstitute.com/blog/ai-trends-in-digital-advertising-for-gaming

Çeber, B. (2024). Reklam ajanslarında yapay zekâ kullanımı: Sektör profesyonellerinin chatGPT ve midjourney deneyimlerine yönelik bir araştırma. *Erciyes İletişim Dergisi, 11*(2), 583–606. DOI: 10.17680/erciyesiletisim.1439479

Çeber, B. (2024). Yapay zekâ etiği bağlamında reklamcılık sektörü üzerine uygulamalı bir araştırma. *Intermedia International e-Journal, 11*(20), 63–84. DOI: 10.56133/intermedia.1462312

Çeber, B. (2025). Yapay zekâ "Sora" ile üretilen reklamların McLuhan'ın "Araç mesajdır" perspektifinden incelenmesi: Toys "R" Us reklam örneği. *Yeni Medya Elektronik Dergisi, 9*(2), 171–200.

Chaney, I. M., Lin, K.-H., & Chaney, J. (2004). The effect of billboards within the gaming environment. *Journal of Interactive Advertising*, *5*(1), 54–69. DOI: 10.1080/15252019.2004.10722092

Changmai, T. (2024). Programmatic advertising technology and social marketing trend on game industrial in 2024. In N. V. Mançurova et al. (Eds.), *İş dünyası. Eğitim. Ekonomi: V. Uluslararası bilimsel-pratik konferans bildirileri (Minsk, 4–5 Nisan 2024)* (ss. 445–450). Belarus Devlet Üniversitesi İşletme Enstitüsü.

Chen, Y. (2024). Advertising in the era of artificial intelligence. *Proceedings of 3rd International Conference on Interdisciplinary Humanities and Communication Studies*. DOI: 10.54254/2753-7064/39/20242180

Connolly, T. M. (2008). Using alternate reality games to support the teaching of modern foreign languages. *Webist 2008: Proceedings of the Fourth International Conference on Web Information Systems and Technologies, 01*, 428-434.

Consalvo, M. (2005). Cheating can be good for you: Educational games and multiple play styles. *On the Horizon, 13*(2), 95–100. DOI: 10.1108/10748120510608124

Culnan, M., & Clark, C. (2009). How ethics can enhance organizational privacy: Lessons from the ChoicePoint and TJX data breaches. *Management Information Systems Quarterly, 33*(4), 673–687. DOI: 10.2307/20650322

Disrupted. (2024). *AI-powered personalization in in-game advertising: Tailoring ads to enhance user experience*. Disrupted Logic. 2 Ağustos 2025 tarihinde https://disruptedlogic.com/ai-powered-personalization-in-in-game-advertising-tailoring-ads-to-enhance-user-experience/ adresinden alındı.

Dix, S. R., & Phau, I. (2017). Predictors of commercial zapping during live prime-time television: An observation-based study identifies factors that drive TV channel switching. *Journal of Advertising Research, 57*(1), 15–27. DOI: 10.2501/JAR-2017-010

Du, S., & Xie, C. (2021). Paradoxes of artificial intelligence in consumer markets: Ethical challenges and opportunities. *Journal of Business Research, 129*, 961–974. DOI: 10.1016/j.jbusres.2020.08.024

Duan, L., Xu, Y., Tsang, I. W., & Luo, J. (2019). Collaborative generated hashing for market analysis and fast cold-start recommendation. *IEEE Intelligent Systems, 35*(5), 84–95. DOI: 10.1109/MIS.2020.3025197

El-aasy, H. A. (2023). Employing artificial intelligence (AI) technology in advertising design on social media. *Journal of Design Sciences and Applied Arts, 4*(2), 247–263. DOI: 10.21608/jdsaa.2023.194906.1260

Epstein, Z., Hertzmann, A., Herman, L., Mahari, R., Frank, M., Groh, M., Schroeder, H., Smith, A., Akten, M., Fjeld, J., Farid, H., Leach, N., Pentland, A., & Russakovsky, O. (2023). Art and the science of generative AI: A deeper dive. *arXiv*. https://doi.org//arXiv.2303.13336DOI: 10.48550

Ferguson, C. J., Rueda, S. M., Cruz, A. M., Ferguson, D. E., Fritz, S., & Smith, S. M. (2008). Violent video games and aggression: Causal relationship or byproduct of family violence and intrinsic violence motivation? *Criminal Justice and Behavior, 35*(3), 311–332. DOI: 10.1177/0093854807311719

Fitria, T. N. (2023). Artificial intelligence (AI) technology in OpenAI ChatGPT application: A review of ChatGPT in writing English essay. *ELT Forum: Journal of English Language Teaching, 12*(1), 44–58.

Gao, B., Wang, Y., Xie, H., Hu, Y., & Hu, Y. (2023). Artificial intelligence in advertising: Advancements, challenges, and ethical considerations in targeting, personalization, content creation, and ad optimization. *SAGE Open, 13*(4), 21582440231210759. DOI: 10.1177/21582440231210759

Gentile, D. A., Lynch, P. J., Linder, J. R., & Walsh, D. A. (2004). The effects of violent video game habits on adolescent hostility, aggressive behaviors, and school performance. *Journal of Adolescence, 27*(1), 5–22. DOI: 10.1016/j.adolescence.2003.10.002 PMID: 15013257

Ghirvu, A. (2012). In-game advertısıng: Advantages and limitations for advertısers. *The USV Annals of Economics and Public Administration, 12*(1), 114–119.

Glass, Z. (2007). The effectiveness of product placement in video games. *Journal of Interactive Advertising*, *8*(1), 23–32. DOI: 10.1080/15252019.2007.10722134

Grigorovici, D., & Constantin, C. (2004). Experiencing ınteractive advertising beyond rich media: Impacts of ad type and presence on brand effectiveness in 3d gaming ımmersive virtual environments. *Journal of Interactive Advertising*, *5*(1), 22–36. DOI: 10.1080/15252019.2004.10722091

Gujar, P., Paliwal, G., & Panyam, S. (2024). Generative AI and the future of interactive and immersive advertising. *Proceedings of the 2024 IEEE Eighth Ecuador Technical Chapters Meeting (ETCM)*, Cuenca, Ecuador, 1-6. DOI: 10.1109/ETCM63562.2024.10746166

Hanbazazah, A., Reeve, C., & Abuljadail, M. (2022). Advergames and consumer behaviour: A quantitative comparative analysis of the United Kingdom and Saudi Arabia. *International Journal of Marketing Studies*, *14*(2), 113–120. DOI: 10.5539/ijms.v14n2p113

Hilton, T. (2006). Gaming as an educational tool. *Young Consumers*, *7*(2), 14–19. DOI: 10.1108/17473610610701457

Ioni ă, C. G., Leovaridis, C., & Popescu, G. (2025). Use of artificial ıntelligence in advertising agencies: Opportunities and challenges. *Management Dynamics in the Knowledge Economy*, *13*(1), 38–51. DOI: 10.2478/mdke-2025-0003

Jayakanthan, R. (2002). Application of computer games in the field of education. *The Electronic Library*, *20*(2), 98–102. DOI: 10.1108/02640470210697471

Jong, M. S. Y., Shang, J., Lee, F.-L., & Lee, J. H. M. (2008). Harnessing computer games in education. *International Journal of Distance Education Technologies*, *6*(1), 1–9. DOI: 10.4018/jdet.2008010101

Joygame Publishing. (2024, August 19). *The power of AI in mobile game advertising*.

Kadry, A. (2024). Exploring gamification advertising and its role in audience engagement. *International Design Journal*, *14*(1), 163–173. DOI: 10.21608/idj.2024.329267

Kietzmann, J., Paschen, J., & Treen, E. (2018). Artificial intelligence in advertising: How marketers can leverage artificial intelligence along the consumer journey. *Journal of Advertising Research*, *58*(3), 263–267. DOI: 10.2501/JAR-2018-035

Kingma, D. P., & Ba, J. (2014). Adam: A method for stochastic optimization. *arXiv*. https://arxiv.org/abs/1412.6980

Kretchmer, S. B. (2005). Changing views of commercialization in digital games: In-game advertising and advergames as worlds in play. *DiGRA '05 - Proceedings of the 2005 DiGRA International Conference: Changing Views: Worlds in Play*.

Kumar, V., Ashraf, A. R., & Nadeem, W. (2024). AI-powered marketing: What, where, and how? *International Journal of Information Management*, *77*, 102783. DOI: 10.1016/j.ijinfomgt.2024.102783

Kwon, J. W. (2015). A study on element features and research frames of game trailer. *Cartoon and Animation Studies*, *41*(), 187–222. DOI: 10.7230/KOSCAS.2015.41.187

Lee, M., & Faber, R. J. (2007). Effects of product placement in on-line games on brand memory: A perspective of the limited-capacity model of attention. *Journal of Advertising*, *36*(4), 75–90. DOI: 10.2753/JOA0091-3367360406

Li, H. (2019). Special Section Introduction: Artificial Intelligence and Advertising. *Journal of Advertising*, *48*(4), 333–337. DOI: 10.1080/00913367.2019.1654947

Li, T. (2024). AI empowered personalized digital advertising marketing. *Frontiers in Business, Economics and Management*, *15*(2), 439–442. DOI: 10.54097/k0wjgk28

Louro, M., & Cunha, P. (2001). Brand management paradigms. *Journal of Marketing Management*, *17*(7-8), 849–875. DOI: 10.1362/026725701323366845

Mallinckrodt, V., & Mizerski, D. (2007). The effects of playing an advergame on young children's perceptions, preferences, and requests. *Journal of Advertising*, *36*(2), 87–100. DOI: 10.2753/JOA0091-3367360206

Martínez-Martínez, I. J., Aguado, J.-M., & Boeykens, Y. (2017). Ethical implications of digital advertising automation: The case of programmatic advertising in Spain. *El Profesional de la Información*, *26*(2), 201–210. DOI: 10.3145/epi.2017.mar.06

McStay, A. (2017). Micro-Moments, Liquidity, Intimacy and Automation: Developments in Programmatic Ad-tech. In Siegert, G., Rimscha, M. B., & Grubenmann, S. (Eds.), *Commercial Communication in the Digital Age* (pp. 143–159). DOI: 10.1515/9783110416794-009

Mete, M. H. (2021). Dijital medyada programatik reklamcılık ve etik sorunlar. *TRT Akademi*, *6*(12), 426–448. DOI: 10.37679/trta.876044

Moor, M., Banerjee, O., Abad, Z. S. H., Krumholz, H. M., Leskovec, J., Topol, E. J., & Rajpurkar, P. (2023). Foundation models for generalist medical artificial intelligence. *Nature*, *616*(7956), 259–265. DOI: 10.1038/s41586-023-05881-4 PMID: 37045921

Moore, S., Bulmer, S., & Elms, J. (2022). The social significance of AI in retail on customer experience and shopping practices. *Journal of Retailing and Consumer Services*, *64*, 102755. DOI: 10.1016/j.jretconser.2021.102755

Morandini, S., Fraboni, F., De Angelis, M., Puzzo, G., Giusino, D., & Pietrantoni, L. (2023). The impact of artificial intelligence on workers' skills: Upskilling and reskilling in organisations. *Informing Science*, *26*, 39–68. DOI: 10.28945/5078

Murugan, T. S., & Kumar, C. M. (2024). Unveiling the evolution: Impact of artificial intelligence on consumer buying behaviors in online retail purchase. *Educational Administration: Theory and Practice*, *30*(5), 1072–1078. DOI: 10.53555/kuey.v30i5.3011

Nelson, M. R., Keum, H., & Yaros, R. (2004). Advertainment or adcreep? game players' attitudes toward advertising and product placements in computer games. *Journal of Interactive Advertising*, *5*(1), 3–21. DOI: 10.1080/15252019.2004.10722090

Nicovich, S. (2005). The effect of involvement on ad judgment in a video game environment: The mediating role of presence. *Journal of Interactive Advertising*, *6*(1), 29–39. DOI: 10.1080/15252019.2005.10722105

Özdemir, H. (2022). Kullanımlar ve doyumlar yaklaşımı bağlamında tüketicilerin online alışveriş eğilimlerini belirleyen nitel bir araştırma. İletişim ve Toplum Araştırmaları Dergisi, 2(2), 138-153. DOI: 10.29228/itamder.3

Palfreyman, B. M. (2025, March 4). *AI-powered video game advertising: Regulatory and IP challenges*. Harris Beach PLLC. https://www.harrisbeachmurtha.com/insights/ai-powered-video-game-advertising-regulatory-and-ip-challenges/

Patil, D. (2024). Generative artificial intelligence in marketing and advertising: Advancing personalization and optimizing consumer engagement strategies. *Journal of Marketing Analytics*, *12*(3), 145–158.

Patil, D., Rane, N. L., & Rane, J. (2024). Applications of ChatGPT and generative artificial intelligence in transforming the future of various business sectors. In *The Future Impact of ChatGPT on Several Business Sectors* (ss. 1-47). Deep Science Publishing. DOI: 10.70593/978-81-981367-8-7_1

Peng, W., Liu, M., & Mou, Y. (2008). Do aggressive people play violent computer games in a more aggressive way? Individual difference and idiosyncratic game-playing experience. *Cyberpsychology & Behavior*, *11*(2), 157–161. DOI: 10.1089/cpb.2007.0026 PMID: 18422407

Penrose, R. (2023). *Kralın Yeni Aklı, Bilgisayar, Zekâ ve Fizik Yasaları* (T. Dereli, Çev.). Koç Üniversitesi Yayınları. (Orijinal çalışma basım tarihi 1989).

Peters, S., & Leshner, G. (2013). Get in the game: The effects of game product congruity and product placement proximity on game players' processing of brands embedded in advergames. *Journal of Advertising*, *42*(2-3), 113–130. DOI: 10.1080/00913367.2013.774584

Prendergast, G., Cheung, W. L., & West, D. (2010). Antecedents to advertising avoidance in China. *Journal of Current Issues and Research in Advertising*, *32*(2), 87–100. DOI: 10.1080/10641734.2010.10505287

Qin, X., & Jiang, Z. (2019). The impact of AI on the advertising process: The Chinese experience. *Journal of Advertising*, *48*(4), 338–346. DOI: 10.1080/00913367.2019.1652122

Rane, J., Mallick, S. K., Kaya, O., & Rane, N. L. (2024). Artificial general intelligence in industry 4.0, 5.0, and society 5.0: Applications, opportunities, challenges, and future direction. In *Future Research Opportunities for Artificial Intelligence in Industry 4.0 and 5.0* (ss. 207-235). Deep Science Publishing. DOI: 10.70593/978-81-981271-0-5_6

Rodgers, S. (2021). Themed Issue Introduction: Promises and Perils of Artificial Intelligence and Advertising. *Journal of Advertising*, *50*(1), 1–10. DOI: 10.1080/00913367.2020.1868233

Rodgers, W., & Nguyen, T. (2022). Advertising benefits from ethical artificial intelligence algorithmic purchase decision pathways. *Journal of Business Ethics*, *178*(4), 1043–1061. DOI: 10.1007/s10551-022-05048-7

Rohr-Sendlmeier, U. A., Gotze, I., & Stichel, R. (2008). Parental education concerning their children's use of modern media: Family rules and motives, extent and effects of using the computer, watching television and playing video games. *Zeitschrift für Familienforschung*, *20*(2), 107–130.

Sancaklı, P., & Sarı, Ü. (2025). Use of artificial ıntelligence ın digital games and current trends in the example of the 'F.E.A.R' game. *Communicata*, *29*, 87–98. DOI: 10.32952/communicata.1628205

Say, C. (2024). *50 Soruda Yapay Zekâ.* Bilim ve Gelecek Kitaplığı.

Sebastian, A., Núñez, M., & Muñoz, D. (2016). New business models for advertisers: The video game sector in Spain. Advergaming Vs In-game Advertising. *Icono 14, 14*(2), 256–279. DOI: 10.7195/ri14.v14i2.964

Singhal, A. (2024). The role of artificial ıntelligence in enhancing ad personalization: A study on programmatic advertising. [JAIGS]. *Journal of Artificial Intelligence General Science*, *3*(1), 431–445. DOI: 10.60087/jaigs.v3i1.246

Smith, R., Kelly, B., Yeatman, H., Moore, C., Baur, L., King, L., Boyland, E., Chapman, K., Hughes, C., & Bauman, A. (2020). Advertising placement in digital game design influences children's choices of advertised snacks: A randomized trial. *Journal of the Academy of Nutrition and Dietetics, 120*(3), 404–413. DOI: 10.1016/j.jand.2019.07.017 PMID: 31892500

Speck, P. S., & Elliott, M. T. (1997). Predictors of advertising avoidance in print and broadcast media. *Journal of Advertising, 26*(3), 61–76. DOI: 10.1080/00913367.1997.10673529

Sreejesh, S., Ghosh, T., & Dwivedi, Y. K. (2021). Moving beyond the content: The role of contextual cues in the effectiveness of gamification of advertising. *Journal of Business Research, 132*, 88–101. DOI: 10.1016/j.jbusres.2021.04.007

Stevens, A., Rau, A., & McIntyre, M. (2016). Integrated campaign planning in a programmatic world. In *Programmatic Advertising* (ss. 193–210). Springer. DOI: 10.1007/978-3-319-25023-6_16

Technavio. (2025). *In-Game Advertising (IGA) Market Analysis North America, APAC, Europe, Middle East and Africa, South America - US, Canada, China, Japan, Germany, India, UK, South Korea, France, Italy - Size and Forecast 2025-2029*. 10 Ağustos 2025 tarihinde https://www.technavio.com/report/in-game-advertising-market-industry-analysis adresinden alındı.

Thomas, D. (2005). Messages and mediums: Learning to teach with videogames. *On the Horizon, 13*(2), 89–94. DOI: 10.1108/10748120510608115

Tian, X. (2024). AI applications in video games and future expectations. *Applied and Computational Engineering, 54*(1), 161–170. DOI: 10.54254/2755-2721/54/20241484

Türksoy, N. (2022). The future of public relations, advertising and journalism: How artificial ıntelligence may transform the communication profession and why society should care? *Türkiye İletişim Araştırmaları Dergisi*, (40), 394–410. DOI: 10.17829/turcom.1050491

Türnüklü, D. A. (2000). Eğitimbilim Araştırmalarında Etkin Olarak Kullanılabilecek Nitel BirAraştırma Tekniği: Görüşme. *Kuram ve Uygulamada Eğitim Yönetimi, 24*(24), 543–559.

Valin, J., & Gregory, A. (2020). Ethics Guide to Artificial Intelligence in PR. Chartered Instıtute of Public Relations, https://cipr.co.uk/common/Uploaded%20files/Policy/AI/AIinPR_Ethics_Guide_UK.pdf

van Berlo, Z. M., & Chen, X. (2024). Advergames and consumer brand engagement: Experiential satisfaction as a mediator of gamified advertising effects. *Journal of Interactive Advertising*, *24*(3), 238–246. DOI: 10.1080/15252019.2024.2335398

Viant Technology, L. L. C. (2025, March 3). *Why in-game advertising is a game-changer for digital marketing*. Viant. https://www.viantinc.com/insights/blog/in-game-advertising-brand-engagement/

Wang, H., & Kosinski, M. (2018). Deep neural networks are more accurate than humans at detecting sexual orientation from facial images. *Journal of Personality and Social Psychology*, *114*(2), 246–257. DOI: 10.1037/pspa0000098 PMID: 29389215

Wang, X. (2020). Screening soft information: Evidence from loan officers. *The RAND Journal of Economics*, *51*(4), 1287–1322. DOI: 10.1111/1756-2171.12357

Wei, R. (2007). Effects of playing violent videogames on Chinese adolescents' pro-violence attitudes, attitudes toward others, and aggressive behavior. *Cyberpsychology & Behavior*, *10*(3), 371–380. DOI: 10.1089/cpb.2006.9942 PMID: 17594261

White, G. R. T., & Samuel, A. (2019). Programmatic Advertising: Forewarning and avoiding hype-cycle failure. *Technological Forecasting and Social Change*, *144*, 157–168. DOI: 10.1016/j.techfore.2019.03.020

Winkler, T., & Buckner, K. (2006). Receptiveness of gamers to embedded brand messages in advergames: Attitudes towards product placement. *Journal of Interactive Advertising*, *7*(1).

Xu, H. (2025). Applications of artificial ıntelligence in advertising and marketing. *Journal of Fintech and Business Analysis*, *2*(1), 50–54. DOI: 10.54254/3049-5768/2025.21631

Yang, M., Roskos-Ewoldsen, D. R., Dinu, L., & Arpan, L. M. (2006). The effectiveness of "in-game" advertising: Comparing college students' explicit and implicit memory for brand names. *Journal of Advertising*, *35*(4), 143–152. DOI: 10.2753/JOA0091-3367350410

Yıldırım, A., & Şimşek, H. (2011). *Sosyal Bilimlerde Nitel Araştırma Yöntemleri*. Seçkin Yayıncılık.

Yu, Y. (2021). The role and influence of artificial intelligence on advertising industry. In *Proceedings of the 2021 International Conference on Social Development and Media Communication (SDMC 2021)* (ss. 190–194). Atlantis Press. DOI: 10.2991/assehr.k.220105.037

Zagni, L. M., Baima, G., Do, B., & Nguyen, L. D. X. (2025). Convergence and divergence in digital game-based advertising: A systematic review of advergames and in game advertising. *Review of Managerial Science*. Advance online publication. DOI: 10.1007/s11846-025-00876-z

Zagni, L. M., & Pera, R. (2024). From immersion to invasion: a netnographic exploration of consumers' responses' to in-game advertising. In *NETNOCON 2024 conference proceedings*.

Zhang, C., Zhang, C., Zheng, S., Zhang, M., Qamar, M., Bae, S.-H., & Kweon, I. S. (2023). A survey on audio diffusion models: Text to speech synthesis and enhancement in generative AI. *arXiv*. https://doi.org//arXiv.2303.13336DOI: 10.48550

Zhang, Y.-S., & Kim, Y.-J. (2023). Exploring the Potential of ChatGPT in Advertising Photography: A Case Study and Validity Research on Elements in Each Production Stage. The journal of the convergence on culture technology, 9(3), 205-211. DOI: 10.17703/JCCT.2023.9.3.205

Zhou, F., & Li, J. (2020). Current status and prospects of artificial intelligence application in game development. *China Management Informatization*, *23*, 183–185.

ADDITIONAL READING

Agrawal, A., Gans, J., & Goldfarb, A. (2019). *Prediction machines: The simple economics of artificial intelligence*. Harvard Business Review Press. DOI: 10.7208/chicago/9780226613475.001.0001

Agrawal, S., & Raikwar, Y. (2025, May). AI-driven content creation in gaming: Opportunities, challenges, and monetization. *Gyan Ganga College of Technology, Yash Raikwar's Lab*. DOI: 10.13140/RG.2.2.31586.24007

Bostrom, N. (2014). *Superintelligence: Paths, dangers, strategies*. Oxford University Press.

Gujar, P., Paliwal, G., & Panyam, S. (2024). Generative AI and the future of interactive and immersive advertising. In *Proceedings of the 2024 IEEE Eighth Ecuador Technical Chapters Meeting (ETCM)* (pp. 1–6). Cuenca, Ecuador. DOI: 10.1109/ETCM63562.2024.10746166

Iansiti, M., & Lakhani, K. R. (2020). *Competing in the age of AI: Strategy and leadership when algorithms and networks run the world*. Harvard Business Review Press.

Jovanović, M., & Campbell, M. (2022). Generative artificial intelligence: Trends and prospects. *Computer, 55*(10), MC.2022.3192720107-112. https://doi.org//DOI: 10.1109

Qin, X., & Jiang, Z. (2019). The impact of AI on the advertising process: The Chinese experience. *Journal of Advertising*, *48*(4), 338–346. DOI: 10.1080/00913367.2019.1652122

Reese, B. (2020). *Yapay zekâ çağı: Akıllı robotlar, bilinçli bilgisayarlar ve insanlığın geleceği* [The Fourth Age: Smart Robots, Conscious Computers, and the Future of Humanity]. Say Yayınları.

Tian, X. (2024). AI applications in video games and future expectations. *Applied and Computational Engineering*, *54*(1), 161–170. DOI: 10.54254/2755-2721/54/20241484

Yu, Y. (2022). The role and influence of artificial intelligence on advertising industry. In *Proceedings of the 2021 International Conference on Social Development and Media Communication (SDMC 2021)* (pp. 190–194). DOI: 10.2991/assehr.k.220105.037

KEY TERMS AND DEFINITIONS

Artificial Intelligence (AI): A technology that enables computers to perform tasks such as thinking or learning, which are normally carried out by humans.

Generative Artificial Intelligence: A type of AI capable of producing new content such as text, images, or audio.

Digital Advertising: Refers to advertising activities conducted through the internet and digital platforms.

Video Game Advertising: The use of video games as an advertising medium for brands to reach users.

In-Game Advertising: Advertisements embedded within games that players notice while playing.

Game Advertising: The design of advertisements directly through games themselves or game mechanics.

Personalization: The adaptation of content or advertisements specifically to a user's tastes and preferences.

APPENDIX

Figure 1.

Figure 2.

Figure 3.

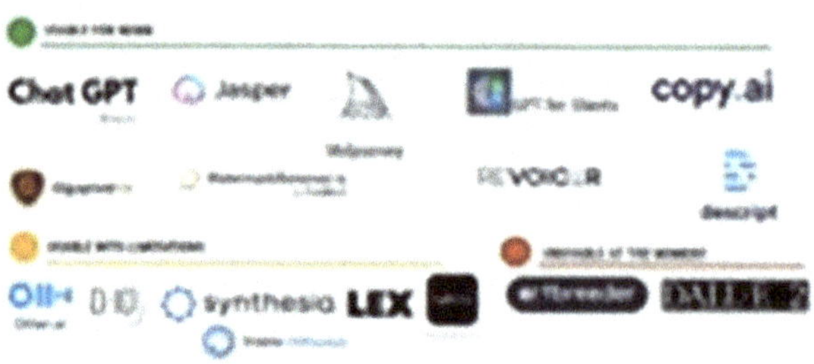

Chapter 6
Voice Assistants and Gamified Advertising:
A New Dimension in Artifiicial Intelligence Powered Brand Interactions

Zihni Can Çamur
http://orcid.org/0009-0005-0404-1015
Ondokuz Mayıs Üniversitesi, Turkey

ABSTRACT

Advertising and marketing communication are undergoing a fundamental transformation alongside technological developments. While traditional advertising formats were based on a one-way communication model and a passive audience approach, interactive, user-centered, and experience-focused methods are now coming to the fore. The main reason for this is the indifference and ad blindness that users have developed towards classic advertising messages. Brands need more innovative strategies to attract consumers' attention and increase engagement. The aim of this study is to examine gamified advertising strategies conducted through voice assistants and to evaluate the effects of these strategies on user behavior, brand loyalty, and interaction levels. The study will proceed through literature review, case studies, and future projections.

INTRODUCTION

The rapid development of digital technologies has brought about fundamental changes in advertising and marketing communications. Although this transforma-

DOI: 10.4018/979-8-3373-6309-7.ch006

tion is frequently discussed in the literature, it is difficult to say that interaction and experience-focused approaches are equally effective for every sector and every user group. In particular, consumers' growing indifference to traditional advertising messages over time and the perceptual resistance defined in the literature as "advertising blindness" stand out as one of the key dynamics of this transformation (Akıllıbaş & Ceylan, 2020). This resistance should be considered not only as a technical problem but also as a psychological threshold that must be overcome. This situation is driving brands to develop new communication strategies that enable them to build stronger and more sustainable relationships with their target audiences.

At this point, the gamification strategy stands out as a noteworthy approach to overcoming the limitations of traditional methods. As Özkan and Samur (2017) also point out, gamification refers to the adaptation of game mechanics to non-game contexts. However, the decisive factor here is not just scoring or reward systems, but the ability to tap into the user's intrinsic motivation. From a marketing communication perspective, gamification goes beyond being a tool that entertains the user; it contributes to establishing an emotional bond between the brand and the user, strengthening brand loyalty, and increasing the level of interaction (Demir & Gök Demir, 2020). In this sense, gamification can be considered a communication practice that removes the user from a passive recipient position and actively involves them in the process. However, treating gamification as a neutral tool that increases user motivation in all circumstances carries the risk of overlooking the concept's directive and ideological dimensions.

On the other hand, artificial intelligence-based voice assistant technologies are becoming increasingly visible within the digital communication ecosystem. Voice assistants such as Amazon Alexa, Google Assistant, and Apple Siri are integrating into users' daily life practices by facilitating access to information, content consumption, and online service usage through voice commands. Studies show that voice assistants transform the user experience and create new dynamics in the way users interact with media thanks to their interaction-based structures (Ergül, 2025). These developments make it necessary to consider voice assistants not only as a technological innovation but also as a new area for advertising and brand interaction in terms of marketing communication.

The personalized and interaction-focused structure offered by voice assistants enables brands to establish more direct, experience-based, and dialogue-centered communication with users. These AI-powered systems offer significant opportunities for strengthening customer relationships, increasing interaction levels, and ensuring user satisfaction in digital marketing processes (Şaylan, Taşkın & Abdulwahid, 2025). However, evaluating the use of voice assistants in advertising and marketing solely based on technical infrastructure is not considered sufficient; it is emphasized that psychosocial factors such as user trust, perceived benefit, and technology acceptance are also decisive in this process (Gelibolu, 2024).

The main objective of this study is to examine gamified advertising strategies conducted through voice assistants and to evaluate the potential effects of these strategies on user behavior, brand loyalty, and interaction levels. The research is structured within a conceptual framework based on literature review and case studies. While voice assistant technologies are addressed from a general perspective, in-depth case analyses are methodologically limited to the Amazon Alexa platform. This preference is related to Alexa's open developer ecosystem, its "Skills" infrastructure that enables brand integrations, and the fact that gamified interactions are technically more visible and feasible (Gelibolu, 2024). Google Assistant and Apple Siri are discussed in the study to provide a comparative background, but are evaluated in a secondary position in the context of case studies.

THE CONCEPT OF GAMIFICATION AND ITS FUNCTION IN MARKETING COMMUNICATION

As a social activity as old as human history, games play an important role in the formation of cultural structures and their transmission from generation to generation (Bolat, 2023). This historical and cultural continuity also forms the background for the use of the concept of gamification as an effective strategy in non-game areas such as marketing and advertising today. Games are not only considered an entertainment-based activity but also a practical field where cultural meanings are produced, shared, and reinterpreted.

Huizinga and Caillois, among classical game theorists, evaluate games as one of the founding components of culture and emphasize that game practices are directly related to social meaning production processes. According to this approach, games offer a cultural experience space where individuals voluntarily participate within certain rules, produce symbolic meanings, and enable social interaction. Digital games and gamification applications can also be considered extensions of this cultural framework today. It is particularly evident that the fundamental principles of games are heavily utilized in strategies aimed at increasing user interaction (Erdem, 2019).

Gamification is defined as an approach that aims to make an experience more motivating, enjoyable, and interactive by using game-specific dynamics and mechanics outside the game context (Deterding et al., 2011). Elements such as collecting points, earning badges, leveling up, leaderboards, reward systems, and completing tasks are among the basic components of gamification. These elements enable behavioral guidance by triggering individuals' tendencies to compete, achieve, and be rewarded. This multi-layered structure of interaction and motivation elevates gamification beyond a simple entertainment element, transforming it into a strategic tool in marketing and brand communication.

In the context of marketing communication, gamification is widely used, especially in digital environments, to strengthen user interaction with brands. The Starbucks Rewards program effectively applies gamification mechanics by awarding users points with every purchase, strengthening the consumer's relationship with the brand on a continuous basis (Huotari & Hamari, 2017). The ability for users to access different rewards through the points they accumulate creates a structure that also encourages repeat purchasing behavior. Similarly, the Nike Run Club app increases loyalty to both the platform and the brand through badge and level systems that track running distances.

Research shows that gamification in marketing communication is not limited to creating entertainment; it also has a decisive impact on brand loyalty, user motivation, and customer experience (Hamari, Koivisto & Sarsa, 2014). Digital natives, such as Generation Z, respond more positively to interactive and personalized experiences than to traditional advertising formats. This trend has influenced brands to place gamification at the center of their marketing strategies. However, effective gamification design should not be limited to superficial rewards such as points and badges; it must also consider the psychological processes that fuel users' intrinsic motivation.

At this point, self-determination theory provides an important theoretical framework for explaining the motivational foundations of gamification. According to Deci and Ryan (2000), individuals' intrinsic motivation is shaped around three basic psychological needs: autonomy, competence, and relatedness. Badges, leaderboards, and reward systems used in gamification designs address these needs at different levels, enabling users to engage more deeply with the brand experience. For example, in the Nike Run Club app, users' ability to set personal goals strengthens their sense of competence, while social sharing and interaction features support their need for relatedness.

In addition to all this, flow theory argues that the balance between “ability” and “difficulty” must be maintained for individuals to have an optimal experience (Csikszentmihalyi, 1990). From a marketing communication perspective, this balance is established through goals designed in a way that neither overwhelms nor bores the user. Duolingo's leveled language learning system stands out as an example that increases both learning motivation and platform loyalty by keeping the user in a constant state of “flow.”

The relationship between gamification and media consumption can be evaluated within the framework of the Uses and Gratifications approach. According to this approach, individuals are motivated to use media to satisfy needs such as entertainment, information acquisition, and socialization (Katz, Blumler & Gurevitch, 1974). Gamification activates these motivations in a more visible and powerful way, extending the duration of users' interaction with the brand and deepening the experience. This motivational structure enables brands to establish more sustainable and interaction-based relationships with users.

Today, many brands apply gamification strategies in different sectors to increase customer loyalty. McDonald's Monopoly campaign created the possibility of winning big prizes by offering users Monopoly cards with every purchase, and this strategy led to significant increases in sales (Kim, 2018). Similarly, Sephora's "Beauty Insider" program offers special gifts and VIP access by awarding points per purchase; this structure strengthens users' emotional attachment to the brand.

Gamification is not limited to marketing communications; it is also widely used in different areas such as education and health. Duolingo's structure, supported by daily series, virtual currencies, and badges, encourages users to use the application regularly, while Fitbit motivates behavioral change with badges and social competition elements based on daily step goals (Lister et al., 2014).

However, critical approaches to gamification also occupy an important place in the literature. Bogost (2015) addresses gamification through the concept of "exploitationware," arguing that user behavior is manipulated and consumption is artificially encouraged. Similarly, Kim (2018) points out that gamification can raise ethical issues and lead users to excessive consumption. In this context, it is emphasized that gamification should be approached by brands not only as a tool to increase sales but also within the framework of long-term, sustainable, and ethical customer relationships.

TRANSFORMATION OF USER EXPERIENCE IN THE CONTEXT OF VOICE ASSISTANT TECHNOLOGIES

Voice assistants can be defined as digital systems that enable users to perform various tasks through voice commands, thanks to advances in artificial intelligence and natural language processing (NLP) technologies. Today, Amazon Alexa, Google Assistant, and Apple Siri are among the most widely used examples of voice assistants. These systems offer numerous functions through a single interface, such as obtaining information, listening to music, managing smart home devices, shopping, and establishing entertainment-focused interactions (Hoy, 2018). This multifaceted structure transforms voice assistants from mere technological products into digital interfaces that must be evaluated in terms of user experience and accessibility.

The level of interaction achieved by voice assistant technologies today is the result of a long technological development process. The origins of this process lie in the early speech recognition systems developed in the 1960s and 1970s. Due to their limited vocabularies and low accuracy rates, these systems were mostly usable in controlled laboratory environments. Nevertheless, they represented an important historical milestone in demonstrating that human-machine interaction could be designed around voice-based communication (Jurafsky & Martin, 2021).

The increased processing power of computers, the proliferation of mobile devices, and the strengthening of internet infrastructure in the 2000s made it possible for voice command technologies to reach a wider user base. Particularly after 2010, the integration of smartphones into everyday life and the development of cloud-based systems have been decisive in transforming voice assistants into practical and continuously used digital tools (Hoy, 2018; McTear, Callejas & Griol, 2016).

The most critical stage of this transformation has been driven by advances in artificial intelligence and natural language processing. Thanks to machine learning-based algorithms, voice assistants have evolved from systems that merely execute given commands into interactive interfaces capable of interpreting context, learning user habits, and providing personalized responses. This development has paved the way for voice assistants to be positioned as digital actors capable of engaging in dialogue with users, rather than passive tools for conveying information (Lopatovska & Williams, 2018).

From a user experience perspective, one of the most notable features of voice assistants is that they offer hands-free use and natural speech-based interaction. Users can access information or use a service without looking at a screen or performing any manual actions. This makes voice assistants tools that save time and simplify everyday life practices. In addition, user experience studies reveal that voice assistants also play an important role in terms of accessibility. Especially for visually impaired individuals and users with limited motor skills, these technologies are considered a critical interface that facilitates access to digital services (Pradhan, Mehta & Findlater, 2018).

The literature frequently emphasizes that personalized experience plays a decisive role in voice assistant usage (Luger & Sellen, 2016). Artificial intelligence algorithms analyze users' previous interactions to tailor suggestions and responses to individual preferences. For example, if a user frequently searches for recipes via Alexa, the system may make related sponsored content or products more visible. Such applications enable micro-targeting strategies in advertising and offer brands the opportunity to respond more directly to user needs (Shankar, 2018).

From this perspective, voice assistants are gaining a new dimension in terms of marketing and consumer behavior. The concept of voice commerce refers to a form of shopping where users can search for products, create shopping carts, and complete payment transactions solely through voice commands (Schweidel & Moe, 2019). This structure brings with it a market dynamic where shopping decisions are accelerated, more instant consumption behaviors emerge, and the relationship between brands and consumers takes on a more personal nature . However, this convenience and personalization also simultaneously raise ethical issues and data security debates.

When examining the limitations of voice assistant usage, it is evident that privacy and data security issues are decisive factors in users' cautious approach to these technologies. According to a study by Purington et al. (2017), approximately 45% of voice assistant users believe that the devices are constantly listening to them. Similarly, Lau, Zimmerman, and Schaub (2018) found that a significant proportion of users prefer to use voice assistants only in specific contexts due to the possibility of conversations being recorded and shared with third parties.

All these features transform voice assistants from merely functional technologies into a new user experience-centric touchpoint for brands. While voice assistant technologies offer important advantages such as speed, convenience, and personalization, data security and ethical debates directly affect users' perception of trust in these systems. From an advertising perspective, this situation creates new opportunities for more personal and direct brand interaction on the one hand, while on the other hand, it necessitates careful consideration of sensitivities regarding the protection of consumer privacy.

COMPARISON OF MAJOR VOICE ASSISTANT PLATFORMS IN TERMS OF STRUCTURE AND FUNCTIONALITY

Voice assistant technologies are among the applications of artificial intelligence-based human-computer interaction that have been integrated into everyday life most rapidly. These systems, which enable access to information, use of services, and performance of various tasks through voice commands, pave the way for new forms of interaction in the contexts of communication, marketing, and user experience (Ergül, 2025; Gelibolu, 2024). In this context, voice assistants stand out as interfaces that necessitate a rethinking of the relationship between users and technology in digital communication practices.

The main voice assistant platforms highlighted in studies are Amazon Alexa, Google Assistant, and Apple Siri. Although these platforms offer similar features in terms of basic functions, they differ significantly in terms of their technical infrastructure, ecosystem structure, and the opportunities they offer to developers. It is stated that these structural differences directly affect how voice assistants are used in digital marketing and advertising (Mohammadabbasi & Değermen, 2023; Şaylan, Taşkın & Abdulwahid, 2025).

, with its open developer ecosystem and "Skills" infrastructure, stands out as a platform that offers extensive opportunities for third-party applications and brand integrations. This flexible structure makes it relatively easy to design and implement gamified interactions; it allows for the integration of game elements such as quiz-based applications, task chains, and reward mechanisms into the environment. For this reason, Alexa is frequently cited in the literature as an example due to its structure, which is conducive to interaction-based and experience-focused advertising applications (Ergül, 2025).

Google Assistant, on the other hand, operates within an ecosystem integrated with Google's search engine, map services, and user data. This integrated structure provides significant advantages in terms of contextual suggestions and personalized information delivery, offering users a fast, context-sensitive experience. However, it is noted that it offers a more limited space for third-party developers to design gamified interactions compared to Amazon Alexa. This situation causes Google Assistant to stand out more for its information access and navigation functions rather than brand-centered gamification applications (Mohammadabbasi & Değermen, 2023).

Apple Siri, on the other hand, is positioned within a relatively closed ecosystem structure that focuses on privacy and data security. Apple's strict policies regarding the sharing of user data make Siri's advertising and gamification integrations more limited compared to other platforms. However, its provision of a trust-based user experience makes Siri a notable alternative platform, particularly in the context of ethical, privacy, and data security discussions (Gelibolu, 2024).

The comparison between these platforms reveals that the emphasis on Amazon Alexa examples in the study is not coincidental but a conscious methodological choice. Alexa's open ecosystem structure ensures that gamified advertising applications are more visible, developable, and analyzable from a technical and conceptual perspective. In contrast, Google Assistant and Apple Siri, which hold significant positions in terms of user numbers and daily usage, exhibit a more limited structure in terms of the technical capabilities they offer for brand-centric gamified advertising applications. Although these differences offer complementary perspectives on the future of voice assistant advertising for all three platforms, they indicate that Amazon Alexa provides a more favorable research ground for in-depth case studies.

The technical capabilities and ecosystem structures offered by voice assistant platforms differ significantly in terms of their contribution to gamified advertising applications. Studies examining the effects of voice-activated artificial intelligence applications on user interaction and communication dynamics indicate that the interaction-focused structure of these technologies brings new user behaviors in media and communication practices (Ergül, 2025). Similarly, research focusing on the effects of digital assistants on customer satisfaction and marketing performance reveals that voice assistants are becoming an increasingly important marketing tool for businesses (Mohammadabbasi & Değermen, 2023).

It is emphasized that in the adoption process of voice assistants, not only the technical infrastructure but also psychosocial factors such as the perception of innovation and user trust are decisive. How consumers evaluate these technologies in the context of shopping and everyday usage practices is largely associated with perceptions of trust and technology acceptance (Gelibolu, 2024). These findings necessitate that the use of voice assistants in marketing and advertising be considered within the framework of user attitudes and perceptions, along with technical capabilities.

In this context, the role of voice assistant platforms in advertising and interaction-focused applications should be evaluated within a holistic approach that considers the technical flexibility of the platforms, user behaviors, and the strategic preferences of businesses.

ADVERTISING APPLICATIONS AND INTERACTION-BASED APPROACHES IN VOICE ASSISTANT ENVIRONMENTS

Although voice assistants are still in the development phase in the field of advertising, they are emerging as a new communication medium that is gaining increasing attention due to their interaction potential. Unlike visual or written advertising formats, advertising messages in voice assistant environments are presented through dialogue with the user and within an interaction-based structure. For example, when a user requests a recipe from Amazon Alexa, the system may offer a sponsored brand suggestion or directly direct the user to purchase a related product. This structure allows advertising messages to become a natural part of everyday interaction, ensuring brand visibility without interrupting the user experience.

In recent years, gamification elements have become increasingly prominent in advertising applications conducted through voice assistants. Quiz-based applications developed on the Amazon Alexa platform, in particular, enable users to establish a fun and interactive relationship with specific brands. Users can earn points through correct answers, access various rewards, or obtain discount codes. For brands, such applications are considered strategic tools that not only increase user loyalty but also have the potential to generate data on user behavior. Similarly, audio advertising formats used on digital platforms such as Spotify encourage users to take active action; for example, they are encouraged to give voice commands to participate in a campaign. This contributes to the voice advertising experience taking on a more participatory and gamified structure (Güngör, 2022). These interaction-focused applications demonstrate that voice assistants have gained significant importance in recent years in terms of personalized and targeted advertising strategies.

The interactive structure offered by voice assistants also enables brands to take their personalized marketing strategies to a higher level. Through AI-based algorithms, users' past interactions are analyzed, and sponsored content can be delivered at more appropriate times and to more accurate target audiences based on the data obtained (Kaplan & Haenlein, 2019). For example, presenting a user who frequently searches for and interacts with sports products with personalized running recommendations related to the Nike brand via a voice assistant increases the perceived value of the advertisement and strengthens the bond between the consumer and the brand.

Another prominent feature of voice assistant advertising is that the interaction established between the brand and the user is relatively more natural and fluid. This finding is consistent with academic studies focusing on user perception (Lopatovska & Williams, 2018; Shankar, 2018). This situation allows advertising content to go beyond merely informative messages and create a holistic brand experience. However, concerns about privacy and data security may also cause users to develop a more cautious attitude towards such interactions (Luger & Sellen, 2016).

A large portion of the studies in the literature focus on the motivations for using voice assistants, user perceptions, and privacy issues (Hoy, 2018; Purington et al., 2017). In contrast, there appears to be a limited number of comprehensive and in-depth studies focusing on how gamification elements integrate with voice assistant advertising. This points to a significant research gap regarding studies that address voice assistant technologies and gamified advertising strategies together.

THE INTERSECTION OF GAMIFICATION AND VOICE ASSISTANT TECHNOLOGIES

Voice assistant technologies and gamification approaches stand out as two fundamental dynamics that complement each other in the transformation of digital advertising and marketing communication. AI-based voice assistants create new communication opportunities for brands thanks to their ability to interact with users through natural language and offer personalized recommendations; gamification transforms this interaction into a fun, motivating, and sustainable experience. The convergence of these two areas enables the development of innovative advertising formats that actively engage users in the process, moving them away from a passive listener role (Önder, 2021).

The dialogue-based structure offered by voice assistants allows for the interaction, feedback, and reward mechanisms that form the basis of gamification applications to be presented in a more natural flow. The inclusion of users in the system through voice commands is one of the most important elements that distinguishes the gamified advertising experience from classic digital advertising formats. Voice assistants move gamification beyond being merely an attention-grabbing tool and place it at the center of the user experience.

APPLICATION OF GAME MECHANICS IN VOICE ASSISTANT ENVIRONMENTS

Gamification in voice assistant environments is implemented by adapting game-specific design elements and mechanics to voice-based interaction processes, independent of the visual interface. In gamification literature, this approach is defined as the use of game design elements to increase user motivation and participation in non-game contexts (Deterding et al., 2011). Specifically for voice assistants, these mechanics aim to ensure the continuity of interaction with the brand by integrating them into users' daily routines. The main game mechanics that stand out in the literature and application examples are quizzes and knowledge contests, task-based progression systems, and random reward mechanisms.

Quizzes and knowledge contests stand out as one of the most common forms of gamification strategies implemented through voice assistants. In these applications, users are asked questions about the brand, product, or a specific theme; in exchange for correct answers, rewards such as points, digital badges, or discount coupons are offered. Voice applications (Alexa Skills) developed specifically for Amazon Alexa demonstrate that quiz-based gamification designs are effective in increasing user engagement (Bräuer & Mazarakis, 2022). For example, a competition with a "coffee knowledge" theme developed by a coffee brand allows users to win discount coupons in exchange for correct answers. Such applications allow users to establish a fun and interactive connection with the brand while also contributing to reinforcing brand knowledge.

Another gamification approach commonly used in voice assistants is task chains and level-up mechanisms. In these systems, users are assigned tasks that must be completed within specific time intervals; completing the tasks unlocks new levels or content. Voice assistants, especially in health and fitness-focused applications, support this mechanism by providing users with daily exercise reminders, motivational messages, and progress feedback. It is stated that such task-based gamification approaches applied in voice environments increase user motivation and positively affect long-term usage behavior (Bräuer, 2024). Regular completion of tasks by the user strengthens the motivation to achieve personal goals while transforming the interaction established with the brand into a continuous relationship.

Another important game mechanism used in voice assistant environments is surprise reward and random reinforcement systems. In this approach, users encounter unpredictable rewards after using certain voice commands or performing certain interactions. For example, a user who says "Alexa, recommend me a coffee" on certain days may receive a surprise discount coupon or digital reward. Gamification literature emphasizes that random rewards increase interaction frequency by keeping users' curiosity and anticipation alive (Hamari et al., 2014). This mechanism is considered an important motivational factor that encourages the repeated use of voice assistants.

These game mechanics should not be considered solely as entertainment-based applications. Research shows that gamified interactions increase brand awareness, extend the time users spend on the platform, and have a positive impact on brand loyalty (Teskeredzic et al., 2025). From this perspective, the intersection of voice assistants and gamification is considered a strategic area that enables brands to establish long-term and sustainable relationships with users ().

GAMIFICATION IN VOICE ASSISTANTS WITHIN THE FRAMEWORK OF FLOW THEORY AND THE USAGE-SATISFACTION APPROACH

Flow theory, as defined by Csikszentmihalyi (1990), is an optimal experience state in which an individual is intensely focused on an activity, their sense of time diminishes, and the activity itself becomes rewarding. This theoretical framework is among the approaches frequently used to explain user experience, particularly in digital and interactive environments. Structures that sustainably direct users' attention to the activity in digital media environments support the formation of the flow experience (Csikszentmihalyi, 1997).

Gamification elements used in voice assistant environments provide a fertile ground for flow to emerge by exposing users to tasks with increasing levels of difficulty. Task-based progression, instant feedback, and reward mechanisms, in particular, focus the user's attention on the voice interaction process. The balance established between the user's level of competence and the difficulty level of the tasks presented increases the sustainability of motivation, one of the fundamental components of flow theory, and supports the continuity of interaction. In this context, voice assistants have the potential to produce flow experiences through cognitive engagement, independent of visual stimuli (Bräuer, 2024).

The Uses and Gratifications Approach argues that individuals consciously use media tools to meet specific needs (Katz, Blumler & Gurevitch, 1974). In line with this approach, users select and use media content according to their own expectations and requirements rather than passively consuming it. Within this framework, voice assistants are considered interactive media tools that offer different types of satisfaction, such as acquiring information, entertainment, practicality, and simplifying daily life.

The integration of gamification elements into voice assistant technologies enhances these types of satisfaction and makes the user experience more meaningful. Through quizzes, tasks, and reward mechanisms, users not only obtain a functional output but also experience hedonic satisfactions such as fun, curiosity, and a sense of achievement. When evaluated within the Uses and Gratifications Approach, this explains why users engage in longer and more repetitive interactions with voice assistants (Sundar & Limperos, 2013).

Although Flow Theory provides a powerful theoretical framework for explaining the voice assistant experience, it may be misleading to assume that every user interaction creates a seamless "flow" experience. Misinterpretation of voice commands, technical glitches, or contextual mismatches can disrupt the flow state. Therefore, rather than evaluating the voice assistant experience solely from a flow perspective, it is necessary to adopt a multidimensional approach that also considers users' expectations and satisfaction-seeking behaviors.

When Flow Theory and the Uses-Satisfactions Approach are considered together, it is seen that gamification in voice assistants provides both hedonic and functional satisfaction. While users enjoy a fun, engaging, and flow-like experience, they also gain practical benefits. This dual structure increases the likelihood of users interacting with voice assistants repeatedly and stands out as an important element that supports the continuity of the relationship established with users from the perspective of brands.

GAMIFICATION STRATEGIES THAT ENHANCE BRAND ENGAGEMENT IN VOICE ASSISTANT-BASED CAMPAIGNS

Gamification strategies used in voice assistant-based advertising and marketing campaigns are designed by adapting game-specific mechanics to the marketing communication context in order to increase user engagement. Gamification is gaining increasing importance in digital marketing as a motivational tool that directs users towards specific behaviors. In this context, gamified advertising applications deepen the interaction established with the brand by transforming the user from a passive recipient to an active participant (Huotari & Hamari, 2017).

Personalized tasks are at the heart of these strategies. Tasks based on users' past interactions, preferences, and behavioral data ensure that the experience is tailored to the individual and strengthen participation motivation. Digital marketing literature reveals that personalized gamification applications have positive effects on user participation and interaction time (Rashid & Zeebaree, 2025). Adapting tasks offered through voice assistants to user habits allows advertising messages to be incorporated into the experience in a more natural and sustainable way.

Another prominent element in gamified campaigns is social competition and sharing mechanisms. The ability for users to share their points, badges, or achievements on social media platforms increases individual motivation and expands brand visibility. Various studies emphasize that gamification applications with a strong social interaction dimension have a meaningful impact on brand awareness and user loyalty (Naumovska & Petrusevska, 2025).

However, limited-time campaigns are another strategy frequently used in the context of gamification advertising. Tasks or rewards limited to a specific period create a sense of urgency in users, encouraging rapid participation. These time-pressure-based mechanisms are considered effective tools for increasing interaction intensity in the short term (Rashid & Zeebaree, 2025).

Storytelling-based gamification strategies, on the other hand, transform users from passive message recipients into active subjects of the narrative. Interactive stories delivered through voice assistants allow users' decisions to influence the course of the narrative, making the experience more personal, emotional, and memorable. Narrative-based interactions have been found to have positive effects on brand perception and user loyalty, particularly in experience-oriented industries (Lundqvist et al., 2012). Such applications, used in industries such as automotive and travel, contribute to users forming deeper and more meaningful connections with the brand.

Gamification strategies applied in voice assistant-based advertising and marketing campaigns strengthen the relationship between the user and the brand through mechanics such as personalized tasks, social sharing, time-limited interactions, and storytelling. These strategies are not only aimed at attracting short-term attention; they also enable users to establish a sustainable and experience-based relationship with the brand.

PSYCHOLOGICAL EFFECTS AND THE MOTIVATION DIMENSION

Gamification applications in voice assistants support user motivation in a multidimensional way within the framework of self-determination theory (Deci & Ryan, 1985). Users being able to determine when and how they interact strengthens their sense of autonomy. Completing tasks and earning points or badges increases the perception of competence, creating a sense of achievement. Elements of social competition and sharing contribute to establishing bonds between users by meeting the need for relatedness.

In addition, the dopamine effect triggered by reward mechanisms has the potential to develop habits in user behavior. This allows brands to increase repeat engagement rates while also increasing the strategic importance of gamification.

SECTORAL USES OF GAMIFICATION APPLICATIONS THROUGH VOICE ASSISTANTS

Gamification applications designed through voice assistants are used in various forms across different sectors in today's digital environments. In the retail sector, the integration of voice assistants with marketing has become part of gamification strategies that increase user participation by offering customers points, badges, or similar rewards for interacting with products. Research shows that such voice interactions positively influence users' purchasing behavior and interaction with the brand (Flavián et al., 2023).

In the food and beverage sector, reward mechanisms integrated into voice ordering processes make the user's purchasing experience more interactive. When voice assistants are associated with gamification components such as post-order feedback or task completion, in addition to ordering, they can increase users' desire to reuse them. This approach transforms voice interaction from merely a functional shopping tool into an interactive experience (Acikgoz et al., 2023).

In the field of education, voice assistants are used with gamification components, particularly in foreign language learning, pronunciation exercises, and question-and-answer-based interactions. In such voice-based educational applications, interactive voice feedback, leveling, and task completion processes are identified as important factors that increase participation in learning processes (Bräuer, 2024). In educational applications offered through voice assistants, users encounter mechanics such as answering questions, earning points, or tracking progress, which strengthen learning motivation and participation.

Health and fitness applications are also one of the areas that integrate gamification components with voice assistants. Health and fitness applications developed for smart assistants allow users to track their exercises, monitor their daily goals, or receive health-related educational content through voice commands. A content scan of 309 different voice assistant-based health and fitness applications shows that these applications span categories such as health education, exercise, and fitness tracking (Chung et al., 2018). These studies reveal that voice assistants can function not only as providers of information but also as interactive tools for changing individuals' healthy lifestyle behaviors.

These application examples demonstrate that voice assistants do not merely provide information but transform the user experience into an interactive platform. The potential of digital gamification approaches to increase user engagement has also been particularly emphasized in marketing and digital platform studies (Yücel, 2023; Duğan, 2022).

GAMIFICATION IN VOICE ASSISTANTS FROM THE PERSPECTIVE OF BEHAVIORAL ECONOMICS AND MOTIVATION THEORY

The behavioral economics approach argues that individuals do not always behave completely rationally in their decision-making processes; they are guided by cognitive biases, emotional responses, and contextual factors (Thaler & Sunstein, 2008). From this perspective, gamification applications used in voice assistants have the potential to guide user behavior through "gentle nudges" without directly coercing them. Specifically, reward-focused, time-limited, or progress-emphasizing voice prompts can trigger behavioral tendencies such as fear of missing out and loss aversion in users, encouraging quick decision-making processes (Lades & Delaney, 2022).

When evaluated from the perspective of nudge theory, the default options, suggestion patterns, and directive statements offered by voice assistants stand out as important elements that shape the user's choice architecture. Highlighting specific goals in voice interactions, using linguistic structures that invite user participation, or presenting certain behaviors as "recommended options" are considered effective tools that indirectly guide decision-making processes (Caraban et al., 2019). Such micro-guidance has the capacity to create behavioral change without forcing user awareness.

Gamification in voice assistants is considered not only as a design approach that enhances interaction and user experience, but also as a strategic communication practice that structures decision-making processes. Rewards, progress indicators, and feedback provided through gamification align with the nudging mechanisms highlighted in behavioral economics literature, making voice assistants an effective interface for shaping user preferences (Caraban et al., 2019).

SYSTEM 1 AND SYSTEM 2 PROCESSES IN VOICE INTERACTION

Daniel Kahneman's System 1 and System 2 model of decision-making processes reveals that individuals' responses to stimuli encountered in daily life cannot be explained by a single, homogeneous cognitive mechanism (Kahneman, 2011). According to this model, System 1 represents a form of thinking that is fast, automatic, intuitive, and requires low cognitive effort, while System 2 refers to decision-making processes that are slower, conscious, analytical, and based on rational evaluations. Kahneman emphasizes that a large portion of individuals' daily decisions are made through System 1, while System 2 typically comes into play in situations that require attention, time, and cognitive resources.

Voice assistant technologies offer a largely System 1-focused cognitive experience thanks to the natural language-based and instantaneous interaction structure they establish with users. Unlike visual interfaces, voice assistants create a form of communication that expects quick responses from the user, shortens decision-making time, and encourages intuitive responses. The user's ability to interact with a short, everyday voice command without looking at the screen leads to the automation of the decision-making process and, in most cases, the conscious evaluation stage taking a back seat (Luger & Sellen, 2016).

The integration of gamification elements into voice assistants further strengthens this System 1-dominated interaction structure. For example, a voice assistant suggesting to the user, "You can earn extra points by participating in today's coffee quiz. Would you like to start?" triggers a quick and intuitive decision-making process. Such statements prompt the user to act based on the expectation of immediate reward and motivation for entertainment rather than directing them to perform a rational cost-benefit analysis. In this respect, gamification's logic of rapid feedback, rewards, and progress creates an experience that aligns with the way System 1 operates (Hamari, Koivisto & Sarsa, 2014).

Expectation of reward and entertainment elements are among the key factors contributing to System 1 becoming dominant in the context of voice interaction. While the user acts on the appeal of potential gain, they may not feel the need to evaluate the long-term consequences of their behavior or alternative options. This situation shows that gamified tasks offered through voice assistants have the potential to direct users toward certain behavior patterns without engaging them in a detailed thought process (Laran, Dalton & Andrade, 2011). However, it would be incorrect to say that these interactions have the same level of impact on all users; individuals with high digital literacy, in particular, are able to evaluate these prompts more consciously.

Nevertheless, it is not possible to say that voice assistant interactions completely bypass System 2. In situations involving higher risk, such as privacy, data security, or spending decisions, users' analytical thinking processes are seen to be reactivated. However, when it comes to everyday interactions, small rewards, and entertainment-focused tasks, voice assistants largely create a System 1-based decision-making environment. In this respect, Kahneman's model provides a powerful theoretical framework for explaining the effects of voice assistants and gamified advertising applications on user behavior. If the interaction is repeated or the tasks become more complex, it is more likely that users will switch to a more solution-oriented evaluation process, engaging System 2.

GAMIFICATION IN VOICE ASSISTANTS IN THE CONTEXT OF EXPECTANCY THEORY AND REWARD PERCEPTION

The Expectancy Theory developed by Kahneman and Tversky (1979) reveals that individuals do not evaluate gains and losses symmetrically in their decision-making processes, and that the psychological impact of losses is felt more strongly than that of gains. This approach emphasizes that individuals act based on perceived risk and emotional responses rather than rational expectations. In digital marketing applications, and particularly in voice assistant-based gamification strategies, this theoretical framework provides an important explanatory basis for understanding user behavior (Kahneman & Tversky, 1979).

In gamified interactions delivered through voice assistants, the possibility of losing a reward has become one of the key factors determining user motivation, just as much as winning a reward. For example, sending a message to the user such as "If you don't complete today's task, you will miss out on an extra 50 points" directs behavior by emphasizing potential loss rather than the promise of gain. This can be considered a direct reflection of the loss aversion principle of Expectancy Theory in the voice interaction environment (Peng, 2025).

Similarly, messages emphasizing limited access, such as "Special reward for the first 100 users," reinforce the perception of scarcity, causing users to make quick and intuitive decisions. Presenting reward mechanisms in an ambiguous manner, i.e., not providing the user with clear information about the content or size of the reward, increases individuals' risk-taking tendencies. Such surprise reward structures align with the Expectancy Theory's explanation of individual behavior under conditions of uncertainty. Therefore, gamification in voice assistants is not merely an entertainment-oriented design choice; it emerges as a strategic communication practice that consciously guides user behavior (Loukopoulou, 2025).

Such surprise reward structures and uncertainty-focused gamification elements are not merely design options for entertainment purposes. On the contrary, they can be considered behavioral guidance strategies that align with the key principles of Expectancy Theory explaining human behavior. These strategies shape the motivations of voice assistant users based on the avoidance of loss and the psychological weight given to uncertain situations; thus, gamification organizes interaction as a strategic communication element and guides user behavior (McDermott, 2024).

CASE STUDIES AND APPLICATION EXAMPLES

Although the integration of voice assistants and gamification is still in its developmental stage in the field of digital marketing, some brands have begun to implement noteworthy applications in this area. This section examines existing applications using the examples of Amazon Alexa, Starbucks, and Nike; it also discusses the potential applications of voice assistant-based gamification through a conceptual example designed specifically for Spotify.

Amazon Alexa: Quiz-Based Interaction Model

Amazon offers brands the opportunity to provide gamified interactions through its "Skills" infrastructure developed on the Alexa platform. In these quiz-based applications, users earn points by answering questions posed by the voice assistant and receive rewards such as discount coupons when they reach certain thresholds. This interaction model keeps user motivation constantly alive through task completion, point earning, and surprise reward mechanics.

Such applications increase the time users spend with Alexa while also strengthening the brand's mental accessibility. The literature also emphasizes that points and reward-based gamification mechanics increase user motivation and interaction levels (Akıllıbaş & Ceylan, 2020; Özkan & Samur, 2017).

Starbucks: Voice Assistant-Supported Loyalty Experience

Starbucks' Alexa-integrated voice ordering system demonstrates that voice assistants can go beyond being merely functional convenience tools and become a component of experience-focused marketing strategies. This structure becomes more meaningful when evaluated in conjunction with the gamification elements offered under the Starbucks Rewards program. Digital badges, limited-time campaigns, and reward-based interaction mechanisms encourage users to engage regularly with the brand ecosystem. As emphasized in gamification literature, time-limited rewards and goal-oriented interactions increase user motivation and transform the experience into a continuous structure (Deterding et al., 2011; Hamari, Koivisto & Sarsa, 2014). In practice, the voice ordering process evolves from being merely a transactional convenience into an interactive and emotional relationship with the brand.

This approach points to the potential of gamification to create habits and develop brand loyalty. Indeed, marketing literature frequently mentions that gamified loyalty programs increase repeat usage behavior and consumer loyalty (Demir & Gök Demir, 2020).

Nike: Personalized Tasks and Flow Experience

In the Nike Run Club example, gamification is used to create a deeper and more long-term user experience. Task chains determined based on the user's past performance, progressive goals, and badge systems support both the perception of competence and motivation. The increasing difficulty of tasks enables the "flow" experience in the context of Flow Theory, while the emphasis on reward loss when tasks are missed creates behavioral pressure through loss avoidance.

Such gamification structures extend the relationship between the user and the brand beyond short-term interactions, creating a more sustainable foundation for loyalty. Previous studies have also shown that task-based gamification applications strengthen user participation and emotional attachment (Yıldız & Demir, 2023).

Spotify Voice Challenge: A Conceptual Application Example

The Spotify Voice Challenge example is not analyzed as an existing application within the scope of this study; rather, it is approached as a conceptual scenario designed to demonstrate how voice assistants and gamification can be integrated into entertainment-based digital platforms. This scenario was created by the author of this study as a conceptual thought experiment based on gamification and voice interaction practices defined in the literature. This model, based on users guessing songs, earning points, and accessing premium benefits through voice commands, reveals how gamification can guide user behavior through dopamine-based pleasure and reward expectations. Furthermore, it is crucial to note that the effects of such an application on users may yield different results under real conditions and must be supported by experimental data.

These types of entertainment-focused gamification applications extend the time users spend on the platform and support conversion goals such as premium membership. The literature also indicates that reward- and entertainment-based gamification strategies positively affect user engagement and purchase intent (Yıldız & Demir, 2023).

Interpreting Theoretical Frameworks in Case Studies

The effectiveness of gamification-based marketing applications conducted through voice assistants is not limited to technical infrastructure and interaction design. The ability of such applications to create a lasting impact on users also depends on their relationship with psychological motivation processes and media usage practices. Based on this, the cases examined were evaluated within the framework of the theoretical approaches discussed in the previous sections; the effects of gamification mechanics on the user experience were interpreted based on theoretical foundations.

When evaluated within the context of Flow Theory, quiz-based gamification applications offered through Amazon Alexa exhibit a structure that keeps the user in constant interaction with progressively increasing levels of difficulty. The flow experience, as defined by Csikszentmihalyi (1990), refers to a state in which the individual is intensely focused on the activity they are performing and their perception of time is diminished. The quizzes offered through Alexa combine elements of competition and reward, enabling users to enter this flow state. However, from the perspective of the Uses and Gratifications Approach, it is seen that these applications offer not only entertainment but also different types of gratification, such as acquiring knowledge, experiencing a sense of achievement, and winning rewards (Katz, Blumler & Gurevitch, 1974). Thus, users can satisfy multiple needs within a single interaction.

In the Starbucks example, gamification strategies are seen to be more directly related to the processes of guiding user behavior and supporting intrinsic motivation. The fact that interactions offered through the voice assistant are conveyed to the user with non-coercive, suggestive statements points to light nudging strategies that can be evaluated within the framework of Nudge Theory (Thaler & Sunstein, 2008). This approach aims to guide users toward certain behavior patterns without exposing them to overt coercion, while preserving their perception of free choice. However, reward-based interactions, daily goals, and point-earning mechanisms, when considered within the framework of Self-Determination Theory, support intrinsic motivation by offering the user a sense of autonomy, competence, and achievement (Deci & Ryan, 1985). This shows that Starbucks positions its voice assistant-based gamification applications not only to generate instant interactions but also to transform user habits into continuous experiences.

In the Nike Run Club example, gamification is structured through frameworks that aim to create a longer-term user experience. When evaluated within the Flow Theory, the task chains and progressive goals offered to users create a flow experience that supports the sustainability of motivation. In addition, the emphasis on reward loss if tasks are not completed activates the loss aversion principle of Prospect Theory (Kahneman & Tversky, 1979). The statement "you lose if you don't complete it" rather than "you win if you complete today's task" more strongly directs user behavior. From this perspective, the Nike example demonstrates that gamification offers a comprehensive strategy that uses both hedonic and behavioral motivation elements together.

The conceptual example developed for Spotify, on the other hand, presents an interaction model that is more entertainment-focused and based on quick decision-making processes. When evaluated within the framework of Kahneman's System 1–System 2 model (), the gamified structure based on song prediction directs the user towards an intuitive and automatic decision-making process (Kahneman, 2011). The user is expected to respond without thinking for a short time, which activates System 1's fast and emotional decision-making mechanism. At the same time, such interactions enhance hedonistic satisfaction by highlighting the entertainment and pleasure aspects of the music listening experience. This demonstrates that gamification can create user loyalty not only through reward acquisition but also through motivations such as enjoyment and entertainment.

Overall, the case studies analyzed suggest that gamification in voice assistants cannot be limited to a temporary marketing approach. On the contrary, these applications emerge as multi-layered strategies built on psychological processes that guide user behavior, motivation theories, and media usage habits. In this regard, voice assistant-based gamification offers a new generation approach to marketing communication that centers human behavior.

FUTURE RESEARCH DIRECTIONS

This study aimed to discuss attention economy, user experience, and behavioral guidance concepts within a holistic framework by examining new-generation product placement applications on digital platforms from a sensory marketing perspective. The findings show that advertising strategies combining gamification, artificial intelligence, and sensory stimuli offer a structure that increases user engagement and enables a deeper connection between the brand and the consumer (Esgin, 2022). However, the rapidly changing nature of digital media indicates that research in this field should not be limited to singular and static approaches.

The fact that this study is primarily based on a conceptual framework provides an important starting point for future research. The use of empirical methods such as experimental designs, content analyses, and neuromarketing techniques in future studies will contribute to revealing the effects of sensory stimuli on consumer behavior in a more concrete and measurable way. In particular, supporting the role of sensory elements such as color, sound, rhythm, and movement in product placement strategies with scientific data has the potential to fill an important gap in the literature.

On the other hand, it should be noted that digital content consumption does not exhibit a homogeneous structure. Variables such as age, generation, cultural background, digital literacy level, and media usage habits directly affect advertising perception and interaction patterns. Studies that comparatively examine the sensory attention patterns of Generation Z and Generation Alpha and their responses to gamified advertising experiences are expected to make important contributions to future research.

The integration of gamification strategies with voice assistants holds strong potential for the future of marketing communications (Gelibolu, 2024). Thanks to AI-powered personalization mechanisms, it appears possible to develop dynamic task structures and reward systems based on user history and preferences. In addition, the integration of augmented reality applications with voice interaction may pave the way for new gamified advertising scenarios, ranging from in-store campaigns to digital experience areas. The proliferation of voice loyalty programs and the use of voice interaction in metaverse environments in conjunction with gamification are also among the trends expected to emerge in the future.

However, these technological developments inevitably bring ethical and privacy debates to the forefront (Furtın Kaya & Yıldız, 2025). The heavy reliance on data usage in AI-based personalization strategies necessitates a more comprehensive examination of issues such as advertising ethics, user consent, and perceptual steering. Future studies examining these issues not only through user perception but also in the context of content creators, brand strategists, and platform policies will contribute to a more holistic understanding of the digital advertising ecosystem.

Sensory marketing, gamification, and AI-powered advertising applications on digital platforms are constantly evolving alongside technological innovations, user psychology, and cultural transformations. Interdisciplinary studies conducted at the intersection of these fields have the capacity to make unique contributions to the advertising and marketing communications literature in terms of both theoretical depth and application potential.

CONCLUSION

The digital marketing environment faces structural problems such as decreasing user attention, increasing ad blindness, and rising content density. Under these conditions, it has become inevitable for brands to turn to interaction-focused and experience-based strategies in order to establish more meaningful and lasting relationships with their target audiences. This study reveals that the convergence of voice assistants and gamification strategies offers a significant area of transformation that addresses this need in the field of advertising.

As the research shows, voice assistants are evolving beyond being mere digital tools for conveying information, transforming into brand experience platforms through the natural and continuous dialogues they establish with users. Integrating gamification elements into this experience increases user motivation, supports the establishment of an emotional connection with the brand, and ensures continuity of interaction. This demonstrates that advertising has evolved from a passive message delivery process into an experience area based on user participation.

From a theoretical perspective, gamification applications in voice assistants support users' optimal experience and intrinsic motivation levels within the framework of Flow Theory and Self-Determination Theory. At the same time, within the context of the Nudging Theory and Expectancy Theory, it is seen that user behaviors can be subtly and often imperceptibly guided. These findings reveal that advertising is no longer just a field based on producing persuasive messages, but requires strategic designs that are compatible with behavioral psychology.

From a sectoral perspective, gamified advertising based on voice assistants offers brands significant opportunities for personalization and differentiation. These strategies are expected to be particularly effective for user groups that are more open to interactive experiences, such as Generation Z and digital natives. However, if users' sensitivities regarding privacy and data security are ignored, the sustainability of these applications may be at risk. Therefore, gamification designs based on ethical principles, transparency, and user-centricity are expected to be a fundamental success criterion for brands in the future.

Overall, this study reveals that the intersection of voice assistants and gamification is one of the critical areas shaping the future of digital advertising. In addition to its conceptual contributions to the academic literature, it offers applicable examples and strategic insights for marketing professionals. Future empirical studies are expected to further deepen this field by examining users' responses to gamified voice advertising experiences in different cultural contexts.

REFERENCES

Acikgoz, F., Perez-Vega, R., Okumus, F., & Stylos, N. (2023). Consumer engagement with AI-powered voice assistants: A behavioral reasoning perspective. *Psychology and Marketing*, *40*(11), 1–18. DOI: 10.1002/mar.21873

Akıllıbaş, E., & Ceylan, K. E. (2020). Oyunlaştırmanın Pazarlamadaki Gücü. *Anasay*, *14*(14), 43–80. DOI: 10.33404/anasay.755465

Bogost, I. (2015). Why gamification is bullshit. In Walz, S. P., & Deterding, S. (Eds.), *The gameful world: Approaches, issues, applications* (pp. 65–79). MIT Press. DOI: 10.7551/mitpress/9788.003.0005

Bolat, N. (2023). Dijital Oyunlarda Kültürel Görsel Kodlarla Kültürün Yeniden Üretimi: Uruz Er Kişinin Dönüşü. *Middle Black Sea Journal of Communication Studies*, *8*(2), 165–178. DOI: 10.56202/mbsjcs.1361429

Bräuer. Paula. (2024). Audio-Gamification: How Gamification Can Improve the Use of Intelligent Virtual Assistants. DOI: 10.13140/RG.2.2.14811.17445

Bräuer, P., & Mazarakis, A. (2022). "Alexa, can we design gamification without a screen?" - Implementing cooperative and competitive audio-gamification for intelligent virtual assistants. *Computers in Human Behavior*, *135*, 107362. DOI: 10.1016/j.chb.2022.107362

Caraban, A., Karapanos, E., Gonçalves, D., & Campos, P. (2019). *23 ways to nudge: A review of technology-mediated nudging in human–computer interaction*. In *Proceedings of the 2019 CHI Conference on Human Factors in Computing Systems* (CHI '19) (Paper 503, pp. 1–15). Association for Computing Machinery. https://doi.org/DOI: 10.1145/3290605.3300733

Chung, A. E., Griffin, A. C., Selezneva, D., & Gotz, D. (2018, September 24). Health and Fitness Apps for Hands-Free Voice-Activated Assistants: Content Analysis. *JMIR mHealth and uHealth*, *6*(9), e174. DOI: 10.2196/mhealth.9705 PMID: 30249581

Csikszentmihalyi, M. (1990). *Flow: The psychology of optimal experience*. Harper & Row.

Deci, E. L., & Ryan, R. M. (2000). Self-determination theory and the facilitation of intrinsic motivation, social development, and well-being. *The American Psychologist*, *55*(1), 68–78. DOI: 10.1037/0003-066X.55.1.68 PMID: 11392867

Demir, M. Ö., & Gök Demir, Z. (2020). Gamification Characteristics' Effects On Brand Loyalty. *Yaşar Üniversitesi E-Dergisi, 15*(58), 270–287. DOI: 10.19168/jyasar.558862

Deterding, S., Dixon, D., Khaled, R., & Nacke, L. (2011, September). From game design elements to gamefulness: Defining "gamification". In *Proceedings of the 15th International Academic MindTrek Conference: Envisioning Future Media Environments* (pp. 9–15). ACM. DOI: 10.1145/2181037.2181040

Duğan, Ö. (2022). Dijital Çağda Öğrenme Aracı Olarak Oyunlaştırmanın Sağlık Okuryazarlığı Üzerindeki Rolü. *TRT Akademi, 7*(14), 262–285. DOI: 10.37679/trta.960815

Erdem, M. N. (2019). Dijital Oyunlarda Şiddetin Estetiği: League of Legends Oyunu Üzerine Bir İnceleme. *Middle Black Sea Journal of Communication Studies, 4*(2), 115–139.

Ergül, N. (2025). Voice-Activated AI and The Evolution of Communication Etiquette. *Intermedia International E-journal, 12*(22), 266–282. DOI: 10.56133/intermedia.1614189

Esgin, Y. (2022). "Oyunlaştırmada Hedeflenen Etki Düzeylerinin Pazarlama İletişimi Bağlamında Kullanımı Üzerine Bir İnceleme". *İstanbul Arel Üniversitesi İletişim Çalışmaları Dergisi*, 10(21), pp. 113-135.

Flavián, C., Akdim, K., & Casaló, L. V. (2023). Effects of voice assistant recommendations on consumer behavior. *Psychology and Marketing, 40*(2), 328–346. DOI: 10.1002/mar.21765

Furtın Kaya, E., & Yıldız, S. (2025). "Reklam Profesyonellerinin Gözünden Veriye Dayalı Reklamcılığın Bugünü ve Geleceği". *İletişim Kuram ve Araştırma Dergisi*, (71), pp. 153-179. DOI: 10.47998/ikad.1755301

Gelibolu, M. (2024). "Yapay Zekâ Temelli Sesli Asistanların Alışveriş Amaçlı Kullanma Niyetinde Yenilikçilik ve Algılanan Güvenin Etkisi", İşletme Araştırmaları Dergisi, 16 (4), pp. 2383-2398.

Güngör, A. (2022). Oyunlaştırma ve Oyun İçerikli Reklamlarda İllüstrasyonun Etkisi. *Art-e Sanat Dergisi, 15*(29), 437–467. DOI: 10.21602/sduarte.1080446

Hamari, J., Koivisto, J., & Sarsa, H. (2014). "Does gamification work? – A literature review of empirical studies on gamification". *Proceedings of the 47th Hawaii International Conference on System Sciences*, pp. 3025–3034. DOI: 10.1109/HICSS.2014.377

Hoy, M. B. (2018). Alexa, Siri, Cortana, and more: An introduction to voice assistants. *Medical Reference Services Quarterly*, *37*(1), 81–88. DOI: 10.1080/02763869.2018.1404391 PMID: 29327988

Huotari, K., & Hamari, J. (2017). A definition for gamification: Anchoring gamification in the service marketing literatüre. *Electronic Markets*, *27*(1), 21–31. DOI: 10.1007/s12525-015-0212-z

Jurafsky, D., & Martin, J. H. (2021). Speech and language processing (3rd ed.). Draft version. Stanford University.

Kahneman, D. (2011). *Thinking, fast and slow*. Farrar, Straus and Giroux.

Kahneman, D., & Tversky, A. (1979). Prospect theory: An analysis of decision under risk. *Econometrica*, *47*(2), 263–291. DOI: 10.2307/1914185

Kaplan, A., & Haenlein, M. (2019). Siri, Siri, in my hand: Who's the fairest in the land? On the interpretations, illustrations, and implications of artificial intelligence. *Business Horizons*, *62*(1), 15–25. DOI: 10.1016/j.bushor.2018.08.004

Katz, E., Blumler, J. G., & Gurevitch, M. (1974). Utilization of mass communication by the individual. In Blumler, J. G., & Katz, E. (Eds.), *The uses of mass communications: Current perspectives on gratifications research* (pp. 19–32). Sage.

Katz, E., Blumler, J. G., & Gurevitch, M. (1974). Uses and gratifications research. *Public Opinion Quarterly*, *37*(4), 509–523. DOI: 10.1086/268109

Kim, T. W. (2018). Gamification ethics: Exploitation and manipulation. *Computers in Human Behavior*, *80*, 246–254. DOI: 10.1016/j.chb.2017.11.022

Lades, L., & Delaney, L. (2022). Nudge FORGOOD. *Behavioural Public Policy*, *6*(1), 75–94. DOI: 10.1017/bpp.2019.53

Laran, J., Dalton, A. N., & Andrade, E. B. (2011). The Curious Case of Behavioral Backlash: Why Brands Produce Priming Effects and Slogans Produce Reverse Priming Effects. *The Journal of Consumer Research*, *37*(6), 999–1014. DOI: 10.1086/656577

Lau, J., Zimmerman, B., & Schaub, F. (2018). "Alexa, are you listening? Privacy perceptions, concerns and privacy-seeking behaviors with smart speakers". Proceedings of the ACM on Human-Computer Interaction, 2(CSCW), pp. 1–31. DOI: 10.1145/3274371

Lister, C., West, J. H., Cannon, B., Sax, T., & Brodegard, D. (2014). Just a fad? Gamification in health and fitness apps. *JMIR Serious Games*, *2*(2), e9. DOI: 10.2196/games.3413 PMID: 25654660

Lopatovska, I., & Williams, H. (2018). "Personification of the Amazon Alexa: BFF or a mindless companion". *Proceedings of the 2018 Conference on Human Information Interaction & Retrieval*, pp. 265–268. DOI: 10.1145/3176349.3176868

Loukopoulou, E. C. (2025). "Prospect Theory and Loss Aversion: A Cognitive Perspective on Economic Behavior". Doi:DOI: 10.17605/OSF.IO/J8QFA

Luger, E., & Sellen, A. (2016). "Like having a really bad PA: The gulf between user expectation and experience of conversational agents". *Proceedings of the 2016 CHI Conference on Human Factors in Computing Systems*, pp. 5286–5297. DOI: 10.1145/2858036.2858288

Lundqvist, A., Liljander, V., Gummerus, J. & van Riel, A. (2012). "The impact of storytelling on the consumer brand experience: The case of a firm-originated story". *Journal of Brand Management,* 20, pp. 283–297 (2013). DOI: 10.1057/bm.2012.15

McDermott, R. (2024). "Prospect Theory". *Encyclopedia Britannica.* https://www.britannica.com/topic/prospect-theory

McTear, M., Callejas, Z., & Griol, D. (2016). *The conversational interface: Talking to smart devices.* Springer., DOI: 10.1007/978-3-319-32967-3

Mohammadabbasi, M., & Değermen, A. (2023). "Dijital Asistanların Müşteri Memnuniyeti Üzerindeki Etkisi: Yapay Zekâ Uygulamaları Türkiye Örneği". *1. Uluslararası Sosyal ve Ekonomik Çalışmalar Dergisi, 4*(2), 225–248. DOI: 10.62001/gsijses.1371527

Naumovska, L., & Petrusevska, G. (2025). Gamification in Marketing: Analyses of the Impact Beyond Play and Fun. *European Journal of Behavioral Sciences, 8*(2), 45–57. DOI: 10.33422/ejbs.v8i2.1585

Önder, B. A. (2021). "Reklam Kampanyalarında Etkileşimli İletişimin Silahı: Oyunlaştırma". *İstanbul Aydın Üniversitesi Sosyal Bilimler Dergisi*, 13(1), pp. 1-40.

Özkan, Z., & Samur, Y. (2017). Oyunlaştırma Yönteminin Öğrencilerin Motivasyonları Üzerine Etkisi. *Ege Eğitim Dergisi, 18*(2), 857–886. DOI: 10.12984/egeefd.314801

Peng, K. (2025). The Impact of Loss Aversion on Decision-Making in Marketing and Financial Markets. *Advances in Economics, Management and Political Sciences, 149*(1), 157–163. DOI: 10.54254/2754-1169/2024.19247

Pradhan, A., Mehta, K., & Findlater, L. (2018). "Accessibility came by accident: Use of voice-controlled intelligent personal assistants by people with disabilities". *Proceedings of the 2018 CHI Conference on Human Factors in Computing Systems*, pp. 1–13. DOI: 10.1145/3173574.3174033

Purington, A., Taft, J. G., Sannon, S., Bazarova, N. N., & Taylor, S. H. (2017). "Alexa is my new BFF": Social roles, user satisfaction, and personification of the Amazon Echo. Proceedings of the 2017 CHI Conference Extended Abstracts on Human Factors in Computing Systems, pp. 2853–2859. DOI: 10.1145/3027063.3053246

Saber Rashid, N., & Zeebaree, R. M., S. (2025). Gamification in digital marketing for e-commerce: A review of strategies to boost engagement and sales. *International Journal of Scientific World, 11*(1), 95–103. DOI: 10.14419/bfmn7r29

Şaylan, O., Taşkın, E., & Abdulwahid, O. I. A. (2025). Yapay Zekanın Dijital Pazarlama Stratejileri Üzerindeki Etkisi: Kavramsal Bir Çalışma. *Uluslararası Sosyal ve Ekonomik Çalışmalar Dergisi*, *6*(1), 350–367. DOI: 10.62001/gsijses.1687324

Schweidel, D. A., & Moe, W. W. (2019). Listening in on conversations: Speech-based marketing intelligence and consumer privacy. *The Journal of Consumer Research*, *46*(4), 595–622. DOI: 10.1093/jcr/ucz017

Shankar, V. (2018). How artificial intelligence (AI) is reshaping retailing. *Journal of Retailing*, *94*(4), vi–xi. DOI: 10.1016/S0022-4359(18)30076-9

Sundar, S. S., & Limperos, A. M. (2013). Uses and Grats 2.0: New Gratifications for New Media. *Journal of Broadcasting & Electronic Media*, *57*(4), 504–525. DOI: 10.1080/08838151.2013.845827

Teskeredzic, E., Paric, M., Sestic, A., Fribert, P., Lukac, A., Hadzic, H., & Lacic, E. (2025, September). Vocalize: Lead Acquisition and User Engagement through Gamified Voice Competitions. In *Proceedings of the 2025 Adjunct Proceedings of the 36th ACM Conference on Hypertext and Social Media* (pp. 35-39).

Thaler, R. H., & Sunstein, C. R. (2008). *Nudge: Improving decisions about health, wealth, and happiness*. Yale University Press.

Yıldız, S. Y., & Demir, D. (2023). Oyunlaştırmanın Satın Alma Davranışını Şekillendirmedeki Gücü. *Toplum Ekonomi ve Yönetim Dergisi*, *4*(2), 336–358. DOI: 10.58702/teyd.1350934

Yücel, E. (2023). "Pazarlamada Oyunlaştırma Uygulamaları: Türkiye ve Dünya'dan Oyunlaştırma Örnekleri". *İzmir Yönetim Dergisi*, 4(1), pp. 20-30. DOI: 10.56203/iyd.1267187

ADDITIONAL READING

Bălan, C. (2023). Chatbots and voice assistants: Digital transformers of the company–customer interface—A systematic review of the business research literature. *Journal of Theoretical and Applied Electronic Commerce Research*, *18*(2), 995–1019. DOI: 10.3390/jtaer18020051

Calahorra-Candao, G., & Martín-de Hoyos, M. J. (2024). From typing to talking: Unveiling AI's role in the evolution of voice assistant integration in online shopping. *Information (Basel)*, *15*(4), 202. DOI: 10.3390/info15040202

Hamacher, K., & Buchkremer, R. (2022). Measuring online sensory consumer experience: Introducing the Online Sensory Marketing Index (OSMI) as a structural modeling approach. *Journal of Theoretical and Applied Electronic Commerce Research*, *17*(2), 751–772. DOI: 10.3390/jtaer17020039

Huang, M.-H., & Rust, R. T. (2021). A strategic framework for artificial intelligence in marketing. *Journal of the Academy of Marketing Science*, *49*(1), 30–50. DOI: 10.1007/s11747-020-00749-9

McLean, G., & Osei-Frimpong, K. (2019). Hey Alexa … examine the variables influencing the use of artificial intelligent in-home voice assistants. *Computers in Human Behavior*, *99*, 28–37. DOI: 10.1016/j.chb.2019.05.009

McLean, G., Osei-Frimpong, K., & Barhorst, J. (2021). Alexa, do voice assistants influence consumer brand engagement? Examining the role of AI powered voice assistants in influencing consumer brand engagement. *Journal of Business Research*, *124*, 312–328. DOI: 10.1016/j.jbusres.2020.11.045

Poushneh, A. (2021). Impact of auditory sense on trust and brand affect through auditory social interaction and control. *Journal of Retailing and Consumer Services*, *58*, 102281. DOI: 10.1016/j.jretconser.2020.102281

Pradhan, A., Findlater, L., & Lazar, A. (2019). "Phantom friend" or "just a box with information": Personification and ontological categorization of smart speaker-based voice assistants by older adults. Proceedings of the ACM on Human-Computer Interaction, 3(CSCW), Article 214.

Prentice, C., Loureiro, S. M. C., & Guerreiro, J. (2023). Engaging with intelligent voice assistants for wellbeing and brand attachment. *Journal of Brand Management*, *30*(5), 449–460. DOI: 10.1057/s41262-023-00321-0

Zhang, J., Zou, Y., Wang, S., & Xiang, Y. (2025). Consumer experience and perception in gamification marketing: Evidence from a user survey of POPMART. *Frontiers in Communication*, *10*, 1388020. DOI: 10.3389/fcomm.2025.1388020

KEY TERMS AND DEFINITIONS

Advertising: Communication activities aimed at promoting products or services to the target audience and increasing brand awareness.

Artificial Intelligence: The ability of computer systems to learn, make decisions, and solve problems with human-like intelligence. It enables personalization in advertising and user experience.

Brand Engagement: The emotional, cognitive, and behavioral connection that consumers actively establish with a brand. It can be enhanced through gamification and digital tools.

Digital Marketing: Marketing activities conducted via the internet and digital platforms. This includes social media, mobile applications, email, and voice assistants.

Gamification: The use of game design elements in non-game contexts (e.g., marketing, education). The goal is to increase user motivation and enhance engagement.

Voice Assistants: Artificial intelligence-based software that interacts with users through voice commands. Examples: Amazon Alexa, Google Assistant, Siri.

Chapter 7
The Power of Digital Recreation:
The Rise of Gaming, Virtual Reality and Mobile Advertising

Fatma Sisli
http://orcid.org/0000-0002-3417-2404
Independent Researcher, Turkey

Yelda Ulker
http://orcid.org/0000-0001-8105-2686
Istanbul Gelisim University, Turkey

Kivanc Nazlim Tuzel Uraltas
http://orcid.org/0000-0001-7682-2164
Marmara University, Turkey

ABSTRACT

Recreation refers to voluntary activities individuals pursue outside work to renew themselves physically and mentally. Digital recreation, a modern extension of this concept, involves leisure activities conducted through digital platforms-such as video games, VR and AR applications, online education, social media, and mobile apps. With technological advancements, digital environments have become key spaces for entertainment, learning, and socialization. As individuals increasingly spend their free time online, brands have integrated advertising into these platforms, particularly through digital games, VR, AR, and mobile applications.These environments allow brands to reach audiences directly and deliver interactive, personalized, and engaging advertising experiences.Methods like in-game ads and advergames embed marketing messages naturally into user experiences, enhancing brand interaction,

DOI: 10.4018/979-8-3373-6309-7.ch007

loyalty, and recall.Thus, digital recreation offers advertisers opportunities for targeted communication, creative engagement and data-driven strategy development across diverse digital touchpoints.

INTRODUCTION

In recent years, the rapid advancement of digital technologies has transformed the operations of businesses and organizations and reshaped individuals' daily lives (Matt, Trenz, Cheung, & Turel, 2019). These technological changes have not only influenced work and communication but have also begun to reshape the ways in which people spend their leisure time. Today, individuals' communication, lifestyle, and leisure habits have undergone significant transformation, and the natural flow of everyday life has become faster, easier, and more convenient through tools such as smartphones, digital entertainment applications, and social media platforms (Annisawati, Gaffar, Hurriyati, & Widjajanta, 2024). These technological advancements have also influenced how people organize their leisure activities, giving rise to a variety of new forms of entertainment and reshaping the digital world. This shift has changed individuals' understanding of leisure, with traditional forms of recreation increasingly being replaced by digital alternatives. The concept of leisure refers to the time individuals spend engaging in activities that provide enjoyment, relaxation, socialization, or personal development. In other words, leisure consists of activities pursued for personal interest and benefit. For instance, activities that contribute to personal growth provide both enjoyment and fulfillment of individual needs. The periods during which people engage in such activities amid their busy routines—such as work—are referred to as recreation (Suhartanto, Brien, Primianac, Wibisono, & Triyuni, 2019).

Recreation, which encompasses activities that allow individuals to renew themselves physically, mentally, and emotionally, enables people to use their leisure time productively and enjoyably. Such activities help reduce stress while meeting social and psychological needs (Güncan, 2021). In contemporary society, where individuals often experience the pressures of work and urban life, recreational activities offer valuable opportunities for relaxation and well-being. In other words, recreation enhances quality of life, supports physical and mental health, and fosters the development of more active and balanced social relationships. Historically, recreational activities have played a central role in societies, and their significance continues to grow in the modern era. With the rise of digital technologies, traditional recreational activities—once confined to physical environments—have increasingly found new forms in virtual spaces. These digital activities not only provide opportunities for mental and physical relaxation but also promote skill development and social interaction. By removing temporal and spatial constraints, digital recreation offers a more accessible and flexible entertainment experience, allowing individuals to engage in leisure activities without being limited by physical location or time. The relevance of digital recreation became particularly pronounced during the COVID-19 pandemic, when outdoor activities were restricted and individuals increasingly relied on digital platforms for leisure. The pandemic not only limited individuals' daily lives but also triggered changes in the recreation sector (Pan, Chen, & Shiau, 2022). These restrictions led to digital transformations within the sector, prompting people to shift activities traditionally conducted outdoors to digital platforms. Even after the pandemic, not only did individuals' work and lifestyle patterns change, but the ways in which digital technologies were consumed also evolved (Santiago, Loureiro, Langaro, & Ali, 2024). These shifts have set the stage for the growing role of digital technologies in shaping recreational experiences.

Within this context, from the perspectives of marketing and advertising, the digital transformation of leisure has also led to changes in the ways brands communicate with consumers, while digital recreational platforms have become increasingly prominent within advertising and marketing communication. In particular, gamified forms of advertising have become more common in digital leisure environments such as digital games, mobile applications, and interactive platforms. In these environments, the inclusion of game-related elements—such as tasks, rewards, narratives, and interactive mechanics—allows advertising content to be integrated into recreational activities. Consequently, individuals encounter marketing and advertising messages while engaging in leisure activities, which blurs the boundaries between entertainment and advertising within digital recreational contexts.

The rapid proliferation of digital technologies has transformed how individuals engage in recreation. As shown in recent studies, digital literacy strongly correlates with increased participation in virtual leisure activities and the perceived benefits derived from them (Türkmen, Akgül, & Durhan, 2024). Meanwhile, digital games—now enjoyed by nearly three billion users worldwide—have been credited with addressing social, cognitive, and psychological needs (Gonzalez-Ibanez, Macıas-Caceres, & Paucar, 2025). However, the increasing integration of virtual reality (VR), mobile gaming, and in-game advertising into everyday life raises serious questions about their broader socio-cultural and ethical implications. Building on these developments, this study aims to investigate the following research question: How do digital recreation practices—including digital games, VR/AR experiences, and mobile applications—transform individuals' leisure experiences, consumption behaviors, and interactions with digital advertising?

THE CONCEPT OF DIGITAL RECREATION

The term recreation originates from the English verb *create* combined with the prefix *re*, meaning "to create again" or "to restore." It encompasses re-creation, revitalization, enjoyment, entertainment, and relaxation (Hazar, 2009; Metin, Kesici, & Kodaş, 2013; Karaküçük, 2014; Akten, 2003). According to the *Dictionary of Sociology*, recreation is defined as "any activity, individual or collective, pursued during leisure time, freely chosen and enjoyable, possessing its own intrinsic appeal and not directed by any reward" (Torkildsen, 2005). Clawson and Knetsch (1974) describe it as the time individuals spend engaging in activities alone or in groups outside the hours dedicated to essential living tasks. Similarly, Yukic (1970) emphasizes that fulfilling social and psychological needs during leisure time contributes to one's sense of freedom.

According to the Turkish Language Association Dictionary (https://sozluk.gov.tr/), recreation is defined as "activities voluntarily participated in by individuals during their leisure time for purposes of entertainment or sport" and as "the process of preparing an area for the recreational use of people." Recreation activities, characterized by voluntariness and performed during free time, foster social renewal while excluding actions that may negatively affect individuals or constitute criminal behavior (Kaya, Güdek, & Uygur, 2023). Recreation refers to voluntary activities carried out during leisure time to protect mental and physical health affected by intense work life or adverse environmental conditions and to derive pleasure and satisfaction from life (Karaküçük, 2014). In this context, recreation can be briefly defined as the activities individuals engage in during their free time (Karaküçük & Başaran, 1996). Bucher (1972) emphasizes that recreation is fundamentally distinct from work. As a leisure-time activity, recreation does not aim for profit but also provides social benefits beyond personal satisfaction. Considering the defining characteristics of recreation—as voluntary activities performed during free time (Tütüncü, 2012) —voluntariness is fundamental. Participation is determined by the individual's own decision, with no obligation to continue, and activities can occur throughout the year in both indoor and outdoor settings. These activities enhance creativity and allow for self-expression. Research indicates that urban residents particularly favor activities that enable them to utilize their non-working days, especially during spring and summer. Saturdays and Sundays are the most preferred days for recreation (Akten, 2003; Tolunay, Alkan, & Korkmaz, 2004). According to Çoruh and Karaküçük (2014), male participants are generally less inclined to spend leisure time compared to women, which has been attributed to the patriarchal structure of Turkish culture and men's perceived work obligations. The study also found that men felt psychologically unprepared for recreational activities due to perceived risks of injury or harm.

Recreation is a universal concept that should align with a society's culture and values. While offering enjoyment, recreational activities positively affect physical health and improve quality of life. Consequently, recreation supports mental development, morale, motivation, and self-confidence (Can, 2015; Aslan, 1993; Karaküçük, 2014). Individuals may engage actively or passively in these activities (Lu & Hu, 2005). Active recreation involves physical exertion, such as football, tennis, swimming, climbing, and camping (Schwilgin, Arch, & Arch, 1974), whereas passive recreation does not, including activities like picnicking, fishing, and museum visits (Mansuroğlu, 2002). Kurar and Baltacı (2014) report that most participants prefer spending leisure time with friends and in outdoor settings. Mansuroğlu's (2002) study of university students revealed an average of five hours of free time on weekdays and ten hours on weekends; however, participants were not sufficiently engaged in recreational activities despite lacking major time or income constraints. Only 27.7% participated in outdoor recreation daily, and increasing distance to recreational areas raised costs, reducing participation among lower-income groups. Lu and Hu (2005) found that personality influences recreational behavior. Generally, individuals satisfied with their lives engage more actively in recreational activities. Extroverted individuals experience greater satisfaction from recreation, whereas those with neurotic traits enjoy leisure less. Extroverted participants also gain positive effects on happiness through recreational engagement. Lu and Argyle (1993) demonstrated that prolonged television viewing increases boredom and reduces leisure satisfaction, whereas engaging in serious and committed leisure activities enhances both satisfaction and overall happiness.

Recreational activities are categorized into outdoor and indoor settings. Outdoor recreation occurs in open spaces, such as parks, trails, urban forests, and nature reserves, often accessible to the public (Hazar, 2009; Abbasi, Alalouch, & Bramley, 2016). Technological advancements have increasingly integrated digital tools into outdoor recreation, including smartphones, smartwatches, action cameras, drones, GPS devices, laptops, and tablets (Ekinci, 2023). Indoor recreation occurs in homes or enclosed spaces specifically designed for leisure, often including sporting or cultural activities (Kaya, Metin, & Kozak, 2015; Peker, 2017). The transformation of both outdoor and indoor recreation due to technology has facilitated the transition to digital environments, allowing individuals to engage in leisure pursuits more conveniently and enjoyably. Digital technology has enabled novel outdoor experiences and "electronic leisure," including online learning, e-commerce, digital dating, blogging, television, music, and e-books (Nimrod & Adoni, 2012). Güncan (2021) describes this phenomenon as the "electronification" of leisure, distinguishing between "electronic leisure activities," "virtual recreation," and "digital recreation." Kozak and Özkeroğlu (2018) define virtual recreation as experiences creating a sense of reality independent of time and space, often occurring in virtual environments such as VR platforms and online games that include social interactions and collaborative or competitive elements. Consequently, many activities once conducted in physical environments are now experienced virtually or in hybrid (physical-digital) spaces. For example, golf can be played entirely with virtual equipment supported by augmented reality (Aylan & Aylan, 2020). Electronic leisure refers to activities performed in electronic environments using the internet, computers, or digital gaming devices (Güncan, 2021). Bayram and Kavlak (2021) define digital recreation as active or passive participation, individually or in groups, in online or offline activities to achieve mental or physical pleasure during leisure time. It encompasses computer games, virtual events, video streaming, and online community engagement. Technological advancement has made leisure activities independent of time and place (Sintas, de Francisco, & Alvarez, 2015), shaping online leisure experiences (Gallistl & Nimrod, 2019). Individuals can now engage in leisure remotely, unconstrained by physical boundaries, and select with whom to share these experiences (Topsakal, 2020; Kraut et al., 2002; Anderson et al., 2002; Abbott-Chapman & Robertson, 2001).

Digital transformations have also allowed differentiated leisure experiences within the same household. For example, family members may simultaneously watch different films or play separate computer games. The development of digital technologies has expanded individuals' freedom to choose preferred activities at home (López-Sintas, Rojas-DeFrancisco, & García-Álvarez, 2017; Esentaş, Güzel, & Vural, 2018). Internet-connected devices—including smartwatches, smart homes, mobile and wearable devices, QR applications, multi-sensory technologies, VR, AR, biotechnology, nanotechnology, and drones—enrich leisure experiences. Research indicates that digital games can divert attention from life's challenges and reduce stress, serving as coping mechanisms (Kneer, Rieger, Ivory, & Ferguson, 2014). Video and computer games also contribute to youth socialization (Esentaş, Güzel, & Vural, 2018). In addition to self-expression, problem-solving, and virtual interactions, technology provides leisure via music streaming and video platforms. In the past decade, mobile devices such as smartphones, tablets, and satellite phones have enabled access to information anytime, anywhere (Bolliger & Shepherd, 2016), making leisure more accessible and enjoyable. Gaming applications enhance cognitive and strategic skills, travel and tourism apps simplify planning, location-based services support outdoor activities, and social media platforms allow users to discover new interests and connect with others. Digital recreation thus facilitates both enjoyment and social expansion, demonstrating the increasing diversity and accessibility of leisure engagement in the digital era.

THE NEW DOMAIN OF DIGITAL RECREATION: DIGITAL GAMES

Playing games—an activity that is neither obligatory nor goal-oriented but rather performed during one's leisure time (Huizinga, 2023) —is regarded as a form of recreation and relaxation. Since the 1970s, *digital games* have increasingly gained popularity, evolving into a significant medium of entertainment and recreation. Having achieved mass popularity, digital games now compete with other forms of recreation such as television, film, and music. Moreover, they are accessible through laptops and mobile phones, making gaming a more integrated part of daily life. Consequently, digital games have emerged as an appealing *advertising platform* for brands, functioning as a contemporary form of digital recreation (De Pelsmacker, Dens, & Verberckmoes, 2019). As screen time has significantly increased, gaming has transformed into a domain that brands perceive as worth investing in. According to a study conducted by the Turkish Statistical Institute (TÜİK) in 2021, 94.7% of children aged 6–15 play digital games almost every day. The rate among girls is 91.8%, while it rises to 96.2% among boys (*Information Technologies Usage Survey on Children*, 2021).

The digital transformation and shifts in leisure-time activities and recreation practices reveal that electronic applications—now integral to daily human life—have introduced a new way of spending leisure time (Güncan, 2021). Bayram and Kavlak (2021) approach the concept of digital recreation from a different perspective, classifying it as *E-recreation* (electronic recreation) and *EoE-recreation* (exclude of electronic recreation). *E-recreation* refers to online leisure activities conducted through internet-connected devices such as computers, mobile phones, and gaming consoles. In contrast, *EoE-recreation* encompasses offline leisure activities carried out individually or in groups using digital devices without requiring internet access. In this context, the act of playing digital games as a recreational domain has attracted the attention of brands, leading to the emergence of *gamification* practices in advertising. Gamification transforms routine and monotonous activities into engaging and enjoyable experiences, thereby encouraging greater consumer interaction with brands (Huotari & Hamari, 2017; Eppmann, Bekk, & Klein, 2018). Gamification provides several benefits for advertisements, including:

1. **Making routines enjoyable:** Activities that consumers typically perceive as tedious are transformed into fun and interactive experiences through gamification (Helpshift, 2023).
2. **Enhancing awareness and loyalty:** Gamification increases brand awareness and fosters customer loyalty (Xi & Hamari, 2019).

3. **Building connections:** It enables stronger emotional and experiential connections with potential target audiences (Stewens, Schlager, Häubl, & Herrmann, 2016).
4. **Developing positive attitudes:** By enhancing the hedonic value of advertisements, gamification encourages more favorable consumer attitudes toward the ad (Mishra & Malhotra, 2020).

With the growth of the gamification market, advertisers have increasingly focused on gaming platforms. Various strategies are employed when incorporating gamification into advertisements. Among these strategies are game advertising, virtual reality, augmented reality, and mobile gaming applications.

TYPES OF ADVERTISING IN THE CONTEXT OF DIGITAL RECREATION

Game Advertising

In the context of digital recreation, the primary element in creating interaction between brands and players is entertainment. Game advertising, as a tool of digital recreation, allows brands to communicate with their target audiences in a fun and non-traditional way. It encompasses advertising activities and product placement within digital games (Erdem & Urfalı, 2022). Game advertising can be divided into two main categories: advergames and in-game advertising. In-game advertising is a strategy in which advertising messages are integrated into video or computer games. This allows advertisers to convey their messages through static or dynamic visuals. In-game ads appear on billboards in racing games, on sponsorship boards in sports games, or in scenes where game characters interact with branded products (Smith, Sun, Sutherland, & Mackie, 2014). In-game ads can be dynamic or static. Dynamic ads, which advertisers can continuously optimize, can be integrated at any stage of the game. Because they can be updated regularly, dynamic ads facilitate message modifications over time (Ghirvu, 2012). Static in-game ads, on the other hand, are coded directly into the game during its design. These elements cannot be changed or removed until a new version of the game is released. Product and brand placement in digital games also enhances the realism of the gaming experience (Smith, Sun, Sutherland, & Mackie, 2014). When delivering messages through in-game advertising, attention must be paid to the relationships among the game, the player, and the brand. Communication depends on the interaction of these three components. The brand uses an interactive tool to convey its message, aiming to ensure that players interpret it correctly. In the game-brand relationship, the brand integrates its message into the game to create an experiential context. In the player-game relationship, the player makes personal choices while playing. Consequently, the interpretation of the brand's message is influenced by the style of the advertisement and the player's in-game performance (Conde-Pumpido, 2014). Research indicates that participants' attitudes toward the game directly affect their attitudes toward the brand (Mau, Silberer, & Constien, 2008).

Another digital recreation tool specifically designed for brands is advergames. Advergames are digital games created for a particular brand, with narratives shaped according to the advertiser's requirements (Tham, Rodgers, & Thorson, 2017; Smith, Sun, Sutherland, & Mackie, 2014). They are among the most widely used applications within digital games. Advergames link brand messages with products, enhance product and brand awareness, and strengthen consumer perception. They are particularly favored due to their relatively low cost. Through advergames, brands can access information such as the number of players, gameplay duration, and website visit frequency. Users who remain engaged during gameplay are more likely to adopt the brand, product, or service as a result of their immersive virtual experience (Tosun, 2010). In other words, the brand occupies a central position in advergames, and the game's narrative is structured around the message the brand wishes to convey. Consequently, while users continue playing, they simultaneously learn about the product or brand. Various sectors, including automotive, fashion, banking, and food and beverage, utilize advergames.

Virtual and Augmented Reality Advertising

With the integration of digital technologies into consumers' lives, experiences have increasingly shifted from physical environments to virtual and digital spaces. In this context, virtual and augmented reality applications have emerged within digital communication technologies, becoming an integral part of daily life. One of these applications is virtual reality (VR). The term *virtual* refers to creating an illusion in which something that does not exist appears to exist through the manipulation of perceptions (Ağca & Kozbekçi Ayranpınar, 2021). Virtual reality, in contrast, is a digital environment offering dynamic, interactive experiences and generating a sense of presence (Bayraktar & Kaleli, 2007). It can also be defined as a computer-generated simulation that immerses the user in the environment, providing experiences through one or more senses. Users interact with this simulated environment as if it were real (Wedel, Bigné, & Zhang, 2020). VR technologies immerse individuals in an artificial environment, temporarily disconnecting them from the real world (Ağca & Kozbekçi Ayranpınar, 2021). Moreover, VR generates a physical sense of presence within the virtual environment, allowing users to become absorbed in the fictional setting and experience a perception of reality distinct from their physical surroundings (Aydoğan & Kaplanoğlu, 2020).

Virtual reality consists of four key elements: immersion, interaction, imagination, and presence (Wedel, Bigné, & Zhang, 2020; Wohlgenannt, Simons, & Stieglitz, 2020). *Presence* refers to the feeling of physically existing in a location different from one's actual environment, while *interaction* denotes the user's ability to control and manipulate the virtual environment. *Immersion* reflects the user's full absorption in the virtual world (Wedel, Bigné, & Zhang, 2020; Wohlgenannt, Simons, & Stieglitz, 2020). VR applications enable a wide range of experiences, including virtual fashion shows, in-store promotions, and window displays (Ağca & Kozbekçi Ayranpınar, 2021). For instance, brands such as Dior have implemented projects to create their own virtual experiences. In 2016, Dior presented the virtual fashion show *Dior Eyes*, allowing users to virtually access its runway shows (Ağca & Kozbekçi Ayranpınar, 2021). Similarly, Gucci collaborated with the avatar application Zepeto, enabling users to dress their avatars in Gucci outfits and experience the brand virtually (see campaign visual at https://tinyurl.com/ywb3rpar). In this way, users engaged with a luxury brand experience through their avatars, enjoying an aspirational interaction in a virtual setting. These opportunities make VR experiences more engaging and attractive for consumers (Uncu, 2024). Burberry, for example, partnered with the game *Honor of Kings* to design a platform where users could purchase and try digital clothing items. The garments, created by creative director Riccardo Tisci, were accessible only to users who participated in a raffle, emphasizing the integration of virtual experiences with brand interaction (see campaign visual at https://tinyurl.com/ywb3rpar).

Another strategy in the digital recreation domain involves augmented reality (AR) applications. AR allows virtual objects to be placed in physical environments, enabling users to interact with and manipulate their perception of reality (Özer & Çolak, 2022). The convergence of digital technologies and the blending of virtual and real environments have influenced brands' communication strategies. Brands use AR to provide informative, supportive, and entertaining experiences to their target audiences (Köse & Yengin, 2018; Cevher, 2023). AR is defined as a technology that combines computer-generated virtual images with physical objects in real-time (Başer & Sever, 2023). Azuma et al. (2001) describe AR as the integration of virtual and real objects in real environments, merging entities in three-dimensional space. According to Poushneh and Vasquez-Parraga (2017), AR merges the real with the virtual to provide a sense of reality. AR applications are increasingly used in advertising, reshaping brand-consumer communication (Javornik, 2016; Dacko, 2017; Hilken De Ruyter, Chylinski, Mahr, & Keeling, 2017). Their use in campaigns positively affects consumer-brand interaction during digital recreation (Owyang, 2010). AR is especially effective for reaching younger audiences due to their frequent interaction with smartphones, which serve as a platform for mobile AR. This technology provides an interactive environment controlled by the user (Singh & Pandey, 2014). In digital recreation, AR applications make communication with consumers both functional and entertaining (Shankar, Venkatesh, Hofacker, & Naik, 2010). Additionally, AR enables personalized advertising experiences, fostering individualized engagement and a stronger brand connection (Erdem, 2021). For example, consumers can try on accessories or clothing via AR rather than imagining how they would look (Akın & Demirel, 2024). Brands have also implemented virtual fitting rooms, smart mirrors, and holographic LED systems (Çelik, 2021). Cadbury, for instance, integrated an AR game into its *Qwak Smack* chocolate during the London Olympics "Spots vs. Stripes" campaign (see game at https://tinyurl.com/nb5tvbdu). Users interacted with the game via smartphones, selecting stripes or circles and tapping appearing ducks to score points (Öndeş, 2011).

AR in advertising enhances the enjoyment of consumers' digital leisure time. As smartphone usage increases, brands leverage these platforms to influence consumer preferences during digital recreation. There are distinctions between VR and AR: VR immerses users entirely in a computer-generated environment, while AR places virtual objects within real environments, enhancing perception of reality (Özer & Çolak, 2022). In other words, VR transfers reality into a virtual world, whereas AR enriches the real world with virtual elements (Somyürek, 2014). Through VR and AR, people have begun socializing and spending their free time in new digital recreation spaces. These technologies provide opportunities for shopping, gaming, learning, and social interaction. With digitalization, social lives and experiences are increasingly transferred into virtual spaces, encompassing not only consumption-oriented activities but also social interactions. Individuals can now engage in shopping, learn musical instruments, or pursue artistic skills within digital environments. Consequently, many activities previously limited to the physical realm have moved into the digital world, creating a comprehensive digital recreation space (Uncu, 2024).

Mobile Game Advertising

Digital games, which people generally play to spend their leisure time, enjoy themselves, and escape the stresses of daily life, have gradually been adopted by brands as an advertising tool. Digital games, having become part of people's daily routines, are perceived as an attractive marketing and advertising medium because they can deliver brand messages without disturbing the user. Considered a leisure activity, digital games have entered our pockets through smartphones, transforming into an advertising platform. In addition to computers and gaming consoles, digital games are widely played on mobile devices, offering users an immersive gaming experience.

Recent digital transformations in the advertising sector, along with the development of new technologies and the widespread use of smartphones, have increased the use of digital games as advertising channels. Recognizing the opportunities provided by the growing mobile gaming sector, brands have begun leveraging mobile game advertising, which has evolved into a digital recreation tool, and investments in advertising through mobile games have increased (Aydoğan, 2021). With the rapid growth and importance of the smartphone market, the mobile gaming market increased from $372 million in 2020 to $400 million in 2021. The accessibility, convenience, and lack of additional hardware requirements of smartphones have contributed to a rise in the number of mobile games played (Başev, 2022). Mobile games, which are rapidly growing globally and in Turkey and gaining importance in the advertising industry, are viewed as a popular leisure activity across all demographic groups (Merdin, 2023). Both worldwide and in Turkey, the number of mobile gamers has increased. In Turkey, 78% of adults play mobile games, and 46% of these players spend at least 10 hours per week gaming (Gaminginturkey, 2021). Research indicates that 55% of mobile gamers are women and 45% are men. While most players are over 34 years old, the average age is 36. Mobile gamers include 34% of the Baby Boomer generation, 54% of Generation X, 73% of Generation Y, and 77% of Generation Z. Female players spend 25% more time gaming than males and are more likely to make in-app purchases. On average, 11% of users' time on mobile devices is spent on mobile games (Telyakar, 2022). Because mobile games are one of the easiest ways to reach target audiences, collaborations between games and brands have become increasingly significant (Kadaifçı, Bozdağ, & Işıklı, 2024). One successful example is the mobile game *Pokémon Go*. The goal of the game is to find and capture Pokémon characters (see campaign visual at https://tinyurl.com/3amy3t92). When released in the summer of 2016, *Pokémon Go* surpassed 550 million downloads worldwide. The game offers promotions such as free Wi-Fi and discounts for showing captured Pokémon. Additionally, McDonald's restaurants in Japan partnered with *Pokémon Go*, integrating their locations into the game as Pokémon gyms (Wu, 2017).

The widespread use of smartphones in all aspects of consumers' lives has made mobile game advertising a more powerful tool. Through mobile game advertisements, brands can interact directly with consumers and, thanks to the portability of mobile devices, reach their target audiences anywhere and at any time. Therefore, mobile game advertising is expected to become increasingly important (Şen, 2024). In other words, mobile games, which allow users to spend time anytime and anywhere with devices that are always at hand, have become a highly profitable platform for the advertising and marketing sector (Kadaifçı, Bozdağ, & Işıklı, 2024). Moreover, augmented reality (AR) and virtual reality (VR) technologies have significantly influenced the mobile game market. The adaptation of gaming habits to mobile technologies alongside AR and VR has transformed mobile games into a major market area (Şen, 2024).

FUTURE RESEARCH DIRECTIONS

Future studies could further expand on the relationship between digital recreation and advertising by exploring users' motivations, behavioral patterns, and emotional responses across different digital environments. Although current research emphasizes entertainment and interaction, examining the cognitive and social dimensions of digital recreation would provide a more comprehensive understanding of users' engagement processes.

Comparative analyses between various digital recreation platforms—such as virtual reality, augmented reality, and mobile games—could help determine which contexts most effectively foster brand interaction and loyalty. Moreover, investigating cross-cultural differences in digital recreation practices could reveal how cultural values influence users' attitudes toward brand-related content and advertising strategies.

As emerging technologies such as artificial intelligence, metaverse platforms, and virtual influencers continue to shape digital spaces, future research should also consider how these developments transform the dynamics of recreation, consumption, and communication. Ethical considerations, including data privacy and digital well-being, will remain critical topics that deserve deeper investigation.

Finally, longitudinal and mixed-method studies could offer valuable insights into the long-term effects of digital recreation on consumer–brand relationships. Understanding how sustained exposure to digital recreational environments impacts users' perceptions, trust, and loyalty will guide marketers in designing more meaningful, value-driven, and user-centered experiences.

CONCLUSION

Producers of countless similar goods and services engage in a wide range of marketing and promotional activities to ensure that their products and brands stand out in the minds of target consumers. Among these activities, advertising plays a central role in securing a lasting place for the brand in consumers' minds. To ensure that consumers prefer their brand over competitors in product choices, businesses increasingly adopt innovative, striking, and novel forms of advertising, investing significant effort in developing advertising strategies. Therefore, advertisers must closely monitor changes in consumers' cultural, social, economic, and personal characteristics, and adapt their marketing activities accordingly. At this point, recreation and digital recreation activities gain importance. Defined as voluntary activities undertaken during free time—apart from work, obligations, or tasks for income—these activities aim to facilitate physical and mental renewal. Traditional recreation activities, such as nature walks, sports, and cultural events, were once limited to physical and group-based experiences. However, with advances in digital technologies, these activities have increasingly shifted to digital platforms. In this new form, digital recreation offers a wide range of activities, including video games, online courses, virtual reality experiences, and digital content consumption, providing participants with opportunities for physical and mental relaxation. By eliminating limitations of time and place, digital recreation provides more accessible and flexible experiences, allowing individuals to socialize, develop new skills, and enjoy mental relaxation. Digital recreation, which began in the 1970s and 1980s with the emergence of early video games played at home, gained real momentum in the early 2000s with the proliferation of the internet and expanded through online games, digital content creation, and social media platforms. Particularly since the 2010s, mobile games, virtual reality, and augmented reality have rapidly gained popularity, creating a substantial market over the past 20–25 years. Major technological advancements, such as the widespread availability of high-speed internet (e.g., 5G), greater accessibility of VR and AR applications, enhanced video game graphics, and more powerful mobile devices, have increased the significance of digital recreation. Consequently, the quality of time spent on digital platforms has improved, and individuals' approaches to leisure and entertainment have increasingly shifted toward digital channels.

For marketers, these technological developments offer significant opportunities. Digital game advertising is widely used by businesses to generate revenue through both free and premium (freemium) features. In-game advertisements are integrated into players' experiences while simultaneously encouraging users to discover new content. By combining these experiences with advertising, brands enable users to engage directly with their messages. This form of advertising provides unprecedented interactive experiences, capturing users' attention and fostering deeper connections with the brand. The internet offers many benefits, such as simplifying daily tasks and providing broader access to information and entertainment. However, alongside these advantages, concerns related to screen addiction and the impact of social media on mental health have increasingly gained attention (Fu Chen & Shian Chen, 2010). In the context of digital interactions, attention is drawn to the potential risks associated with emerging forms of digital recreation. For example, VR-based games have been shown to generate higher levels of stress, cognitive load, and emotional arousal than traditional screen-based games, often resulting in discomfort, reduced feelings of control, and heightened physiological strain for users (Vatsal et al., 2023). Beyond VR environments, mobile games introduce another layer of concern due to the widespread use of dark patterns. Design features such as time pressure, artificial scarcity, limited-time offers, and repetitive reward loops intentionally prolong gameplay and elevate players' stress levels. Furthermore, monetization elements—including microtransactions and premium in-game currencies—create financial pressures, while psychological mechanisms such as social comparison, competition, and fear of missing out (FOMO) intensify addictive tendencies, particularly among young and vulnerable users. Consequently, mobile games function not merely as tools for entertainment but as consumption-driven platforms built upon manipulative design strategies that target users' time, attention, and financial resources (Niknejad, Mildner, Zargham, Putze, & Malaka, 2024). Moreover, although digital games offer cognitive and entertainment-related benefits, excessive or compulsive use has been linked to a range of negative outcomes. Game addiction is associated with social isolation, neglect of daily responsibilities, irregular sleep and eating habits, and psychological difficulties such as anxiety, depression, and hopelessness. These risks are amplified for young individuals and those with fragile mental health, who may be more easily influenced by the reinforcing structure of digital games. Extended gameplay can also affect physical well-being, as prolonged sedentary behavior and poor posture may diminish overall quality of life. Collectively, these findings underscore that digital games possess both beneficial and harmful potentials, and that the nature and intensity of use play a crucial role in determining negative effects (Darvenkumar & Rajasekaran, 2024). Within this landscape, VR games warrant particular attention due to their strong emotional impact. Compared with flat-screen games, VR environments can trigger more intense negative emotions, stress responses, and anxiety, and these emotional reactions may persist even after gameplay, contributing to mental strain throughout the day. Additionally, exposure to violent or trauma-related VR content can evoke feelings of guilt, shame, and psychological discomfort, raising further ethical and emotional concerns (Lavoie, Main, King, & King, 2021).

In addition, digital recreation offers opportunities for socialization and skill development. Through digital recreation, users can connect with individuals from diverse cultures worldwide, independent of their physical location. Educational games, virtual student experiences, and online courses not only expand knowledge but also help users develop various skills, providing experiences that are both enjoyable and educational. Digital recreation has become accessible to large audiences thanks to technological advances and can offer personalized experiences. Areas such as game advertising, virtual reality experiences, and mobile game advertisements are key factors shaping the future of digital recreation. The evolving forms of entertainment enabled by digital technologies are driving significant changes in advertising and marketing. The expanding digital recreation market allows brands to establish deeper and more interactive relationships with users. Advertisements integrated into video games, VR, and AR experiences are more interactive and targeted than traditional methods, allowing brands not only to capture attention but also to foster emotional connections with consumers. Because digital recreation can serve educational, personal development, and social purposes—not just entertainment—it is important for marketers to support content and experiences that contribute to users' growth, rather than focusing solely on entertainment. By engaging in areas valued by users, brands can enhance trust and build long-term brand loyalty. Advertisers and marketers should continue to leverage the opportunities offered by digital recreation advertising, developing interactive, personalized, and value-driven strategies. Such approaches will both enhance user experiences and shape the future success of the brands.

REFERENCES

Abbasi, A., Alalouch, C., & Bramley, G. (2016). Open space quality in deprived urban areas: User perspective and use pattern. *Procedia: Social and Behavioral Sciences, 216*, 194–205. DOI: 10.1016/j.sbspro.2015.12.028

Abbott-Chapman, J., & Robertson, M. (2001). Youth, leisure and home: Space, place and identity. Loisir et Société. *Society and Leisure, 24*(2), 485–506. DOI: 10.7202/000192ar

Ağca, G., & Kozbekçi Ayranpınar, S. (2021). Moda sektöründe artırılmış gerçeklik ve sanal gerçeklik (Augmented Reality and Virtual Reality in the Fashion Industry). Sanat. *Tarim Bilimleri Dergisi, 25*, 1–15.

Akın, T., & Demirel, M. (2024). Açık hava reklamcılığında artırılmış gerçekliğin önemi ve uygulamaları (The Importance and Applications of Augmented Reality in Outdoor Advertising). *Sanat ve Tasarım Araştırmaları Dergisi, 5*(8), 82–97.

Akten, M. (2003). Isparta ilindeki bazı rekreasyon alanlarının mevcut potansiyellerinin belirlenmesi (Determining the Current Potential of Some Recreation Areas in Isparta). *Süleyman Demirel Üniversitesi Orman Fakültesi Dergisi*, (2), 115–132.

Anderson, B., Gale, C., Gower, A. P., France, E. F., Jones, M., Lacohee, H. V., McWilliam, A., Tracey, K., & Trimby, M. (2002). Digital living- people-centred innovation and strategy. *BT Technology Journal, 20*(2), 11–29. DOI: 10.1023/A:1015632120289

Annisawati, A., Gaffar, V., Hurriyati, R., & Widjajanta, B. (2024). Muslim Loyalty in Halal Digital Recreation: The Role of Experience Quality and Value. *Proceedings of the 8th Global Conference on Business, Management, and Entrepreneurship (GCBME 2023)*, pp. 710-718. DOI: 10.2991/978-94-6463-443-3_93

Aslan, Z. (1993). Sanayileşme ve kentleşmenin doğada rekreasyon faaliyetlerine duyulan gereksinimi arttırıcı etkisi (The Effect of Industrialization and Urbanization on the Need for Recreation Activities in Nature). *Ekoloji Çevre Dergisi, 2*(8), 22–24.

Aydoğan, D., & Kaplanoğlu, L. (2020). *Sanal gerçeklik kapsamında sanat (Art within the Scope of Virtual Reality). 7. Uluslararası İletişim Günleri*. Üsküdar Üniversitesi İletişim Fakültesi.

Aydoğan, H. (2021). Dijital oyunlar aracılığıyla reklamcılık: Ürün ve hizmet simülasyonlarının ötesine bakmak (Advertising through Digital Games: Beyond Product and Service Simulations). *Uluslararası Halkla İlişkiler ve Reklam Çalışmaları Dergisi, 4*(1), 58–71.

Aylan, K., & Aylan, S. (2020). Sanal gerçeklik ve artırılmış gerçeklik uygulamalarının rekreatif faaliyetlere yansıması: Dijital rekreasyon (Reflection of Virtual and Augmented Reality Applications on Recreational Activities: Digital Recreation). *Türk Turizm Araştırmaları Dergisi*, *4*(3), 2746–2760. DOI: 10.26677/TR1010.2020.507

Azuma, R., Baillot, Y., Behringer, R., Feiner, S., Julier, S., & MacIntyre, B. (2001). Recent advances in augmented reality. *IEEE Computer Graphics and Applications*, *21*(6), 34–47. DOI: 10.1109/38.963459

Başer, E., & Sever, N. (2023). Artırılmış gerçeklik tabanlı reklamların etkileri (The Effects of Augmented Reality-Based Advertisements). In Söğütlüler, T. (Ed.), *Sinema ve Reklam Çalışmalarında Güncel Yaklaşımlar* (pp. 151–170). Eğitim Yayınevi.

Başev, S. E. (2022). Game-based advertisement: Uludag Lemonade and Lipton Ice Tea example. *Journal of Erciyes Communication*, *9*(1), 77–95.

Bayraktar, E., & Kaleli, F. (2007). *Sanal gerçeklik ve uygulama alanları (Virtual Reality and Its Application Areas). IX. Akademik Bilişim Konferansı*. Dumlupınar Üniversitesi.

Bayram, A. T., & Kavlak, H. T. (2021). Rekreasyon ve teknoloji (Recreation and Technology). In Güneş, G., & Varol, F. (Eds.), *Rekreasyon: Disiplinlerarası Yaklaşım ve Örnek Olaylar* (pp. 383–400). Nobel Yayıncılık.

Bolliger, D. U., & Shepherd, C. E. (2016). Instructor and adult learner perceptions of the use of Internet-enabled devices in residential outdoor education programs. *British Journal of Educational Technology*, •••, 1–10.

Bucher, C. (1972). *Foundations of physical education*. C.V. Mosby Company.

Can, E. (2015). Boş zaman, rekreasyon ve etkinlik turizmi ilişkisi (The Relationship Between Leisure, Recreation, and Event Tourism). *Istanbul Journal of Social Sciences*, *10*, 1–17.

Çelik, Z. (2021). Fijital (Phygital) Pazarlama (Phygital Marketing). In Sağlam, M. (Ed.), *Dijitalleşen Dünyada Pazarlama* (pp. 297–317). Atlas Akademik Basım.

Cevher, M. F. (2023). Fijital pazarlama: Geleneksel ve dijital pazarlamanın kesişimi (Phygital Marketing: The Intersection of Traditional and Digital Marketing). *Pearson Journal of Social Sciences & Humanities*, *8*(25), 520–535.

Clawson, M., & Knetsch, J. L. (1974). Leisure in modern America. In Murphy, J. F. (Ed.), *Concepts of Leisure*. Prentice-Hall.

Conde-Pumpido, T. d. (2014). *Persuasive structures in advergames*. Utrecht University.

Çoruh, Y., & Karaküçük, S. (2014). Üniversite öğrencilerinin cinsiyet değişkenliğine göre rekreasyonel eğilimleri ve rekreasyonel etkinliklere katılımına engel olan faktörler (Recreational Tendencies of University Students According to Gender and Factors Hindering Participation in Recreational Activities). *International Journal of Science Culture and Sport, 1*, 854–862.

Dacko, S. G. (2017). Enabling smart retail settings via mobile augmented reality shopping apps. *Technological Forecasting and Social Change, 124*, 243–256. DOI: 10.1016/j.techfore.2016.09.032

Darvenkumar, T., & Rajasekaran, W. (2024). Disorder and rehabilitation: The paradox of digital games and vulnerabilities. *Journal of Education and Health Promotion, 13*(1), 13–64. DOI: 10.4103/jehp.jehp_923_23 PMID: 38559475

De Pelsmacker, P., Dens, N., & Verberckmoes, S. (2019). How ad congruity and interactivity affect fantasy game players' attitude toward in-game advertising. *Journal of Electronic Commerce Research, 20*(1), 55–74.

Ekinci, E. (2023). Açık alan rekreasyon aktivitelerinde dijital teknolojilerin kullanımı (The Use of Digital Technologies in Outdoor Recreational Activities). *Spor ve Rekreasyon Araştırmaları Dergisi, 5*(2), 108–124. DOI: 10.52272/srad.1353789

Eppmann, R., Bekk, M., & Klein, K. (2018). Gameful experience in gamification: Construction and validation of a gameful experience scale [GAMEX]. *Journal of Interactive Marketing, 43*(1), 98–115. DOI: 10.1016/j.intmar.2018.03.002

Erdem, M., & Urfalı, M. (2022). Neden game-vertising? Gelenekselden dijitale oyun ve reklam ilişkisi. In Erdem, M. N. (Ed.), *Game-vertising Dijital Çağda Oyunlaştırma ve Reklam* (pp. 12–25). Eğitim Yayınevi.

Erdem, S. (2021). Sanal gerçekliğin reklam stratejilerinde kullanılmasına yönelik bir değerlendirme (An Evaluation of the Use of Virtual Reality in Advertising Strategies). *Atatürk Üniversitesi Güzel Sanatlar Enstitüsü Dergisi, 27*(46), 241–248. DOI: 10.32547/ataunigsed.836847

Esentaş, M., Güzel, P., & Vural, M. (2018). Popüler kültürde rekreatif bir etkinlik olarak dijital sporlar (Digital sports as a recreational activity in popular culture). *Atatürk Üniversitesi Beden Eğitimi ve Spor Bilimleri Dergisi, 20*(1), 71–79.

Fu Chen, C., & Shian Chen, F. (2010). Experience Quality, Perceived Value, Satisfaction and Behavioral Intentions for Heritage Tourists. *Tourism Management, 31*(1), 29–35. DOI: 10.1016/j.tourman.2009.02.008

Gallistl, V., & Nimrod, G. (2019). Media-based leisure and wellbeing: A study of older internet users. *Leisure Studies*, •••, 1–16.

Gaminginturkey. (2021). Türkiye Oyun Sektörü Raporu 2021 Yayında. Retrieved November 2024, from https://www.gaminginturkey.com/tr/turkiye-oyun-sektoru-raporu-2021-yayinda/

Ghirvu, A. (2012). In-game advertising: Advantages and limitations for advertisers. *The USV Annals of Economics and Public Administration, 12*(1[15]), 114–119.

Gonzalez-Ibanez, R., Macıas-Caceres, J., & Paucar, M. (2025, October 22). LifeSync-Games: Toward a Video Game Paradigm for Promoting Responsible Gaming and Human Developmen. *Computer Science. Psychology (Irvine, Calif.).*

Güncan, Ö. (2021). Elektronik boş zaman uygulamaları "sanal rekreasyon" mudur yoksa "dijital rekreasyon" mu? (Are electronic leisure applications considered 'virtual recreation' or 'digital recreation'?) *Sosyal. Beşerî ve İdari Bilimler Dergisi, 4*(2), 163–181.

Hazar, A. (2009). *Rekreasyon ve animasyon (*Recreation and Animation). Ankara: Detay Yayıncılık.

Helpshift. (2023). App gamification: 12 examples of mobile apps using gamification. Retrieved October 2024, from https://www.helpshift.com/blog/app-gamification-9-examples-of-mobile-apps-using-gamification/

Hilken, T., De Ruyter, K., Chylinski, M., Mahr, D., & Keeling, D. (2017). Augmenting the eye of the beholder: Exploring the strategic potential of augmented reality to enhance online service experiences. *Journal of the Academy of Marketing Science, 45*(6), 884–905. DOI: 10.1007/s11747-017-0541-x

Huizinga, J. (2023). *Homo ludens: Oyunun toplumsal işlevi üzerine bir deneme* (Kılıçbay, M. A., Ed.). Doğu Batı Yayınları. DOI: 10.30965/9783846766781

Huotari, K., & Hamari, J. (2017). A definition for gamification: Anchoring gamification in the service marketing literature. *Electronic Markets, 27*(1), 21–31. DOI: 10.1007/s12525-015-0212-z

Javornik, A. (2016). Augmented reality: Research agenda for studying the impact of its media characteristics on consumer behaviour. *Journal of Retailing and Consumer Services, 30,* 252–261. DOI: 10.1016/j.jretconser.2016.02.004

Karaküçük, S. (2014). *Rekreasyon: Boş zaman değerlendirme*. Bağırgan Yayınevi.

Karaküçük, S., & Başaran, Z. (1996). Stresle başa çıkmada rekreasyon faktörü. *Gazi Beden Eğitimi ve Spor Bilimleri Dergisi, 4,* 55–64.

Kaya, B., Güdek, O., & Uygur, S. M. (2023). Oryantiring ve çöp topla-koş (plogging) eko rekreasyon faaliyetleri için dijital oyun modeli geliştirme. *Turizm Akademik Dergisi, 10*(1), 119–131.

Kaya, B., Metin, T., & Kozak, M. A. (2015). Kapalı rekreasyon tesislerinde kullanıcıların akış deneyimi. *Seyahat ve Otel İşletmeciliği Dergisi, 12*(2), 6–25.

Kneer, J., Rieger, D., Ivory, J. D., & Ferguson, C. (2014). Awareness of risk factors for digital game addiction: Interviewing players and counselors. *International Journal of Mental Health and Addiction, 12*(5), 1–15. DOI: 10.1007/s11469-014-9489-y

Köse, N., & Yengin, D. (2018). Dijital pazarlamadan fijital pazarlamaya geçişe örnek olarak artırılmış gerçeklik ve sanal gerçeklik uygulamalarının pazarlama üzerindeki katkılarının incelenmesi. *İstanbul Aydın Üniversitesi Dergisi, 10*(1), pp. 77-111.

Kozak, M. A., & Özkeroğlu, Ö. (2018). Turizm ve rekreasyon kavramları: Sanal bakış ile değerlendirme. In *II* (pp. 399–409). Uluslararası Sürdürülebilir Turizm Kongresi.

Kraut, R., Kiesler, S., Boneva, B., Cummings, J., Helgeson, V., & Crawford, A. (2002). Internet paradox revisited. *The Journal of Social Issues, 58*(1), 49–74. DOI: 10.1111/1540-4560.00248

Kurar, İ., & Baltacı, F. (2014). Halkın boş zaman değerlendirme alışkanlıkları: Alanya örneği. *International Journal of Science Culture and Sport*, pp. 39-52.

Lavoie, R., Main, K., King, C., & King, D. (2021). Virtual Experience, Real Consequences: The Potential Negative Emotional Consequences of Virtual Reality Gameplay. *Virtual Reality (Waltham Cross), 25*(2), 69–81. DOI: 10.1007/s10055-020-00440-y

López-Sintas, J., Rojas-DeFrancisco, L., & García-Álvarez, E. (2017). Home-based digital leisure: Doing the same leisure activities, but digital. *Cogent Social Sciences, 3*(1), 1–14. DOI: 10.1080/23311886.2017.1309741

Lu, L., & Argyle, M. (1993). *TV watching, soap opera and happiness*. Kaohsiung J Med.

Lu, L., & Hu, C.-H. (2005). Personality, leisure experiences and happiness. *Journal of Happiness Studies, 6*(3), 325–342. DOI: 10.1007/s10902-005-8628-3

Mansuroğlu, S. (2002). Akdeniz Üniversitesi öğrencilerinin serbest zaman özellikleri ve dış mekan rekreasyon eğilimlerinin belirlenmesi. *Akdeniz Üniversitesi Ziraat Fakültesi Dergisi, 15*(2), 53–62.

Matt, C., Trenz, M., Cheung, C., & Turel, O. (2019). The digitization of the individual: Conceptual foundations and opportunities for research. *Electronic Markets, 29*(3), 315–322. DOI: 10.1007/s12525-019-00348-9

Mau, G., Silberer, G., & Constien, C. (2008). Communicating brands playfully: Effects of ingame advertising for familiar and unfamiliar brands. *International Journal of Advertising, 27*(5), 827–851. DOI: 10.2501/S0265048708080293

Merdin, M. (2023). Dijital oyun reklamlarında oyuncular tarafından üretilen nefret söylemleri. *Selçuk İletişim Dergisi, 16*(1), 34–62. DOI: 10.18094/josc.1203241

Metin, T. C., Kesici, M., & Kodaş, D. (2013). Rekreasyon olgusuna akademisyenlerin yaklaşımları. *Journal of Yasar University, 30*(8), 5021–5048.

Mishra, S., & Malhotra, G. (2020). The gamification of in-game advertising: Examining the role of psychological ownership and advertisement intrusiveness. *International Journal of Information Management, 61*(3), 1–13. PMID: 33012944

Niknejad, S., Mildner, T., Zargham, N., Putze, S., & Malaka, R. (2024). (Level Up or Game Over: Exploring How Dark Patterns Shape Mobile Games). *In International Conference on Mobile and Ubiquitous Multi- media (MUM '24)*, pp. 1-4. DOI: 10.1145/3701571.3701604

Nimrod, G., & Adoni, H. (2012). Conceptualizing E-leisure. *Loisir et Société. Society and Leisure, 35*(1), 31–56. DOI: 10.1080/07053436.2012.10707834

Öndeş, A. (2011, August 22). Cadbury: Qwak Smack *Ambalaj üzeri augmented reality oyun*. Retrieved November 2024, from https://bigumigu.com/haber/cadbury-qwak-smack-ambalaj-uzeri-augmented-reality-oyun/

Owyang, J. (2010, January 26). The New Reality Will Be Augmented. Retrieved November 2024, from https://www.destinationcrm.com/Articles/Columns-Departments/Connect/The-New-Reality-Will-Be-Augmented-60593.aspx

Özer, S., & Çolak, A. (2022). Dijital çağın meta-tüketicilerini anlamaya yönelik kavramsal bir değerlendirme. In Uğurhan, Y. Z. (Ed.), *Dijitalleşme Bağlamında Birey, Toplum ve İletişim* (pp. 7–29). Eğitim Yayınevi.

Pan, H., Chen, M., & Shiau, W.-L. (2022). Exploring post-pandemic struggles and recoveries in the rural tourism based on Chinese situation: A perspective from the IAD framework. *Journal of Hospitality and Tourism Technology, 13*(1), 120–139. DOI: 10.1108/JHTT-11-2020-0300

Peker, G. (2017, April 1). Rekreasyonun sınıflandırılması. Retrieved from https://www.rekreasyonist.com/rekreasyonunsiniflandirilmasi/#:~:text=Kapal%C4%B1%20Alan%20Rekreasyon%20Etkinlikleri,bu%20ama%C3%A7larla%20yap%C4%B1lan%20tesislerde%20geli%C5%9Fir

Poushneh, A., & Vasquez-Parraga, A. (2017). Discernible impact of augmented reality on retail customer's experience, satisfaction, and willingness to buy. *Journal of Retailing and Consumer Services*, *34*(3), 229–234. DOI: 10.1016/j.jretconser.2016.10.005

Santiago, M., Loureiro, S., Langaro, D., & Ali, F. (2024). Adoption of smart technologies in the cruise tourism services: A systematic review and future research agenda. *Journal of Hospitality and Tourism Technology*, *15*(3).

Schwilgin, F. A., Arch, B., & Arch, M. (1974). *Town planning guidelines*. Department of Public Works.

Şen, H. (2024). *Mobil oyun reklamlarında reklam çekiciliklerinin kullanımı: Mafia City oyun reklamları örneği* (Unpublished master's thesis). Konya, Turkey.

Shankar, V., Venkatesh, A., Hofacker, C., & Naik, P. (2010). Mobile marketing in the retailing environment: Current insights and future research avenues. *Journal of Interactive Marketing*, *24*(2), 111–120. DOI: 10.1016/j.intmar.2010.02.006

Singh, P., & Pandey, M. (2014). Page augmented reality advertising: An impactful platform for new age consumer engagement. *IOSR Journal of Business and Management*, *16*(2), 24–28. DOI: 10.9790/487X-16222428

Sintas, J. L., de Francisco, L. R., & Alvarez, E. G. (2015). The nature of leisure revisited. *Journal of Leisure Research*, *47*(1), 79–101. DOI: 10.1080/00222216.2015.11950352

Smith, M., Sun, W., Sutherland, J., & Mackie, B. (2014). Game advertising: A conceptual framework and exploration of advertising prevalence. *The Computer Games Journal*, *3*(2), 95–124. DOI: 10.1007/BF03395948

Somyürek, S. (2014). Öğretim sürecinde Z kuşağının dikkatini çekme: Artırılmış gerçeklik. *Eğitim Teknolojisi Kuram ve Uygulama*, *4*(1), 63–80. DOI: 10.17943/etku.88319

Stewens, J., Schlager, T., Häubl, G., & Herrmann, A. (2016). Gamified information presentation and consumer adoption of product innovations. *Journal of Marketing*, *81*(2), 8–24. DOI: 10.1509/jm.15.0396

Suhartanto, D., Brien, A., Primianac, I., Wibisono, N., & Triyuni, N. (2019). Tourist loyalty in creative tourism: The role of experience quality, value, satisfaction, and motivation. *Current Issues in Tourism*, *23*(12), 1–13.

Telyakar, E. (2022). *Yaşam karmaşasının mobil oyun tercihlerine etkisi (The Effect of Life Complexity on Mobile Game Preferences)*. Yüksek Lisans Tezi, Sosyal Bilimler Enstitüsü, Yıldız Teknik Üniversitesi.

Tham, S., Rodgers, S., & Thorson, E. (2017). Trends and opportunities for digital advertising research. In Rodgers, S., & Thorson, E. (Eds.), *Digital Advertising* (pp. 31–44). DOI: 10.4324/9781315623252-3

Tolunay, A., Alkan, H., & Korkmaz, M. (2004). *Kent ormanlarında rekreasyonel etkinlikler açısından ziyaretçi profilinin belirlenmesi (Determining Visitor Profile in Urban Forests in Terms of Recreational Activities). Türkiye Ormancılar Derneği.* I. Kent Ormancılığı Kongresi.

Topsakal, Y. (2020). Rekreasyon ve dijitalleşme (Recreation and Digitalization). In Y. Yağmur & Ü. Gaberli (Eds.), Rekreasyon: Tarihsel Gelişim, Teoriler, Farklı Alanlarla İlişkiler ve Güncel Gelişmeler (pp. 453-463). Ankara: Nobel Bilimsel Eserler.Torkildsen, G. (2005). Leisure and recreation management. London: Routledge, Taylor and Francis Group.

Tosun, N. B. (2010). *İletişim temelli marka yönetimi (Communication-Based Brand Management)*. Beta Yayınevi.

Türkmen, E., Akgül, B., & Durhan, T. (2024). Dijital okuryazarlığın sanal rekreasyon etkinliklerine katılım sıklığına ve rekreasyon faydaya etkisi. *Tourism and Recreation*, *6*(1), 22–29. DOI: 10.53601/tourismandrecreation.1301883

Tütüncü, Ö. (2012). Rekreasyon ve rekreasyon terapisinin yaşam kalitesindeki rolü (The Role of Recreation and Recreation Therapy on Life Quality). Anatolia. *Turizm Araştırmaları Dergisi*, *23*(2), 248–252.

Uncu, G. (2024). Fijitalizm & metaverse evreninde, markaların pazarlama faaliyetleri (Marketing Activities of Brands in the Fijitalism & Metaverse Universe). *Akademik Sosyal Araştırmalar Dergisi*, *12*(153), 50–70.

Vatsal, R., Mishra, S., Thareja, R., Chakrabarty, M., Sharma, O., & Shukla, J. (2023). (*An Analysis of Physiological and Psychological Responses in Virtual Reality and Flat Screen Gaming*). Communication and Media.

Wedel, M., Bigné, E., & Zhang, J. (2020). Virtual and augmented reality: Advancing research in consumer marketing. *International Journal of Research in Marketing*, *37*(3), 443–465. DOI: 10.1016/j.ijresmar.2020.04.004

Wohlgenannt, I., Simons, A., & Stieglitz, S. (2020). Virtual reality. *Business & Information Systems Engineering*, *62*(5), 455–461. DOI: 10.1007/s12599-020-00658-9

Wu, T. (2017). Pokémon Go: Marketing implications for mobile video game. In Tang, J., & Hung, P. (Eds.), *Computing in Smart Toys* (pp. 7–20). Springer Cham. DOI: 10.1007/978-3-319-62072-5_2

Xi, N., & Hamari, J. (2019). Does gamification satisfy needs? A study on the relationship between gamification features and intrinsic need satisfaction. *International Journal of Information Management*, *46*, 210–221. DOI: 10.1016/j.ijinfomgt.2018.12.002

Yukic, T. S. (1970). *Fundamentals of recreation*. Harper & Row.

ADDITIONAL READING

Ardahan, F., Turgut, T., & Kaplan Kalkan, A. (2016). *Her yönüyle rekreasyon*. Detay Yayıncılık.

Cauberghe, V., Hudders, L., & Poels, K. (2021). Digital advertising and consumer engagement: A conceptual framework. *Journal of Interactive Advertising*, *21*(2), 79–92. DOI: 10.1080/15252019.2021.1892251

de la Hera, T. (2019). *Digital gaming and the advertising landscape*. Palgrave Macmillan. DOI: 10.2307/j.ctvnp0j4g

Domínguez, A., Saenz-de-Navarrete, J., de-Marcos, L., Fernández-Sanz, L., Pagés, C., & Martínez-Herráiz, J. J. (2013). Gamifying learning experiences: Practical implications and outcomes. *Computers & Education*, *63*, 380–392. DOI: 10.1016/j.compedu.2012.12.020

Grimley, M. (2012). Digital leisure-time activities, cognition, learning behaviour and information literacy: What are our children learning? *E-Learning and Digital Media*, *9*(1), 13–28. DOI: 10.2304/elea.2012.9.1.13

Hollebeek, L. D., & Macky, K. (2019). Digital content marketing's role in fostering consumer engagement, trust, and value. *Journal of Interactive Marketing*, *45*(1), 27–41. DOI: 10.1016/j.intmar.2018.07.003

Özel, Ç. H., & Can, İ. İ. (2021). COVID-19 pandemisi sürecinde boş zaman aktivitelerinin dönüşümü. *Turar Turizm ve Araştırma Dergisi, 10*(2), 63–98. Retrieved from https://dergipark.org.tr/tr/pub/turar/issue/64627/986946

KEY TERMS AND DEFINITIONS

Advergame: A digital game designed for advertising purposes in which brand messages or products are integrated into the gameplay. These games combine entertainment with brand promotion to enhance user engagement.

Augmented Reality (AR): A technology that overlays digital images onto the real world, making physical spaces more interactive and visually engaging for users.

Digital Leisure: Leisure activities conducted in digital environments for entertainment, learning, or social interaction. They provide users with flexible, personalized, and time- and location-independent experiences.

Digital Recreation: Activities that individuals perform through digital platforms to spend their leisure time, relax, or entertain themselves. These activities enable users to experience interactive and immersive forms of recreation in virtual environments.

Gamification: The application of game design elements to non-game contexts such as services and advertising. By incorporating game dynamics, it transforms ordinary experiences into more engaging and motivating interactions.

Mobile Advertising: A type of digital marketing that enables brands to reach consumers directly through personalized or location-based messages delivered via mobile devices.

Virtual Reality (VR): A digital simulation that immerses users in a three-dimensional environment, allowing them to interact as if they were physically present in that space.

Chapter 8
Enhancing Marketing Communication Through Gamification in the Fashion Industry

Neetu Singh
http://orcid.org/0000-0002-0338-9846
Symbiosis Institute of Design, Symbiosis International University, Pune, India

ABSTRACT

Gamification is changing how fashion interacts with consumers by leading them into new XR dimensions, challenging traditional marketing communication tools, resulting in heightened consumer engagement and improving marketing metrics like brand identification, enhanced favorability, and purchase intent. This research aims to analyze the application of Gamification in the fashion industry, identifying the benefits and challenges of gamification technologies powered by Augmented reality, Virtual Reality, and Mixed realities and their impact on consumers' fashion purchase experience. By analyzing secondary data and various fashion brand case studies, this research aspires to understand the marketing communication strategies of fashion brands employing Gamification to create immersive experiences by proposing three categories: Gamification in fashion, fashion games, and fashion in games.

INTRODUCTION

Gamification is changing our interactions with the World. What started as a gaming obsession, creating idealistic versions of ourselves, tackling challenging situations in an imaginary fantastical world, is now leading us into new XR dimensions, even

DOI: 10.4018/979-8-3373-6309-7.ch008

propelling us towards making actual purchases. The marketing world has been quick to capitalize on the gaming trend with social media trends, in particular, Instagram gamification, leading consumer engagement through content creation, stories, and gamified posts, engaging over 800 million users, with 33% users confirming positive purchase intentions through gamified engagement (Reflectdigital, 2025). Fashion brands have been experimenting with various modes of entertainment, such as film, television, sports, music, museums, and photography, as marketing communication channels for decades. However, the recent digital and AR (Augmented Reality), VR (Virtual Reality), and MR (Mixed Reality) advancements have made gaming a viable marketing communication channel through emerging opportunities, and enhanced engagement resulting in positive purchase intentions. Catch the critters is an interactive, fun, and pretty oasis game keeping up with the brand's playful image. The game entails swiping and matching a minimum of three critters to score points and progress to the next level while engaging consumers through point accumulation. ASOS's collaboration with The Sims created a limited fashion-savvy game for users. The game available on the user's mobile as an app gives leeway to consumer imagination, allowing them to organize their very own fashion show by dressing and styling characters in Asos garments. Several apps are now engaging in unique games, leading to incentives and winning prizes.

METHODOLOGY

By analyzing secondary data and various fashion brand case studies, this research aspires to understand the marketing communication strategies of fashion brands employing Gamification to create immersive experiences by proposing three categories: Gamification in fashion, fashion games, and fashion in games.

GAMIFICATION IN FASHION

Fashion is undergoing a transformative change through Gamification aided by VR, AR, and 3D visualization technologies, encouraging consumers' psychological purchase motivations, increased consumption, positive word of mouth, and brand loyalty (Hamari et al., 2020; Koivisto & Hamari, 2019).Defined as "the addition of game-related elements to on game contexts" (Basten, 2017, p. 76), the global gamification market valued at \$6.33 Bln in 2019, growing at a CAGR 0f 24.8% is projected to reach \$37 Bln by 2027 and \$89.75 Bln by 2031(Insights, 2025). Implementation of Gamification has been found to have positive effect in the fields of consumer behaviour, marketing and education by enhancing consumer engagement and customer experience through enhanced gamified business processes, with the gamification element points, badges and leader boards known as PBL triad showing high effectiveness in creating favourable attitude of consumer towards a specific behaviour(Douglas & Brauer, 2021; Mulcahy et al., 2021; Subhash & Cudney, 2018). The Technology Acceptance Model (TAM),as an offshoot of Fishbein & Ajzen's (1975 theory of reasoned action, verifies the relationship between consumers' perceived usefulness of a technology in relation to intention and adoption of innovative technology by users (Davis, 1989; Davis et al., 1989).Adding another variable of playfulness validates the application of TAM in the Gamification of fashion, verifying the relationship between consumers' technological innovativeness and fashion innovativeness (Hur et al., 2017). Hence, consumers displaying a high degree of technological innovativeness find pleasure in engaging in Gamification, with their fashion innovativeness getting bolstered by its usage, deriving enjoyment, and ultimately adopting it for continuous brand engagement .SDT or Self-determination theory by Ryan & Deci, 2000 further elucidates human motivation towards engaging in specific behaviour, denoting competence, autonomy, and relatedness as needs controlling behavioural outcomes (Cedrola & Giovannetti, 2024).The difference between traditional marketing communication and Gamified marketing communication is listed below in Table 1.

Table 1. Difference between Traditional marketing communication and gamified marketing communication.

Aspect	Traditional Marketing communication	Gamified Marketing Communication
Use Engagement	Passive-Exposure to advertisements and posts leads to limited outcomes.	Active Engagement by the user.
Consumer Retention	Low-Depending on the nature, quality and engagement provided by the created content.	High retention, due to reward motivation.
Data collection	Low as the exact impact of marketing communication cannot be tapped. Limited to clicks ,forms and surveys which the consumer may or may not subscribe to.	High as consumer gaming preferance,behaviour and actions can be ascertained and quantified as data.
Consumer Experience	Limited to dissemination of information	High consumer experience due to active involvement immersive story play and reward motivation.
Conversion Strategy	Hard selling leads towards conversion.	Indirect but highly Impactful strategy via achievements, rewards, points and benefits.
Brand Recall	Low ,requiring continuous exposure to the brand.	High due to the consumers active participation and involvement in the gamified world.
Cost	Variable, requiring continuous spending to maintain consumer recall and brand preference.	High development costs but high ROI due to consumers high engagement.
Potential to amplify	Content is limited to hashtags and sharing of posts.	High amplification due to social motivation through leaderboards, badges and achievements.

The gamification pioneer, Yu-Kai Chou, elaborated eight key drivers through an Octalysis framework, indicating different consumer motivations(Chou Yu-Kai, 2016; Kai-Yu, 2023). The eight core drivers indicating different consumer motivations through Gamification are

- Epic means and calling-Desire to participate, pursue a mission or goal, or achieve greatness. Hence, various challenges within a game satisfy the user's quest to achieve greatness by challenging the unattainable(Korn et al., 2017).
- Accomplishment and Development -Overpowering one's limits by meeting goals of increasing complexity. Hence, points, badges, rankings, and progress scales meet this requirement in Gamification and contribute to increasing motivation.
- Empowerment of creativity and feedback: Self-expression enables people to customize or try new creative outlets, for example, dressing up digital Avatars in games like Lego or Roblox, usually stemming from a need to receive positive feedback in a social space.
- Ownership and possession: Tap into human need for ownership, which in a game is satisfied through acquiring points, badges, or other credentials.

- Social influence and Relatedness- These are the manifestations of human need for acceptance in a community or society, peer recognition, status, and reciprocity. Fashion within Gamification enables consumers to seek social gratification through their choice of clothing and accessories. It also allows them to augment their self-concept and strive to become a self that they are not in their real lives.
- Scarcity & Impatience: Stressing scarcity leads to an increase in the value of products as consumers tend to increase purchases driven by fear or anxiety, feeling that the product or service is limited. Strategies such as a countdown in marketing communication yield positive results, relying on the time scarcity factor. In gamification techniques, such as "Appointment", scarcity is based, giving the players a limited opportunity through some predetermined moments when the game offers advantages to the players.
- Unpredictability and Curiosity: This factor relies on psychological and medical concepts where unpredictability of an act results in curiosity and engagement. Thus, gambling, betting, and bonuses such as "Easter eggs" in Gamification entice the consumers by generating surprise and evoking their curiosity(Van Rooij et al., 2010; Zendle & Cairns, 2018).
- Avoidance and Loss: Fear of loss is an innate motivation propelling the user to avoid failures or adverse events. When applied in Gamification, negative reinforcement or malus drives engagement through the fear of loss, engaging the users through an urgency or fear of losing progress (Ozturkcan & Şengün, 2016).

A recent mobile app behaviour study done by Digital Turbine and Apptobia concluded that 70% of new-age consumers are mobile gamers spending more time playing mobile games (28 minutes) as compared to Facebook (20 minutes) or TikTok (17 minutes) (Turbine, 2025). Thus, Gamification is a viable proposition for engaging consumers, especially young consumers, towards monetization.(Sue Jeff, 2025). Virtual reality-based fashion app games such as Taobao Life or Roblox challenge all three behaviours, competence, autonomy, and relatedness while playing games, winning points, and using the points to initiate purchase behaviour. Balenciaga's collaboration with Fortnite showcased authentic Balenciaga digital fashion, and Fontography featured In-game, challenging their intrinsic competitive behaviour and autonomy while designing and customizing their own fashion (Jill, 2021; Lau & Ki, 2021). Similar gaming apps by brands like GAP, called Dressing Room, enable consumers to get dressed virtually according to their tastes, and Animal Crossing allows them to dress their digital avatars. Listing of various gaming motivations resulting in desired consumer outcomes is found in Table 2.

Table 2. Game mechanics and motivations resulting in desired outcomes

Game mechanics	Motivation	Objectives	Desired Outcome
Points,ladders and Leader boards	Epic meaning and calling	Engage Employees.Impart brand information to employees.	Employee,Engagement,Learning & development
Quizzes & Badges	Development and Accomplishment	Challenge the user	Motivation to engage in gaming behaviour,Engagement
Stories and challenges	Empowerment of creativity and feedback	Increase participation. Brand storytelling	Increase user Brand experience. Self Expression linked to the need of positive feedback.
Badges, Leaderboards and Status symbols and points	Ownership and Possession	Increase user participation	Increase Social relatedness, engagement
Group quests,teams,conformity anchors,mentorship.Leaderboards badges, certificates and levels	Social influence and Relatedness	User interface in a social setup.	Brand -consumer relationship building. Brand community building
Limited Period "Appointment"	Scarcity and Impatience	Increase scarcity	Marketing communication, Introduction to limited period capsule collections. Brand awareness and Brand loyalty.
Prize draws,contests,bets and lotteries. Random rewards like mystery boxes or loot boxes.	Unpredictability and Curiosity	Generation of surprise and "Wow" element	Leading to brand curiosity and excitement amongst consumers. Rewarding the consumer resulting in Brand loyalty.
Expiring points, Gift points	Loss and Avoidance	Negative reinforcement	Fear of loss

Customer Engagement

Augmented Reality enhances consumers' shopping experience by overlaying digital objects and information onto the real World. Virtual Reality creates a virtual environment for consumers in a real-world setting using computer hardware, software, and head-mounted devices, enabling consumers to have realistic sensory engagements through technology (Dwivedi et al., 2022). These technologies, when used for high involvement product categories like fashion, result in both hedonic and utilitarian benefits for the consumers through SOR, resulting in telepresence (consumers' sensory arousal, control, and immersion) (Stimulus organism response) mechanism (Li et al., 2023; Mehrabian & Russell, 1976). Telepresence reflects a heightened psychological framework after interaction with a VR/AR/MR gaming environment, indicating consumers' sensory. cognitive arousal, control and immersion(J.-H. Kim et al., 2021; Nikhashemi et al., 2021).

The presence /absence of avatars in a digital fashion environment is considered a potential antecedent of perceived presence in a stimulated fashion gaming environment(Zhao et al., 2021). The Gamification of fashion enables consumers to interact in 3D with virtual malls, test drive cars, or watch avatars in a gaming world, changing their fashion rapidly(M. J. Kim et al., 2020; Wang, 2021). The interactive XR technologies involved in Gamification through immersive and non-immersive technologies define interactivity and vividness as two main contributors to evoke telepresence. In the virtual World, interactivity refers to the extent to which a user can modify the form and content of an environment in real-time. In 2023, Gucci sold a virtual bag at Roblox, showcasing that a digital product can be perceived as valuable as a real one. Limited edition products increase hype, create engagement, and enhance brand loyalty (Dressx, 2025). By creating game-like elements in non-gaming contexts, brands in exceptionally high involvement categories like fashion can encourage high engagement, which is critical in enhancing customers' lifetime value, creating active and engaged customers and not passive(Sue Jeff, 2025).

Create the Perfect Fit

The new age fashion now uses AR and VR devices, imbuing consumers with high hedonic and utilitarian values, resulting in high immersion compared to an actual physical world(Ricci et al., 2023). Virtual fitting rooms enable consumers to assess how clothing appears on them using AR, VR, AI, smartphones, tablets, and digital devices (Başeğmez & Tuncali Yaman, 2022). Consumers' accuracy of fit, measurement, and appearance differ between redefined and actual body shape and size, so innovations in Image Interactive Technology (IIT) address this challenge by simulating real-world interactions with products (Yaoyuneyong et al., 2016). These technologies enable the user to view the product item features and angles effectively, providing an engaging shopping experience akin to a physical store try-on.

Amongst some of the new promising developments in this field are Virtual try-on technologies leveraging web interface, Virtual Reality, Augmented Reality, and digital avatars to ensure that the customers experience a seamless apparel fitting experience(Alcantara & Alcantara, 2022; Kang et al., 2020). Brands like Amazon, Outfit-VITON, My-virtual model, and Fit-room allow the users to try on one outfit at a time virtually eventually proving to be strong antecedents to customers satisfaction and repurchase intention(J. V. Chen et al., 2023; Tandon & Ertz, 2024).

In contrast, fashion sites by brands, such as Guess, Taobao, and Uniqlo, enable users to try on several outfits at a time(J. V. Chen et al., 2023; Deeplearning.AI, 2020; Fitroom, 2025). Gamification in virtual try on integrates gaming elements while trying on fashion using digital avatars, interactive display and features, point accumulation, badges, and challenges for heightened user involvement, engagement, interaction, and motivation resulting in customer satisfaction and repurchase intention (Risso & Paesano, 2021; Tandon & Ertz, 2024). Gamification in a virtual dressing room, Fashion Island has enhanced customers' shopping experience while they dress up their avatars through dresses and accessories they would like to purchase (Donatiello et al., 2018). Christian Louboutin, a French-Egyptian designer, has collaborated with Korean app Zepeto to create the Loubi world, displaying their 2021 fashion collection, where users can try on clothing and accessories and attend virtually through their avatars. Victoria's Secret app, The Pink Nation, also uses

Gamification, where users unlock badges while rummaging through the lingerie catalogues, building fashion visuals, and winning prizes(Abdul, 2021). Through Gamification, the brands can communicate their accessible, fun side while challenging consumers' desire to participate and win, thereby creating an engaging and lasting brand experience.

Democratization of Fashion

The digitization of fashion has democratized the fashion industry by offering digital fashion at a lower price than its actual physical version, enabling access to all types of consumers (Noris et al., 2021).Another aspect of fashion within games is the fairness and inclusivity aspect, ensuring that enabling users of all ages, sizes, genders, nationalities, and physiques have equal access to fashion and can make their choices, resulting in a rewarding experience. Virtual fashion is now available to consumers anywhere using IoT,5G, and metaverse technologies(Se Jin Kim, 2023). Luxury fashion brand Balenciaga showcased its Human Destiny themed collection through an online interactive video game, taking users on a gaming journey set in 2031. Video games now allow users to acquire digital clothing for their avatars, giving them access to luxury fashion that they would otherwise not be able to afford in the real World (Reydar, 2021). Players recreated their looks as avatars in games such as Animal Crossing and Sandy's Island Shop, creating digital ensembles with brands such as Chanel, Gucci, Saint Laurent, Off-white, Noah, Calvin Klein, Marc Jacobs, and Valentino, to name a few(Obi, 2020). Globally, there are approximately 3.32 billion video game players(53% of males are gamers and 52% subscribe to at least one gaming service), with Asian gamers totalling to $1.5 Bln and numbers growth showing a staggering $691 Bln estimate by year 2029(Fabio, 2025). These numbers allow fashion brands to make fashion available across digital and non-digital mediums, improving marketing metrics like brand identification, favourability, and consumers' purchase intention.

Tapping into this vast market by fashion brands was imperative, especially during the pandemic when retail stores were inaccessible. During this time, fashion brands increased gamification elements like points, badges, rewards, and virtual experiences to engage them and diversify the sales channel (Cedrola & Giovannetti, 2024). Louis Vuitton partnered with Riot Games to present a League of Legends capsule collection, presenting the games across T-shirts, sneakers, pants bags and other accessories ranging from US$170 up to US$5,600 for a leather jacket(Apparel, 2023a).H&M, Moschino, and Asos released outfits for the Sims series with the Sims characters adorning Marine Serre. Telfar and LaQuan Smith make fashion accessible (Obi, 2020).

Sustainability

Consumers change their fashion preferences quickly, discarding old fashion for new, creating waste, surplus, and landfills, which are highly hazardous to the environment.(X. Chen et al., n.d.; Norum, 2017).Consumers' desire to "fit in" amongst peers leads to increased consumption of fashion clothing and accessories, and finding a viable solution is imperative. Lesser and second-hand consumption are solutions that have been considered unappealing, time-consuming, and inconvenient by consumers, creating a barrier to the circular fashion industry (Denizel & Schumm, 2024; Zhang et al., 2023). A better approach towards sustainability would be to ensure that second-hand garments have a prolonged life cycle and make sustainable fashion products attractive. Massively Multiplayer online role-playing games (MMORPG) build a narrative around characters in games, the role of storytelling, and game satisfaction. Gamification thus has significant potential for facilitating sustainable fashion through gaming elements like storytelling, badges, challenges, and rewards, thus encouraging sustainable fashion consumption. "Eco-gamification" or "green gamification" is a concept which aims towards developing sustainable behaviour amongst users by making it fun rewarding and fulfilling (Deterding et al., 2011; Kai-Yu, 2019).Various game design elements can trigger different motivational outcomes for users, employing an organismic metatheory within self-determination theory(SDT) highlighting the importance of humans inner resources for personality development and self-regulation (Sailer et al., 2017).Thus a total of three needs relatedness, competence and autonomy when built within a gaming mechanism can challenge the intrinsic psychology of the consumer and be utilized to for behaviour change in several contexts like self-management, productivity, education, finance, news, entertainment and environment sustainability amongst many other. Thus green games apply elements to make sustainability fun promoting environmentally friendly behaviours(Md & Azhar, 2017).Brands can use game mechanics, tapping into human motivation like purpose, mastery, and social connection, to foster deeper engagement and behaviour change. Brands can use the generated data to understand user preference towards sustainable fashion and Gamification using Gamification to educate users towards sustainable practices towards purchase of eco-friendly garments, disposal, participating in clothes swapping, and styling using existing options instead of overconsuming (Singh, 2024b; Sustainability, 2025; Waydel-Bendyk, 2020).

Diversified Revenue Streams

Gamification elements like rewards, leader boards, and badges imbibe the users with a sense of achievement, resulting in loyalty for the users. Gaming incentives make the consumer feel valued, encouraging repeat engagement and conversion of users towards long-term patronage and improved customer loyalty. According to the theory of affordance by James J.Gibson, the environment provides opportunities for action where affordance implies actionable properties shared between an object and actor, which in this case is Gamification and consumer perception resulting from a heightened emotional state while engaging in the same(Gibson, 1978, 2014; Huotari & Hamari, 2017). Hence, the gamification mechanism captures and embeds consumers' perceptions into contexts with instrumental intent (Liu et al., 2017). Since the core of gamification experience is intended to provide relaxation and entertainment, the concept can be replicated to shopping experiences that are equally relaxing, fun, and playful (Jayasooriya et al., 2020).Consumers' interaction and experience with fashion brands within a game also supplements their offline behaviour, with consumers preferring the brand in both online and offline contexts (Belghiti et al., 2018). Cross collaboration between the actual and gaming worlds brings an additional revenue stream to brands, capturing users' attention through enhanced digital experiences. Burberry's 2019 interactive experience to sell its puffer jacket collection and Louis Vuitton League of Legends skin outfits, along with a physical limited edition capsule collection, are examples of brands capitalizing on different media to gain the attention of young consumers(Cunningham & Ribeiro, 1997). Brands like Dolce and Gabbana released a one-of-a-kind collection known as Collezione Genesi, a museum-grade collection of nine pieces presented both as an NFT and a physical collection (Fashinnovation, 2025; UNXD, 2020).

Cost Efficiency

Digital platforms, showcasing fashion rely on social connections, online recommendation engines and other enabling technologies especially gamification to enhance consumer experience by making online shopping pleasant and enjoyable (Karać & Stabauer, 2017).Gamified platforms not only provide the consumer with an additional avenue of purchase but the usage of game thinking mechanisms in a non-game context, influences the consumer motivation more specifically as eight core drivers explained through an Octalysis analysis(Kai-Yu, 2023). The fashion industry is rethinking consumer engagement through Gamification, weaving game-like elements in its marketing strategies. This move has resulted in cost-effective methods of increasing brand visibility, collecting consumer data, lead generation, and driving consumer engagement towards brand loyalty(Scratcher, 2024). Message, a multi-brand fashion retailer, has been using Gamification, translating into a significant boost through their campaign, resulting in more than 32000 participants,80% conversion of attendees, and consolation prizes towards driving revenue. Technology and digitization are enabling the development of size and fit for clothing. Using 3D models,3D body scanning, and virtual models with gamification elements enables understanding of fit and appearance on various body types and perfect product creation, highlighting the value of anthropometric information (Gill et al., 2022). Digitizing fit and sizing tools enhances customer satisfaction, reduces consumer returns, increases sales conversions, and bridges physical and digital assessment of clothing (Miell et al., 2018).

Counterfeit Prevention

Gamified fashion on digital networks requires maintenance of the brand's core identity, enabling customer affiliation. The metaverse presents fashion brands with an opportunity to enhance their brand narratives through immersive and interactive experiences through gamified recreation of iconic brand moments, showcasing exquisiteness and craftsmanship, and connecting with the brand's values and heritage through virtual tours of iconic historical spaces, thereby communicating brand authenticity and enabling consumers to connect with the brand. (Koles et al., 2024). Digital transparency company Everledger, through its latest counterfeiting report, estimated losses of nearly $100 Bln due to counterfeits, raising the importance of protecting brand authenticity (Shemona, 2024).

Blockchain, with its decentralized and secure ledger technology, safeguards the exclusivity of digital fashion products in the metaverse and digital domains by creating a digital record for a product, enabling consumers to verify its authenticity by tracing its supply chain from manufacturing to sale, thereby preventing counterfeits. (Lu et al., 2022; Marco et al., 2024).NFT or Non-fungible Tokens, the digital currency through which digital assets are traded and recorded on the blockchain, is a secure peer-to-peer network ensuring transactional security(Sung et al., 2023).

Fashion Games

Fashion plays a crucial role in evolution of culture and society, interestingly with consumers having dual viewpoints, conformists think what is popular is fashion while rebels believe that being different formulates the essence towards fashion. (Cao et al., 2013).These viewpoints formulate the basis of two fundamental social interactions; coordination and anti-coordination simultaneously making fashion games integral to gaming theory also called "strictly competitive games"(Osborne & Rubinstein, 1994, p. 21).When two conformists meet a rebel they play zero sum matching pennies game which is considered pure competition. When two conformists(rebels) meet they play anti coordination game as pure cooperation. Fashion games therefore are considered Common interest games (team games) and are stellar examples of cooperation entailing same ranking of preference for all players of the game. Fashion game simulation shows “that simple social interactions greatly promote cooperation: in most cases people can reach an extraordinarily high level of cooperation, through a selfish, myopic, naive, and local interacting dynamic (the best response dynamic).(Cao et al., 2013, p. 1).

The commonality between Marc Jacobs, Sandy Liang, Valentino, Gucci, and Ted Baker is that these brands dress fashion game characters like Animal Crossing, where simple character options have been converted into intense marketing communication and digital interactions(Duncan Catherine, 2023). Fashion games attract the user's attention, making them aware of the fashion scene and giving them a sense of fashion being something they can get attracted to. Fashion games predominantly deal with dressing up, styling, and makeovers, like girlsgogames.com and stardoll.com entail dressing up or making over a person with storylines leading the player towards a two-way influence, with the player influencing the character and the character reverse-influencing the player too(girlsgogames.com, 2025; stardoll.com, 2025).The intersection of fashion gaming creates a novel personal expression akin to the transformative mechanics of a puzzle, manifesting their individual style and creativity (Bhuyan et al., 2025).Fashion in games thus gives the user a creative outlet to craft their work, personalize their character, and socialize. Games like Dress X and XR Couture enable users to express their originality through virtual collections and allow them to explore their identities, aligning naturally with the fundamental essence of fashion, which is self-expression, influencing everyone around them, even in a virtual setup (Fashinnovation, 2025).

Fashion in Games

Fashion researchers Susan Kaiser and Denise Green discuss the intersectional role of fashion and identity, where on one hand fashion incorporates a person's boundaries (gender, country, age, ethnicity, etc) and on the other spectrum is a means of realizing the self they are trying to become(Denise, 2021). Various fashion discourse spread across media, and digital channels create an aspirational image in the mind of consumers which they emulate or try to reach as close as possible hence to reach as close to “real me” as possible people try to change their appearance, clothing, face bodies etc through diets, color change, cosmetic surgery or clothing etc (Koma, 2023). Metaverse, the most prominent convergence of physical and virtual spaces through Virtual Reality (VR), Augmented Reality (AR), and Mixed Reality (MR), was coined in 1992 in Snow Crash, a dystopian alternate sci-fi world by Neil Stephenson(Appinventiv.com, 2024; J. Kim, 2021).

Virtual spaces such as the metaverse, which are rapidly emerging, enable users to get closer to the self they are trying to become in the virtual World, unrestricted by boundaries, free to follow their desires and become the person they want to be. The

US in-game advertising research 2022 by Anzu on American gamers reveals many fashion enthusiasts becoming gamers, with 76% following influencers and fashion companies, and 66% engaging in upscale brands. Most gamers who participated in the study showed an affinity for fashion brands, with 47% buying Gucci,43% purchasing Dior, and 29% engaging in Chanel(Anzu, 2022). Fashion in a Branded Virtual world(BVW) utilizes the gaming world platforms to create an immersive experience uniquely tailored to specific brands, creating new avenues of brand engagement and ultimately becoming a strategic marketing strategy for fashion brands (Emily, 2021; Wongkitrungrueng & Suprawan, 2024). Another advantage of fashion in games is that the collection can be highly innovative and versatile, using either difficult or unattainable techniques to create in real life, nurturing high design creativity and innovation (Fashinnovation, 2025).

Virtual Identity in Digital Spaces

Factors influencing consumers' adoption of technology through AR,VR, Mixed Reality, Gamification, or mobile apps have been identified as technological innovativeness (inclination to try new technology)and fashion innovativeness(evolving changes in consumption patterns) (Hur et al., 2017). Consumer attitude encompassing their beliefs, feelings, and intentions towards an object determines whether it satisfies consumers' intrinsic needs (competence, relatedness, and autonomy), motivating them towards a behavioural intention(Lau & Ki, 2021; Trivedi & Trivedi, 2018).The characters in the gaming platforms represent the gamers, reflecting the personal identity style and aesthetic sensibility for the users through character representations.(Sang Jin Kim et al., 2012). Fashion one wears is a unique way of identity representation as "clothing and fashion are one of the most important ways of expressing identity because of their full of signs, codes, and meanings inside them" (Akdemir, 2018, p. 1396). Fashion is the main symbol of constructing and reconstructing player identities, with fashion as a means of expressing affinity and as part of a social phenomenon allowing individuals to showcase their personal values, as it brings in solidarity or difference within a social setting(Castaldo Lundén, 2020). Players therefore engage in virtual outfits to showcase their unique personalities, akin to real-life fashion(Katie, 2023). Customization, thus, remains the gamers' top priority as it enables them to reflect their identity and enhances their gaming experience, as stated by 75% of Roblox players(Roblox, 2024).

Metaverse and Fashion Communication

The evolving relationship between fashion, technology, and digital environments, focusing on interactions of fashion within the gaming or metaverse World, can be explained by the concept of Social presence. Virtual fashion on the metaverse is created using, VR, AR and Artificial Intelligence (AI) software's and monetized through a digital currency known as Non fungible Tokens(NFT), enabling brands to auger their image, enhance creativity, increase customer recall, build brand value and brand loyalty amongst young consumers(Linda & John, 2024; program-ace.com, 2024).Numerous fashion brands ranging from high street to luxury, makeup, and accessories such as Gap, Adidas, Burberry, Gucci, Dolce & Gabbana, Balmain, Louis Vuitton. Clinique and Nars have made their foray into the metaverse, with 17% of brands on the index having worked with NFTs as of Winter 2021 (Maghan & Madeleine, 2024). Brand collaborations, such as art projects, digital partnerships, digital collectibles, and tokens granting special perks to the users, have started to capitalize on digital currency usage, bestowing a unique digital identity to products using blockchain. Hence the first recorded sale of a fashion NFT was the iridescent dress created by the Fabricant and sold for $9500 in May 2019, while the first luxury bard entrant was the Gucci Aria film auctioned for a whopping $25000 in May 2021, making fashion on the metaverse, accessible and an extension of its existing brand image enabling consumer patronage (Oleksandra, 2022). Fashion in the metaverse adopts the play culture, where it moves beyond self-adornment, enhancing consumers' social presence and relatedness with "Presence signaling", gratifying their feeling of relatedness by enabling them to feel connected, harbour a sense of belonging and feel supported by the co-digital community (Bilali & Papahristou, 2024; Koma, 2023; Park & Chun, 2023).

In-Game Advertisements

80% of the gaming titles are "free to play," making them accessible to a wide range of audience(Iion.io, 2024). the evolving gaming advertisements are getting more and more immersive and relatable to the gaming players resulting in significant brand engagement. Branded virtual worlds with strong narrative and high social presence increase brand immersion, enabling consumers to connect with the brand. Brand immersion, in turn, mediates the positive effect of brand narrative engagement on consumers' intention to purchase the brand(Romero et al., 2025). Character customization enables players to customize their avatars (gender, skin colour, clothing, accessories) and experience flow (high concentration with intrinsic enjoyment), resulting in avatar identification and subsequent player loyalty(Teng, 2021).Developers craft the in-game fashion items like clothing, accessories, and skins, and players can either purchase them or win them through achievements, points, or special events, making it aspirational for the players. Frequent collaborations between fashion brands and game developers also create a special want for these limited-edition fashion items, with players wanting to get these items and appear similar to their aspirational character, as in games like Fortnite and Roblox, creating NFL, DC. Star Wars and Marvel-based fashion seasons (Paul, 2021). These fashion items use 3D design software, augmented Reality (AR), or digital representations within the metaverse. Once bought, digital fashion is traded using Non-fungible tokens (NFTs) on a blockchain. Gaming merchandise on digital gaming platforms enables fans to express their love for gaming in the real World by purchasing game-inspired fashion lines like clothing, accessories, and shoes, blurring the line between virtual and fashion worlds (iion, 2024). The market for apparel collaborations does exceptionally well, especially capsule collections, which do well when combined with hit games. Levi's with the help of Anzu's gaming advertising solution advertised their 501 jeans brand across multiple gaming platforms like Trackmania, Tennis Clash and Gravity Rider zero resulting in 6 percent increase in brand consideration and 16 percent increase in brand recall, with about two third of gamers after viewing their in-game advertisements visited their website or an online store(Apparel, 2023b). Epic game collaboration with fast fashion giant Uniqlo to create a new fashion collection for the game Fortnite, launched in December 2020, was a massive success, with merchandise featuring characters from the game. Diesel, H&M, and Moschino have partnered with the Sims game franchise to create similar capsules(Apparel, 2023a).

CONCLUSION AND FUTURE RECOMMENDATIONS

The future of fashion is definitely Gamification, especially with the democratization of fashion and the requirement of enhanced sustainability with physical fashion resulting in enormous resource wastage, landfills, and environmental unsustainability(Dominick, 2023; Halicki et al., 2024; Singh, 2024a). Fashion supply chains will benefit immensely through enhanced marketing communication by maintaining brand identity online through consumer engagement, leading towards brand loyalty from digital natives who are otherwise hard to please. Gamification also enables fashion brands to replicate the in-game relaxing, fun, and playful interaction through their offline brick-and-mortar stores, ensuring the consumer connects with the brand through all channels (Zofia, 2023). The interface of Gamification with fashion has become a universal language. It might lead towards fashion becoming a virtual commodity due to digital dependency, reducing consumerism, pollution, and enhancing sustainability through waste reduction. With the advancement in Artificial Intelligence (AI) and Machine learning technologies(ML), Gamification in fashion is enabling a uniquely tailored experience for consumers, analysing a vast amount of data towards understanding and interpreting the precise customer requirements(Kanishka, 2024). Therefore, the shift towards hyper-personalisation enables unique data-driven personalised customer experiences that resonate deeply with the consumer, enabling brand engagement at a superior level and surpassing existing marketing communication strategies.

An ethical concern regarding Gamification is addiction and overuse, where, due to the continuous reward motivation mechanism, the consumers are encouraged to repeat use. Overuse plays a vital role in consumer engagement but can also result in compulsive behaviour when left unchecked. Hence, marketers need to ensure mindful usage of Gamification through time mechanisms like frequent reminders of overuse or options to avoid excessive screen time.

REFERENCES

Abdul, S. B. (2021). *Gamification In Fashion Is Influencing Fashion Freaks*. Mycred. Me. https://mycred.me/blog/gamification-in-fashion-influencing-fashion-freaks/

Akdemir, N. (2018). Visible Expression of Social Identity: The Clothing and Fashion. *Gaziantep University Journal of Social Sciences, 17*(4), 1371–1379. DOI: 10.21547/jss.411181

Alcantara, H., & Alcantara, C. (2022). The future of shopping - Changing Consumers' Mindset through Metaverse Immersive Experiences: hibe Case Study. *Usability and User Experience. AHFE International Conference*. DOI: 10.54941/ahfe1001733

Anzu. (2022). *The US in-game advertising report 2022*.

Apparel, R. (2023a). *Gamification of fashion: A combination that is fast becoming a hit | Apparel Resources*. Apparelresources.Com. https://apparelresources.com/business-news/retail/gamification-fashion-combination-fast-becoming-hit/

Apparel, R. (2023b). *Gamification of fashion: A combination that is fast becoming a hit | Apparel Resources*. Apparelresources.Com. https://apparelresources.com/business-news/retail/gamification-fashion-combination-fast-becoming-hit/

Appinventiv.com. (2024). *What is Metaverse and how is it reshaping the AR/VR world?* Advertising in the Metaverse: Research Agenda. https://appinventiv.com/blog/what-is-metaverse/

Başeğmez, H. & Tuncali Yaman, T. (2022). The Role Of Virtual Try-on Technology In Online Purchasing Decision. *Journal of Research in Business, 7*(IMISC2021 Special Issue), 165–176. DOI: 10.54452/jrb.1023619

Basten, D. (2017). Gamification. *IEEE Software, 34*(5), 76–81. DOI: 10.1109/MS.2017.3571581

Belghiti, S., Ochs, A., Lemoine, J.-F., & Badot, O. (2018). The Phygital Shopping Experience: An Attempt at Conceptualization and Empirical Investigation. In *Developments in Marketing Science: Proceedings of the Academy of Marketing Science* (pp. 61–74). DOI: 10.1007/978-3-319-68750-6_18

Bhuyan, F. A., Rahman, M., Akram, W., & Talim, T. (2025). *Turning puzzle games into fashion: Exploring personal outfits through symbol-based clothing assembly. Fashion, Style & Popular Culture, Online fir(Online First)*. Online First., DOI: 10.1386/fspc_00293_1

Bilali, T., & Papahristou, E. (2024). Analyzing the Impact of Digital Fashion, Gaming, and the Metaverse on Social Presence in Digital Worlds Through a Literature Review. In *Driving Green Marketing in Fashion and Retail* (1st ed., pp. 226–250). IGI Global., DOI: 10.4018/979-8-3693-3049-4.ch014

Cao, Z., Gao, H., Qu, X., Yang, M., & Yang, X. (2013). Fashion, Cooperation, and Social Interactions. *PLoS One*, *8*(1), e49441. DOI: 10.1371/journal.pone.0049441 PMID: 23382799

Castaldo Lundén, E. (2020). Exploring Fashion as Communication: The Search for a new fashion history against the grain. In *Popular Communication*. DOI: 10.1080/15405702.2020.1854952

Catherine, D. (2023). *Growing Playings: Childhood Video Games' Influence on Current Style — STITCH*. Stitchfashion.Com. https://www.stitchfashion.com/home// growing-playings-childhood-video-games-influence-on-current-style

Cedrola, E., & Giovannetti, M. (2024). Fashion and Gamification. In *Digital Transformation for Fashion and Luxury Brands* (pp. 423–442). Palgrave Macmillan., DOI: 10.1007/978-3-031-35589-9_20

Chen, J. V., Ha, Q. A., & Vu, M. T. (2023). The Influences of Virtual Reality Shopping Characteristics on Consumers' Impulse Buying Behavior. *International Journal of Human-Computer Interaction*, *39*(17), 3473–3491. DOI: 10.1080/10447318.2022.2098566

Chen, X., Memon, H. A., Wang, Y., Marriam, I., & Tebyetekerwa, M. (n.d.). Circular Economy and Sustainability of the Clothing and Textile Industry. *Materials Circular Economy*, *1*, 3. DOI: 10.1007/s42824-021-00026-2

Chou, Y.-K. (2016). Actionable Gamification: Beyond points, badges and leaderboards. *Revista Internacional de Organizaciones*, *18*(18), 137–144. DOI: 10.17345/rio18.137-144

Cunningham, P. A., & Ribeiro, A. (1997). The Art of Dress: Fashion in England and France 1750 to 1820. *The William and Mary Quarterly*, *54*(2), 430. Advance online publication. DOI: 10.2307/2953289

Davis, F. D. (1989). Perceived usefulness, perceived ease of use, and user acceptance of information technology. *MIS Quarterly: Management. Management Information Systems Quarterly*, *13*(3), 319–340. Advance online publication. DOI: 10.2307/249008

Davis, F. D., Bagozzi, R. P., & Warshaw, P. R. (1989). User Acceptance of Computer Technology: A Comparison of Two Theoretical Models. *Management Science*, *35*(8), 982–1003. DOI: 10.1287/mnsc.35.8.982

Deeplearning.AI. (2020). *Amazon's Outfit-Viton Generates Apparel Images On Demand*. Deeplearning.Ai. https://www.deeplearning.ai/the-batch/clothes-make-the-model/

Denise, K. B. S., & Green, N. (2021). *Fashion and Cultural Studies* (2nd ed.). Bloomsbury Publishing., https://books.google.co.in/books/about/Fashion_and_Cultural_Studies.html?id=fds_EAAAQBAJ&redir_esc=y

Denizel, M., & Schumm, C. Z. (2024). Closed loop supply chains in apparel: Current state and future directions. *Journal of Operations Management*, *70*(2), 190–223. DOI: 10.1002/joom.1274

Deterding, S., Dixon, D., Khaled, R., & Nacke, L. (2011). From game design elements to gamefulness: Defining "gamification." *Proceedings of the 15th International Academic MindTrek Conference: Envisioning Future Media Environments, MindTrek 2011*. DOI: 10.1145/2181037.2181040

Dominick, A.-F. (2023). *The Fashion Industry Needs to Reduce Its Carbon Footprint | Industry Insights*. Ana.Net. https://www.ana.net/miccontent/show/id/ii-2023-01-sustainable-fashion

Donatiello, L., Morotti, E., Marfia, G., & Di Vaio, S. (2018). Exploiting Immersive Virtual Reality for Fashion Gamification. *IEEE International Symposium on Personal, Indoor and Mobile Radio Communications, PIMRC, 2018-September*, 17–21. DOI: 10.1109/PIMRC.2018.8581036

Douglas, B. D., & Brauer, M. (2021). Gamification to prevent climate change: a review of games and apps for sustainability. In *Current Opinion in Psychology*. DOI: 10.1016/j.copsyc.2021.04.008

Dressx. (2025). *Gaming Meets Fashion: The Rise of Virtual Outfits in the Metaverse - DRESSX | World's leader in digitral fashion technologies*. Dressx.Com. https://dressx.com/news/gaming-meets-fashion-the-rise-of-virtual-outfits-in-the-metaverse?srsltid=AfmBOoqdMHjB9BMKUvLsz3KL9 Gm6A7EXZ1YAyhqJzpIS-r0E4ls6CBmTe

Dwivedi, Y. K., Hughes, L., Baabdullah, A. M., Ribeiro-Navarrete, S., Giannakis, M., Al-Debei, M. M., Dennehy, D., Metri, B., Buhalis, D., Cheung, C. M. K., Conboy, K., Doyle, R., Dubey, R., Dutot, V., Felix, R., Goyal, D. P., Gustafsson, A., Hinsch, C., Jebabli, I., & Wamba, S. F. (2022). Metaverse beyond the hype: Multidisciplinary perspectives on emerging challenges, opportunities, and agenda for research, practice and policy. *International Journal of Information Management, 66*, 102542. Advance online publication. DOI: 10.1016/j.ijinfomgt.2022.102542

Emily, D. S. (2021). *Branded virtual worlds.* Vml.Com. https://www.vml.com/insight/branded-virtual-worlds

Fabio, D. (2025). *How Many Gamers Are There? (New 2025 Statistics).* Explodingtopics.Com. https://explodingtopics.com/blog/number-of-gamers

Fashinnovation. (2025). *Fashion Gamification: The Power and Rise.* Fashinnovation. Nyc. https://fashinnovation.nyc/fashion-gamification-the-power-and-rise/

Fishbein, M., & Ajzen, I. (1975). *Belief, attitude, intention, and behavior : an introduction to theory and research.* Addison-Wesley Pub. Co. https://books.google.co.in/books/about/Belief_Attitude_Intention_and_Behavior.html?id=8o0QAQAAIAAJ&redir_esc=y

Fitroom. (2025). *Virtual Try On Clothes Online - AI Clothes Changer | FitRoom.* Fitroom.App. https://fitroom.app/

Gibson, J. J. (1978). The Ecological Approach to the Visual Perception of Pictures. *Leonardo, 11*(3), 227. DOI: 10.2307/1574154

Gibson, J. J. (2014). The Ecological Approach to Visual Perception. In M. Tomasello (Ed.), *The Ecological Approach to Visual Perception* (Classic). Psychology Press. DOI: 10.4324/9781315740218

Gill, S., Januszkiewicz, M., & Ahmed, M. (2022). Digital fashion technology: a review of online fit and sizing. In *Digital Manufacturing Technology for Sustainable Anthropometric Apparel* (pp. 135–163). Elsevier., DOI: 10.1016/B978-0-12-823969-8.00008-3

girlsgogames.com. (2025). *Girls games - Play free online games for girls at girlsgogames.com.* Girlsgogames.Com. https://www.girlsgogames.com/

Halicki, D., Zaborek, P. & Meylan, G. (2024). Sustainable Fashion Choices: Exploring European Consumer Motivations behind Second-Hand Clothing Purchases. *Administrative Sciences 2024, Vol. 14, Page 174, 14*(8), 174. DOI: 10.3390/admsci14080174

Hamari, J., Thibault, M., & Hassan, L. (2020). Introduction to the Minitrack on Gamification. *Proceedings of the 53rd Hawaii International Conference on System Sciences*. DOI: 10.24251/HICSS.2020.148

Huotari, K., & Hamari, J. (2017). A definition for gamification: Anchoring gamification in the service marketing literature. *Electronic Markets*, *27*(1), 21–31. DOI: 10.1007/s12525-015-0212-z

Hur, H. J., Lee, H. K., & Choo, H. J. (2017). Understanding usage intention in innovative mobile app service: Comparison between millennial and mature consumers. *Computers in Human Behavior*, *73*, 353–361. DOI: 10.1016/j.chb.2017.03.051

iion. (2024). *Fashion in the Gaming Industry*. Iion.Io. https://www.iion.io/blog/fashion-in-the-gaming-industry

Iion.io. (2024). *Fashion in the Gaming Industry*. Iion.Io. https://www.iion.io/blog/fashion-in-the-gaming-industry

Insights, F. B. (2025). *Gamification Market Size, Share & Growth Analysis Report, 2032*. Fortunebusinessinsights.Com. https://www.fortunebusinessinsights.com/industry-reports/gamification-market-100632

Jayasooriya, S., Alles, T., & Thelijjagoda, S. (2020). Demystifying the concept of IoT enabled gamification in retail marketing: An exploratory study. *Proceedings - International Research Conference on Smart Computing and Systems Engineering, SCSE 2020*. DOI: 10.1109/SCSE49731.2020.9313039

Jeff, S. (2025). *How Gamification Is Changing the Game for Brands*. Mintegral. https://www.mintegral.com/en/blog/how-gamification-is-changing-the-game-for-brands

Jill, M. (2021). *Fashion embraces gaming and the direct-to-avatar model*. Glossy. https://www.glossy.co/fashion/fashion-briefing-fashion-embraces-gaming-and-the-direct-to-avatar-model/

Kai-Yu, C. (2019). *Actionable Gamification: Beyond Points, Badges, and Leaderboards eBook : Chou, Yu-kai: Amazon.in: Kindle Store* (reprint). Octalysis Media. https://www.amazon.in/Actionable-Gamification-Beyond-Points-Leaderboards-ebook/dp/B00WAOGY4U

Kai-Yu, C. (2023). *The Octalysis Framework for Gamification & Behavioral Design*. Yukaichou.Com. https://yukaichou.com/gamification-examples/octalysis-complete-gamification-framework/

Kang, H. J., Shin, J., & Ponto, K. (2020). How 3D Virtual Reality Stores Can Shape Consumer Purchase Decisions: The Roles of Informativeness and Playfulness. *Journal of Interactive Marketing*, *49*(1), 70–85. DOI: 10.1016/j.intmar.2019.07.002

Kanishka, T. (2024). *Future Of Gamification 2024 Trends - My Framer Site*. Nudgenow.Com. https://nudgenow.com/blogs/future-of-gamification-trends

Karać, J., & Stabauer, M. (2017). Gamification in e-commerce a survey based on the octalysis framework. *Lecture Notes in Computer Science (Including Subseries Lecture Notes in Artificial Intelligence and Lecture Notes in Bioinformatics), 10294 LNCS*, 41–54. https://doi.org/DOI: 10.1007/978-3-319-58484-3_4/FIGURES/3

Katie, M. (2023). *New Roblox report finds Gen Z users prioritize styling their virtual avatars over themselves in the physical world*. Yahoo.Com. https://www.yahoo.com/lifestyle/new-roblox-report-finds-gen-z-users-prioritize-styling-their-virtual-avatars-over-themselves-in-the-physical-world140100522.html?guccounter=1&guce_referrer=aHR0cHM6Ly93d3cuZ29vZ2xlLmNvbS8&guce_referrer_sig=AQAAAGaFVDhPKzhM

Kim, J. (2021). Advertising in the Metaverse: Research Agenda. *Journal of Interactive Advertising*, *21*(3), 141–144. DOI: 10.1080/15252019.2021.2001273

Kim, J.-H., Kim, M., Park, M., & Yoo, J. (2021). How interactivity and vividness influence consumer virtual reality shopping experience: The mediating role of telepresence. *Journal of Research in Interactive Marketing*, *15*(3), 502–525. DOI: 10.1108/JRIM-07-2020-0148

Kim, M. J., Lee, C. K., & Jung, T. (2020). Exploring Consumer Behavior in Virtual Reality Tourism Using an Extended Stimulus-Organism-Response Model. *Journal of Travel Research*, *59*(1), 69–89. Advance online publication. DOI: 10.1177/0047287518818915

Kim, S. J., Kim, K. H., & Mattila, P. (2012). The role of fashion in the characters of online games. *Journal of Global Fashion Marketing*, *3*(2), 81–88. DOI: 10.1080/20932685.2012.10593110

Kim, S. J. (2023). Virtual fashion experiences in virtual reality fashion show spaces. *Frontiers in Psychology*, *14*, 1–13. DOI: 10.3389/fpsyg.2023.1276856 PMID: 38046109

Koivisto, J., & Hamari, J. (2019). The rise of motivational information systems: A review of gamification research. In *International Journal of Information Management*. DOI: 10.1016/j.ijinfomgt.2018.10.013

Koles, B., Audrezet, A., Moulard, J. G., Ameen, N., & McKenna, B. (2024). The authentic virtual influencer: Authenticity manifestations in the metaverse. *Journal of Business Research, 170*, 114325. Advance online publication. DOI: 10.1016/j.jbusres.2023.114325

Koma, K. (2023). Fashion and Identity in Virtual Spaces. In *The Other Bodies as an Avatar in Animal Crossing* (pp. 187–202). Springer., DOI: 10.1007/978-981-99-0349-8_12

Korn, O., Muschick, P., & Schmidt, A. (2017). *Gamification of production? A study on the acceptance of gamified work processes in the automotive industry*. Advances in Intelligent Systems and Computing., DOI: 10.1007/978-3-319-41661-8_42

Lau, O., & Ki, C.-W. (2021). Can consumers' gamified, personalized, and engaging experiences with VR fashion apps increase in-app purchase intention by fulfilling needs? *Fashion and Textiles, 8*(1), 36. DOI: 10.1186/s40691-021-00270-9

Li, H., Ding, Y., Zhao, B., Xu, Y., & Wei, W. (2023). Effects of immersion in a simulated natural environment on stress reduction and emotional arousal: A systematic review and meta-analysis. *Frontiers in Psychology, 13*, 1058177. Advance online publication. DOI: 10.3389/fpsyg.2022.1058177 PMID: 36698558

Linda, T., & John, M. (2024). *What is the Metaverse? An Explanation and In-Depth Guide*. Techtarget.Com. https://www.techtarget.com/whatis/feature/The-metaverse-explained-Everything-you-need-to-know

Liu, D., Santhanam, R., & Webster, J. (2017). Toward meaningful engagement: A framework for design and research of gamified information systems. In *MIS Quarterly*. Management Information Systems., DOI: 10.25300/MISQ/2017/41.4.01

Lu, W., Jiang, Y., Chen, Z., & Ji, X. (2022). Blockchain adoption in a supply chain system to combat counterfeiting. *Computers & Industrial Engineering, 171*, 108408. DOI: 10.1016/j.cie.2022.108408

Maghan, M., & Madeleine, S. (2024). *The Vogue Business NFT Tracker: Vintage pieces from Prada, Comme des Garcons unveil their stories through NFTs and NFCs*. Vogue Business. https://www.voguebusiness.com/technology/the-vogue-business-nft-tracker

Marco, M. F., Rumen, P., & Della Irene, S. (2024). Sinergie-SIMA 2024 Management Conference. *Sinergie-SIMA 2024 Conference Management of Sustainability and Well-Being for Individuals and Society, 1*(1), 267–287. DOI: 10.7433/SRECP.LP.2024.01

Md, R., & Azhar, A. (2017). Article 1 Applying Green Gamification to Support Green Campus Initiatives in Reducing Carbon Emissions. [JCRINN]. *Journal of Computing Research and Innovation*, *2*(4), 1–6.

Mehrabian, A., & Russell, J. A. (1976). An approach to environmental psychology. In *The MIT Press*. M.I.T. Press.

Miell, S., Gill, S., & Vazquez, D. (2018). Enabling the digital fashion consumer through fit and sizing technology. *Journal of Global Fashion Marketing*, *9*(1), 9–23. DOI: 10.1080/20932685.2017.1399083

Mulcahy, R. F., McAndrew, R., Russell-Bennett, R., & Iacobucci, D. (2021). "Game on!" Pushing consumer buttons to change sustainable behavior: A gamification field study. *European Journal of Marketing*, *55*(10), 2593–2619. Advance online publication. DOI: 10.1108/EJM-05-2020-0341

Nikhashemi, S. R., Knight, H. H., Nusair, K., & Liat, C. B. (2021). Augmented reality in smart retailing: A (n) (A) Symmetric Approach to continuous intention to use retail brands' mobile AR apps. *Journal of Retailing and Consumer Services*, *60*, 102464. DOI: 10.1016/j.jretconser.2021.102464

Noris, A., Nobile, T. H., Kalbaska, N. & Cantoni, L. (2021). Digital Fashion: A systematic literature review. A perspective on marketing and communication. *Journal of Global Fashion Marketing*. DOI: 10.1080/20932685.2020.1835522

Norum, P. S. (2017). *Towards sustainable clothing disposition: Exploring the consumer choice to use trash as a disposal option*. Sustainability., DOI: 10.3390/su9071187

Obi, A. (2020). *Animal Crossing Fashion: Valentino, Marc Jacobs Get Into the Game*. Wwd.Com. https://wwd.com/fashion-news/sportswear/feature/animal-crossing-new-horizons-nintendo-switch-fashion-world-1203628365/

Oleksandra, B. (2022). *What is Fashion NFT and How Brands are Capitalizing on it?* Techpacker.Com. https://techpacker.com/blog/design/how-fashion-brands-are-taking-advantage-of-nfts/

Osborne, M. J., & Rubinstein, A. (1994). *A Course in Game Theory*. The MIT Press.

Ozturkcan, S., & Şengün, S. (2016). Gaining Reward vs. Avoiding Loss. In *Emerging Research and Trends in Gamification* (pp. 48–71). IGI Global., DOI: 10.4018/978-1-4666-8651-9.ch003

Park, J., & Chun, J. (2023). Evolution of Fashion as Play in the Digital Space. *Fashion Practice*, *15*(2), 256–278. DOI: 10.1080/17569370.2022.2149837

Paul, T. (2021). *Fortnite's Metaverse Assembles: The Complete List Of Licensed Skins*. Forbes. https://www.forbes.com/sites/paultassi/2021/02/28/fortnites-metaverse-assembles-the-complete-list-of-licensed-skins/

program-ace.com. D. (2024). *Fashion in the Metaverse: Trends, Examples, and More*. Program-Ace.Com. https://program-ace.com/blog/fashion-in-the-metaverse/

Reflectdigital, D. (2025). *A gamified fashion world... | Reflect Digital*. Reflectdigital.Co.Uk. https://www.reflectdigital.co.uk/blog/a-gamified-fashion-world

Reydar. (2021). *Fashion Gamification: Why Brands Are Gaming in 2021 | REYDAR*. Reydar.Com. https://www.reydar.com/fashion-gamification-balenciaga/

Ricci, M., Evangelista, A., Di Roma, A., & Fiorentino, M. (2023). Immersive and desktop virtual reality in virtual fashion stores: A comparison between shopping experiences. *Virtual Reality (Waltham Cross)*, *27*(3), 2281–2296. Advance online publication. DOI: 10.1007/s10055-023-00806-y PMID: 37360805

Risso, M., & Paesano, A. (2021). Retail and Gamification for a New Customer Experience in Omnichannel Environment. [IJEB]. *International Journal of Economic Behavior*, *11*(1), 109–128. https://doi.org/https://doi.org/ 10.14276/2285-0430.3238

Roblox. (2024). Roblox - Roblox Reports First Quarter 2024 Financial Results. In *roblox.com*. https://ir.roblox.com/news/news-details/2024/Roblox-Reports-First-Quarter-2024-Financial-Results/default.aspx

Romero, P. M., Lim, R. E., & Park, H. (2025). Branded virtual worlds in fashion gaming: Examining the role of brand narratives and social presence in consumer engagement. *Computers in Human Behavior*, *164*, 108505. DOI: 10.1016/j.chb.2024.108505

Ryan, R. M., & Deci, E. L. (2000). Self-determination theory and the facilitation of intrinsic motivation, social development, and well-being. *The American Psychologist*, *55*(1), 68–78. Advance online publication. DOI: 10.1037/0003-066X.55.1.68 PMID: 11392867

Sailer, M., Hense, J. U., Mayr, S. K., & Mandl, H. (2017). How gamification motivates: An experimental study of the effects of specific game design elements on psychological need satisfaction. *Computers in Human Behavior*, *69*, 371–380. DOI: 10.1016/j.chb.2016.12.033

Scratcher. (2024). *Gamification in Fashion: What's Actually Working - Scratcher*. Scratcher.Io. https://scratcher.io/gamification-marketing-in-fashion-industry/

Shemona, S. (2024). *Can blockchain put an end to fakes and ripping-off ideas in fashion? - Just Style*. Just-Style.Com. https://www.just-style.com/news/can-blockchain-put-an-end-to-fakes-and-ripping-off-ideas-in-fashion/

Singh, N. (2024a). Building Sustainability in Textile and Apparel Supply Chains. In *Eco-Innovation and Sustainable Development in Industry 5.0* (pp. 198–222). IGI Global., DOI: 10.4018/979-8-3693-2219-2.ch010

Singh, N. (2024b). Circular Economy in Textile and Apparel Supply Chains. In *Innovation and Sustainability Through Circular Economy in Businesses* (1st ed., pp. 25–64). IGI Global., DOI: 10.4018/979-8-3693-4123-0.ch002

stardoll.com. (2025). *Dress Up Games for Girls - Stardoll | English*. Stardoll.Com. https://www.stardoll.com/en/

Subhash, S., & Cudney, E. A. (2018). Gamified learning in higher education: A systematic review of the literature. *Computers in Human Behavior*, *87*, 192–206. Advance online publication. DOI: 10.1016/j.chb.2018.05.028

Sung, E., Kwon, O., & Sohn, K. (2023). NFT luxury brand marketing in the metaverse: Leveraging blockchain-certified NFTs to drive consumer behavior. *Psychology and Marketing*, *40*(11), 2306–2325. Advance online publication. DOI: 10.1002/mar.21854

Sustainability, D. (2025). *Gamification Sustainable Fashion Consumption Behaviors Scenario*. Prism.Sustainability-Directory.Com. https://prism.sustainability-directory.com/scenario/gamification-sustainable-fashion-consumption-behaviors/

Tandon, U., & Ertz, M. (2024). Modelling gamification, virtual-try-on technology, e-logistics service quality as predictors of online shopping: An empirical investigation. *Current Psychology (New Brunswick, N.J.)*, *43*(16), 14289–14303. DOI: 10.1007/s12144-023-05379-2

Teng, C. I. (2021). How can avatar's item customizability impact gamer loyalty? *Telematics and Informatics*, *62*, 101626. Advance online publication. DOI: 10.1016/j.tele.2021.101626

Trivedi, J. P., & Trivedi, H. (2018). Investigating the Factors That Make a Fashion App Successful: The Moderating Role of Personalization. *Journal of Internet Commerce*, *17*(2), 170–187. DOI: 10.1080/15332861.2018.1433908

Turbine, D. (2025). Mobile App Habit Report | Digital Turbine. In *digitalturbine.com*. https://www.digitalturbine.com/insight/mobile-app-habit-report-2022

UNXD. (2020). *UNXD: Digital Luxury & Culture NFTs*. Unxd.Com. https://unxd.com/drops/collezione-genesi

Van Rooij, A. J., Meerkerk, G.-J., Schoenmakers, T. M., Griffiths, M., & van de Mheen, D. (2010). Video game addiction and social responsibility. *Addiction Research and Theory, 18*(5), 489–493. DOI: 10.3109/16066350903168579

Wang, C. L. (2021). New frontiers and future directions in interactive marketing: Inaugural Editorial. *Journal of Research in Interactive Marketing, 15*(1), 1–9. Advance online publication. DOI: 10.1108/JRIM-03-2021-270

Waydel-Bendyk, M. (2020). Evaluating Potential of Gamification to Facilitate Sustainable Fashion Consumption. In *Lecture Notes in Computer Science (including subseries Lecture Notes in Artificial Intelligence and Lecture Notes in Bioinformatics): Vol. 12204 LNCS* (pp. 205–215). Springer. DOI: 10.1007/978-3-030-50341-3_16

Wongkitrungrueng, A., & Suprawan, L. (2024). Metaverse Meets Branding: Examining Consumer Responses to Immersive Brand Experiences. *International Journal of Human-Computer Interaction, 40*(11), 2905–2924. DOI: 10.1080/10447318.2023.2175162

Yaoyuneyong, G., Foster, J., Johnson, E., & Johnson, D. (2016). Augmented Reality Marketing: Consumer Preferences and Attitudes Toward Hypermedia Print Ads. *Journal of Interactive Advertising, 16*(1), 16–30. Advance online publication. DOI: 10.1080/15252019.2015.1125316

Zendle, D., & Cairns, P. (2018). Video game loot boxes are linked to problem gambling: Results of a large-scale survey. *PLoS One, 13*(11), e0206767. Advance online publication. DOI: 10.1371/journal.pone.0206767 PMID: 30462669

Zhang, D., Frei, R., Wills, G., Gerding, E., Bayer, S., & Senyo, P. K. (2023). Strategies and practices to reduce the ecological impact of product returns: An environmental sustainability framework for multichannel retail. *Business Strategy and the Environment, 32*(7), 4636–4661. DOI: 10.1002/bse.3385

Zhao, Y., Baghaei, N., Schnack, A., & Stemmet, L. (2021). Assessing Telepresence, Social Presence and Stress Response in a Virtual Reality Store. *2021 IEEE International Symposium on Mixed and Augmented Reality Adjunct (ISMAR-Adjunct)*, 52–56. DOI: 10.1109/ISMAR-Adjunct54149.2021.00020

Zofia, Z. (2023). *Fashion brands evolve NFC tag strategies to provide more value, exclusivity - Glossy*. Glossy.Co. https://www.glossy.co/fashion/why-implementing-nfc-tags-for-fashion-items-isnt-enough/

ADDITIONAL READING

Bazaki, E., & Wanick, V. (2023). *Reinventing fashion retailing : digitalising, gamifying, entrepreneuring* (1st ed.). Palgrave Macmillan., https://books.google.com/books/about/Reinventing_Fashion_Retailing.html?id=IdekEAAAQBAJ DOI: 10.1007/978-3-031-11185-3

Burke, B. (2014). *Gamify: How Gamification Motivates People to Do Extraordinary Things* (1st ed.). Routledge., https://www.routledge.com/Gamify-How-Gamification-Motivates-People-to-Do-Extraordinary-Things/Burke/p/book/9781937134853

Cedrola, E., & Giovannetti, M. (2024). Fashion and Gamification. In *Digital Transformation for Fashion and Luxury Brands* (1st ed., pp. 423–442). Springer International Publishing., DOI: 10.1007/978-3-031-35589-9_20

Gupta, S., Nagina, R., Paruthi, M., & Gupta, G. (2024). *Marketing and Gamification* (1st ed.). Routledge., DOI: 10.4324/9781032694238

Hyzy, M., Wardle, B., & Zichermann, G. (2023). *Gamification for product excellence : make your product stand out with higher user engagement, retention, and innovation* (1st ed.). Packt Publishing., https://www.packtpub.com/en-us/product/gamification-for-product-excellence-9781837638383

Moreira, A. C., Bernades, O., & Amorim, V. (2022). Handbook of Research on Cross-Disciplinary Uses of Gamification in Organizations. In *IGI Global* (1st ed.). IGI Global., https://www.igi-global.com/book/handbook-research-cross-disciplinary-uses/276508

Osborne, M. J., & Rubinstein, A. (1994). *A Course in Game Theory* (1st ed.). The MIT Press., https://mitpress.mit.edu/9780262650403/a-course-in-game-theory/

Santos, J. D., & Sousa, B. M. (2022). Promoting Organizational Performance Through 5G and Agile Marketing. In Santos, J. D., & Sousa, B. M. (Eds.), *Promoting Organizational Performance Through 5G and Agile Marketing*. IGI Global., DOI: 10.4018/978-1-6684-5523-4

Sutherland, K. E., & Barker, R. (2023). Transmedia brand storytelling: Immersive experiences from theory to practice. In *Transmedia Brand Storytelling: Immersive Experiences from Theory to Practice* (1st ed.). Springer Nature. https://doi.org/DOI: 10.1007/978-981-99-4001-1/COVER

Wang, C. L. (2023). The Palgrave Handbook of Interactive Marketing. In Wang, C. L. (Ed.), *The Palgrave Handbook of Interactive Marketing* (1st ed.). Springer International Publishing., DOI: 10.1007/978-3-031-14961-0_43

KEY TERMS AND DEFINITIONS

AI (Artificial Intelligence): Artificial Intelligence is the human-like capability of computers towards learning, reasoning, perception, analysis, problem solving, and decision-making tasks, such as large learning models, language processing, robotics, and large data analysis.

AR (Augmented Reality): An interactive experience where enhancement of real-time information happens through computer-generated visual elements,3D models, or texts through smartphones, tablets, and digital devices.

Blockchain: Blockchain is a decentralized digital ledger that securely records transactions across computers, enhancing data transparency and tamper-proof.

ML (Machine Learning): ML is a subset of Artificial Intelligence, enables computers to analyze, learn, and improve from existing data without requiring programming to conduct those tasks.

MMORPG (Massively Multiplayer Online Role-Playing Games): Massively multiplayer online role-playing games enable many players to interact with each other, engage, customize, and create new characters, play games, and meet challenges all online in a digital gaming world.

NFTs (Non-fungible tokens): These are unique digital identifiers stored on a blockchain. NFTs are unique and different from cryptocurrencies as they are not interchangeable, each having an exceptional value that is impossible to replicate.

SDT: Self-determination theory by Ryan & Deci, 2000 elucidates human motivation towards engaging in specific behaviour, denoting competence, autonomy, and relatedness as needs controlling behavioural outcomes.

SOR: Stimulus Organism response model frameworks the relationship between the external stimuli (S)within an environment, impacting the emotional state of an individual or organism (O), resulting in a behavioral response (R).

TAM-Technology Acceptance Model: This model explores variables influencing consumers' acceptance of new technologies, finding a relationship between users' beliefs about a technology's usefulness and the attitude and intention to use that technology.

VR-Virtual Reality: VR technologies simulates a real-world environment using computer modeling, which can be explored and interacted with by a person using special headsets and devices.

Chapter 9

Personalizing the Customer Journey Across Phygital Touchpoints: Sephora's Gamification Strategies

Sandeep Shede
http://orcid.org/0009-0004-8483-958X
Alliance School of Business, Alliance University, India

Biswa Prakash Jena
http://orcid.org/0000-0002-5691-4130
Alliance School of Business, Alliance University, India

Indu Sharma
Alliance School of Business, Alliance University, India

ABSTRACT

As global beauty retail is evolving continuously due to rapid digital disruption and changing consumer expectations, Sephora has emerged as a global leader in leveraging gamification - game mechanics such as rewards, challenges, interactive content, and status 3-tiers loyalty program to create highly immersive, and data-driven hyper-personalised experiences that complement simultaneously and bridge in-store and online environments. This chapter investigates Sephora's strategic use of gamification for adapting customer-centric game designs to enhance retail innovation. The study analyses the gamified beauty insider program, website pages, mobile app features, social media platforms, augmented reality tools, and interactive in-store technologies to understand how Sephora's gamification serves as marketing tool and provides dynamic customer centric framework which operates with valuable

DOI: 10.4018/979-8-3373-6309-7.ch009

customer behavioural data-driven hyper-personalization engine that personalize the customer journey, increase engagement, deepens loyalty, and enhance brand engagement across phygital retail landscapes.

INTRODUCTION

In the rapidly evolving retail landscape, Sephora, emerges as a global beauty leader by offering wide range of body, cosmetics, skincare, hair, fragrance, and accessories (Jain, 2025) from both its own private label 'Sephora Collection' and over 340 carefully curated premium global beauty brands (Smith, 2024) that exemplifies company's integration of strategic innovation in phygital ecosystem through a seamless blend of physical and digital experiences by leveraging power of gamification for redefining customer engagement and long-term loyalty (Lukic, López & Pagès, 2024). This fusion of the physical and digital worlds, customer-centric personalization approach and gamification integration by Sephora aims to deliver data-driven hyper-personalized, immersive experiential beauty shopping journeys that appeal to modern beauty consumers' personal expectations for utmost convenience, recommendations as per individual preferences, and meaningful interactivity with brand through bidirectional communication with greater speed and agility (McKinsey, 2025a).

Sephora's phygital ecosystem includes physical stores, website, mobile app, social media platforms, and online and offline events (Tate, 2023). Sephora uses gamification strategies - such as points, challenges, rewards, and interactive experiences within its phygital ecosystem to successfully navigate omnichannel marketing challenges to create a unified, playful, and personalized beauty shopping experience for all (Grzybowska, 2025). In gamified phygital retail, a global benchmark is created by Sephora through industry first adoption of technological innovations, including interactive features, unique 3-tiered instant discount and point based loyalty program, and data-driven hyper-personalized engagement tactics (McKinsey, 2025b). Sephora's integration of game mechanics in phygital ecosystems often hyper-personalizes the customer beauty journey in innovative ways that drive customers brand affinity, increases the potential for repeat purchase, amplification of user generated content (UGC) through social media sharing and constructive efforts for beauty community development (Rebiere & Mavoori, 2021).

In the US it is found that 78% of all purchases are made in-store (Think with Google, 2024a) and 73% of consumers are channel-agnostic. Majority of Sephora customers beauty journeys start online through information searches that increasingly influences their beauty product decision and further reinforces purchasing behaviour in physical stores (Think with Google, 2024b). Sephora's 'Delivered to

Beauty' campaign provides prominence to physical retail operations to encash the power of personalized beauty experience to improve consumer engagement, increase customer satisfaction, foster brand loyalty (Power Commerce, 2025) and compete in the global beauty market (Patov, 2024). The familiarity and tailored personalized beauty experiences by beauty consultants in Sephora's physical store shape customers future behaviour for increasing online shopping to enjoy benefits of digital touchpoints thereby providing opportunity to the company to target altogether new customer segments with latent beauty needs (Tate, 2023).

Sephora's website and mobile app are designed to be user-friendly and engaging (Marketing Explainers, 2024). The company's mobile app is a cornerstone of the omnichannel ecosystem (Deloitte, 2021b) that intends to work as personal shopping assistant or a Sephora sales associate and offers one-stop shop by providing educational information to interested users (Patov, 2024). Sephora's mobile app is the most used app in the history of retail recording a 3X increase in mobile shopping globally. App users purchase 2X more frequently and spend 2X more annually than the average customer (Nguyen, 2024). Sephora's mobile app feature allows customers to view their beauty insider points, and search products that are available in the nearest store or purchase them online (Honigman, 2025). Sephora research has found that most Gen Z and millennial consumers journey commonly begin and end on a mobile device (CXNet, 2025), but in-store experiential experience is also very significant touchpoint (Das, Kalia & Kuijpers, 2023). Over 57% of Sephora consumers have used in-store mobile app feature inside retail store (42signals, 2024).

This study explores how Sephora's gamified touchpoints integrate customers psychological triggers such as achievement, curiosity, and social connection by drawing from theories of customer engagement, experiential marketing, and human-computer interaction. The study unpacks how Sephora strategically uses user experience analysis, and customer journey mapping across phygital touchpoints to better align the integration of game-like elements by involving key decision points in the shopping journey highlighting mainly product discovery, trial to purchase and post-purchase engagement. It also examines how gamification supports Sephora's broader omnichannel strategy framework by fostering hyper-personalised customer experience continuity and global brand cohesion across app interfaces, e-commerce platforms, and physical retail spaces. Sephora's success lies in its ability to continuously adapt and localize gamified experiences to meet the expectations of diverse country markets and target customer segments. The study critically evaluates potential risks and limitations highlighting gamification fatigue, privacy concerns, and the digital divide.

THEORETICAL BACKGROUND OF PHYGITAL RETAIL, PERSONALIZATION, AND GAMIFICATION

Theoretical Background of Phygital Retail

Globally, retail dynamics is no longer confined to the most riveting sensory pleasure of physical storefront or convenient digital website and mobile app but incorporates an integrated ecosystem where customer interactions cross seamlessly between online and offline channels (Lopienski, 2024). This phenomenon, termed 'phygital', responds to fast changing consumer habits where existing loyal shoppers expect to move fluidly between browsing on a smartphone, experiencing products in-store, effective faster checkout with one touch payment integration, enjoy unique buying experiences, and sharing personal moments on social media platforms (Rebiere & Mavoori, 2021). Phygital retail ecosystem focuses on customers emotions and provides immediate service and satisfaction to customer with unmatched speed, utmost convenience and better responsiveness (Watt & Lester, 2025) by managing adequate inventory and complexities of green last mile logistics operations that offer a seamless shopping journey across different touchpoints (Kornilov, 2024) without sacrificing service quality resulting in increased touchpoints interactions and transactions thereby strengthening brands emotional bonding (Rukavina, 2025).

Theoretical Background of Personalization

Marketing personalization is the process of using data coming from different touchpoints to target and retarget leads with a synchronous brand message that speaks directly to customer considering that specific customers' interests, demographics, and past buying behaviour (Adobe, 2024). The retail companies for effective personalization utilize many strategies like leverage big data and analytics to understand target customers (develop 360-degree customer profile from contextual, transactional, behavioural, and preference data coming from all touchpoints), use users contextual cues and touchpoints interactions to tailor coherent brand messaging (users previous search history used for most tailored product recommendations, and suggest customized cross-sell offers), provide hyper-personalized recommendations and offers (uses past purchase history data to provide highly relevant products and offers), build emotional connections with customers through relevant content (individual's needs and interests based content), design individually hyper-customized products and service (tailored to each customer's unique style and needs), and adopt an organization-wide focus on personalization (more holistic, highly coordinated, and consistent across touchpoints). Also retail companies face many challenges like obtaining accurate, ethical customer data, achieving personalization at rapid scale, maintaining data security, user privacy and transparency, and managing rising costs and technology resources required for smooth and efficient marketing operations (EHL Holding SA, 2024).

Theoretical Background of Gamification

Gamification involves the application of game design elements in non-game contexts (Santos, Dias & Bairrada, 2024). Gamification is the process of creating a game-like environment to non-game settings like a website or application (Zhang et al., 2025), which acts as a critical customer driver to elevate passive consumption into active participation, and leading to stronger emotional engagement (Li, Zubielqui & Hill, 2025). Gamified elements are making the shopping process interactive, fun, and rewarding (Faster Capital, 2025). Gamification in marketing used as stickiness for sharing, content creation, and purchases across different touchpoints (Abraham, 2020). Gamification marketing technique offers points, badges, leaderboards, challenges, rewards, prizes, discounts, and exclusive offers to customers (Khoros, 2025). Gamification disrupted how younger consumers shop more openly by reinforcing self-representation with digital identities in the virtual world (Locke, 2025).

Gamification tactics blend into human psychology for tapping human desires for fun, challenge, achievement, recognition, status, competition and social interaction by creating memorable gamified experiences by transforming mundane real-world activities tasks into engaging game-like adventures and rewarding desired behaviours to achieve goals through motivational drivers highlighting brand reinforcements and personal emotions for developing lasting brand impression on customers (Faster Capital, 2025). Gamified elements integration makes buying goods more interactive, fun, and a satisfying task to complete. Customers are incentivized to keep "playing" as they progress to a higher level in their membership or unlock special rewards and getting points (Abraham, 2020). Company utilizes website, app and social media platforms to provide gamified contests and challenges to customers and encourages them to participate (Dowdall, 2024). Physical stores transform into adventure spaces to overcome customers challenges, and customers become brand protagonists through UGC (CAAD Retail Design, 2025).

Psychologist Mihaly Csikszentmihalyi's Flow Theory (FT) of gamification utilise the practice of designing an immersive and challenging shopping experience that induces a human motivational state into more organised 'flow channel' for improving focused user engagement and enjoyment for the shoppers (Chakraborty & Rana, 2025). Psychologists Edward Deci and Richard Ryan's Self-Determination Theory (SDT) provide a framework that defines intrinsic and varied extrinsic sources of human motivation in cognitive, social and personality development through enhanced performance, persistence, and creativity. SDT also highlight well-being, quality of performance, social and cultural factors related to individual's experience of autonomy, competence, and relatedness that facilitate or undermine persons sense of volition and initiative (Self-Determination Theory, 2025). Yukai Chou's Octalysis (8 core drives) framework for gamification & behavioural design include - epic meaning and calling, development and accomplishment, empowerment of creativity and feedback, ownership and possession, social influence and relatedness, scarcity and impatience, unpredictability and curiosity and loss and avoidance (Chou, 2025).

Gamification in Retail Marketing

The gamification retail industry was estimated at US$21.81 billion in 2024 and expected to reach US$145.75 billion by 2032 (Beri, 2023). The integration of gamification can increase retail customer acquisition, customer retention and engagement by up to 700%, 22% and between 100% – 150% respectively (CAAD Retail Design, 2025). The customer undertakes gamification participation by writing a review, completing a purchase, or answering a peer's question, there by building community and the brand (Khoros, 2025). The usage of gamification into customer engagement strategies increases meaningful engagement, brand loyalty and brand awareness by 47%, 22% and 15% respectively (Sandler, 2023). Adoption of gamification strategies benefit businesses with growing brand reputation and image, enhance the user experience, drive social media engagement, attract new customers to their stores, influencing customer behaviour, increasing customer confidence, creating online value for products, awareness, increase user participation, enhancing purchases, customer satisfaction, improve loyalty, rewards motivate customers to boost sales, and cut marketing costs (Dowdall, 2024).

Augmented Reality (AR) retail market was US$4.0 billion in 2023 growing at 29.9% annually and projected to reach US$54.7 billion by 2033 (Mattan 2025b). AR storefronts technology uses interactive gamification to transform traditional static retail displays into interactive, engaging tools for attracting customers with three times higher foot traffic (Mattan, 2025c) and turning passive window shopping into active product exploration (Mattan, 2024a). AR-enabled storefronts provide 11 times higher engagement rates than static displays, and 70% of consumers take immediate action after engaging with AR outdoor advertising. Customers can virtually try on or access detailed product information through smartphone interactions with storefront displays. Implementation costs range from US$50,000 to US$200,000 for complete storefront AR systems, with ROI typically realized within 6-12 months through increased foot traffic and sales. Almost 91.75% of Generation Z demand AR-enabled shopping experiences. AR retail applications deliver business performance with 31% sales growth, 90% higher conversion rates, and 22-40% reductions in return rates (Mattan, 2025b).

RESEARCH METHODOLOGY

This chapter adopts a qualitative method of research design. The research utilizes a thorough review methodology for drawing inferences by synthesizing available trusted information from existing literature and research reports to provide a comprehensive overview of Sephora's gamification challenges and opportunities within the framework of the phygital ecosystems and personalization across customers life cycle journey. A multi-stage content search strategy was used to ensure the availability of trustworthy literature for undertaking comprehensive research coverage. A selection of old and recent studies was considered and included if they were highly essential to the analysis and scientific discourse. The methodology is based on a desk review of existing openly available trustworthy literature and is subject to all sources inherent author bias, research study limitations and ultimate source material used by them to derive a conclusion. The exclusion of non-English language publications published mainly by Sephora's holding company in French and other European Union based local researchers in local European languages might have limited the study's wider scope. While every effort was made by researchers to identify and include relevant literature, meaning this research cannot capture every single initiative / challenge and offer respective strategies / solutions to manage it effectively and efficiently.

RESULTS / FINDINGS

The results / findings section includes, a) Sephora company background, b) Sephora's integration of phygital retail, personalization and gamification, c) Sephora's in-store gamification technologies, d) Sephora's digital gamification technologies extending to physical experiences and e) the beauty insider loyalty program as a gamified phygital hub. These topics were explained briefly under each heading for better clarity of content presentations.

SEPHORA COMPANY BACKGROUND

In 1969, 'Shop 8' beauty retail store was founded by Dominique Mandonnaud with the unique concept of "try before you buy" that targets prospective customers to experience beauty products before buying. He purchased the Sephora chain in 1993 and Louis Vuitton Moët Hennessy (LVMH) purchased Sephora in 1997 (Tate, 2023). In 2024, Sephora operated in 35 countries with 2,700 retail stores and had US$17 billion in annual revenue. The company offers 45,000 beauty products from 340 big beauty brands and its own private label 'Sephora Collection'. Sephora's clean beauty products initiative started in 2018 (Sephora, 2025a) includes high ingredient safety standards signifying clear focus on providing sustainable beauty options for catering growing demand globally (Marketing Explainers, 2024). Planet Aware at Sephora' was started in 2023 (Sephora, 2025b). Sephora US was started in 1998 and has over 500 stores. The company's global ecommerce website and mobile app was introduced in 1999 and 2010 respectively. Sephora beauty insider loyalty program and client loyalty program started in 2003 and 2007 respectively (Sephora, 2025a).

Sephora's adoption of the Phygital retail model with technology integration is way ahead of competitors. Phygital model expanded its customer reach and provided unique personalized shopping experiences across customers life cycle journey (Marketing Explainers, 2024). Sephora customers spend time in physical store to explore, experiment, and engage with a wide variety of beauty products (Marketing Maverick, 2024). The "try before you buy" initiative with integration of instore technology (Tate, 2023) is whole heartedly supported by in-store beauty advisors to provide personalized beauty consultation and live experiences without any purchase obligations from customers (Deloitte, 2021a). The in-store technologies like Color IQ analyse customers skin tone for selecting suitable beauty shades, and interactive kiosks provide virtual try-ons of these shades (Tate, 2023). The company periodically launches new beauty products and offers exclusive tiered discounts to existing loyal customer base through Beauty Insider loyalty program (Cezim, 2025).

SEPHORA'S PHYGITAL RETAIL, PERSONALIZATION AND GAMIFICATION

This section briefly explains the a) Sephora's phygital retail, b) Sephora's personalized phygital customer journey, and c) Sephora's gamification strategies for emotional engagement and loyalty management. These topics were explained briefly under each heading for better clarity of content presentations.

Sephora's Phygital Retail: Sephora's Truly Phygital Strategy

Sephora's Phygital touchpoints penetrate in highly competitive global beauty market by creating value for customers through unique personalized beauty experiences by offering convenient shopping experience (KPMG, 2025b), build more deeper relationships with loyal customers that bridges divide between immersive digital and riveting in-store features by creating a unified customer journey smoothly and intuitively, where each channel complements the other rather than compete with it (Power Commerce, 2025). Beauty retail companies need to ensure consistent quality across phygital as over 63% of customers shopping journeys start online

(Kornilov, 2024). Sephora's Phygital model includes 'Buy Online, Pick Up In Store' (BOPIS) where customers browse and buy beauty product online and pick them in a convenient store (Silvia, 2024). It encourages online buying and store visits result in further impulse buying. Another initiative 'Reserve Online, and Try In-Store', where customers browse and reserve products online and try them in store (42signals, 2024) or schedule consultations with in-store beauty associates before buying or vice versa (Ellis, 2025).

Sephora's 'Beauty Insider loyalty' program offers 3-tiered upfront discounts (Lindecrantz, Gi, & Zerbi, 2020) and opportunity to accumulate loyalty points after purchases and redeem them in phygital ecosystems (Smith, 2024). The company's integration of single, centralized seamless mobile payment application from J.P. Morgan having high volumes processing capacity across phygital ecosystems helps them to manage customers purchases, exchanges and returns across different touchpoints. It also resulted in beauty advisors spending more time with customers, increase in average purchase value, and improved checkout experience (J.P. Morgan, 2024). Sephora customers review available on website and mobile app help other customers to make informed buying decisions before purchases but it also offers an opportunity for Sephora to integrate direct feedback to improve beauty products portfolio and service quality across different touchpoints (Patov, 2024). The company has been a beauty industry pioneer in embedding AI and gamified experiences that enhances the brand's omnichannel approach, helping beauty customers feel personally connected with the brand and motivated to simultaneously engage in both online and offline channels (Edmonds et al., 2025).

Sephora's In-Store Experience: A Beauty Playground

The conversion of Sephora's strategically accessible, attractive and captivating 'Store of the Future' physical locations design layout into immersive digital playgrounds for beauty enthusiasts of all demographics (Smith, 2024) by combining cutting-edge technology integration thereby creating seamless blend of physical and digital elements create a seamless omnichannel strategy to builds trust and allows customers to make more informed purchasing decisions (Briedis et al., 2021). Sephora's 'Delivered to Beauty' campaign offers US$20 for encouraging customers to visit stores to understand consumers changing expectations and provide tailored personalized beauty consultations from expert beauty advisors to foster human connection (Hammers, 2025). This encompasses the 'Get Beauty from People Who Get Beauty' initiative. Sephora store offers unique and memorable shopping environment that highly reinvents personalized experiences with 15-minute skin scans & skincare treatments (Jain, 2025), 60-minute makeup application, exclusive discounts, product sampling (Power Commerce, 2025), beauty classes and community activities (Zhu, 2025) as per individual needs and preferences (Meyer, 2023).

Sephora Store (LVMH, 2023)

The Sephora's neutral stores having multiple brands are go-to destination for beauty lovers and designed to provide adventurous delightful environment that boosts customer satisfaction and engagement with kiosks (Deslandes, 2017), augmented reality stations, virtual try-on stations, thoughtfully positioned interactive displays (Smith, 2024), and beauty advisors personalized advice on tutorials and makeovers and product recommendations that teach and inspire customers to learn new beauty techniques in self-expressive manner thereby allowing them to discover, search, explore, learn, touch, test, play and engage with beauty products in hands-on immersive, experiential and interactive novel way with self-checkout kiosks (Marketing Explainers, 2024) and one touch mobile payment 'Tap to Pay on iPhone' options for purchases, exchanges and returns (J.P. Morgan, 2024) that cannot be replicated online (Power Commerce, 2025).

Most beauty customers are frustrated as they buy wrong beauty product that was not the right fit for them. Sephora's in-store 'Pocket Contour' classes offer beauty tips about how to use products properly and also suggest the right fit considering skin tones (Nguyen, 2024). Mobile devices and iPad enable beauty advisors to offer individualized beauty suggestions, display product reviews and provide up-to-date product information (McKinsey, 2025b). Some Sephora stores offer immersive AR and VR experiences that gamify product education and brand storytelling, enhancing emotional connection and customer delight (Super AGI, 2025). Sephora customers can use digital tools to choose their personal interest beauty product color by using Color IQ, that provide more useful information and confidence to make informed decisions when making purchases in-store (Worldwide Business Research, 2025). Sephora physical stores provides the intuitive consumer experience by integrating digital tools inside store setting by blending digital convenience with concierge in-store service relevance and appeal (Zhu, 2025).

Sephora's Digital Experience: Website, Mobile Platforms and Social Media

Website

Sephora's website provides personalized product recommendations, virtual try-on tools, and educational content like beauty tutorials (Tate, 2023), skincare and makeup tips, and customers product reviews and ratings to enhance the online shopping experience, customer satisfaction and build brand loyalty (Patov, 2024). Sephora websites have a Beauty Insider online community involving people from diverse skin types, beauty goals, and personal needs. Community members connect, share, and support each other on their social feeds by creating social proof in action by user generated content like reviews, asking and answering questions, and join themed beauty groups (Deloitte, 2021b; Cezim, 2025).

Sephora Website (Sephora, 2025d)

Mobile Application

Sephora's mobile app data provides consumer information about their personal beauty preferences and buying habits across different touchpoints to undertake effective marketing campaigns (Deloitte, 2021b). The app is mostly used by customers to browse products, make purchases, track orders, and avail customer service. The mobile app also has in-store features used to integrate in-store technology for one touch payments, encash digital loyalty coupons, and avail delivery services (Lopienski, 2024). Sephora's mobile app offers personalized product recommendations, customer product reviews and ratings, product performance lessons, trending beauty news, pricing information, virtual try-on tools and professional guidance to enhance the online shopping experience, customer satisfaction and build brand loyalty (Deloitte, 2021b; Mani & Narayanan, 2025). The Virtual Artist feature in app uses augmented reality (AR) to simulate beauty experience from smartphone to virtually try on things to see how different beauty products look on their faces with product suggestions or AI-generated makeup trends for inspiration and experimenting beauty looks with shades of lipstick, eyeshadow, and more (Honigman, 2025) for making the shopping experience more interactive and fun (Marketing Explainers, 2024).

Sephora Mobile Application (Sephora, 2025g)

Social Media Platforms

Sephora social media focuses on building a strong online community with a sense of belonging to drive repeat purchases and improve referrals. The company provides expert beauty influencers and makeup artists created authentic, and relatable beauty content like tutorials, product demos, and customer reviews on social media pages (Lopienski, 2024). The localized influencer marketing strategy #SephoraSquad works with a diverse group of local influencers having a sizable follower base on their own social media channels to create platform-specific beauty content to ensure maximum target audience reach, engagement, loyalty and build global brand image (Jain, 2025). Sephora focuses on beauty content creation for customers consumption, sharing, and engagement, across Instagram (visual brand storytelling), TikTok (community-driven discourse), YouTube (long-form engagement) and Snapchat (ephemeral stories). Sephora has over 22 million and 1.7 million followers on Instagram and TikTok respectively. It has 1.4 million subscribers on YouTube (Cezim, 2025).

Sephora Instagram Page (Sephora, 2025f)

Mapping Sephora's Personalized Phygital Customer Journey

Sephora's customers adopt phygital touchpoints with exploring products on websites or mobile app, virtually trying on makeup, visiting stores for personalized consultations, attending beauty classes, and participating in loyalty programs (Deloitte, 2021b). These touchpoint utilization behaviours highlight how Sephora needs to manage a customer journey by crafting a more detailed, coherent phygital brand narrative that allows seamless movement of target customers through discovery, evaluation, purchase, and advocacy stages with immersive, interactive, gamified incentives. Each of these touchpoints having customers movement provide an opportunity for Sephora to introduce gamified elements that personalize and enrich the experience (Rebiere & Mavoori, 2021).

Sephora's gamification success is driven by mapping customer journey across physical and digital interfaces and integration of technologies for transforming customer journey into an immersive, interactive, experiential and unique gamified adventure. Augmented Reality (AR) and Virtual Reality (VR) technologies play a significant role in Sephora's gamified phygital experiences that enhance both customer experience and conversion rates (KPMG, 2025b). Sephora is exploring possibilities for using Mixed Reality (MR) or Extended Reality (XR) experiences that will further gamify the beauty journey across digital and physical spaces (Meta, 2025). Over 80% of consumers prefer personalized brand experiences before deciding purchase resulting revenue growth of 5-15% (Patov, 2024).

Understanding the Customer: Catering to Gen Z - Phygital Generation

Generations Alpha and Z are hyperconnected digital natives. Generation Z expects brands to deliver cohesive, comprehensive and engaging personalized interactive experiences when they seamlessly move between digital convenience and sensory pleasure of in-store shopping (KPMG, 2025a). Over 60% of Gen Z and millennials play games at least once a week (Sandler, 2023). Gen Z value gamification shopping experience with AR mirror displays highlighting their preferences for intersection of beauty, mobility, technology, entertainment and fun lifestyle (Power Commerce, 2025) for building brand relationships and loyalty that will last forever (Kornilov 2024). Inside the Sephora store, over 16% of Gen Z customers want hyper-personalized offers on mobile (Lopienski, 2024). Mobile is used for discounts, compare prices, read product reviews and search products (Silvia, 2024). Generation Z avoids waiting for checkout and uses mobile payments at beauty advisors in shops or online (Meyer, 2023).

Gen Z preference for J.P. Morgan 'Tap to Pay on iPhone' payments account 33% in-store transactions, 25% of all payments, increased in sales by 7%, and 2X faster checkout resulting in higher frequency, and better retention (J.P. Morgan, 2024). Over

65% of all retail customers now prefer phygital shopping, over 75% of Generation Z customers prefer AR-enabled experiences, and over 40% of customers willing to pay premium prices with AR products experience (Mattan, 2025b).

Marketing Data to Manage Customers Personalize Lifetime Journey and Emphasize Unique Experience

Sephora’s use of data and technology highlight their commitment for personalization to provide tailored beauty experiences designed to be seamless and engaging across customers lifecycle journeys (Patov, 2024) as customers move seamlessly across in-store, online and mobile strategies (Honigman 2025). This often highlights that customer journey starts online then try and buy in store or vice versa or usage of only one channel and then after-sales services managed digitally (Lopienski, 2024). Customers use mobile in store to look for recommendations, reviews and better product prices (CX Network, 2023). Sephora’s personalization commitment in customer journey start from data collection (Deloitte, 2024) data attribution and data measurement across in-store, website, mobile, and social media (Marketing Explainers, 2024) for developing 360-degree customer profiles across touchpoints to find possible synergies (Honigman, 2025).

Data related to customers shopping behaviours, beauty concerns, product preferences, purchases history (Rukavina, 2025), engagement levels across touchpoints were collected to better understand customers’ changing beauty needs and lifestyle desires (Honigman, 2025). This data is used for personalizing future user experience, predicting future purchasing decisions, optimizing product mix, designing informative content, and undertaking more personalized marketing efforts (Jain, 2025). When customers log into their Sephora accounts, it displays products based on previous purchases, browsed items, and beauty interests. (42signals, 2024). Over 50% and 20% of customers visited the mobile and desktop website respectively and undertook buying in store within 24 hours highlighting 13% increase in average order values. Sephora online advertising was driving in-store purchases creating a 3X increase in conversion rates and 3.9X higher return on ad spend (ROAS) (Honigman, 2025).

Sephora's Beauty Insider program, which rewards 34 million members globally accounting 80% of sales with instant 3-tiered discounts and reward points for purchases (Masternak, 2025), also delivering hyper-personalized recommendations for targeted product promotions, and exclusive offers through emails, in app messages or online advertisements and alerts for loyalty points redemption and upcoming rewards to create a more individualized shopping experience. Other benefits offered include beauty classes, meeting influencers, and participating in makeup masterclasses (42signals, 2024). Beauty Insider program enhances customers memorable experience (Marketing Explainers, 2024), increases engagement, optimizes inventory, customer satisfaction, improves loyalty and creates more tailored effective marketing campaigns (Patov, 2024). Color IQ technology uses AI for digital quizzes and recommends products based on skin tone in in-store kiosks for perfect foundation matches. Similarly, Skin IQ uses AI to recommend skincare routines based on customers' specific skin concerns (Cezim, 2025).

Sephora utilizing the 'Google Analytics 360 Suite' to better understand customer journey across different touchpoints that finally led to a sale in online or offline purchase when that customer has seen ad either online or on mobile. Sephora integrates data across online and in-store transactions to Analytics 360 to connect purchases to existing customer journeys (Honigman, 2025).

Sephora's Gamification – Emotional Engagement and Loyalty Management

Sephora utilizes gamification elements to balance challenge with intense focus on immersion to create loss of self-consciousness and increasing sense of control for providing unique metaverse experiences by offering surprise rewards for managing sustainable challenges (Authors Research).

Table 1. Sephora's Gamification Elements Incorporate Theoretical Background of Customer Lifecycle Journey Phases Across Phygital Touchpoints

Gamification Theoretical Background	Sephora's Gamification Element	Customer Lifecycle Journey Phases
Social Influence and Relatedness	Beauty insider community, Beauty insider challenges, Sephora squad, social media contests and quizzes, community features - beautyfeed, leaderboards	Product discovery, trial to purchase and post-purchase
Surprise and Novelty	Surprise rewards, rotating item in rewards, beauty advisors in-store help, Sephoria events, "swipe it. shop it", in-store skin studio, in-store live beauty studio	Product discovery, trial to purchase
Achievement and Accomplishment	Tiered status, beauty insider challenges, points and rewards, progress tracking, skill challenges	Product discovery, trial to purchase and post-purchase
Scarcity, Impatience and Exclusivity	Limited-time offers, time-bound challenges, exclusive rewards, early exclusive access to new products	Product discovery, trial to purchase and post-purchase
Empowerment of Creativity, Clear Goals and Feedback	Virtual artist and AR tools (Color IQ, Skin IQ and fragrance IQ, store mirrors), customization of profile avatar and personalization quizzes, in-app messages	Product discovery, trial to purchase and post-purchase

continued on following page

Table 1. Continued

Gamification Theoretical Background	Sephora's Gamification Element	Customer Lifecycle Journey Phases
Ownership and Possession	Product collections, customizable avatars	Trial to purchase and post-purchase
Unpredictability and Curiosity	"Spin-to-win" pop-ups, mystery gifts, free-to-play with optional purchase	Product discovery, trial to purchase and post-purchase

SEPHORA'S IN-STORE GAMIFICATION TECHNOLOGIES

Sephora's e-commerce presence has grown extraordinarily but its awe-inspiring physical stores with diversified product portfolio are cornerstone of phygital strategy that complements virtual digital interactions on website and mobile app (Power Commerce, 2025). Overcrowded Sephora stores and busy beauty advisors deter many potential shoppers. Sephora's physical stores have integrated in-store digital gamification tools like in-store kiosk, iPad and mobile app and beauty advisors' personal consultation approach significantly enhances the physical retail environment, creating memorable product exploration, beauty discovery and offers more personalized shopping experience. Over 82% of customers agree that in-store use of digital tools enhances their shopping experience significantly (Jain, 2025).

Interactive Kiosks, iPad, and Tablets

In-store Sephora offers online product catalogue, product availability, product tutorials, product reviews (Patov, 2024), digital quizzes, and challenges accessible via incorporated digital tools like kiosks, iPads and tablets. Customers might complete a gamified skincare quiz that offers more personalized beauty routines or unlock limited-time rewards for trying new products (Cezim, 2025).

Sephora's Virtual Try-On: AR Virtual Artist In-Store Kiosks and Mobile App

Sephora Virtual Artist mobile app feature also available in in-store is developed in partnership with AR company ModiFace (ModiFace, 2025). AI driven Virtual Artist program has integrated over 10,000 unique customers data and test cases that replicates the in-store beauty advisor provided test makeup experience virtually to customers hesitant to try products in-store or online by offering a photo upload or live video try-on experience by scanning persons face to track facial feature, lips and eyes to provide compatible lipstick shade and beauty products. Apps also allow purchase of products or provide details of the nearest store (Sephora Malaysia, 2025). Customers experimenting with different makeup designs and trends can share instantly through social sharing buttons resulting in increased awareness, increased conversions, user engagement and brand engagement (Abukhadra, 2021).

In-store AR Virtual Artist In-Store Kiosks (T Australia, 2022)

Integration of Mobile App with In-Store Shopping

Sephora's mobile app acts as a personal shopping assistant or a Sephora sales associate by offering a cohesive brand and convenient in-store shopping experience. With geotargeting, customers are prompted to switch mobile apps to 'Store Mode' that provide access to many in-store features like 'Sephora to Go' that send personalized notifications (Deloitte, 2021b). Many Sephora customers use mobile app instore for browsing online product catalogue, product availability, product tutorials, product recommendations, product reviews (Patov, 2024), past purchases, wish list, personalized offers, loyalty card, gift cards, product in abandoned cart and better prices before confidently deciding on correct beauty product while considering purchase in-store (Lamb, 2025) which help Sephora analyse customers' online behaviours in-store resulting in increasing sales in phygital ecosystems (Nguyen, 2024).

Color IQ Technology

Sephora's in-store Color IQ technology, AR tool scans a customer's skin tone to recommend precise personalized foundation and concealer shades recommendations. Color IQ functions as a gamified beauty assistant, by providing product matching in a more personalized interactive way thereby rewarding customers with saving time and enthusing greater confidence in choices to avoid decision paralysis. ColorIQ utilizes a patented algorithm having over 10000 skin tones database highlighting Diversity, Equity, and Inclusion commitments (Abukhadra, 2021).

In-store Color IQ Technology (Sephora, 2014)

Fragrance IQ Technology

Sephora customers create their online scent profile highlighting personal choices for fragrances. Fragrance IQ InstaScent technology has an integrated dry air delivery system that lets customers test 18 different scents without actually trying them (Abukhadra, 2021).

In-store Fragrance IQ Technology (Duan, 2015)

In-Store AR Mirrors Bring Digital Experiences

In-store lifelike realism with AR mirrors replaces changing rooms in retail store by allowing touchless and rapid try-ons of numerous products in more engaging, interactive and informative way by addressing customers choice overload, personal hygiene concerns, and inadequate trial time. AR adoption in beauty retail industry has shown consistent yearly performance of over 300% ROI across major implementations. Sephora's AR mirror deployment conversion rates increased by 90% by AR try-on features with increase in average basket size resulting in 31% growth in sales from trial users (Mattan, 2025a). Sephora stores having interactive mirrors provide a more tactile and hands-on shopping experience that allows customers to explore product details, beauty tutorials, and try on products virtually (Patov, 2024). AR mirrors stores have shown 5X longer customer stay time thereby creating more opportunities for cross-selling and brand education. (Mattan, 2025b). AR mirror displays with RFID tag readers enables customers to independently, and extensively research beauty products in-store by putting product on the reader area and receive detailed product information and authentic product reviews online (Meyer, 2023).

In-Store AR Mirrors (Marin-Lopez, 2024)

Sephora's AR Mirrors Boosting Window Shopping into Interactive Experiences

Interactive gamification integrated product price tags include product QR codes that convert stores into a shopping attraction allowing customers to explore and purchase thereby increasing sales. Customers walk to window, scanning a QR code with their phones to interact or control stores window display even when a retail store is closed (Silvia, 2024) to browse products, view sales promotions, save product in cart or purchase from outside store and getting home delivery without ever entering the store (Silvia, 2024). QR code increases foot traffic to stores, customers step inside the store, scanning the QR code redirected to a special website where the game was explained allowing Sephora to collect relevant customer data in a GDPR-compliant manner for future marketing. The captivating game mechanic was designed to allow users to tap as many virtual lipsticks dropping on a customized website screen. At the end users collect points and position in the ranking was displayed. Customers filled out forms, participated in lucky draws, and sign up for the newsletter that generated valuable leads and strengthened Sephora's position as a pioneer in customer-centric marketing strategies (Vyndo, 2025).

Beauty Events, Beauty Studio, Skin Studio, Beauty Workshops, and Beauty Classes

Sephora's in-store events gamify learning by incorporating challenges, leaderboards, and social sharing. Participants can earn badges or points by attending beauty tutorials or sharing their looks online, blending education with playful competition (Sephora Malaysia, 2025).

Sephoria Gamified Beauty Event - Hybrid In-Person and Virtual

Sephoria started in 2018 in US has adopted hybrid in-person and virtual immersive event involving diverse community members in US, Canada, France and China that takes customers on a well-crafted Sephora's world of beauty journey to provide "immersive virtual experience" on a 3D gaming-like platform with a "unique, playful and socially driven approach" by presenting Sephora's products from more than 50 global beauty brands. Virtual attendees create personal avatars and play a series of games, to earn Beauty Insider loyalty points. Customers receive a unique free Non-Fungible Token (NFT) or Proof of Attendance Protocol (POAP) that is added to digital wallets. Silver Key and Gold Key sold for US$99 for US$349 per session respectively. Attendees having the highest tier ticket receive US$1,000 worth of beauty products. Customers attend the Sephoria virtual event for free and have the option to buy US$300 worth beauty products for US$65 (King, 2023). Each event provides exclusive product access, beauty influencer meetups, and hands-on personal and unforgettable beauty experiences (Cezim, 2025). Sephora gathers its community in the Beauty Live Studio for exclusive events or masterclasses. (Meyer, 2023).

Sephoria Gamified Beauty Event (Sephoria 2025)

In-store Skin Studio (Duan, 2015)

In-store Beauty Live Studio (Duan, 2015)

Sephora's Digital Gamification Technologies Extending to Physical Experiences

Sephora's tinder inspired fun filled "Swipe it. Shop it" gamification feature targeting Gen Z and millennials makes the shopping experience more enjoyable by reducing customers anxiety while choosing a select few products in online stores and mobile app (Ufford, 2023). Sephora's digital gamification drives traffic and engagement across physical stores, strengthening omnichannel presence and thriving on the fluid integration between digital and physical realms (KPMG, 2025b).

"Swipe it. Shop it" Gamification (Ufford, 2023)

Mobile Apps Gamified Features

The Sephora app allows users to earn points and advance through a 3-tiers loyalty program by purchasing products, writing reviews, or completing challenges. The brand's mobile app allows customers to shop online, book in-store appointments, and access beauty tutorials (Jain, 2025). Sephora app offers gamified shopping experience with Beautyfeed that provide community beauty advice by scroll through endlessly. A color correction tool takes a quiz-style gamified approach to sell where customers choose an avatar most similar to their skin tone, provide beauty intention to achieve and it answers what color would resolve the condition. The user guessed with three chances to choose the correct color and then redirected to instructional video explaining how to resolve the problem. Also suggest a Sephora product that will fix their problem and encourage them to share their experiences on social media. beauty customers' key core drivers used into gamification include epic meaning and calling "elitism / feeling special by inclusion in an exclusive club or group development" and accomplishment "progressing up the ranks of a special program", and ownership and possession "the ability to buy even more with member-based discounts / promotions" (Abraham, 2020). Virtual Artist integrates AI for facial recognition, so customers virtually try makeup products and better know the product applications (KPMG, 2025b).

Sephora's Virtual Try-On App: AR Virtual Artist

Sephora's augmented reality tool Virtual Artist feature in mobile app allows customers to test products digitally by uploading a photo (Brodowicz, 2025) or virtually try on makeup in real time or find perfect shade of lipstick from anywhere thereby making the entire experience more personalized and convenient (Ellis, 2025). Customers can purchase and get delivery to home or pick up from the nearest store (Silvia, 2024). This playful, gamified experience often leads users to visit stores for further exploration or purchase, bridging the digital experience with real-world actions. Customers can try on thousands of products virtually via their mobile devices, blending playfulness with personalization. This gamified try-on experience reduces purchase hesitation by allowing experimentation in a low-risk environment (KPMG, 2025b).

Virtual Try-On App (Carman, 2017)

Sephora's Physical Beauty Calendar

Customers signed up for Sephora's 2024 physical Beauty Calendar created to build excitement and ultimately drive customer acquisition and loyalty by integrating gamification into their Christmas Marketing strategy, but customers were not opting in to know when the calendar will be released. Sephora assesses the impact of opt-in text and gamified experiences within the app would get more opt-ins messaging text. Sephora created a 24-day interactive calendar on the Sephora app communicated via in app messages, emails and socials. Customers are encouraged to go find the reward of the day and reveal their prize. A/B split testing feature to test different opt in texts supercharged opt-in and traffic to the website and app. Gets 272k entries and 11k average daily entries. gained a 60% uplift from test B of the A/B testing in 2024.

demonstrating the power of clear, targeted messaging. maximise both immediate revenue and long-term customer relationships (Odicci, 2025b).

Sephora Used a Gamified Snapchat AR game

Gamified Snapchat AR game used by Sephora in Saudi Arabia during the religious festival of Ramadan. In Ramadan many competitors heavy advertising and promotional offers competing with each other for getting customers short lived attention to increase sales by meaningful engagement. Sephora's AR game once played offers a coupon code as reward to players and is redeemed on the website. The game delivered an extraordinary 2.39X ROI accounting 5% of all sales on Sephora website. In 4 weeks of campaign lens experience delivered average 37s lens playtime, over 1200 transactions, and over 15% lift in advertising awareness (Digital Training Academy, 2020).

Gamified Snapchat AR game (Snap Inc, 2025)

Push Notifications and Challenges

Sephora digital push notifications and prompt messages encourage Sephora customers to visit nearby stores, complete makeup looks, participate in seasonal quizzes and contests, creating a supplementing hyperloop where digital engagement fuels physical store traffic and vice versa (Kamat, 2025).

In-App Message Gamification

In 2020, Sephora Southeast Asia used in-app memorable customized gamification messages in competitive, and saturated Malaysian market by imitating tradition of 'Ang Paos' gifting signifying good fortune and luck delivered with data streaming capabilities to capture customers attention in 30 days of campaign period. Malasia market achieves a 132% growth in revenues from participating customers. Game participants received insignificant prizes after winning the game that provided the highest revenue. The game was responsible for sales conversions, rather than the monetary incentive offered as a win. Customers open surprised gifts from cash vouchers to loyalty points. Sephora collected customers personal details in GDPR complaint way (Braze, 2025).

In-App Message 'Ang Paos' Gamification (Braze, 2025)

Sephora's 'Pay Day' Gamified Experiences

Sephora tested out gamification within the app every six weeks, to compare engagement rates from the app vrs CRM alone. incorporated 'Pay Day' gamified experiences at the end of every month. Sephora gamification achieved a 27% increase in mobile app sales in 2024. New customer acquisition and engagement gained a surprisingly 330% increase in entries and a 68% increase from their combined email and app experiences taken together. Sephora used gamification in the app to acquire more customer traffic, increased product sales, cross-selling, and higher average order values. enhance brand visibility, foster customer loyalty, and collect valuable data for personalizing user experiences (Odicci, 2025a).

Pay Day' Gamified Experiences (Odicci, 2025a)

Social Media Integration for Gamified Challenges

Sephora's gamified campaigns encourage customers to share photos or videos of their makeup looks, turning user-generated content into a community challenge that blurs online and offline boundaries (Soto, 2025). Customer shared brand stories through UGC are featured in the brand's online and store's offline marketing campaigns (Beri, 2023). Sephora customers often post AR experiences to social media platforms through social sharing that expand brand reach (Meyer, 2023).

Social Media Interactive Quiz (Vox Media, 2025)

The Beauty Insider Loyalty Program as a Gamified Phygital Hub

This section briefly explains, a) Beauty Insider Loyalty Program, and b) Sephora Beauty Insider Challenges. These topics were explained briefly under each heading for better clarity of content presentations.

Beauty Insider Loyalty Program

In 2024, Sephora's Beauty Insider program having over 34 million members accounting 80% of total sales (Masternak, 2025) gamifies loyalty, making it a central, personalized hub in Sephora's phygital strategy (Smartico, 2025). Over 17 million members are in North America (Sobhi, 2024). These 34 million members are frequently active across phygital touchpoints and spend 2X more than non-members (42signals, 2024). Sephora's Beauty Insider program available on Sephora website and Mobile app launched in 2007 is free to join and provides a 3-tiered loyalty system that offers incentives through purchases, with each level gaining more exclusive access. and inspires customers to enjoy benefits and privileges for brand association. These digital achievements unlock in-store perks, exclusive events, and early access to new products, motivating users to visit physical stores (Tate, 2023). This 3-tiered system aspires and motivates customers to achieve the next level to unlock rewards (42signals, 2024).

Beauty Insider (Sephora, 2025e)

Sephora's Beauty Insider program is a core pillar of its gamification efforts, designed as a tiered, point-based system that spans both digital and physical channels. The program's rewards and challenges work seamlessly whether customers shop online or in-store, fostering a unified brand experience Tiered Levels as Customers progress from free to join Insider (spend US$50+ annually) to Very Important Beauty (VIB - spend US$350+ annually) to Rouge (spend US$1,000+ annually) by accumulating points through purchases and engagement, unlocking increasingly valuable rewards such as exclusive products, birthday gifts, free samples, events, and personalized offers. Points and rewards earned online, or in-store can be redeemed for discounts, samples, and experiences, incentivizing repeat purchases and fostering brand loyalty. Higher tiers gain exclusive access to private events and early product launches, creating a sense of community and exclusivity. In Beauty Insiders program customers accumulate 1 point for every US$1 spent across phygital touchpoints. In seasonal sales promotion all customers belonging to different spending tiers are entitled to more points (42signals, 2024). Sephora's Beauty Insider offers skincare masterclasses, private shopping nights, and beauty tutorials (Woolnough-Rai, 2025).

Sephora Beauty Insider Challenges

Gamified experience in Beauty Insider loyalty program, called "Beauty Insider Challenges," on both website and mobile app create seamless experiences to engage Gen Z, younger, and tech-savvy customers by offering reward points for completing various purchase and non-purchase related tasks. Sephora's challenge "Ready, Set, Sephora" offers 100 points for each task that encourages users to enrol for text alerts, interest in samples, and utilize tools like Color IQ (Masternak, 2025). The customers receive 500 points worth US$10 for completing the full challenge, which can be redeemed in next purchase. Gamification uses spin-to-win, bingo and prediction, and leaderboards. Beauty insider challenges enhance data collection, increase participation, provide meaningful engagement, build long-term loyalty, and amplify brand message (Snipp, 2025).

Beauty Insider Challenges (Sephora, 2025h)

Sephora Spin-To-Win (Milled, 2022)

DISCUSSION

This section provides brief explanation of authors perspective on the Sephora's, a) Phygital Retail, b) Personalization and c) Gamification. These topics were explained briefly under each heading for better clarity of content presentations.

Sephora's Truly Phygital Strategy

Sephora has adopted innovative approaches to create strong phygital retail strategy in a highly competitive global beauty retail market. The over-reliance on adopting beauty retail industry first innovative technology and data integration tools across phygital operations increases the high costs of maintenance. Sephora's heavy investment in digital innovation such as AR try-ons, AI-driven hyper personalization, and app integrations. It potentially results in data collection overload and may alienate less tech-savvy beauty customers. The digital tools adopted offers a competitive advantage but can sometimes feel more impersonal after repetitive usage. The technology initiatives can drastically overshadow the company's core in-store human experiential element as imbibed in "try before you buy" philosophy. The excessive tech adoption may potentially diminish many customers emotional brand connection and eroding the long-term loyalty. The company's data driven hyper-personalization algorithms come with the risk of becoming personally intrusive or altogether inaccurate due to tech obsolescence thereby impacting user brand trust. Sephora's over-reliance on data-driven hyper-personalization subsequently raises immediate concerns around users' privacy, ethical artificial intelligence (AI) use, and consumer trust. The seamless integration of omnichannel green logistics strategy across physical stores, mobile applications and e-commerce platforms remains highly complex and extremely cost-intensive.

Sephora's competitors, Ulta Beauty (phygital operations with strong loyalty programs and salon services) and Amazon (online operations with superior logistics and hyper-personalization technology) offer highly competitive environment in primary US market. The Sephora's competing companies are rapidly enhancing their own phygital strategies thereby intensifying further pressure on managing customer expectations. The future challenges for brand Sephora in phygital operations includes staying well ahead in AI-driven hyper-personalization, satisfy customers sustainability expectations, and manage evolving Gen Z segments beauty products preferences. Sephora in phygital operations has to crucially maintain brand relevance with Gen Z, navigate them seamlessly across channels to avoid the digital fatigue, and deliver most authentic sustainability promises through product portfolio. Sephora must continuously adopt technology for innovating operations without compromising intimacy, inclusivity, and experiential richness across different touchpoints. Although

Sephora's focus on most vibrant sophisticated digital innovation may dilute meaningful highly personal in-store experiences and managing the perfect balance between two methodologies will always going to be more complex. In future direct and indirect beauty retail competition will heats up exponentially and consumers everchanging personal needs will further change the beauty buying behaviour drastically. In such scenario brand Sephora must always ensure its phygital business model evolves simultaneously to satisfy everchanging needs of target segments without losing its human in-store touch and brand intimacy.

Sephora's Personalized Phygital Customer Journey

Sephora's adaptive hyper-personalization strategy for managing customers journey across the phygital touchpoints is often celebrated by the luxury retail industry strategists. The brand Sephora's heavy reliance on data-based algorithm-driven hyper-personalized product recommendations are offering utmost convenience to existing customers. But it simultaneously also raises most complex strategic and ethical concerns for the company operations. This data-based dependency can misfire or create risks of reducing individuality and may overshadow need for personal beauty consultations thereby reinforcing most homogenized beauty ideals. In extreme cases it will altogether narrow the beauty standards, and unintentionally exclude diverse skin tones, textures, and identities. The Sephora's key target demographics across the globe may alienate if hyper-personalization strategy lacks country / regional specific beauty nuance and integration of local cultural sensitivity. The company undertake seamless integration of loyalty data, browsing behaviour, and social media engagement. In an increasingly regulated US digital landscape, it can lead to creating data driven hyper-targeting that exceeds intrusive personal surveillance thereby creating data ethics and user privacy issues.

The brand Sephora's hyper-personalization strategy across its phygital operations may also trigger data overload. The user data collection will become more pervasive across in-store, apps, websites, and social media platforms. The synchronizing real-time personalization across multiple global markets having country specific astute beauty standards, cultural ethos and consumer expectations poses extreme challenge. The Ulta beauty focused on the customer centric approach by imbibing emotional connect with target customers through offering in-store experiential beauty services and community driven loyalty programs. On the other hand, Amazon uses predictive data driven AI for hyper-personalizing customer journey and provides last mile connectivity with inherent global supply chain dominance. Likewise, Sephora must balance AI for hyper-personalization to imbibe customers emotional brand relevance, ethical data privacy responsibility, and localizing human touch considering customers cultural relevance. The brand Sephora while hyper-personalising customer journey across phygital touchpoints must address customers digital fatigue and inclusivity gaps. It must address the technological integration for meaningful, authentic and human centric customer engagement to deliver emotionally driven non-intrusive brand experiences.

Sephora's In-Store Gamification Strategies

Sephora's in-store gamification technologies are highly innovative and enhances customer engagement. The gamification technologies increase the risks of undermining the core human centered beauty retail experiences provided by Sephora through prioritizing technology enabled fun entertainment over the beauty product utility. The personal gamification experiences provided to customers by Sephora can sometimes feel gimmick and may distract many informed customers seeking quick, and highly purposeful store visits. In-store AR mirrors and gamified interactive displays mostly provide superficial engagement. The interactive gamified technologies excessive adoption increase the risk of converting existing customers experiential shopping journey into short-term novelty rather than building long-term loyalty. The gamification technology tools underestimate the capabilities of highly experienced in-store beauty advisors personal relationship approach with customers thereby reducing meaningful customer engagement. These technological tools excessive uses may isolate potential customers interested in seeking highly personal trustworthy expert guidance and most sensory beauty product interaction that create more personalised intimate brand experience. The sophisticated gamified tools AR features adopted by Sephora are still under continuous development and mostly struggle to accurately reflect diverse skin tones and facial features of target segments. The lack of inclusivity criteria's resulted in further alienation of many customers instead of offering them complete ownership and empowerment in beauty buying.

The high cost of Sephora's gamification technologies conceptualizing, wide scale implementation and periodic maintenance across different store formats are increasingly raising concerns related to return on investment (ROI), operational flexibility, faster scalability, and environmental sustainability. The well-established competitor, Ulta beauty offers a more grounded in-store experience with deepened service-driven focus in beauty retailing by providing highly personalized consultations, human-led product experiences, and integrated salon services that. Amazon on other hand involves highly effective AI driven tech integration for personalization and focuses on utmost customer convenience. The global beauty consumers wide changing beauty expectations are shifting towards authenticity and inclusivity. The Sephora majorly risks being trapped into the hollow digital-first beauty retail business model that excessively overlooks brand authenticity, social equity, and emotional brand resonance in highly competitive global market. Sephora's future challenges in global market includes customers digital fatigue, tech obsolescence, technology accessibility gaps, and maintaining beauty product relevance across generational and cultural target segments. So, brand Sephora must ensure gamification increasingly enhances human connection for product education and does not replace it completely.

Sephora's Digital Gamification Strategies

Sephora has creatively integrated gamification technologies across its website, apps, and social media platforms. The gamification strategy of Sephora faces increasing criticism for prioritizing superficial and manipulative short-term customer engagement over meaningful long-term brand association. The customers may feel gamification strategies are more designed to extract their personal data for tailoring future marketing activity rather than to enhance the personalized customer journey. The adoption of high technology enabled gamification elements can potentially belittle the customers personalized beauty experiences by reducing it to mere symbolic loyalty consideration of few points, badges, and challenges. The younger Gen Z consumers may initially engage vigorously, but digital fatigue and scepticism around "reward-based loyalty" approach can fully diminish the long-term loyal association and overall brand impact. These gamified systems more often fail to reflect complete inclusivity of target segments. The AR and gamified quizzes often lack personal nuance for customers diverse skin tones, gender, and personal beauty preferences. Sephora's gamification tactics highly risks reducing personal beauty to a mere transactional game. The commodifying personal beauty self-expression of customers into gamified reward loops mostly favour user addiction rather than overall beauty empowerment. Many global critics argue this type of gamified approach adopted by Sephora exploits customers psychological triggers similar to the social media algorithms thereby fostering compulsive user behaviour and offer very little substantive value in return.

Many gamified features adopted by Sephora may remain exclusionary and grossly fails to accurately represent customers diverse identities, body types, and skin tones. They largely reinforce the narrow beauty ideals under the guise of gamified "fun" approach. The competitors like Ulta beauty are investing in service-based loyalty and authentic brand communities and Amazon uses predictive AI to deliver seamless convenience without creating gamified distractions at large. The informed beauty customers' expectations nowadays shift toward more meaningful, and personalized engagement. In looking toward current developments brand Sephora must reassess the depth and purpose of its gamification tools. Sephora's future challenge includes maintaining brand relevance, avoiding user disengagement, and aligning gamification where necessary to provide only genuine customer value. Otherwise, brand

Sephora risks alienating critical audiences unless it rethinks gamification as a tool for social equity, and not for customer exploitation.

FUTURE RESEARCH DIRECTIONS

The further research can provide the long-term effectiveness of the gamification strategies for enhancing the customer experience and loyalty across phygital touch-points in the beauty retail industry. This Sephora study highlights the connection between customers short-term participation and customers meaningful engagement. The further research can provide insight whether personalized gamified experiences resulted in customer lifetime value and strong brand advocacy over a period of time. In addition to that it is interesting to investigate whether different cultural and country / region specific markets could reveal how consumers will respond to gamification tactics based on digital maturity, competitive rivalry and local retail laws.

The further research may also need to find the ethical implications of data driven hyper personalization strategies that may result in privacy concern, transparency issues, and erosion of consumer trust. The evolving role of artificial intelligence, augmented reality, and virtual reality to develop gamification designs and systems for phygital touchpoints provides promising research avenue. The empirical research using the mixed method research designs can unearth deeper insights related to how consumers perceive such brands and emotionally respond to the gamified elements while seamlessly moving across customer journey from online to offline and vice versa. This will offer a highly valuable guidelines for retail companies interested in using gamification elements to optimize the phygital customer engagement and loyalty strategies.

CONCLUSION

Sephora's strategic business model is way ahead of its global competitors as annual revenue has grown from US$13.64 billion in 2018 (Deloitte, 2021b) to US$17 billion in 2024 (Sephora, 2025a). Also, in the US market Sephora brand has achieved a 14th position in 2022 in experiential customer experience as against 94th position in 2018 (KPMG, 2022). This signifies that in a highly competitive beauty retail industry, Sephora's adoption of innovative phygital gamification strategy and data-driven customer centric personalization across customers lifecycle journey delivers multiple benefits by building deep and long-lasting relationships with target customers and making collective approach more relevant and highly rewarding for each customer (KPMG, 2018). Sephora has undertaken omnichannel consistency by seamless technology integration across digital and physical touchpoints (Lindecrantz, Gi, & Zerbi, 2020) by capitalising on customer data with prompt collection and synthesis in real time to analyse customer behaviour in online (Deloitte, 2021), in-store, quiz responses, and loyalty program activity (Cezim, 2025) to create a 360-degree customer profile (Honigman, 2025).

Sephora's adoption of AI-powered algorithms generates personalized hyper-relevant recommendations in real time across phygital touchpoints by offering tailored product suggestions, reward offers, and gamified challenges based on individual customers behaviours, preferences, purchase history and other past interactions (Ellis, 2025). Gamification has enhanced customer engagement by transforming routine purchase into an immersive, interactive and enjoyable shopping experience thereby increasing the time and money customers spend with the brands multiple touchpoints (Li, Zubielqui & Hill, 2025). Through gamified 'Beauty Insider loyalty program' customer sense beauty progression with rewards and personalized incentives that increases sales by reducing barriers to purchase and encouraging repeat buying (Tate, 2023) and their participation in online communities fosters long-term relationships with brands (Masternak, 2025). Customers participation in shareable gamified challenges across touchpoints and user-generated content (Soto, 2025) create social buzz, amplify brand visibility and customer advocacy to build and develop a cohesive global brand identity (Snipp, 2025).

Sephora's innovative phygital gamification strategy brings multiple challenges of technological integration for transfer of customer data to ensure smooth interoperability between phygital ecosystems (KPMG, 2018). Sephora must manage 'User Experience Balance' by keeping brand content fresh, attractive and trustful by continuously innovating gamified experiences across touchpoints to maintain customer interest for meaningful engagement and avoiding over-gamification that might frustrate or fatigue customers (Kamble, 2025). Sephora's ability to deliver personalized gamified experiences across phygital touchpoints in future relies heavily on sophisticated data analytics and artificial intelligence (AI) to offer personalized experiences (KPMG, 2025b). Navigating country or regional data privacy regulations and addressing customer personal data expectations and concerns about data security while maintaining transparency, trust and ethical standards is highly important for hyper-personalized experience delivery (McKinsey, 2025a). Looking forward, emerging trends such as AI-powered real-time gamification, MR/XR immersive experiences, and hyper-personalization will shape Sephora's ongoing evolution (Meta, 2025).

Sephora's gamification strategies have been highly successful and demonstrate the power of blending physical and digital experiential experiences (Kamble, 2025) to create a highly personalized, and more engaging customer journey by integrating innovative technologies, loyalty programs, and interactive brand content (McKinsey,

2025b). Sephora's Beauty Insider program is a core pillar of its gamification strategy, designed as a 3-tiered instant discount, and point-based loyalty system applicable across digital and physical touchpoints (42signals, 2024). Sephora's Beauty Insider loyalty program adapts customized real-time data driven dynamic adjustments to provide the gamified content and eligible rewards thereby improving customer engagement and satisfaction (Li, Zubielqui & Hill, 2025). Sephora provides its well-established global phygital retail experiences and strategic framework to beauty retail companies to connect with today's dynamic global consumers. The brand Sephora provides a lesson that the future of successful global phygital retail lies in gamified data-driven hyper-personalization for providing seamless user experiences across customer's life cycle journey. In nutshell, Sephora is leading the way through its own 'Sephora Way'.

REFERENCES

Abraham, V. (2020). *Gamification: A digital marketing strategy in the beauty industry*. Retrieved from https://www.linkedin.com/pulse/gamification-digital-marketing-strategy-beauty-industry-abraham

Abukhadra, S. (2021). *Sephora leading the way with augmented reality*. Retrieved from https://medium.com/marketing-in-the-age-of-digital/sephora-leading-the-way-with-augmented-reality-c117eed0faa0

Adobe. (2024). *Guide to marketing personalization — benefits, examples, and more*. Retrieved from https://business.adobe.com/blog/basics/marketing-personalization

Australia, T. (2022). *How AI and AR is shaping the post-pandemic beauty industry*. Retrieved from https://taustralia.com.au/ai-ar-beauty-industry/

Beri, S. (2023). *Gamified kiosks and in-store experiences - the future of retail*. Retrieved from https://ogmento.io/blog/gamified-kiosks-and-in-store-experiences-the-future-of-retail/

Braze. (2025). *Sephora SEA used in-app message gamification to increase purchases by 132%*. Retrieved from https://www.braze.com/customers/sephora-sea-case-study

Briedis, H., Gregg, B., Heidenreich, K., & Liu, W. (2021). *Omnichannel: The path to value*. Retrieved from https://www.mckinsey.com/capabilities/growth-marketing-and-sales/our-insights/the-survival-guide-to-omnichannel-and-the-path-to-value

Brodowicz, M. (2025). *Sephora's AI-powered virtual try-on for personalized makeup recommendations*. Retrieved from https://aithor.com/essay-examples/sephoras-ai-powered-virtual-try-on-for-personalized-makeup-recommendations

Carman, A. (2017). *Sephora's latest app update lets you try virtual makeup on at home with AR*. Retrieved from https://www.theverge.com/2017/3/16/14946086/sephora-virtual-assistant-ios-app-update-ar-makeup

Cezim, B. (2025). *How Sephora's marketing strategies & campaigns win over different audiences*. Retrieved from https://digitalagencynetwork.com/sephora-marketing-strategies/

Chakraborty, D., & Rana, N. (2025). *Impulse Buying and Stickiness Using Flow Theory: A Longitudinal Study*. Retrieved from https://www.tandfonline.com/doi/full/10.1080/08874417.2025.2547970

Chou, Y. (2025). The Octalysis Framework for Gamification & Behavioural Design. Retrieved from https://yukaichou.com/gamification-examples/octalysis-complete-gamification-framework/

CXNet. (2025). *Sephora: Inventing an omnichannel strategy to revolutionize the retail experience for cosmetics.* Retrieved from https://cxnet.in/2025/01/31/sephora-inventing-an-omnichannel-strategy-to-revolutionize-the-retail-experience-for-cosmetics/

Das, R., Kalia, S., & Kuijpers, D. (2023). *'Zero consumers': What they want and why it matters.* Retrieved from https://www.mckinsey.com/industries/retail/our-insights/zero-consumers-what-they-want-and-why-it-matters

Deloitte. (2021a). *Sephora's purpose comes to life through action.* Retrieved from https://deloitte.wsj.com/cmo/sephoras-purpose-comes-to-life-through-action-01636124196

Deloitte. (2021b). *Beauty retail - A closer look at current trends impacting beauty specialist retailers.* Retrieved from https://www.deloitte.com/content/dam/assets-shared/legacy/docs/perspectives/2022/gx-beauty-retail-pov-update.pdf

Deloitte. (2024). *Q3 2024 emerging retail & consumer trends.* Retrieved from https://www.deloitte.com/us/en/Industries/consumer/articles/q3-2024-retail-consumer-trends.html

Deslandes, M. (2017). *Sephora tests new 'phygital' store concept in France.* Retrieved from https://ww.fashionnetwork.com/news/Sephora-tests-new-phygital-store-concept-in-france,813370.html

Digital Training Academy. (2020). *Snapchat case study: Sephora gamifies loyalty to boost Ramadan sales.* Retrieved from http://www.digitaltrainingacademy.com/casestudies/2020/02/snapchat_case_study_sephora_gamifies_loyalty_to_boost_ramadan_sales.php

Dowdall, M. (2024). *5 retail gamification ideas to consider in 2024.* Retrieved from https://seamlessxtra.com/5-retail-gamification-ideas-to-consider-in-2024/

Duan, N. (2015). *Hot spot: Sephora's new high-tech workshop.* Retrieved from https://www.yahoo.com/lifestyle/sephora-beauty-tip-workshop-san-francisco-174751572.html

Edmonds, M., Furman, A., Pedersen, K., & Joe, M. (2025). *AI is no longer an option—it's the future of retail.* Retrieved from https://www.pwc.com/gx/en/services/alliances/microsoft/ai-retail-transformation-future.html

EHL Holding SA. (2024). Customer personalization - No longer an option in the digital age? Retrieved from https://hospitalityinsights.ehl.edu/customer-personalization

Ellis, A. (2025). *The rise of phygital retail: Creating seamless experiences across online and offline channels*. Retrieved from https://www.stratfieldconsulting.com/insights/phygital-retail

Faster Capital. (2025). *Successful examples of gamification marketing*. Retrieved from https://fastercapital.com/topics/successful-examples-of-gamification-marketing.html

Grzybowska, K. (2025). *Omnichannel retail loyalty programs in 2025: Top 5 real-world examples*. Retrieved from https://www.openloyalty.io/insider/omnichannel-retail-loyalty-programs

Hammers, J. (2025). *Sephora doles out Lyft credits to transport shoppers to its stores*. Retrieved from https://www.marketingdive.com/news/sephora-doles-out-lyft-credits-to-transport-shoppers-to-its-stores/752153/

Honigman, B. (2025). *How Sephora integrates retail & online marketing*. Retrieved from https://etailwest.wbresearch.com/blog/how-sephora-integrates-retail-online-marketing

Jain, K. (2025). *Sephora: Revolutionizing beauty retail with innovation and personalization*. Retrieved from https://www.linkedin.com/pulse/sephora-revolutionizing-beauty-retail-innovation-kashish-jain-bvskc

Kamat, A. (2025). *Enhancing customer engagement in retail through personalized notifications*. Retrieved from https://www.irjmets.com/uploadedfiles/paper//issue_3_march_2025/69735/final/fin_irjmets1742559517.pdf

Kamble, M. (2025). *Experience: A UX case study on building trust and reducing abandonment*. Retrieved from https://medium.com/@kamble.ma/reimagining-sephoras-shopping-experience-a-ux-case-study-on-building-trust-reducing-d752f1bca950

Khoros. (2025). *What is gamification marketing and 6 examples from top brands*. Retrieved from https://khoros.com/blog/gamification-marketing

King, A. (2023). *Sephora's gamified beauty event Sephoria returns with hybrid in-person and virtual experience*. Retrieved from https://cosmeticsbusiness.com/sephora-s-gamified-beauty-event-sephoria-returns-with-hybrid-in-person-and-virtual-experience-210003

Kornilov, D. (2024). *Phygital retail in action: Real-world examples and insights.* Retrieved from https://ffface.me/media/phygital-retail-where-digital-meets-physical-commerce/

KPMG. (2018). *Tomorrow's experience, today - Harnessing a customer first approach in a changing world.* Retrieved from https://assets.kpmg.com/content/dam/kpmg/pe/pdf/Publicaciones/TL/tomorrows-experience-today-harnessing-a-customer-first-approach.pdf

KPMG. (2022). *Break Out – from ordinary to extraordinary.* Retrieved from https://assets.kpmg.com/content/dam/kpmg/xx/pdf/2023/01/us-customer-experience-excellence-report-2022.pdf

KPMG. (2025a). *2025 retail trends from NRF's big retail show.* Retrieved from https://kpmg.com/ie/en/insights/retail-manufacturing/2025-cge-retail-mfg-trends-nrf.html

KPMG. (2025b). *Intelligent retail - A blueprint for creating value through AI-driven transformation.* Retrieved from https://assets.kpmg.com/content/dam/kpmgsites/xx/pdf/2025/03/intelligent-retail-report.pdf

Lamb, K. (2025). *7 retail advertising trends for 2025: From Ulta to Sephora.* Retrieved from https://www.zappi.io/web/blog/retail-advertising-trends/

Li, W., Zubielqui, G., & Hill, S. (2025). *Gamification impact on brand strategies: A systematic review.* Retrieved from https://www.tandfonline.com/doi/full/10.1080/08874417.2025.2503954

Lindecrantz, E., Gi, M., & Zerbi, S. (2020). *Personalizing the customer experience: Driving differentiation in retail.* Retrieved from https://www.mckinsey.com/se/~/media/McKinsey/Industries/Retail/Our%20Insights/Personalizing%20the%20customer%20experience%20Driving%20differentiation%20in%20retail/Personalizing-the-customer-experience-Driving-differentiation-in-retail.pdf

Locke, J. (2025). *The digital transformation of the beauty industry: AI, gamification and the metaverse.* Retrieved from https://medium.com/digital-society/the-digital-transformation-of-the-beauty-industry-ai-gamification-and-the-metaverse-926b5c2fdb08

Lopienski, K. (2024). *Is phygital retail the future of retail and ecommerce?* Retrieved from https://www.shipbob.com/blog/phygital-retail/

Lukic, A., López, M., & Pagès, A. (2024). *Phygital brand experience: Merging physical and digital formats to enhance customer engagement.* Retrieved from https://merit.url.edu/en/publications/phygital-brand-experience-merging-physical-and-digital-formats-to

LVMH. (2023). *Sephora unveils new flagship Champs-Élysées store.* Retrieved from https://www.lvmh.com/en/news-lvmh/sephora-unveils-new-flagship-champs-elysees-store

Mani, R., & Narayanan, V. (2025). *Beauty and the (AI) Beast – The makeover of personalisation, simplicity and trust.* Retrieved from https://www.pwc.com/gx/en/about/pwc-asia-pacific/asia-pacific-blogs/beauty-and-the-ai-beast.html

Marin-Lopez, X. (2024). *Makeup by Mario launches AR mirror at Sephora Times Square.* Retrieved from https://www.retaildive.com/news/makeup-by-mario-ar-mirror-virtual-try-on-sephora-times-square/718688/

Marketing Explainers. (2024). *Sephora's marketing strategy explained.* Retrieved from https://www.marketingexplainers.com/sephoras-marketing-strategy-explained/

Marketing Maverick. (2024). *Sephora is unique because of this and no other brand has ever done it before.* Retrieved from https://marketingmaverick.io/p/marketing-strategies-of-sephora

Masternak, W. (2025). *Sephora's Beauty Insider program: The gold standard in loyalty.* Retrieved from https://www.openloyalty.io/insider/sephora-beauty-insider

Mattan, M. (2024). *How augmented reality storefronts can drive foot traffic.* Retrieved from https://www.brandxr.io/how-augmented-reality-storefronts-can-drive-foot-traffic

Mattan, M. (2025a). *BrandXR research report: How beauty brands are using AR mirrors to increase sales.* Retrieved from https://www.brandxr.io/research-report-how-beauty-brands-are-using-ar-mirrors-to-increase-sales

Mattan, M. (2025b). *Experiences – Blending physical and digital in-store experiences.* Retrieved from https://www.brandxr.io/phygital-retail-experiences-blending-physical-and-digital-in-store-experiences

Mattan, M. (2025c). *AR mirrors vs. traditional retail displays: A conversion rate comparison.* Retrieved from https://www.brandxr.io/ar-mirrors-vs-traditional-retail-displays-a-conversion-rate-comparison

McKinsey. (2025a). How beauty players can scale gen. *AI, 2025*, •••. https://www.mckinsey.com/industries/consumer-packaged-goods/our-insights/how-beauty-players-can-scale-gen-ai-in-2025

McKinsey. (2025b). *The state of fashion: Beauty volume 2*. Retrieved from https://www.mckinsey.com/~/media/mckinsey/industries/consumer%20packaged%20goods/our%20insights/state%20of%20beauty/2025/the-state-of-fashion-beauty-june-2025-f.pdf

Meta. (2025). *What's the difference between AR, VR and MR*? Retrieved from https://forwork.meta.com/gb/blog/difference-between-vr-ar-and-mr/

Meyer, J. (2023). *Sephora's stores of the future*. Retrieved from https://www.euroshop-tradefair.com/en/euroshopmag/sephoras-stores-of-the-future-for-an-immersive-shopping-experience

Milled. (2022). Win prizes at Sephora spin to win. Retrieved from https://milled.com/sephora-sg/win-prizes-at-sephora-spin-to-win-j1YAMIiL5aUYZQy6

ModiFace. (2025). *We deliver beauty tech solutions to help engage, educate, and empower your consumers*. Retrieved from https://modiface.com/#product

Morgan, J. P. (2024). *Sephora delivers a best-in-class omnichannel experience with J.P. Morgan payments*. Retrieved from https://www.jpmorgan.com/insights/payments/acquiring-and-e-commerce/sephora-omnichannel-experience

Network, C. X. (2023). *How Sephora uses digital channels to deliver on customer centricity*. Retrieved from https://www.cxnetwork.com/cx-experience/articles/how-sephora-uses-digital-channels-to-deliver-on-customer-centricity

Nguyen, H. (2024). *Case study – what does Sephora teach us about digital customer experience?* Retrieved from https://savvycomsoftware.com/blog/sephora-case-study/

Odicci. (2025a). *Leading beauty retailer uses always-on gamification to supercharge app acquisition*. Retrieved from https://odicci.com/customer-success-stories/sephora-combining-crm-app/

Odicci. (2025b). *Leading beauty retailer uses Gamification to supercharge their christmas marketing strategy*. Retrieved from https://odicci.com/customer-success-stories/sephora-a-b-testing-calendars/

Patov, A. (2024). *How Sephora enhances customer experience (cx) through personalization and digital innovation*. Retrieved from https://www.renascence.io/journal/how-sephora-enhances-customer-experience-cx-through-personalization-and-digital-innovation

Power Commerce. (2025). *Sephora and Lyft's innovative partnership: Redefining beauty retail in a digital age*. Retrieved from https://powercommerce.com/blogs/ecommerce-hub/sephora-and-lyfts-innovative-partnership-redefining-beauty-retail-in-a-digital-age

Rebiere, P., & Mavoori, H. (2021), *Sephora: Phygital excellence in beauty tech*. Retrieved from https://hal.science/hal-03138790

Retail Design, C. A. A. D. (2025). *Gamification in retail: Playful experiences for generations Alpha and Z*. Retrieved from https://caad-design.com/en/gamification-in-retail-playful-experiences-for-generations-alpha-and-z

Rukavina, A. (2025). *What is phygital marketing? 11 examples of phygital experiences*. Retrieved from https://www.infobip.com/blog/what-is-phygital-marketing

Sandler, E. (2023). *Sephora adds gamified experience to Beauty Insider loyalty program in appeal to Gen Z*. Retrieved from https://www.glossy.co/beauty/sephora-adds-gamified-experience-to-beauty-insider-loyalty-program-in-appeal-to-gen-z/

Santos, P., Dias, J., & Bairrada, C. (2024). *Gamification in marketing: Insights on current and future research directions based on a bibliometric and theories, contexts, characteristics and methodologies analysis*. Retrieved from https://www.sciencedirect.com/science/article/pii/S2405844024080782

Self-Determination Theory. (2025). Theory. Retrieved from https://selfdeterminationtheory.org/theory/

Sephora. (2014). *Sephora Twitter post*. Retrieved from https://x.com/Sephora/status/649252368031346688

Sephora. (2025a). *About Sephora*. Retrieved from https://www.sephora.com/beauty/about-us

Sephora. (2025b). *2024 global impact and progress report*. Retrieved from https://www.inside-sephora.com/sites/default/files/2025-06/SEPHORA_Global%20Impact%20Report%20-%20accessible.pdf

Sephora. (2025c). *Sephora: Buy Makeup & Skincare*. Retrieved from https://play.google.com/store/apps/details?id=com.sephora

Sephora. (2025d). *Website Domian Page*. Retrieved from https://www.sephora.com/

Sephora. (2025e). *Beauty insiders get a free birthday gift set*. Retrieved from https://www.sephora.com/beauty/birthday-gift

Sephora. (2025f). *Sephora Instagram page*. Retrieved from https://www.instagram.com/sephora/?hl=en

Sephora. (2025g). *Sephora - make-up, beauty*. Retrieved from https://play.google.com/store/apps/details?id=fr.sephora.sephorafrance

Sephora. (2025h). *Sephora.* Retrieved from https://sephora.en.aptoide.com/app

Sephora Malaysia. (2025). *Sephora virtual artist.* Retrieved from https://www.sephora.my/pages/virtual-artist

Sephoria. (2025). Sephoria webpage. Retrieved from https://sephoria-1f83b.kxcdn.com/storage/thumbnails/data/Postcard/8/1400-_q-90/Manandwomandressedup.webp

42. signals. (2024). *Sephora's digital strategy: How smart beauty sales & their insider program made them #1*. Retrieved from https://www.42signals.com/blog/sephora-digital-strategy/

Silvia, C. (2024). *Phygital retail: Combining in-store and digital shopping*. Retrieved from https://www.amu.apus.edu/area-of-study/business-administration-and-management/resources/phygital-retail/

Smartico. (2025). *How does Sephora's Gamified Beauty Insider Program succeed?* Retrieved from https://www.smartico.ai/blog-post/how-sephora-gamified-beauty-insider-program-succeed

Smith, C. (2024). *Sephora's store of the future locations are immersive*. Retrieved from https://www.trendhunter.com/trends/sephora-store-of-the-future

Snap Inc. (2025). *Gamified Augmented Reality Lens delivers massive ROI for Sephora*. Retrieved from https://forbusiness.snapchat.com/inspiration/gamified-augmented-reality-lens-delivers-massive-roi-for-sephora

Snipp. (2025). *Gamification in action - 11 examples of gamification for engagement success*. Retrieved from https://www.snipp.com/blog/gamification-examples

Sobhi, N. (2024). *Learn how to retain customers like the world's 14 best beauty loyalty programs*. Retrieved from https://www.gameball.co/blog/best-beauty-loyalty-programs

Soto, I. (2025). *How beauty influencers are transforming the way we shop online*. Retrieved from https://www.bentley.edu/news/how-beauty-influencers-are-transforming-way-we-shop-online

Super, A. G. I. (2025). *Case studies: How top brands are using AI recommendation engines to boost sales and customer satisfaction in 2025.* Retrieved from https://superagi.com/case-studies-how-top-brands-are-using-ai-recommendation-engines-to-boost-sales-and-customer-satisfaction-in-2025/

Tate, S. (2023). *Sephora marketing strategy: 6 tactics to makeup a beauty empire.* Retrieved from https://coschedule.com/marketing-strategy/marketing-strategy-examples/sephora-marketing-strategy

Think with Google. (2024a). *How physical stores can benefit from the surge in online.* Retrieved from https://www.thinkwithgoogle.com/future-of-marketing/digital-transformation/buying-online-new-normal/

Think with Google. (2024b). *Trends to inform your 5-year retail strategy.* Retrieved from https://www.thinkwithgoogle.com/intl/en-emea/consumer-insights/consumer-trends/five-year-retail-strategy-trends/

Ufford, L. (2023). *6 Examples of retail gamification to boost engagement and sales.* Retrieved from https://www.shopify.com/in/retail/6-examples-of-retail-gamification-to-boost-engagement-and-sales

Vox Media. (2025). *This influencer wanted to revamp her skincare routine and discovered the easiest way to do it at Sephora.* Retrieved from https://www.popsugar.com/beauty/sephora-skincare-routine-builder-quiz-first-experience-47643071

Vyndo. (2025). *Sephora.* Retrieved from https://en.vyndo.io/projects/sephora

Watt, T., & Lester, A. (2025), *Phygital service excellence: Reimagining service to create differentiated industry experiences.* Retrieved from https://www.pwc.com/us/en/technology/alliances/salesforce/generative-ai/phygital-service-excellence.html

Worldwide Business Research. (2025). *Future stores: Building 'phygital' brand and in-store experiences.* Retrieved from https://etailasia.wbresearch.com/blog/future-stores-building-phygital-brand-and-in-store-experiences

Zhang, J., Zou, Y., Wang, S., & Xiang, Y. (2025). *Consumer experience and perception in gamification marketing: evidence from the user survey of POPMART.* Retrieved from https://www.frontiersin.org/journals/communication/articles/10.3389/fcomm.2025.1388020/full

Zhu, M. (2025). *Store of the future.* Retrieved from https://www.ideo.com/works/sephora

ADDITIONAL READING

Askari, F., Nekooeezadeh, M., & Esmaeilzadeh, D. (2025;). Optimizing gamification: unveiling customer preferences through neural network and conjoint analysis". Journal of Advances in Management Research, Vol. ahead-of-print No. ahead-of-print. doi: DOI: 10.1108/JAMR-12-2023-0379

Bauer, J. C., Linzmajer, M., Nagengast, L., Rudolph, T., & D'Cruz, E. (2020). Gamifying the digital shopping experience: Games without monetary participation incentives increase customer satisfaction and loyalty. *Journal of Service Management, 31*(3), 563–595. DOI: 10.1108/JOSM-10-2018-0347

Disse, I. K., & Olsson, M. (2023). Uncovering the gamified customer experience in the retail environment. *International Journal of Retail & Distribution Management, 51*(7), 955–971. DOI: 10.1108/IJRDM-07-2022-0268

Ebrahimi, E., Irani, H. R., Abbasi, M., & Abedini, A. (2024). The effect of gamification on brand equity and desirable consumer behaviors in online retail stores: The mediating role of brand engagement. *Interdisciplinary Journal of Management Studies, 17*(2), 379–391. DOI: 10.22059/ijms.2023.352786.675544

Elmashhara, M. G., De Cicco, R., Silva, S. C., Hammerschmidt, M., & Silva, M. L. (2024). How gamifying AI shapes customer motivation, engagement, and purchase behavior. *Psychology and Marketing, 41*(1), 134–150. DOI: 10.1002/mar.21912

Gupta, K., Funk, D., & Kunkel, T. (2026;), "Gameful affordance management for engagement and retention (GAMER) framework: organizational practices to manage consumer affordances in gamified services". *Journal of Service Management*, Vol. ahead-of-print No. ahead-of-print. DOI: 10.1108/JOSM-07-2024-0300

Hulya, A., & Dilaver, T. (2024). The effect of gamification on brand awareness: A study of retail industry and healthy-living applications. *Journal of Digital & Social Media Marketing, 12*(3), 293. Advance online publication. DOI: 10.69554/OHMK3521

Jain, S., Mishra, S., & Saxena, G. (2023). Luxury customer's motivations to adopt gamification. *Marketing Intelligence & Planning, 41*(2), 156–170. DOI: 10.1108/MIP-05-2022-0207

Malik, G., & Pradhan, D. (2025). How does gameful experience foster customer engagement and brand advocacy? Consumer insights into branding in e-tail. *Journal of Consumer Marketing, 42*(2), 205–222. DOI: 10.1108/JCM-04-2024-6764

Neiva, R., Ferreira, H., & Azevedo, A. (2025;), "Understanding the impact of gamification features on user retention: evidence from a mobile payment app". *International Journal of Bank Marketing*, Vol. ahead-of-print No. ahead-of-print. DOI: 10.1108/IJBM-07-2025-0567

Panda, D., Raut, S. K., Rana, S., & Shamsudin, M. N. (2024). Leveraging gamification to enhance persuasive behaviour and streamline online product returns: An approach grounded in multiple case studies. *Journal of Business and Industrial Marketing*, *39*(12), 2684–2698. DOI: 10.1108/JBIM-01-2024-0007

Paschmann, J. W., Bruno, H. A., van Heerde, H. J., Völckner, F., & Klein, K. (2024). Driving Mobile App User Engagement Through Gamification. *Journal of Marketing Research*, 62(2), 249-273. (Original work published 2025)DOI: 10.1177/00222437241275927

Silva, J. H., Mendes, G. H., Teixeira, J. G., & Braatz, D. (2023). Gamification in the customer journey: A conceptual model and future research opportunities. *Journal of Service Theory and Practice*, *33*(3), 352–386. DOI: 10.1108/JSTP-07-2022-0142

Stein, F., Guerreiro, J., Loureiro, S. M. C., & Rodrigues, M. B. (2025). Leveling up coolness: How VR gamification drives experiential values. *Journal of Brand Management*, *32*(5), 438–457. DOI: 10.1057/s41262-025-00390-3

Tien Minh, D., Vu Lan Oanh, L., & Diem Quynh, N. (2023). How gamification affects online shopping behavior: An approach with youngsters (aged 16 – 30). *Cogent Business &amp. Cogent Business & Management*, *10*(3), 2256076. Advance online publication. DOI: 10.1080/23311975.2023.2256076

Vilkaite - Vaitone, N., Kirse, S., Adomaviciute - Sakalauske, K., Dikcius, V., & Zimaitis, I. (2025). The usefulness of gamification for enhancing customer loyalty to small e-tailers. *EuroMed Journal of Business*, *20*(2), 435–452. DOI: 10.1108/EMJB-09-2023-0240

Zafar, A. U., Sajjad, A., Agarwal, R., Lamprinakos, G., & Yaqub, M. Z. (2025). Digital transformation portrays a play or ploy for brands: Exploring the impact of green gamification as a digital marketing strategy. *International Marketing Review*, *42*(4), 585–603. DOI: 10.1108/IMR-04-2024-0110

Zhou, Y., Zang, Z., Wang, K., & Gu, Y. (2025). Enhancing gamified experiences in online service platforms: Exploring the impact of extrinsic gamification design elements. *Electronic Markets*, *35*(1), 101. DOI: 10.1007/s12525-025-00852-1

KEY TERMS AND DEFINITIONS

Artificial intelligence (AI): Artificial Intelligence refers to design of computer systems to mimic the human intelligence like reinforced learning, reasoning, and decision-making. In data driven sustainable marketing, AI is used for developing algorithms for personalization, chatbots, and recommendation to improve operational efficiency and customer experience.

Augmented reality (AR): Augmented reality refers to design of technology that enhances the real-world environment by overlaying digital elements such as images, text, and animations. In data driven sustainable marketing, AR is used for developing algorithms that allows customers to visualize products, access interactive information, and experience brands in phygital touchpoints in innovative and immersive ways using smartphones or AR-enabled devices.

Consumer engagement: Consumer engagement refers to brands connection with customer through emotional, cognitive, and behavioural means that goes beyond transactions. Brands interactions with customers happens through as social media participation, feedback, reviews, and brand advocacy. Company's high brand engagement indicates strong relationship with customers that leads to increased brand association, loyalty and brand advocacy through word of mouth.

Customer journey: Brands deliver cohesive, comprehensive and engaging personalized interactive experiences by building long-lasting customer relationships and loyalty to benefit from customers lifetime value. The company's use data and technology for personalization to provide tailored beauty experiences designed to be seamless and engaging across customers lifecycle journeys as customers move seamlessly across sensory pleasure of in-store shopping, and digital convenience of online and mobile strategies. This often highlights that customer journey starts online then try and buy in store or vice versa or usage of only one channel and then after-sales services managed digitally.

Digital gamification: Brands custom design digital gamification tools within its mobile applications and website designs to make the shopping experience of target customers more enjoyable by reducing customers anxiety while purchasing a product. Digital gamification drives traffic and engagement across physical stores, strengthening omnichannel presence and thriving on the fluid integration between digital and physical realms.

Experiential marketing: Experiential marketing tactics in product / service offering ecosystems focuses on creating a memorable and interactive brand experiences in highly immersive manner that highly involve the target customers. These tactics allow customers to engage with brands events, activities and other immersive experiences either in online or offline touchpoints. These tactics helps brand to build lasting impressions, brand awareness, strong emotional connections and brand loyalty.

Gamification: Gamification involves the application of game design elements in non-game contexts. Gamification is the process of creating a game-like environment to non-game settings like a website or application, which acts as a critical customer driver to elevate passive consumption into active participation, and leading to stronger emotional engagement and satisfaction. Gamified elements are making the shopping process interactive, fun, and rewarding.

In-store gamification: Brands custom design awe-inspiring physical stores with integrated in-store gamification tools like in-store kiosk, iPad, mobile app and beauty advisors' personal consultation approach significantly enhances the physical retail environment, creating memorable product exploration, beauty discovery and offers more personalized shopping experience.

Loyalty programs: Loyalty program's provides rewards and challenges that work seamlessly whether customers shop online or in-store thereby fostering a unified brand experience. Brands offer incentives to customers through purchases, with each level gaining them more exclusive access to unique benefits and privileges for long-term brand association. Sometimes brand uses customers digital achievements to motivate them to visit physical stores to unlock in-store perks, exclusive events, and early access to new products.

Personalization: Marketing personalization is the process of using data coming from different touchpoints to target and retarget leads with a synchronous brand message that speaks directly to customer considering that specific customers' interests, demographics, and past buying behaviour. The Personalization improve marketing content relevance and customers satisfaction by targeted recommendations through curated content and promotional offers. It helps brand to create more meaningful interactions and imbibe emotional connections with target customers.

Phygital touchpoints: Phygital touchpoints is an integrated ecosystem where customer interactions cross seamlessly between online and offline channels from most riveting sensory pleasure of physical storefront to convenient digital website and mobile app. Phygital retail ecosystem responds to fast changing consumer habits, focuses on customers emotions and provides immediate service and satisfaction to customer with unmatched speed, utmost convenience and better responsiveness

Virtual reality: Virtual reality refers to design of technology that enhances the computer-generated environment that creates a fully immersive experience so users can explore and interact with it. The target consumers use VR headsets to experience simulated spaces, products, and scenarios. Virtual reality tools are used for most immersive experiential marketing, product training, and brand storytelling.

Compilation of References

Aaker, D. (2020). Güçlü markalar yaratmak. (Çev: E. Demir). İstanbul: Mediacat Yayınları.

Abbasi, A. Z., Alqahtani, N., Tsiotsou, R. H., Rehman, U., & Ting, D. H. (2023). Esports as playful consumption experiences: Examining the antecedents and consequences of game engagement. *Telematics and Informatics*, *77*, 101937.

Abbasi, A. Z., Asif, M., Hollebeek, L. D., Islam, J. U., Ting, D. H., & Rehman, U. (2021). The effects of consumer esports videogame engagement on consumption behaviors. *Journal of Product and Brand Management*, *30*(8), 1194–1211.

Abbasi, A. Z., Ting, D. H., Hlavacs, H., Costa, L. V., & Veloso, A. I. (2019). An empirical validation of consumer video game engagement: A playful-consumption experience approach. *Entertainment Computing*, *29*, 43–55.

Abbasi, A., Alalouch, C., & Bramley, G. (2016). Open space quality in deprived urban areas: User perspective and use pattern. *Procedia: Social and Behavioral Sciences*, *216*, 194–205. DOI: 10.1016/j.sbspro.2015.12.028

Abbott-Chapman, J., & Robertson, M. (2001). Youth, leisure and home: Space, place and identity. Loisir et Société. *Society and Leisure*, *24*(2), 485–506. DOI: 10.7202/000192ar

Abdul, S. B. (2021). *Gamification In Fashion Is Influencing Fashion Freaks*. Mycred.Me. https://mycred.me/blog/gamification-in-fashion-influencing-fashion-freaks/

Abdulwahid, A., Pattnaik, M., Palav, M. R., Babu, S. T., Manoharan, G., & Selvi, G. P. (2023). Library management system using artificial intelligence. In *2023 Eighth International Conference on Science Technology Engineering and Mathematics (ICONSTEM)* (ss. 1-7). IEEE.

Abraham, V. (2020). *Gamification: A digital marketing strategy in the beauty industry*. Retrieved from https://www.linkedin.com/pulse/gamification-digital-marketing-strategy-beauty-industry-abraham

Abukhadra, S. (2021). *Sephora leading the way with augmented reality*. Retrieved from https://medium.com/marketing-in-the-age-of-digital/sephora-leading-the-way-with-augmented-reality-c117eed0faa0

Acar, B. N. (2024). *The role of experiential marketing in in-game advertising* (Master's thesis, Istanbul Kultur University, Graduate School of Education). Istanbul Kultur University. https://openaccess.iku.edu.tr/entities/publication/38538e4d-cd23-4ec5-9f0e-7b5fe6d1b3c5

Acar, A. (2007). Testing the effects of incidental advertising exposure in online gaming environment. *Journal of Interactive Advertising*, *8*(1), 45–56. DOI: 10.1080/15252019.2007.10722136

Acikgoz, F., Perez-Vega, R., Okumus, F., & Stylos, N. (2023). Consumer engagement with AI-powered voice assistants: A behavioral reasoning perspective. *Psychology and Marketing*, *40*(11), 1–18. DOI: 10.1002/mar.21873

Adobe. (2024). *Guide to marketing personalization — benefits, examples, and more*. Retrieved from https://business.adobe.com/blog/basics/marketing-personalization

Adomavicius, G., & Tuzhilin, A. (2005). Toward the next generation of recommender systems: A survey of the state-of-the-art and possible extension. *IEEE Transactions on Knowledge and Data Engineering*, *17*(6), 734–749. DOI: 10.1109/TKDE.2005.99

Ağca, G., & Kozbekçi Ayranpınar, S. (2021). Moda sektöründe artırılmış gerçeklik ve sanal gerçeklik (Augmented Reality and Virtual Reality in the Fashion Industry). Sanat. *Tarim Bilimleri Dergisi*, *25*, 1–15.

Agrawal, S., & Raikwar, Y. (2025, May). *AI-driven content creation in gaming: Opportunities, challenges, and monetization*. Gyan Ganga College of Technology, Yash Raikwar's Lab. DOI: 10.13140/RG.2.2.31586.24007

Ahmad, M. (2024, March 5). *Exploring the Booming Landscape of In-Game Advertising*. ExchangeWire. https://www.exchangewire.com/blog/2024/03/05/exploring-the-booming-landscape-of-in-game-advertising/

Akalın, M. (2018). *Research techniques in social sciences with sample explanations: Surveys* (2nd ed.). Seçkin Publishing.

Akan, N. A. (2022). Dijital oyunlarda reklam ve etkileri. Ş. Sağıroğlu, Hİ Bülbül, A. Kılıç, M. Küçükali, Ş. Bayzan & Y. Samur (Ed.*), Dijital Oyunlar-2: Araçlar, Metodolojiler, Uygulamalar ve Öneriler* içinde (pp. 215-245). Ankara: Nobel Yayınevi.

Akdemir, N. (2018). Visible Expression of Social Identity: The Clothing and Fashion. *Gaziantep University Journal of Social Sciences, 17*(4), 1371–1379. DOI: 10.21547/jss.411181

Akıllıbaş, E., & Ceylan, K. E. (2020). Oyunlaştırmanın Pazarlamadaki Gücü. *Anasay, 14*(14), 43–80. DOI: 10.33404/anasay.755465

Akın, T., & Demirel, M. (2024). Açık hava reklamcılığında artırılmış gerçekliğin önemi ve uygulamaları (The Importance and Applications of Augmented Reality in Outdoor Advertising). *Sanat ve Tasarım Araştırmaları Dergisi, 5*(8), 82–97.

Akten, M. (2003). Isparta ilindeki bazı rekreasyon alanlarının mevcut potansiyellerinin belirlenmesi (Determining the Current Potential of Some Recreation Areas in Isparta). *Süleyman Demirel Üniversitesi Orman Fakültesi Dergisi*, (2), 115–132.

Aktuğlu, I. K. (2022). *Marka yönetimi: Güçlü ve başarılı markalar için temel ilkeler*. İletişim Yayınları.

Akyol, M. (2010). Game advertising as a brand communication tool: A study on its role in creating brand awareness. T.C. Selçuk University Institute of Social Sciences Department of Advertising and Promotion Public Relations and Promotion Division. Unpublished Doctoral Thesis https://tez.yok.gov.tr/UlusalTezMerkezi/tezDetay.jsp?id=rdrl-PfYM1STPpq62lPmBQ&no=zJ1UNQlaO-xvXUW5D1-ekw

Alcantara, H., & Alcantara, C. (2022). The future of shopping - Changing Consumers' Mindset through Metaverse Immersive Experiences: hibe Case Study. *Usability and User Experience. AHFE International Conference*. DOI: 10.54941/ahfe1001733

Altınbaş, H. (2007). Marketing communication and city marketing: "Branding cities." *Selçuk Communication, 4*(4), 156–162. https://dergipark.org.tr/tr/pub/josc/article/200747?issue_id=19014

Altun, G. (2019). *Advergame Applications as a Marketing Communication Tool: A Study of Advergame Applications in Turkey* (Master's thesis, Sakarya University (Turkey)).

Anderson, C. A., Shibuya, A., Ihori, N., Swing, E. L., Bushman, B. J., Sakamoto, A., . . . Saleem, M. (2010). Effects of violent video games on aggression, empathy, and prosocial behavior in Eastern and Western countries: A meta-analytic review. *Psychological Bulletin, 136(*2), 151–173. https://psycnet.apa.org/doiLanding?doi=10.1037%2Fa0018251

Anderson, B., Gale, C., Gower, A. P., France, E. F., Jones, M., Lacohee, H. V., McWilliam, A., Tracey, K., & Trimby, M. (2002). Digital living- people-centred innovation and strategy. *BT Technology Journal, 20*(2), 11–29. DOI: 10.1023/A:1015632120289

Annetta, L. A. (2008). Video games in education: Why they should be used and how they are being used. *Theory into Practice, 47*(3), 229–239. DOI: 10.1080/00405840802153940

Annisawati, A., Gaffar, V., Hurriyati, R., & Widjajanta, B. (2024). Muslim Loyalty in Halal Digital Recreation: The Role of Experience Quality and Value. *Proceedings of the 8th Global Conference on Business, Management, and Entrepreneurship (GCBME 2023)*, pp. 710-718. DOI: 10.2991/978-94-6463-443-3_93

An, S., & Stern, S. (2011). Mitigating the effects of advergames on children. *Journal of Advertising, 40*(1), 43–56. DOI: 10.2753/JOA0091-3367400103

Anzu. (2022). *The US in-game advertising report 2022.*

Apparel, R. (2023a). *Gamification of fashion: A combination that is fast becoming a hit | Apparel Resources.* Apparelresources.Com. https://apparelresources.com/business-news/retail/gamification-fashion-combination-fast-becoming-hit/

Apparel, R. (2023b). *Gamification of fashion: A combination that is fast becoming a hit | Apparel Resources.* Apparelresources.Com. https://apparelresources.com/business-news/retail/gamification-fashion-combination-fast-becoming-hit/

Appinventiv.com. (2024). *What is Metaverse and how is it reshaping the AR/VR world?* Advertising in the Metaverse: Research Agenda. https://appinventiv.com/blog/what-is-metaverse/

Ar, A. A. (2007). *Marka ve marka stratejileri.* Nobel Yayın Dağıtım.

Aslan, Z. (1993). Sanayileşme ve kentleşmenin doğada rekreasyon faaliyetlerine duyulan gereksinimi arttırıcı etkisi (The Effect of Industrialization and Urbanization on the Need for Recreation Activities in Nature). *Ekoloji Çevre Dergisi, 2*(8), 22–24.

Australia, T. (2022). *How AI and AR is shaping the post-pandemic beauty industry.* Retrieved from https://taustralia.com.au/ai-ar-beauty-industry/

Aydemir, F. (2022). Digital games and their effects on children. *Adıyaman University Journal of Social Sciences Institute,* (41), 40–69. https://doi.org/DOI: 10.14520/adyusbd.1116868

Aydoğan, D., & Kaplanoğlu, L. (2020). *Sanal gerçeklik kapsamında sanat (Art within the Scope of Virtual Reality). 7. Uluslararası İletişim Günleri.* Üsküdar Üniversitesi İletişim Fakültesi.

Aydoğan, H. (2021). Dijital oyunlar aracılığıyla reklamcılık: Ürün ve hizmet simülasyonlarının ötesine bakmak (Advertising through Digital Games: Beyond Product and Service Simulations). *Uluslararası Halkla İlişkiler ve Reklam Çalışmaları Dergisi, 4*(1), 58–71.

Aylan, K., & Aylan, S. (2020). Sanal gerçeklik ve artırılmış gerçeklik uygulamalarının rekreatif faaliyetlere yansıması: Dijital rekreasyon (Reflection of Virtual and Augmented Reality Applications on Recreational Activities: Digital Recreation). *Türk Turizm Araştırmaları Dergisi, 4*(3), 2746–2760. DOI: 10.26677/TR1010.2020.507

Azuma, R., Baillot, Y., Behringer, R., Feiner, S., Julier, S., & MacIntyre, B. (2001). Recent advances in augmented reality. *IEEE Computer Graphics and Applications, 21*(6), 34–47. DOI: 10.1109/38.963459

Baltezarević, R., & Baltezarević, I. (2024). Effects of in-game advertısıng on the world economy. *4th Internatıonal Cankaya Scıentıfic Studıes Congress*, September 7-9, 2024, Ankara-TÜRKİYE.

Bányai, F., Zsila, Á., Griffiths, M. D., Demetrovics, Z., & Király, O. (2020). Career as a professional gamer: Gaming motives as predictors of career plans to become a professional esport player. *Frontiers in Psychology, 11*, 1866. PMID: 32903792

Barnes, S. J. (2002). Wireless digital advertising: Nature and implications. *International Journal of Advertising, 21*(3), 399–420. https://www.tandfonline.com/doi/pdf/10.1080/02650487.2002.11104939. DOI: 10.1080/02650487.2002.11104939

Barsha, S., & Munshi, S. A. (2023). Implementing artificial intelligence in library services: A review of current prospects and challenges of developing countries. *Library Hi Tech News, 41*(1), 7–10. DOI: 10.1108/LHTN-07-2023-0126

Başeğmez, H. & Tuncali Yaman, T. (2022). The Role Of Virtual Try-on Technology In Online Purchasing Decision. *Journal of Research in Business, 7*(IMISC2021 Special Issue), 165–176. DOI: 10.54452/jrb.1023619

Başer, E., & Sever, N. (2023). Artırılmış gerçeklik tabanlı reklamların etkileri (The Effects of Augmented Reality-Based Advertisements). In Söğütlüler, T. (Ed.), *Sinema ve Reklam Çalışmalarında Güncel Yaklaşımlar* (pp. 151–170). Eğitim Yayınevi.

Başev, S. E. (2022). Game-based advertisement: Uludag Lemonade and Lipton Ice Tea example. *Journal of Erciyes Communication, 9*(1), 77–95.

Basten, D. (2017). Gamification. *IEEE Software, 34*(5), 76–81. DOI: 10.1109/MS.2017.3571581

Başyazıcıoğlu, H. N. (2020). Interactive marketing communication and digital advertising. In Üzümlü, A. M. (Ed.), *Integrated marketing communication in all its aspects* (pp. 201–223). Nobel Yayınları.

Bayraktar, E., & Kaleli, F. (2007). *Sanal gerçeklik ve uygulama alanları (Virtual Reality and Its Application Areas). IX. Akademik Bilişim Konferansı*. Dumlupınar Üniversitesi.

Bayram, A. T., & Kavlak, H. T. (2021). Rekreasyon ve teknoloji (Recreation and Technology). In Güneş, G., & Varol, F. (Eds.), *Rekreasyon: Disiplinlerarası Yaklaşım ve Örnek Olaylar* (pp. 383–400). Nobel Yayıncılık.

Bayzan, Ş., & Güneş, A. (2022). History of digital games and Turkish gaming media. In Sağıroğlu, Ş., Bülbül, H. İ., Kılıç, A., Küçükali, M., Bayzan, Ş., & Samur, Y. (Eds.), *Digital games - 1: Tools, methodologies, applications, and recommendations* (pp. 25–83). Nobel Yayınları.

Bechmann, P. A. (2007). "Realizing Cross-media". In Ambivalence towards Convergence: Digitalisation and media change, (Eds.) Storsul, T. and Stuedahl, D., Nordicom, pp. 57-72.

Belch, G. E., & Belch, M. A. (2003). *Advertising and promotion: An integrated marketing communications perspective* (6th ed.). McGraw-Hill., https://www.scribd.com/document/963071761

Belghiti, S., Ochs, A., Lemoine, J.-F., & Badot, O. (2018). The Phygital Shopping Experience: An Attempt at Conceptualization and Empirical Investigation. In *Developments in Marketing Science: Proceedings of the Academy of Marketing Science* (pp. 61–74). DOI: 10.1007/978-3-319-68750-6_18

Benway, J. P., & Lane, D. M. (1998). "Banner Blindness: The Irony of Attention Grabbing on the World Wide Web", *Proceedings of the Human Factors and Ergonomics Society 42nd Annual Meeting*, 1, pp. 463-467. DOI: 10.1177/154193129804200504

Beri, S. (2023). *Gamified kiosks and in-store experiences - the future of retail.* Retrieved from https://ogmento.io/blog/gamified-kiosks-and-in-store-experiences-the-future-of-retail/

Bezjian-Avery, A., Calder, B., & Iacobucci, D. (1998). New media interactive advertising vs. traditional advertising. *Journal of Advertising Research, 38*(4), 23–32. DOI: 10.1080/00218499.1998.12466563

Bhave, K., et al. (2013). "Understanding the Orientatıon of Gen Y Toward Mobile Applications and In-App Advertısıng in India", IJMM Summer, 8(1), pp. 62-74.

Bhuyan, F. A., Rahman, M., Akram, W., & Talim, T. (2025). *Turning puzzle games into fashion: Exploring personal outfits through symbol-based clothing assembly. Fashion, Style & Popular Culture, Online fir(Online First).* Online First., DOI: 10.1386/fspc_00293_1

Bilali, T., & Papahristou, E. (2024). Analyzing the Impact of Digital Fashion, Gaming, and the Metaverse on Social Presence in Digital Worlds Through a Literature Review. In *Driving Green Marketing in Fashion and Retail* (1st ed., pp. 226–250). IGI Global., DOI: 10.4018/979-8-3693-3049-4.ch014

Binark, M., & Bayrakturan, G. (2008). *Digital games as a cultural industry*. Kalkedon Publications.

Block, F., Hodge, V., Hobson, S., Sephton, N., Devlin, S., Ursu, M. F., & Cowling, P. I. (2018, June). Narrative bytes: Data-driven content production in esports. In *Proceedings of the 2018 ACM international conference on interactive experiences for TV and online video* (pp. 29-41).

Bogost, I. (2005). Videogames and the future of education. *On the Horizon, 13*(2), 119–125. DOI: 10.1108/10748120510608151

Bogost, I. (2015). Why gamification is bullshit. In Walz, S. P., & Deterding, S. (Eds.), *The gameful world: Approaches, issues, applications* (pp. 65–79). MIT Press. DOI: 10.7551/mitpress/9788.003.0005

Bolat, N. (2019). "Geleneksel Mecralarda Çapraz Medya ve Transmedya Anlatıları Üzerine Bir İnceleme: Ağır Roman Örneği" (An Examination of Cross-Media and Transmedia Narratives in Traditional Media: The Case of Ağır Roman) [Journal of Selçuk Communication]. *Selçuk İletişim Dergisi, 12*(2), 503–531.

Bolat, N. (2020). "Televizyonun Teknik Dönüşümünün İçeriğe Etkisi" (The Impact of the Technical Transformation of Television on Content). In Yeni, İ. Y. İ. (Ed.), *Sirer, E* (pp. 111–130). LiteraTürk Publications.

Bolat, N. (2023). Dijital Oyunlarda Kültürel Görsel Kodlarla Kültürün Yeniden Üretimi: Uruz Er Kişinin Dönüşü. *Middle Black Sea Journal of Communication Studies, 8*(2), 165–178. DOI: 10.56202/mbsjcs.1361429

Bolliger, D. U., & Shepherd, C. E. (2016). Instructor and adult learner perceptions of the use of Internet-enabled devices in residential outdoor education programs. *British Journal of Educational Technology*, •••, 1–10.

Booth, D., & Koberg, C. (2012). *Display Advertising*. John Wiley & Sons.

Bozkurt, A., & Genç-Kumtepe, E. (2014). *Gamification, game philosophy, and education: Gamification*. Academic Computing '14 - XVI. Academic Computing Conference Proceedings (pp. 147–156). Mersin University.

Bozkurt, Y. (2019). Tutum ve davranış niyeti üzerinde oyun reklam algısının rolü. *Gümüşhane Üniversitesi İletişim Fakültesi Elektronik Dergisi*, *7*(2), 1341–1371.

Brand Safety Institute. (2023, May 25). *AI trends in digital advertising for gaming*. https://www.brandsafetyinstitute.com/blog/ai-trends-in-digital-advertising-for-gaming

Bräuer. Paula. (2024). Audio-Gamification: How Gamification Can Improve the Use of Intelligent Virtual Assistants. DOI: 10.13140/RG.2.2.14811.17445

Bräuer, P., & Mazarakis, A. (2022). "Alexa, can we design gamification without a screen?" - Implementing cooperative and competitive audio-gamification for intelligent virtual assistants. *Computers in Human Behavior*, *135*, 107362. DOI: 10.1016/j.chb.2022.107362

Braze. (2025). *Sephora SEA used in-app message gamification to increase purchases by 132%*. Retrieved from https://www.braze.com/customers/sephora-sea-case-study

Briedis, H., Gregg, B., Heidenreich, K., & Liu, W. (2021). *Omnichannel: The path to value*. Retrieved from https://www.mckinsey.com/capabilities/growth-marketing-and-sales/our-insights/the-survival-guide-to-omnichannel-and-the-path-to-value

Brodie, R. J., Hollebeek, L. D., Jurić, B., & Ilić, A. (2011). Customer engagement: Conceptual domain, fundamental propositions, and implications for research. *Journal of Service Research*, *14*(3), 252–271.

Brodowicz, M. (2025). *Sephora's AI-powered virtual try-on for personalized makeup recommendations*. Retrieved from https://aithor.com/essay-examples/sephoras-ai-powered-virtual-try-on-for-personalized-makeup-recommendations

Brown, E., & Cairns, P. (2004, April). A grounded investigation of game immersion. In *CHI'04 extended abstracts on Human factors in computing systems* (pp. 1297-1300).

Bubna, K., Trotter, M. G., Watson, M., & Polman, R. (2023). Coaching and talent development in esports: A theoretical framework and suggestions for future research. *Frontiers in Psychology*, *14*, 1191801. PMID: 37235101

Bucher, C. (1972). *Foundations of physical education*. C.V. Mosby Company.

Buckner, K., Fang, H., & Qiao, S. (2002). Advergaming: A new genre in Internet advertising. *SoCbytes Journal*, *2*(1), 1–5.

Buijsman, M. (2025). "Global games market to hit $189 billion in 2025 as growth shifts to console". Retrieved from: https://newzoo.com/resources/blog/global-games-market-to-hit-189-billion-in-2025), Date of Access: 12th of September 2025.

Caillois, R. (2001). *Man, play, and games.* University of Illinois press.

Çakır, E. (2023). Metaverse evreninde dijital mimarilerin haber üretimindeki konumsallıkları. E. Güven & İ. Kılınç (Ed.), Yeni çağda dönüşen gazetecilik: Gazetecilikte yeni yaklaşımlar içinde (pp. 263-283). İstanbul: Eğitim Yayınevi.

Çakır, O. (2021, July 19). PUBG Mobile'dan Tesla hayranlarını sevindiren iş birliği. https://shiftdelete.net/pubg-mobiledan-tesla-hayranlarini-sevindiren-isbirligi

Calapez, A., Ribeiro, T., Almeida, V., & Pedragosa, V. (2024). Esports fan identity toward sponsor–sponsee relationship: An understanding of the role-based identity. *International Journal of Sports Marketing & Sponsorship, 25*(1), 42–66.

Can, E. (2015). Boş zaman, rekreasyon ve etkinlik turizmi ilişkisi (The Relationship Between Leisure, Recreation, and Event Tourism). *Istanbul Journal of Social Sciences, 10*, 1–17.

Cao, Z., Gao, H., Qu, X., Yang, M., & Yang, X. (2013). Fashion, Cooperation, and Social Interactions. *PLoS One, 8*(1), e49441. DOI: 10.1371/journal.pone.0049441 PMID: 23382799

Caraban, A., Karapanos, E., Gonçalves, D., & Campos, P. (2019). *23 ways to nudge: A review of technology-mediated nudging in human–computer interaction.* In *Proceedings of the 2019 CHI Conference on Human Factors in Computing Systems* (CHI '19) (Paper 503, pp. 1–15). Association for Computing Machinery. https://doi.org/DOI: 10.1145/3290605.3300733

Carman, A. (2017). *Sephora's latest app update lets you try virtual makeup on at home with AR.* Retrieved from https://www.theverge.com/2017/3/16/14946086/sephora-virtual-assistant-ios-app-update-ar-makeup

Castaldo Lundén, E. (2020). Exploring Fashion as Communication: The Search for a new fashion history against the grain. In *Popular Communication.* DOI: 10.1080/15405702.2020.1854952

Catherine, D. (2023). *Growing Playings: Childhood Video Games' Influence on Current Style—STITCH.* Stitchfashion.Com. https://www.stitchfashion.com/home//growing-playings-childhood-video-games-influence-on-current-style

Cauberghe, V., & De Pelsmacker, P. (2010). Advergames. *Journal of Advertising, 39*(1), 5–18.

Çeber, B. (2024). Yapay zekâ etiği bağlamında reklamcılık sektörü üzerine uygulamalı bir araştırma. *Intermedia International e-Journal, 11*(20), 63–84. DOI: 10.56133/intermedia.1462312

Çeber, B. (2024). Reklam ajanslarında yapay zekâ kullanımı: Sektör profesyonellerinin chatGPT ve midjourney deneyimlerine yönelik bir araştırma. *Erciyes İletişim Dergisi, 11*(2), 583–606. DOI: 10.17680/erciyesiletisim.1439479

Çeber, B. (2025). Yapay zekâ "Sora" ile üretilen reklamların McLuhan'ın "Araç mesajdır" perspektifinden incelenmesi: Toys "R" Us reklam örneği. *Yeni Medya Elektronik Dergisi, 9*(2), 171–200.

Cedrola, E., & Giovannetti, M. (2024). Fashion and Gamification. In *Digital Transformation for Fashion and Luxury Brands* (pp. 423–442). Palgrave Macmillan., DOI: 10.1007/978-3-031-35589-9_20

Çelebi, Ö. (2021). *The reflection of change in marketing communication on experiential marketing: An examination of brand applications from traditional to digital* (Master's thesis, Istanbul University, Institute of Social Sciences). Istanbul University. https://nek.istanbul.edu.tr/ekos/TEZ/ET002178.pdf?utm_source=chatgpt.com

Çelik, Z. (2021). Fijital (Phygital) Pazarlama (Phygital Marketing). In Sağlam, M. (Ed.), *Dijitalleşen Dünyada Pazarlama* (pp. 297–317). Atlas Akademik Basım.

Ceran, Y., & Karaçor, S. (2013). Advertising as a marketing communication tool: Advertising costs and accounting. *Niğde University Journal of Economics and Administrative Sciences, 6*(1), 9–22. https://dergipark.org.tr/tr/pub/niguiibfd/issue/19752/211410?utm_source=chatgpt.com

Cevher, M. F. (2023). Fijital pazarlama: Geleneksel ve dijital pazarlamanın kesişimi (Phygital Marketing: The Intersection of Traditional and Digital Marketing). *Pearson Journal of Social Sciences & Humanities, 8*(25), 520–535.

Cezim, B. (2025). *How Sephora's marketing strategies & campaigns win over different audiences*. Retrieved from https://digitalagencynetwork.com/sephora-marketing-strategies/

Chakraborty, D., & Rana, N. (2025). *Impulse Buying and Stickiness Using Flow Theory: A Longitudinal Study*. Retrieved from https://www.tandfonline.com/doi/full/10.1080/08874417.2025.2547970

Chaney, I. M., Lin, K. H., & Chaney, J. (2004). The effect of billboards within the gaming environment. *Journal of Interactive Advertising, 5*(1), 37–45. https://www.researchgate.net/publication/228701546_The_Effect_of_Billboards_within_the_Gaming_Environment. DOI: 10.1080/15252019.2004.10722092

Chan, G., Huo, Y., Kelly, S., Leung, J., Tisdale, C., & Gullo, M. (2022). The impact of eSports and online video gaming on lifestyle behaviours in youth: A systematic review. *Computers in Human Behavior, 126*, 106974.

Changmai, T. (2024). Programmatic advertising technology and social marketing trend on game industrial in 2024. In N. V. Mançurova et al. (Eds.), *İş dünyası. Eğitim. Ekonomi: V. Uluslararası bilimsel-pratik konferans bildirileri (Minsk, 4–5 Nisan 2024)* (ss. 445–450). Belarus Devlet Üniversitesi İşletme Enstitüsü.

Chang, Y. K., Chen, K., & Li, Z. (2024). Systematic Framework for Esports Training: Informing eSports Training with the Learning Sciences. *Simulation & Gaming, 55*(1), 82–108.

Chen, J., & Ringel, M. (2001). Can advergaming be the future of interactive advertising. *Fast Forward. Available online:* http://www.kpe.com

Chen, J. V., Ha, Q. A., & Vu, M. T. (2023). The Influences of Virtual Reality Shopping Characteristics on Consumers' Impulse Buying Behavior. *International Journal of Human-Computer Interaction, 39*(17), 3473–3491. DOI: 10.1080/10447318.2022.2098566

Chen, X., Memon, H. A., Wang, Y., Marriam, I., & Tebyetekerwa, M. (n.d.). Circular Economy and Sustainability of the Clothing and Textile Industry. *Materials Circular Economy, 1*, 3. DOI: 10.1007/s42824-021-00026-2

Chen, Y. (2024). Advertising in the era of artificial intelligence. *Proceedings of 3rd International Conference on Interdisciplinary Humanities and Communication Studies*. DOI: 10.54254/2753-7064/39/20242180

Chou, Y. (2025). The Octalysis Framework for Gamification & Behavioural Design. Retrieved from https://yukaichou.com/gamification-examples/octalysis-complete-gamification-framework/

Chou, Y.-K. (2016). Actionable Gamification: Beyond points, badges and leaderboards. *Revista Internacional de Organizaciones, 18*(18), 137–144. DOI: 10.17345/rio18.137-144

Chung, A. E., Griffin, A. C., Selezneva, D., & Gotz, D. (2018, September 24). Health and Fitness Apps for Hands-Free Voice-Activated Assistants: Content Analysis. *JMIR mHealth and uHealth, 6*(9), e174. DOI: 10.2196/mhealth.9705 PMID: 30249581

Cicchirillo, V., & Mabry, A. (2016). Advergaming and healthy eating involvement: How healthy eating inclinations impact processing of advergame content. *Internet Research, 26*(3), 587–603. DOI: 10.1108/IntR-04-2014-0091

Clavio, G., Kraft, P. M., & Pedersen, P. M. (2009). Communicating with Consumers through Video Games: An Analysis of Brand Development within the Video Gaming Segment of the Sports Industry. *International Journal of Sports Marketing & Sponsorship*, *10*(2), 39–52. DOI: 10.1108/IJSMS-10-02-2009-B005

Clawson, M., & Knetsch, J. L. (1974). Leisure in modern America. In Murphy, J. F. (Ed.), *Concepts of Leisure*. Prentice-Hall.

Conde-Pumpido, T. d. (2014). *Persuasive structures in advergames*. Utrecht University.

Connolly, T. M. (2008). Using alternate reality games to support the teaching of modern foreign languages. *Webist 2008: Proceedings of the Fourth International Conference on Web Information Systems and Technologies, 01*, 428-434.

Consalvo, M. (2005). Cheating can be good for you: Educational games and multiple play styles. *On the Horizon*, *13*(2), 95–100. DOI: 10.1108/10748120510608124

Cornwell, T. B., Frank, A., & Miller-Moudgil, R. (2024). A research agenda at the intersection of sport sponsorship and service. *Journal of Service Management*, *35*(1), 108–126.

Çoruh, Y., & Karaküçük, S. (2014). Üniversite öğrencilerinin cinsiyet değişkenliğine göre rekreasyonel eğilimleri ve rekreasyonel etkinliklere katılımına engel olan faktörler (Recreational Tendencies of University Students According to Gender and Factors Hindering Participation in Recreational Activities). *International Journal of Science Culture and Sport*, *1*, 854–862.

Crook, A. (2015, October 28). *A fresh look at in-game sponsorships*. Adrian Crook. https://adriancrook.com/a-fresh-look-at-in-game-sponsorships/

Csikszentmihalyi, M. (1990). *Flow: The psychology of optimal experience*. Harper & Row.

Culnan, M., & Clark, C. (2009). How ethics can enhance organizational privacy: Lessons from the ChoicePoint and TJX data breaches. *Management Information Systems Quarterly*, *33*(4), 673–687. DOI: 10.2307/20650322

Cunningham, P. A., & Ribeiro, A. (1997). The Art of Dress: Fashion in England and France 1750 to 1820. *The William and Mary Quarterly*, *54*(2), 430. Advance online publication. DOI: 10.2307/2953289

CXNet. (2025). *Sephora: Inventing an omnichannel strategy to revolutionize the retail experience for cosmetics*. Retrieved from https://cxnet.in/2025/01/31/sephora-inventing-an-omnichannel-strategy-to-revolutionize-the-retail-experience-for-cosmetics/

Dacko, S. G. (2017). Enabling smart retail settings via mobile augmented reality shopping apps. *Technological Forecasting and Social Change*, *124*, 243–256. DOI: 10.1016/j.techfore.2016.09.032

Darvenkumar, T., & Rajasekaran, W. (2024). Disorder and rehabilitation: The paradox of digital games and vulnerabilities. *Journal of Education and Health Promotion*, *13*(1), 13–64. DOI: 10.4103/jehp.jehp_923_23 PMID: 38559475

Darvin, L., Holden, J., Wells, J., & Baker, T. (2021). Breaking the glass monitor: Examining the underrepresentation of women in esports environments. *Sport Management Review*, *24*(3), 475–499.

Darvin, L., Vooris, R., & Mahoney, T. (2020). The playing experiences of esport participants: An analysis of treatment discrimination and hostility in esport environments. *Journal of Athlete Development and Experience*, *2*(1), 3.

Das, R., Kalia, S., & Kuijpers, D. (2023). *'Zero consumers': What they want and why it matters*. Retrieved from https://www.mckinsey.com/industries/retail/our-insights/zero-consumers-what-they-want-and-why-it-matters

Davidson, D.. (2010). *Cross-Media Communications: an Introduction to the Art of Creating Integrated Media Experiences*. ETC Press.

Davis, F. D. (1989). Perceived usefulness, perceived ease of use, and user acceptance of information technology. *MIS Quarterly: Management. Management Information Systems Quarterly*, *13*(3), 319–340. Advance online publication. DOI: 10.2307/249008

Davis, F. D., Bagozzi, R. P., & Warshaw, P. R. (1989). User Acceptance of Computer Technology: A Comparison of Two Theoretical Models. *Management Science*, *35*(8), 982–1003. DOI: 10.1287/mnsc.35.8.982

De Pelsmacker, P., Dens, N., & Verberckmoes, S. (2019). How ad congruity and interactivity affect fantasy game players' attitude toward in-game advertising. *Journal of Electronic Commerce Research*, *20*(1), 55–74.

De Pelsmacker, P., Geuens, M., & Van den Bergh, J. (2013). *Marketing communications: A European perspective*. Pearson Education Limited.

Deeplearning.AI. (2020). *Amazon's Outfit-Viton Generates Apparel Images On Demand.* Deeplearning.Ai. https://www.deeplearning.ai/the-batch/clothes-make-the-model/

Deloitte. (2021a). *Sephora's purpose comes to life through action.* Retrieved from https://deloitte.wsj.com/cmo/sephoras-purpose-comes-to-life-through-action-01636124196

Deloitte. (2021b). *Beauty retail - A closer look at current trends impacting beauty specialist retailers.* Retrieved from https://www.deloitte.com/content/dam/assets-shared/legacy/docs/perspectives/2022/gx-beauty-retail-pov-update.pdf

Deloitte. (2024). *Q3 2024 emerging retail & consumer trends.* Retrieved from https://www.deloitte.com/us/en/Industries/consumer/articles/q3-2024-retail-consumer-trends.html

Demir, M. Ö., & Gök Demir, Z. (2020). Gamification Characteristics' Effects On Brand Loyalty. *Yaşar Üniversitesi E-Dergisi, 15*(58), 270–287. DOI: 10.19168/jyasar.558862

Denise, K. B. S., & Green, N. (2021). *Fashion and Cultural Studies* (2nd ed.). Bloomsbury Publishing., https://books.google.co.in/books/about/Fashion_and_Cultural_Studies.html?id=fds_EAAAQBAJ&redir_esc=y

Denizel, M., & Schumm, C. Z. (2024). Closed loop supply chains in apparel: Current state and future directions. *Journal of Operations Management, 70*(2), 190–223. DOI: 10.1002/joom.1274

Deslandes, M. (2017). *Sephora tests new 'phygital' store concept in France.* Retrieved from https://ww.fashionnetwork.com/news/Sephora-tests-new-phygital-store-concept-in-france,813370.html

Deterding, S., Dixon, D., Khaled, R., & Nacke, L. (2011). From game design elements to "gamefulness": Defining "gamification." *MindTrek '11* [Association for Computing Machinery.]. *Academic MindTrek, 2011*, 9–15. DOI: 10.1145/2181037.2181040

Dichev, C., & Dicheva, D. (2017). Gamifying education: What is known, what is believed and what remains uncertain: A critical review. *International Journal of Educational Technology in Higher Education, 14*(1), 9. DOI: 10.1186/s41239-017-0042-5

Digital Training Academy. (2020). *Snapchat case study: Sephora gamifies loyalty to boost Ramadan sales.* Retrieved from http://www.digitaltrainingacademy.com/casestudies/2020/02/snapchat_case_study_sephora_gamifies_loyalty_to_boost_ramadan_sales.php

Disrupted. (2024). *AI-powered personalization in in-game advertising: Tailoring ads to enhance user experience*. Disrupted Logic. 2 Ağustos 2025 tarihinde https://disruptedlogic.com/ai-powered-personalization-in-in-game-advertising-tailoring-ads-to-enhance-user-experience/ adresinden alındı.

Dix, S. R., & Phau, I. (2017). Predictors of commercial zapping during live prime-time television: An observation-based study identifies factors that drive TV channel switching. *Journal of Advertising Research*, *57*(1), 15–27. DOI: 10.2501/JAR-2017-010

Dominick, A.-F. (2023). *The Fashion Industry Needs to Reduce Its Carbon Footprint | Industry Insights*. Ana.Net. https://www.ana.net/miccontent/show/id/ii-2023-01-sustainable-fashion

Donatiello, L., Morotti, E., Marfia, G., & Di Vaio, S. (2018). Exploiting Immersive Virtual Reality for Fashion Gamification. *IEEE International Symposium on Personal, Indoor and Mobile Radio Communications, PIMRC, 2018-September*, 17–21. DOI: 10.1109/PIMRC.2018.8581036

Douglas, B. D., & Brauer, M. (2021). Gamification to prevent climate change: a review of games and apps for sustainability. In *Current Opinion in Psychology*. DOI: 10.1016/j.copsyc.2021.04.008

Dowdall, M. (2024). *5 retail gamification ideas to consider in 2024*. Retrieved from https://seamlessxtra.com/5-retail-gamification-ideas-to-consider-in-2024/

Dressx. (2025). *Gaming Meets Fashion: The Rise of Virtual Outfits in the Metaverse - DRESSX | World's leader in digitral fashion technologies*. Dressx.Com. https://dressx.com/news/gaming-meets-fashion-the-rise-of-virtual-outfits-in-the-metaverse?srsltid=AfmBOoqdMHjB9BMKUvLsz3KL9 Gm6A7EXZ1YAyhqJzpIS-r0E4ls6CBmTe

Duan, N. (2015). *Hot spot: Sephora's new high-tech workshop*. Retrieved from https://www.yahoo.com/lifestyle/sephora-beauty-tip-workshop-san-francisco-174751572.html

Duan, L., Xu, Y., Tsang, I. W., & Luo, J. (2019). Collaborative generated hashing for market analysis and fast cold-start recommendation. *IEEE Intelligent Systems*, *35*(5), 84–95. DOI: 10.1109/MIS.2020.3025197

Duan, Z., & Jeong, G. (2025). What Drives Continuance Usage Intention Toward Virtual Reality Games? Gamer-Avatar Identification and Experiential Consumption Perspectives. *International Journal of Human-Computer Interaction*, *41*(14), 8581–8592.

Duarte, F. (2025). "How Many Gamers Are There? (New 2025 Statistics)". Retrieved from: https://explodingtopics.com/blog/number-of-gamers, Date of Access: 12th of September 2025.

Duğan, Ö. (2022). Dijital Çağda Öğrenme Aracı Olarak Oyunlaştırmanın Sağlık Okuryazarlığı Üzerindeki Rolü. *TRT Akademi*, *7*(14), 262–285. DOI: 10.37679/trta.960815

Du, S., & Xie, C. (2021). Paradoxes of artificial intelligence in consumer markets: Ethical challenges and opportunities. *Journal of Business Research*, *129*, 961–974. DOI: 10.1016/j.jbusres.2020.08.024

Dwivedi, Y. K., Hughes, L., Baabdullah, A. M., Ribeiro-Navarrete, S., Giannakis, M., Al-Debei, M. M., Dennehy, D., Metri, B., Buhalis, D., Cheung, C. M. K., Conboy, K., Doyle, R., Dubey, R., Dutot, V., Felix, R., Goyal, D. P., Gustafsson, A., Hinsch, C., Jebabli, I., & Wamba, S. F. (2022). Metaverse beyond the hype: Multidisciplinary perspectives on emerging challenges, opportunities, and agenda for research, practice and policy. *International Journal of Information Management*, *66*, 102542. Advance online publication. DOI: 10.1016/j.ijinfomgt.2022.102542

Edmonds, M., Furman, A., Pedersen, K., & Joe, M. (2025). *AI is no longer an option—it's the future of retail.* Retrieved from https://www.pwc.com/gx/en/services/alliances/microsoft/ai-retail-transformation-future.html

Edwards, S., & La Ferle, C. (2000). Cross Media Promotion of the Internet in Television Commercials. *Journal of Current Issues and Research in Advertising*, *22*(1), 1–12. DOI: 10.1080/10641734.2000.10505098

EHL Holding SA. (2024). Customer personalization - No longer an option in the digital age? Retrieved from https://hospitalityinsights.ehl.edu/customer-personalization

Ekinci, E. (2023). Açık alan rekreasyon aktivitelerinde dijital teknolojilerin kullanımı (The Use of Digital Technologies in Outdoor Recreational Activities). *Spor ve Rekreasyon Araştırmaları Dergisi*, *5*(2), 108–124. DOI: 10.52272/srad.1353789

El Oraiby, M., & Kiygi-Calli, M. (2026). Rethinking performance measurement in esports: How games shape coaching priorities for amateur player development. *International Journal of Sports Science & Coaching*, *21*(1), 97-108.

El-aasy, H. A. (2023). Employing artificial intelligence (AI) technology in advertising design on social media. *Journal of Design Sciences and Applied Arts*, *4*(2), 247–263. DOI: 10.21608/jdsaa.2023.194906.1260

Elareshi, M., Ahmed, W., Das, R., Hardey, M., Fenton, A., Chadwick, S., & Alaawad, H. (2025). Esports Interaction and Influencer Impact: Insights from the League of Legends World Championship. In *Tech Fusion in Business and Society: Harnessing Big Data, IoT, and Sustainability in Business* (Vol. 2, pp. 291–300). Springer Nature Switzerland.

Elden, M. (2013). *Reklam ve reklamcılık.* Say Yayınları.

Ellis, A. (2025). *The rise of phygital retail: Creating seamless experiences across online and offline channels.* Retrieved from https://www.stratfieldconsulting.com/insights/phygital-retail

Emily, D. S. (2021). *Branded virtual worlds.* Vml.Com. https://www.vml.com/insight/branded-virtual-worlds

Eppmann, R., Bekk, M., & Klein, K. (2018). Gameful experience in gamification: Construction and validation of a gameful experience scale [GAMEX]. *Journal of Interactive Marketing, 43*(1), 98–115. DOI: 10.1016/j.intmar.2018.03.002

Epstein, Z., Hertzmann, A., Herman, L., Mahari, R., Frank, M., Groh, M., Schroeder, H., Smith, A., Akten, M., Fjeld, J., Farid, H., Leach, N., Pentland, A., & Russakovsky, O. (2023). Art and the science of generative AI: A deeper dive. *arXiv.* https://doi .org//arXiv.2303.13336DOI: 10.48550

Erdal, I. J. (2007). Researching Media Convergence and Crossmedia News Production. *Nordicom Review, 28*(2), 51–61. DOI: 10.1515/nor-2017-0209

Erdem, M. N., & Urfalı, M. M. (2022). Neden game-vertising? Gelenekselden dijitale oyun ve reklam ilişkisi. M. Nur Erdem (Ed.), *Game-vertising dijital çağda oyunlaştırma ve Reklam* içinde (pp. 12-25). İstanbul: Eğitim Yayınevi.

Erdem, M. N. (2018). "Markalar Oyunda! Dijitalde Bir Ürün / Marka Yerleştirme Alanı Olarak Game-Vertising" (Brands are in the Game! Game-vertising as a field of Product / Brand Placement in Digital. In Bolat, N. (Ed.), *Ürün Yerleştirme Uygulamaları (Product Placement Practices)* (pp. 215–266). LiteraTürk Publications.

Erdem, M. N. (2019). Dijital Oyunlarda Şiddetin Estetiği: League of Legends Oyunu Üzerine Bir İnceleme. *Middle Black Sea Journal of Communication Studies, 4*(2), 115–139.

Erdem, M., & Urfalı, M. (2022). Neden game-vertising? Gelenekselden dijitale oyun ve reklam ilişkisi. In Erdem, M. N. (Ed.), *Game-vertising Dijital Çağda Oyunlaştırma ve Reklam* (pp. 12–25). Eğitim Yayınevi.

Erdem, S. (2021). Sanal gerçekliğin reklam stratejilerinde kullanılmasına yönelik bir değerlendirme (An Evaluation of the Use of Virtual Reality in Advertising Strategies). *Atatürk Üniversitesi Güzel Sanatlar Enstitüsü Dergisi*, *27*(46), 241–248. DOI: 10.32547/ataunigsed.836847

Ergül, N. (2025). Voice-Activated AI and The Evolution of Communication Etiquette. *Intermedia International E-journal*, *12*(22), 266–282. DOI: 10.56133/intermedia.1614189

ESA - Entertainment Software Association. (2024, July 16). *Annual ESA study reveals video games' universal appeal across generations.* https://www.theesa.com/annual-esa-study-reveals-video-games-universal-appeal-across-generations

Esentaş, M., Güzel, P., & Vural, M. (2018). Popüler kültürde rekreatif bir etkinlik olarak dijital sporlar (Digital sports as a recreational activity in popular culture). *Atatürk Üniversitesi Beden Eğitimi ve Spor Bilimleri Dergisi*, *20*(1), 71–79.

Esgin, Y. (2022). "Oyunlaştırmada Hedeflenen Etki Düzeylerinin Pazarlama İletişimi Bağlamında Kullanımı Üzerine Bir İnceleme". *İstanbul Arel Üniversitesi İletişim Çalışmaları Dergisi*, 10(21), pp. 113-135.

Esiri, S. (2022). Integrated marketing communication framework for esports brand growth and audience expansion. *Journal of Advance Multidisciplinary Research*, *1*(2), 39–47.

Fabio, D. (2025). *How Many Gamers Are There? (New 2025 Statistics)*. Explodingtopics.Com. https://explodingtopics.com/blog/number-of-gamers

Fashinnovation. (2025). *Fashion Gamification: The Power and Rise*. Fashinnovation. Nyc. https://fashinnovation.nyc/fashion-gamification-the-power-and-rise/

Faster Capital. (2025). *Successful examples of gamification marketing*. Retrieved from https://fastercapital.com/topics/successful-examples-of-gamification-marketing .html

Ferguson, C. J., Rueda, S. M., Cruz, A. M., Ferguson, D. E., Fritz, S., & Smith, S. M. (2008). Violent video games and aggression: Causal relationship or byproduct of family violence and intrinsic violence motivation? *Criminal Justice and Behavior*, *35*(3), 311–332. DOI: 10.1177/0093854807311719

Fernández Galeote, D., Gabrielaitis, L., Guillén, G., & Hamari, J. (2025). Play, games, and gamification to support sustainability transitions: A scoping review and research agenda. *Environmental Innovation and Societal Transitions*, *57*, 101025. Advance online publication. DOI: 10.1016/j.eist.2025.101025

Fill, C., & Turnbull, D. S. (2023). *Marketing communications*. Pearson., https://www.iicseonline.org/marketing_communication_1.pdf

Fishbein, M., & Ajzen, I. (1975). *Belief, attitude, intention, and behavior : an introduction to theory and research*. Addison-Wesley Pub. Co. https://books.google.co.in/books/about/Belief_Attitude_Intention_and_Behavior.html?id=8o0QAQAAIAAJ&redir_esc=y

Fitria, T. N. (2023). Artificial intelligence (AI) technology in OpenAI ChatGPT application: A review of ChatGPT in writing English essay. *ELT Forum: Journal of English Language Teaching, 12*(1), 44–58.

Fitroom. (2025). *Virtual Try On Clothes Online - AI Clothes Changer | FitRoom*. Fitroom.App. https://fitroom.app/

Flavián, C., Akdim, K., & Casaló, L. V. (2023). Effects of voice assistant recommendations on consumer behavior. *Psychology and Marketing*, *40*(2), 328–346. DOI: 10.1002/mar.21765

Flores-Marquez, P. (2025, February 12). *Gen Zers have the highest rate of digital gaming adoption*. eMarketer. Retrieved from https://www.emarketer.com/content/gen-zers-have-highest-rate-digital-gaming-adoption

Fnatic (2020, June 2020). https://fnatic.com/news/fnatic-x-gucci

Fog, K., Budtz, C., Munch, P., & Blanchette, S. (2005). *Storytelling: Branding in practice*. Springer.

Frasca, G. (2001). Rethinking agency and immersion: Video games as a means of consciousness-raising. *Digital Creativity (Exeter)*, *12*(3), 167–174. DOI: 10.1076/digc.12.3.167.3225

Freitas, B. D. A., Contreras-Espinosa, R. S., & Correia, P. Á. P. (2021). The importance of incorporating relevant-added value into esports sponsorships. *Journal of contemporary marketing science, 4*(3), 397-423.

Fu Chen, C., & Shian Chen, F. (2010). Experience Quality, Perceived Value, Satisfaction and Behavioral Intentions for Heritage Tourists. *Tourism Management*, *31*(1), 29–35. DOI: 10.1016/j.tourman.2009.02.008

Funk, D. C., Pizzo, A. D., & Baker, B. J. (2018). eSport management: Embracing eSport education and research opportunities. *Sport Management Review*, *21*(1), 7–13.

Furtın Kaya, E., & Yıldız, S. (2025). "Reklam Profesyonellerinin Gözünden Veriye Dayalı Reklamcılığın Bugünü ve Geleceği". *İletişim Kuram ve Araştırma Dergisi*, (71), pp. 153-179. DOI: 10.47998/ikad.1755301

Gallistl, V., & Nimrod, G. (2019). Media-based leisure and wellbeing: A study of older internet users. *Leisure Studies*, •••, 1–16.

Gaminginturkey. (2021). Türkiye Oyun Sektörü Raporu 2021 Yayında. Retrieved November 2024, from https://www.gaminginturkey.com/tr/turkiye-oyun-sektoru-raporu-2021-yayinda/

Gao, B., Wang, Y., Xie, H., Hu, Y., & Hu, Y. (2023). Artificial intelligence in advertising: Advancements, challenges, and ethical considerations in targeting, personalization, content creation, and ad optimization. *SAGE Open*, *13*(4), 21582440231210759. DOI: 10.1177/21582440231210759

Gelibolu, M. (2024). "Yapay Zekâ Temelli Sesli Asistanların Alışveriş Amaçlı Kullanma Niyetinde Yenilikçilik ve Algılanan Güvenin Etkisi", İşletme Araştırmaları Dergisi, 16 (4), pp. 2383-2398.

Gentile, D. A., Lynch, P. J., Linder, J. R., & Walsh, D. A. (2004). The effects of violent video game habits on adolescent hostility, aggressive behaviors, and school performance. *Journal of Adolescence*, *27*(1), 5–22. DOI: 10.1016/j.adolescence.2003.10.002 PMID: 15013257

Ghirvu, A. (2012). In-game advertising: Advantages and limitations for advertisers. *The USV Annals of Economics and Public Administration*, *12*(1 (15)), 114–119.

Ghirvu, A. (2012). In-game advertısıng: Advantages and limitations for advertısers. *The USV Annals of Economics and Public Administration*, *12*(1), 114–119.

Ghosh, T. S. S., & Dwivedi, Y. K. (2022). Brands in a game or a game for brands? Comparing the persuasive effectiveness of in-game advertising and advergames. *Psychology and Marketing*, *39*(12), 2328–2348.

Giakoni-Ramírez, F., Merellano-Navarro, E., & Duclos-Bastías, D. (2022). Professional esports players: Motivation and physical activity levels. *International Journal of Environmental Research and Public Health*, *19*(4), 2256. PMID: 35206445

Gibson, J. J. (2014). The Ecological Approach to Visual Perception. In M. Tomasello (Ed.), *The Ecological Approach to Visual Perception* (Classic). Psychology Press. DOI: 10.4324/9781315740218

Gibson, J. J. (1978). The Ecological Approach to the Visual Perception of Pictures. *Leonardo*, *11*(3), 227. DOI: 10.2307/1574154

Giles, D. C. (2002). Parasocial interaction: A review of the literature and a model for future research. *Media Psychology*, *4*(3), 279–305.

Gill, S., Januszkiewicz, M., & Ahmed, M. (2022). Digital fashion technology: a review of online fit and sizing. In *Digital Manufacturing Technology for Sustainable Anthropometric Apparel* (pp. 135–163). Elsevier., DOI: 10.1016/B978-0-12-823969-8.00008-3

girlsgogames.com. (2025). *Girls games - Play free online games for girls at girlsgogames.com*. Girlsgogames.Com. https://www.girlsgogames.com/

Glass, Z. (2007). The effectiveness of product placement in video games. *Journal of Interactive Advertising*, *8*(1), 23–32. DOI: 10.1080/15252019.2007.10722134

Gonzalez-Ibanez, R., Macıas-Caceres, J., & Paucar, M. (2025, October 22). LifeSync-Games: Toward a Video Game Paradigm for Promoting Responsible Gaming and Human Developmen. *Computer Science. Psychology (Irvine, Calif.).*

Google. (n.d.). *Overview of rewarded interstitial ad units (Beta)*. Google AdMob Help Center. https://support.google.com/admob/answer/9884467?hl=en

Grigorovici, D., & Constantin, C. (2004). Experiencing ınteractive advertising beyond rich media: Impacts of ad type and presence on brand effectiveness in 3d gaming ımmersive virtual environments. *Journal of Interactive Advertising*, *5*(1), 22–36. DOI: 10.1080/15252019.2004.10722091

Grubor, A., & Milovanov, O. (2017). Brand strategies in the era of sustainability. *Interdisciplinary description of complex systems, 15*(1), 78-88.

Grzybowska, K. (2025). *Omnichannel retail loyalty programs in 2025: Top 5 real-world examples*. Retrieved from https://www.openloyalty.io/insider/omnichannel-retail-loyalty-programs

Gucci (2025). Gucci off the grid X The Sims 4 Community. https://www.gucci.com/us/en/st/stories/article/gucci-off-the-grid-x-the-sims shoppable?srsltid=AfmBOooSSs0BQjPpb-Ttnf_CTjsYvprCU92vjbdp7rXoNEiupzgdFjjV

Gujar, P., Paliwal, G., & Panyam, S. (2024). Generative AI and the future of interactive and immersive advertising. *Proceedings of the 2024 IEEE Eighth Ecuador Technical Chapters Meeting (ETCM)*, Cuenca, Ecuador, 1-6. DOI: 10.1109/ETCM63562.2024.10746166

Gul, O., & Yurtsizoglu, Z. (2025). Development and Validation of the Scale for Analysing the Consumption Behaviours of E-Sports Players Using a Mixed-Methods Approach. *SAGE Open, 15*(3), 21582440251357721.

Güncan, Ö. (2021). Elektronik boş zaman uygulamaları "sanal rekreasyon" mudur yoksa "dijital rekreasyon" mu? (Are electronic leisure applications considered 'virtual recreation' or 'digital recreation'?) *Sosyal. Beşerî ve İdari Bilimler Dergisi, 4*(2), 163–181.

Güneş, A. H. (2012). *Legal and administrative regulation issues of digital games in the context of security* (Master's thesis, Police Academy Institute of Security Sciences, Department of Security Strategies and Management). Ankara. https://tez.yok.gov.tr/UlusalTezMerkezi/tezDetay.jsp?id=sqK-eB3NiJsEzLgOXs415A&no=F7dOig4g63YR7vXJ1RR6iA

Güngör, A. (2022). Oyunlaştırma ve Oyun İçerikli Reklamlarda İllüstrasyonun Etkisi. *Art-e Sanat Dergisi, 15*(29), 437–467. DOI: 10.21602/sduarte.1080446

Gurau, C. (2008). The influence of advergames on players behaviour: An experimental study. *Electronic Markets, 18*(2), 106–116. DOI: 10.1080/10196780802044859

Hackley, C., & Kitchen, P. (1998). IMC: A consumer psychological perspective. *Marketing Intelligence & Planning, 16*(3), 229–235. DOI: 10.1108/02634509810217345

Halicki, D., Zaborek, P. & Meylan, G. (2024). Sustainable Fashion Choices: Exploring European Consumer Motivations behind Second-Hand Clothing Purchases. *Administrative Sciences 2024, Vol. 14, Page 174, 14*(8), 174. DOI: 10.3390/admsci14080174

Hamari, J., Koivisto, J., & Sarsa, H. (2014). "Does gamification work? – A literature review of empirical studies on gamification". *Proceedings of the 47th Hawaii International Conference on System Sciences*, pp. 3025–3034. DOI: 10.1109/HICSS.2014.377

Hamari, J., & Lehdonvirta, V. (2010). Game design as marketing: How game mechanics create demand for virtual goods. *International Journal of Business Science and Applied Management, 5*(1), 14–29. DOI: 10.69864/ijbsam.5-1.48

Hamari, J., & Sjöblom, M. (2017). What is eSports and why do people watch it? *Internet Research, 27*(2), 211–232.

Hamari, J., Thibault, M., & Hassan, L. (2020). Introduction to the Minitrack on Gamification. *Proceedings of the 53rd Hawaii International Conference on System Sciences*. DOI: 10.24251/HICSS.2020.148

Hamilton, W. A., Garretson, O., & Kerne, A. (2014, April). Streaming on twitch: fostering participatory communities of play within live mixed media. In *Proceedings of the SIGCHI conference on human factors in computing systems* (pp. 1315-1324).

Hammers, J. (2025). *Sephora doles out Lyft credits to transport shoppers to its stores*. Retrieved from https://www.marketingdive.com/news/sephora-doles-out-lyft-credits-to-transport-shoppers-to-its-stores/752153/

Hanbazazah, A., Reeve, C., & Abuljadail, M. (2022). Influence of Advergames on brand outcomes and cross-cultural consumer behaviour. *International Business Reseach, 15*(8).

Hanbazazah, A., Reeve, C., & Abuljadail, M. (2022). Advergames and consumer behaviour: A quantitative comparative analysis of the United Kingdom and Saudi Arabia. *International Journal of Marketing Studies*, *14*(2), 113–120. DOI: 10.5539/ijms.v14n2p113

Handheld Museum. (n.d.). *Nintendo DS Pepsi Limited Edition*. Handheld Museum. http://devkits.handheldmuseum.com/NintendoDSPepsi/index.htm

Hansson, L. (2017). *Dynamic in-game advertising: How important is it that ads are dynamic and capable of changing?* (Yüksek lisans tezi, Halmstad University). Halmstad University Open Access Repository. https://hh.diva-portal.org/smash/record.jsf?pid=diva2%3A1065214

Hardy, J. (2010). *Cross-Media Promotion*. Peter Lang. DOI: 10.3726/978-1-4539-0001-7

Hazar, A. (2009). *Rekreasyon ve animasyon (*Recreation and Animation). Ankara: Detay Yayıncılık.

Helpshift. (2023). App gamification: 12 examples of mobile apps using gamification. Retrieved October 2024, from https://www.helpshift.com/blog/app-gamification-9-examples-of-mobile-apps-using-gamification/

Hennig-Thurau, T., Gwinner, K. P., Walsh, G., & Gremler, D. D. (2004). Electronic word-of-mouth via consumer-opinion platforms: What motivates consumers to articulate themselves on the internet? *Journal of Interactive Marketing*, *18*(1), 38–52.

Herrewijn, L., & Poels, K. (2013). Putting brands into play: How game difficulty and player experiences influence the effectiveness of in-game advertising. *International Journal of Advertising*, *32*(1), 17–44. DOI: 10.2501/IJA-32-1-017-044

Herrewijn, L., & Poels, K. (2014). Recall and recognition of in-game advertising: The role of game control. *Frontiers in Psychology*, *5*, 1023. DOI: 10.3389/fpsyg.2013.01023

Hilken, T., De Ruyter, K., Chylinski, M., Mahr, D., & Keeling, D. (2017). Augmenting the eye of the beholder: Exploring the strategic potential of augmented reality to enhance online service experiences. *Journal of the Academy of Marketing Science*, *45*(6), 884–905. DOI: 10.1007/s11747-017-0541-x

Hilton, T. (2006). Gaming as an educational tool. *Young Consumers*, *7*(2), 14–19. DOI: 10.1108/17473610610701457

Hirschman, E. C., & Holbrook, M. B. (1982). Hedonic consumption: Emerging concepts, methods and propositions. *Journal of Marketing*, *46*(3), 92–101.

Hoi, H. T. (2020). "Attractiveness of Online Marketing in the Age of Industry 4.0", in Proceedings of the 2020 The 6th International Conference on E-Business and Applications, Malaysia, Published: ICEBA 2020. pp. 1-4. DOI: 10.1145/3387263.3387264

Holbrook, M. B., Chestnut, R. W., Oliva, T. A., & Greenleaf, E. A. (1984). Play as a consumption experience: The roles of emotions, performance, and personality in the enjoyment of games. *The Journal of Consumer Research*, *11*(2), 728–739.

Holden, J. T., Edelman, M., & Baker III, T. A. (2020). A short treatise on esports and the law: How America regulates its next national pastime. *U. Ill. L. Rev.*, 509.

Holden, J. T., Kaburakis, A., & Rodenberg, R. (2017). The future is now: Esports policy considerations and potential litigation. *Journal of Legal Aspects of Sport*, *27*(1), 46–78.

Hollebeek, L. D., Abbasi, A. Z., Schultz, C. D., Ting, D. H., & Sigurdsson, V. (2022). Hedonic consumption experience in videogaming: A multidimensional perspective. *Journal of Retailing and Consumer Services*, *65*, 102892.

Holmes, R. (2019, March 6). *More than a game, Fortnite is emerging as the best new social network.* Fast Company. https://www.fastcompany.com/90315238/the-best-new-social-network-may-surprise-you

Holt, D. B. (2004). *How brands become icons: The principles of cultural branding.* Harvard Business School Press.

Holt, Douglas B., & Cameron, D. (2012). *Cultural strategy: Using innovative ideologies to build breakthrough brands.* New York: Oxford University Press.

Holt, D. B. (2012). Cultural brand strategy. In Shankar, V., & Carpenter, G. S. (Eds.), *Handbook of Marketing Strategy* (pp. 306–317). Edward Elgar. DOI: 10.4337/9781781005224.00029

Hong, H. J. (2023). eSports: The need for a structured support system for players. *European Sport Management Quarterly*, *23*(5), 1430–1453.

Hong, H. J. (2024). Duty of Care in Esports: Organizational Support for Esports Players' Mental Wellbeing and Physical Health. In *Proceedings of the 57th Hawaii International Conference on System Sciences 2024* (pp. 4443- 4452).

Hong, H. J. (2025). Exploring stakeholders' perspectives on esports players' well-being and career prospects. *Computers in Human Behavior Reports, 17*, 100589.

Honigman, B. (2025). *How Sephora integrates retail & online marketing*. Retrieved from https://etailwest.wbresearch.com/blog/how-sephora-integrates-retail-online-marketing

Horton, D., & Wohl, R. R. (1956). Mass communication and para-social interaction. *Psychiatry, 19*(3), 215–229. PMID: 13359569

Hoy, M. B. (2018). Alexa, Siri, Cortana, and more: An introduction to voice assistants. *Medical Reference Services Quarterly, 37*(1), 81–88. DOI: 10.1080/02763869.2018.1404391 PMID: 29327988

Huang, J. H., & Yang, T. K. (2012). The Effectiveness of In-Game Advertising: The Impacts of Ad Type and Game/Ad Relevance. *International Journal of Electronic Business Management, 10*(1).

Huettermann, M., & Pizzo, A. D. (2022). Esports fan engagement: A comparison of PC and console esports team fans. *Frontiers in Sports and Active Living, 4*, 880294. PMID: 35571745

Huizinga, J. (1970). *Homo Ludens: A study of the play element in culture*. Maurice Temple Smith Ltd.

Huizinga, J. (2023). *Homo ludens: Oyunun toplumsal işlevi üzerine bir deneme* (Kılıçbay, M. A., Ed.). Doğu Batı Yayınları. DOI: 10.30965/9783846766781

Huotari, K., & Hamari, J. (2017). A definition for gamification: Anchoring gamification in the service marketing literature. *Electronic Markets, 27*(1), 21–31. DOI: 10.1007/s12525-015-0212-z

Hur, H. J., Lee, H. K., & Choo, H. J. (2017). Understanding usage intention in innovative mobile app service: Comparison between millennial and mature consumers. *Computers in Human Behavior, 73*, 353–361. DOI: 10.1016/j.chb.2017.03.051

Hussain, A., Hollebeek, L. D., Marder, B., & Ting, D. H. (2025). In-game content purchase motivations (IGCPMs): Conceptualization, scale development, and validation. *Information & Management, 62*(7), 104207.

IAB. (2017). IAB New Standard Ad Unit Portfolio. IAB Technology Laboratory. Retirieved from: www.iab.com/newadportfolio

iion. (2024). *Fashion in the Gaming Industry*. Iion.Io. https://www.iion.io/blog/fashion-in-the-gaming-industry

Iion.io. (2024). *Fashion in the Gaming Industry*. Iion.Io. https://www.iion.io/blog/fashion-in-the-gaming-industry

Ilgın, H. Ö. (2013). Advergaming and brand relationship. The Turkish Online Journal of Design, Art and Communication – TOJDAC, 3(1), 24-33. https://dergipark.org.tr/tr/pub/tojdac/article/156783

Innovationpei (2012). Successful Online Display Advertising. Retrieved from: http://www.gov.pe.ca/photos/original/IPEI_ebiz_ads

Insights, F. B. (2025). *Gamification Market Size, Share & Growth Analysis Report, 2032*. Fortunebusinessinsights.Com. https://www.fortunebusinessinsights.com/industry-reports/gamification-market-100632

Ioni ă, C. G., Leovaridis, C., & Popescu, G. (2025). Use of artificial ıntelligence in advertising agencies: Opportunities and challenges. *Management Dynamics in the Knowledge Economy*, *13*(1), 38–51. DOI: 10.2478/mdke-2025-0003

Iwatsuki, T., Hagiwara, G., & Dugan, M. E. (2022). Effectively optimizing esports performance through movement science principles. *International Journal of Sports Science & Coaching*, *17*(1), 202–207.

Jaffe, J. (2003). *Advergaming Equals Attention. iMedia Connection, May 5.*

Jain, K. (2025). *Sephora: Revolutionizing beauty retail with innovation and personalization*. Retrieved from https://www.linkedin.com/pulse/sephora-revolutionizing-beauty-retail-innovation-kashish-jain-bvskc

Jang, W., & Byon, K. K. (2020). Antecedents and consequence associated with esports gameplay. *International Journal of Sports Marketing & Sponsorship*, *21*(1), 1–22.

Jang, W., Byon, K. K., Baker, T. A., & Tsuji, Y. (2020). Mediating effect of esports content live streaming in the relationship between esports recreational gameplay and esports event broadcast. *Sport, Business and Management*, *11*(1), 90–106.

Jang, W., Choi, W., Kim, M. J., Song, H., & Byon, K. K. (2024). What makes esports consumers watch streamers' esports live-streaming contents? Extending the theory of planned behavior. *International Journal of Sports Marketing & Sponsorship*, *25*(2), 288–309.

Jasrotia, S. S., Kamila, M. K., Chib, S., & Mishra, H. G. (2022). Role of engagement in online gaming: A study of generation Z customers. *Digital Creativity*, *33*(1), 64–76.

Javornik, A. (2016). Augmented reality: Research agenda for studying the impact of its media characteristics on consumer behaviour. *Journal of Retailing and Consumer Services*, *30*, 252–261. DOI: 10.1016/j.jretconser.2016.02.004

Jayakanthan, R. (2002). Application of computer games in the field of education. *The Electronic Library*, *20*(2), 98–102. DOI: 10.1108/02640470210697471

Jayasooriya, S., Alles, T., & Thelijjagoda, S. (2020). Demystifying the concept of IoT enabled gamification in retail marketing: An exploratory study. *Proceedings - International Research Conference on Smart Computing and Systems Engineering, SCSE 2020*. DOI: 10.1109/SCSE49731.2020.9313039

Jeff, S. (2025). *How Gamification Is Changing the Game for Brands*. Mintegral. https://www.mintegral.com/en/blog/how-gamification-is-changing-the-game-for-brands

Jenkins, H. (2006). *Convergence culture: Where old and new media collide*. New York University Press.

Jennett, C., Cox, A. L., Cairns, P., Dhoparee, S., Epps, A., Tijs, T., & Walton, A. (2008). Measuring and defining the experience of immersion in games. *International Journal of Human-Computer Studies*, *66*(9), 641–661. DOI: 10.1016/j.ijhcs.2008.04.004

Jenny, S. E., Keiper, M. C., Taylor, B. J., Williams, D. P., Gawrysiak, J., Manning, R. D., & Tutka, P. M. (2018). eSports venues: A new sport business opportunity. *Journal of Applied Sport Management*, *10*(1), 8.

Jenny, S. E., Manning, R. D., Keiper, M. C., & Olrich, T. W. (2017). Virtual (ly) athletes: Where eSports fit within the definition of "Sport". *Quest*, *69*(1), 1–18.

Jill, M. (2021). *Fashion embraces gaming and the direct-to-avatar model*. Glossy. https://www.glossy.co/fashion/fashion-briefing-fashion-embraces-gaming-and-the-direct-to-avatar-model/

Jong, M. S. Y., Shang, J., Lee, F.-L., & Lee, J. H. M. (2008). Harnessing computer games in education. *International Journal of Distance Education Technologies*, *6*(1), 1–9. DOI: 10.4018/jdet.2008010101

Joygame Publishing. (2024, August 19). *The power of AI in mobile game advertising*.

Jung, S., Chen, J., & Cai, L. A. (2024). Beyond video game competition: Novel dimensions of live esports event experiences through co-creation. *Journal of Hospitality & Tourism Research (Washington, D.C.)*, *48*(8), 1453–1466.

Jurafsky, D., & Martin, J. H. (2021). Speech and language processing (3rd ed.). Draft version. Stanford University.

Kadry, A. (2024). Exploring gamification advertising and its role in audience engagement. *International Design Journal, 14*(1), 163–173. DOI: 10.21608/idj.2024.329267

Kahneman, D. (2011). *Thinking, fast and slow*. Farrar, Straus and Giroux.

Kahneman, D., & Tversky, A. (1979). Prospect theory: An analysis of decision under risk. *Econometrica, 47*(2), 263–291. DOI: 10.2307/1914185

Kai-Yu, C. (2019). *Actionable Gamification: Beyond Points, Badges, and Leaderboards eBook : Chou, Yu-kai: Amazon.in: Kindle Store* (reprint). Octalysis Media. https://www.amazon.in/Actionable-Gamification-Beyond-Points-Leaderboards-ebook/dp/B00WAOGY4U

Kai-Yu, C. (2023). *The Octalysis Framework for Gamification & Behavioral Design*. Yukaichou.Com. https://yukaichou.com/gamification-examples/octalysis-complete-gamification-framework/

Kamat, A. (2025). *Enhancing customer engagement in retail through personalized notifications*. Retrieved from https://www.irjmets.com/uploadedfiles/paper//issue_3_march_2025/69735/final/fin_irjmets1742559517.pdf

Kamble, M. (2025). *Experience: A UX case study on building trust and reducing abandonment*. Retrieved from https://medium.com/@kamble.ma/reimagining-sephoras-shopping-experience-a-ux-case-study-on-building-trust-reducing-d752f1bca950

Kang, H. J., Shin, J., & Ponto, K. (2020). How 3D Virtual Reality Stores Can Shape Consumer Purchase Decisions: The Roles of Informativeness and Playfulness. *Journal of Interactive Marketing, 49*(1), 70–85. DOI: 10.1016/j.intmar.2019.07.002

Kanishka, T. (2024). *Future Of Gamification 2024 Trends - My Framer Site*. Nudgenow.Com. https://nudgenow.com/blogs/future-of-gamification-trends

Kaplan, A., & Haenlein, M. (2019). Siri, Siri, in my hand: Who's the fairest in the land? On the interpretations, illustrations, and implications of artificial intelligence. *Business Horizons, 62*(1), 15–25. DOI: 10.1016/j.bushor.2018.08.004

Karać, J., & Stabauer, M. (2017). Gamification in e-commerce a survey based on the octalysis framework. *Lecture Notes in Computer Science (Including Subseries Lecture Notes in Artificial Intelligence and Lecture Notes in Bioinformatics), 10294 LNCS*, 41–54. https://doi.org/DOI: 10.1007/978-3-319-58484-3_4/FIGURES/3

Karaküçük, S. (2014). *Rekreasyon: Boş zaman değerlendirme*. Bağırgan Yayınevi.

Karaküçük, S., & Başaran, Z. (1996). Stresle başa çıkmada rekreasyon faktörü. *Gazi Beden Eğitimi ve Spor Bilimleri Dergisi, 4*, 55–64.

Karayel Bilbil, E. (2004). Bütünleşik pazarlama iletişimi içerisinde marka kavramı ve bu kavramın halkla ilişkiler boyutu. *İstanbul Üniversitesi İletişim Fakültesi Dergisi, 20, pp.* 197-206.

Karayel Bilbil, E., & Güngör, S. S. (2024). The Impact of Corporate Sustainability Practices on Consumers' Brand Loyalty. *Academıc social resources journal, 8*(51), pp. 2931-2941.

Karayel Bilbil, E., & Şen, T. (2023). Türkiye'de çevreci STK'ların kurumsal kimlik ve imaj bileşenlerinin analizi. *Selçuk İletişim, 16*(1), 166–201.

Kasım, M., & Tunç, P. C. (2024). AN EVALUATION ON THE RISKS AND ETHICAL ISSUES AWAITING CHILD USERS IN DIGITAL ADVERTISEMENTS. *Journal of Communication Studies, 10*(2), 210–240.

Katie, M. (2023). *New Roblox report finds Gen Z users prioritize styling their virtual avatars over themselves in the physical world.* Yahoo.Com. https://www.yahoo.com/lifestyle/new-roblox-report-finds-gen-z-users-prioritize-styling-their-virtual-avatars-over-themselves-in-the-physical-world140100522.html?guccounter=1&guce_referrer=aHR0cHM6Ly93d3cuZ29vZ2xlLmNvbS8&guce_referrer_sig=AQAAAGaFVDhPKzhM

Katz, E., Blumler, J. G., & Gurevitch, M. (1974). Uses and gratifications research. *Public Opinion Quarterly, 37*(4), 509–523. DOI: 10.1086/268109

Katz, E., Blumler, J. G., & Gurevitch, M. (1974). Utilization of mass communication by the individual. In Blumler, J. G., & Katz, E. (Eds.), *The uses of mass communications: Current perspectives on gratifications research* (pp. 19–32). Sage.

Kaya, B., Güdek, O., & Uygur, S. M. (2023). Oryantiring ve çöp topla-koş (plogging) eko rekreasyon faaliyetleri için dijital oyun modeli geliştirme. *Turizm Akademik Dergisi, 10*(1), 119–131.

Kaya, B., Metin, T., & Kozak, M. A. (2015). Kapalı rekreasyon tesislerinde kullanıcıların akış deneyimi. *Seyahat ve Otel İşletmeciliği Dergisi, 12*(2), 6–25.

Kaya, R., & Bayat, M. (2022). Çevrimiçi Dünyada Yükselen Bir Trend: Display (Görüntülü) Reklamlar. *Elektronik Sosyal Bilimler Dergisi, 21*(82), 759–770. DOI: 10.17755/esosder.1031584

Keller, K. L. (2001). Mastering the Marketing Communications Mix: Micro and Macro Perspectives on Integrated Marketing Communication Programs. *Journal of Marketing Management*, *17*(7–8), 819–847.

Keller, K. L. (2013). *Strategic brand management: Building measuring, and managing brand equity* (Global Edition). Pearson Education.

Kemp, S. (2025, January). *Digital 2025: Global Advertising Trends*. Data Reportal. https://datareportal.com/reports/digital-2025-sub-section-global-advertising-trends

Kent, S. L. (2001). *The ultimate history of video games: From Pong to Pokémon and beyond*. Three Rivers Press.

Khoros. (2025). *What is gamification marketing and 6 examples from top brands*. Retrieved from https://khoros.com/blog/gamification-marketing

Kietzmann, J., Paschen, J., & Treen, E. (2018). Artificial intelligence in advertising: How marketers can leverage artificial intelligence along the consumer journey. *Journal of Advertising Research*, *58*(3), 263–267. DOI: 10.2501/JAR-2018-035

Kim, J. (2021). Advertising in the Metaverse: Research Agenda. *Journal of Interactive Advertising*, *21*(3), 141–144. DOI: 10.1080/15252019.2021.2001273

Kim, J.-H., Kim, M., Park, M., & Yoo, J. (2021). How interactivity and vividness influence consumer virtual reality shopping experience: The mediating role of telepresence. *Journal of Research in Interactive Marketing*, *15*(3), 502–525. DOI: 10.1108/JRIM-07-2020-0148

Kim, M. J., Lee, C. K., & Jung, T. (2020). Exploring Consumer Behavior in Virtual Reality Tourism Using an Extended Stimulus-Organism-Response Model. *Journal of Travel Research*, *59*(1), 69–89. Advance online publication. DOI: 10.1177/0047287518818915

Kim, S. J. (2023). Virtual fashion experiences in virtual reality fashion show spaces. *Frontiers in Psychology*, *14*, 1–13. DOI: 10.3389/fpsyg.2023.1276856 PMID: 38046109

Kim, S. J., Kim, K. H., & Mattila, P. (2012). The role of fashion in the characters of online games. *Journal of Global Fashion Marketing*, *3*(2), 81–88. DOI: 10.1080/20932685.2012.10593110

Kim, T. W. (2018). Gamification ethics: Exploitation and manipulation. *Computers in Human Behavior*, *80*, 246–254. DOI: 10.1016/j.chb.2017.11.022

Kim, Y. V., & Ahn, H. (2025). Protecting the Mental Health of Esports Players: A Qualitative Case Study on Their Stress, Coping Strategies, and Social Support Systems. *International Journal of Mental Health Promotion*, *27*(9).

King, A. (2023). *Sephora's gamified beauty event Sephoria returns with hybrid in-person and virtual experience*. Retrieved from https://cosmeticsbusiness.com/sephora-s-gamified-beauty-event-sephoria-returns-with-hybrid-in-person-and-virtual-experience-210003

King, D. L., & Delfabbro, P. H. (2019). Video game monetization (eg,'loot boxes'): A blueprint for practical social responsibility measures. *International Journal of Mental Health and Addiction*, *17*(1), 166–179.

Kingma, D. P., & Ba, J. (2014). Adam: A method for stochastic optimization. *arXiv*. https://arxiv.org/abs/1412.6980

Kirkpatrick, G. (2012). Constitutive tensions of gaming's field: UK gaming magazines and the formation of gaming culture 1981–1995. *Game Studies*, *12*(1), 3.

Kitchen, P. J., & Burgmann, I. (2010). Integrated marketing communication. *Wiley international encyclopedia of marketing*.

Kliatchko, J. G., & Schultz, D. E. (2014). Twenty years of IMC: A study of CEO and CMO perspectives in the Asia-Pacific region. *International Journal of Advertising*, *33*(2), 373–390.

Kneer, J., Rieger, D., Ivory, J. D., & Ferguson, C. (2014). Awareness of risk factors for digital game addiction: Interviewing players and counselors. *International Journal of Mental Health and Addiction*, *12*(5), 1–15. DOI: 10.1007/s11469-014-9489-y

Koivisto, J., & Hamari, J. (2019). The rise of motivational information systems: A review of gamification research. In *International Journal of Information Management*. DOI: 10.1016/j.ijinfomgt.2018.10.013

Koles, B., Audrezet, A., Moulard, J. G., Ameen, N., & McKenna, B. (2024). The authentic virtual influencer: Authenticity manifestations in the metaverse. *Journal of Business Research*, *170*, 114325. Advance online publication. DOI: 10.1016/j.jbusres.2023.114325

Koma, K. (2023). Fashion and Identity in Virtual Spaces. In *The Other Bodies as an Avatar in Animal Crossing* (pp. 187–202). Springer., DOI: 10.1007/978-981-99-0349-8_12

Kordyaka, B., Pumplun, L., Brunnhofer, M., Kruse, B., & Laato, S. (2023). Gender disparities in esports–An explanatory mixed-methods approach. *Computers in Human Behavior, 149*, 107956.

Kornilov, D. (2024). *Phygital retail in action: Real-world examples and insights.* Retrieved from https://ffface.me/media/phygital-retail-where-digital-meets-physical-commerce/

Korn, O., Muschick, P., & Schmidt, A. (2017). *Gamification of production? A study on the acceptance of gamified work processes in the automotive industry.* Advances in Intelligent Systems and Computing., DOI: 10.1007/978-3-319-41661-8_42

Köse, N., & Yengin, D. (2018). Dijital pazarlamadan fijital pazarlamaya geçişe örnek olarak artırılmış gerçeklik ve sanal gerçeklik uygulamalarının pazarlama üzerindeki katkılarının incelenmesi. *İstanbul Aydın Üniversitesi Dergisi, 10*(1), pp. 77-111.

Kotler, P., & Keller, K. L. (2016). *Marketing Management.* Pearson Prentice Hall.

Kozak, M. A., & Özkeroğlu, Ö. (2018). Turizm ve rekreasyon kavramları: Sanal bakış ile değerlendirme. In *II* (pp. 399–409). Uluslararası Sürdürülebilir Turizm Kongresi.

KPMG. (2018). *Tomorrow's experience, today - Harnessing a customer first approach in a changing world.* Retrieved from https://assets.kpmg.com/content/dam/kpmg/pe/pdf/Publicaciones/TL/tomorrows-experience-today-harnessing-a-customer-first-approach.pdf

KPMG. (2022). *Break Out – from ordinary to extraordinary.* Retrieved from https://assets.kpmg.com/content/dam/kpmg/xx/pdf/2023/01/us-customer-experience-excellence-report-2022.pdf

KPMG. (2025a). *2025 retail trends from NRF's big retail show.* Retrieved from https://kpmg.com/ie/en/insights/retail-manufacturing/2025-cge-retail-mfg-trends-nrf.html

KPMG. (2025b). *Intelligent retail - A blueprint for creating value through AI-driven transformation.* Retrieved from https://assets.kpmg.com/content/dam/kpmgsites/xx/pdf/2025/03/intelligent-retail-report.pdf

Kraut, R., Kiesler, S., Boneva, B., Cummings, J., Helgeson, V., & Crawford, A. (2002). Internet paradox revisited. *The Journal of Social Issues, 58*(1), 49–74. DOI: 10.1111/1540-4560.00248

Kretchmer, S. B. (2005). Changing views of commercialization in digital games: In-game advertising and advergames as worlds in play. *DiGRA '05 - Proceedings of the 2005 DiGRA International Conference: Changing Views: Worlds in Play*.

Kumar, V., Ashraf, A. R., & Nadeem, W. (2024). AI-powered marketing: What, where, and how? *International Journal of Information Management*, *77*, 102783. DOI: 10.1016/j.ijinfomgt.2024.102783

Kunz, R. E., Roth, A., & Santomier, J. P. (2022). A perspective on value co-creation processes in eSports service ecosystems. *Sport, Business and Management*, *12*(1), 29–53.

Kuo, A., & Rice, D. H. (2015). Catch and shoot: The influence of advergame mechanics on preference formation. *Psychology and Marketing*, *32*(2), 162–172. DOI: 10.1002/mar.20770

Kurar, İ., & Baltacı, F. (2014). Halkın boş zaman değerlendirme alışkanlıkları: Alanya örneği. *International Journal of Science Culture and Sport*, pp. 39-52.

Kwon, J. W. (2015). A study on element features and research frames of game trailer. *Cartoon and Animation Studies*, *41*(), 187–222. DOI: 10.7230/KOSCAS.2015.41.187

Lades, L., & Delaney, L. (2022). Nudge FORGOOD. *Behavioural Public Policy*, *6*(1), 75–94. DOI: 10.1017/bpp.2019.53

Lamb, K. (2025). *7 retail advertising trends for 2025: From Ulta to Sephora*. Retrieved from https://www.zappi.io/web/blog/retail-advertising-trends/

Laran, J., Dalton, A. N., & Andrade, E. B. (2011). The Curious Case of Behavioral Backlash: Why Brands Produce Priming Effects and Slogans Produce Reverse Priming Effects. *The Journal of Consumer Research*, *37*(6), 999–1014. DOI: 10.1086/656577

Lau, J., Zimmerman, B., & Schaub, F. (2018). "Alexa, are you listening? Privacy perceptions, concerns and privacy-seeking behaviors with smart speakers". Proceedings of the ACM on Human-Computer Interaction, 2(CSCW), pp. 1–31. DOI: 10.1145/3274371

Lau, O., & Ki, C.-W. (2021). Can consumers' gamified, personalized, and engaging experiences with VR fashion apps increase in-app purchase intention by fulfilling needs? *Fashion and Textiles*, *8*(1), 36. DOI: 10.1186/s40691-021-00270-9

Lavoie, R., Main, K., King, C., & King, D. (2021). Virtual Experience, Real Consequences: The Potential Negative Emotional Consequences of Virtual Reality Gameplay. *Virtual Reality (Waltham Cross)*, *25*(2), 69–81. DOI: 10.1007/s10055-020-00440-y

Lee, J., & Hammer, J. (2011). Gamification in education: What, how, why bother? *Academic Exchange Quarterly*, *15*(2), 1–5.

Lee, J., & Shin, D.-H. (2017). Positive side effects of in-app reward advertising: Free items boost sales: A focus on sampling effects. *Journal of Advertising Research*, *57*(3), 272–282. DOI: 10.2501/JAR-2017-036

Lee, M., & Faber, R. J. (2007). Effects of product placement in online games on brand memory: A perspective of the limited-capacity model of attention. *Journal of Advertising*, *36*(4), 75–90. DOI: 10.2753/JOA0091-3367360406

Lee, S. (2021). *The impact of in-game product placement on consumer engagement*. Springer.

LEGO. (2025). *All about LEGO Fortnite*. https://www.lego.com/en-us/service/help-topics/article/all-about-lego-fortnite

Lehnert, K., Walz, A., & Christianson, R. (2022). The booming eSports market: A field day for fans. *The Journal of Business Strategy*, *43*(2), 122–128.

Leith, A. P. (2021). Parasocial cues: The ubiquity of parasocial relationships on Twitch. *Communication Monographs*, *88*(1), 111–129.

Li, W., Zubielqui, G., & Hill, S. (2025). *Gamification impact on brand strategies: A systematic review*. Retrieved from https://www.tandfonline.com/doi/full/10.1080/08874417.2025.2503954

Lieberman, D. A., Fisk, M. C., & Biely, E. (2009). Digital games for young children ages three to six: From research to design. *Computers in the Schools*, *26*(4), 299–313. DOI: 10.1080/07380560903360178

Li, H. (2019). Special Section Introduction: Artificial Intelligence and Advertising. *Journal of Advertising*, *48*(4), 333–337. DOI: 10.1080/00913367.2019.1654947

Li, H., Ding, Y., Zhao, B., Xu, Y., & Wei, W. (2023). Effects of immersion in a simulated natural environment on stress reduction and emotional arousal: A systematic review and meta-analysis. *Frontiers in Psychology*, *13*, 1058177. Advance online publication. DOI: 10.3389/fpsyg.2022.1058177 PMID: 36698558

Lim, J. S., Choe, M. J., Zhang, J., & Noh, G. Y. (2020). The role of wishful identification, emotional engagement, and parasocial relationships in repeated viewing of live-streaming games: A social cognitive theory perspective. *Computers in Human Behavior*, *108*, 106327.

Linda, T., & John, M. (2024). *What is the Metaverse? An Explanation and In-Depth Guide*. Techtarget.Com. https://www.techtarget.com/whatis/feature/The-metaverse-explained-Everything-you-need-to-know

Lindecrantz, E., Gi, M., & Zerbi, S. (2020). *Personalizing the customer experience: Driving differentiation in retail.* Retrieved from https://www.mckinsey.com/se/~/media/McKinsey/Industries/Retail/Our%20Insights/Personalizing%20the%20customer%20experience%20Driving%20differentiation%20in%20retail/Personalizing-the-customer-experience-Driving-differentiation-in-retail.pdf

Lister, C., West, J. H., Cannon, B., Sax, T., & Brodegard, D. (2014). Just a fad? Gamification in health and fitness apps. *JMIR Serious Games*, *2*(2), e9. DOI: 10.2196/games.3413 PMID: 25654660

Li, T. (2024). AI empowered personalized digital advertising marketing. *Frontiers in Business, Economics and Management*, *15*(2), 439–442. DOI: 10.54097/k0wjgk28

Liu, Y., Yu, H., Sonbudak, M. F., Troiano, G. M., & Harteveld, C. (2021, May). "Why are you playing games? You are a girl!": Exploring gender biases in Esports. In *Proceedings of the 2021 CHI conference on human factors in computing systems* (pp. 1-15).

Liu, D., Santhanam, R., & Webster, J. (2017). Toward meaningful engagement: A framework for design and research of gamified information systems. In *MIS Quarterly*. Management Information Systems., DOI: 10.25300/MISQ/2017/41.4.01

Li, W., Corral de Zubielqui, G., & Rao Hill, S. (2025). Gamification Impact on Brand Strategies: A Systematic Review. *Journal of Computer Information Systems*, •••, 1–19. DOI: 10.1080/08874417.2025.2503954

Locke, J. (2025). *The digital transformation of the beauty industry: AI, gamification and the metaverse*. Retrieved from https://medium.com/digital-society/the-digital-transformation-of-the-beauty-industry-ai-gamification-and-the-metaverse-926b5c2fdb08

Lopatovska, I., & Williams, H. (2018). "Personification of the Amazon Alexa: BFF or a mindless companion". *Proceedings of the 2018 Conference on Human Information Interaction & Retrieval*, pp. 265–268. DOI: 10.1145/3176349.3176868

López-Sintas, J., Rojas-DeFrancisco, L., & García-Álvarez, E. (2017). Home-based digital leisure: Doing the same leisure activities, but digital. *Cogent Social Sciences*, *3*(1), 1–14. DOI: 10.1080/23311886.2017.1309741

Lopienski, K. (2024). *Is phygital retail the future of retail and ecommerce?* Retrieved from https://www.shipbob.com/blog/phygital-retail/

Loukopoulou, E. C. (2025). "Prospect Theory and Loss Aversion: A Cognitive Perspective on Economic Behavior". Doi:DOI: 10.17605/OSF.IO/J8QFA

Louro, M., & Cunha, P. (2001). Brand management paradigms. *Journal of Marketing Management, 17*(7-8), 849–875. DOI: 10.1362/026725701323366845

Luger, E., & Sellen, A. (2016). "Like having a really bad PA: The gulf between user expectation and experience of conversational agents". *Proceedings of the 2016 CHI Conference on Human Factors in Computing Systems*, pp. 5286–5297. DOI: 10.1145/2858036.2858288

Lukic, A., López, M., & Pagès, A. (2024). *Phygital brand experience: Merging physical and digital formats to enhance customer engagement.* Retrieved from https://merit.url.edu/en/publications/phygital-brand-experience-merging-physical-and-digital-formats-to

Lu, L., & Argyle, M. (1993). *TV watching, soap opera and happiness.* Kaohsiung J Med.

Lu, L., & Hu, C.-H. (2005). Personality, leisure experiences and happiness. *Journal of Happiness Studies, 6*(3), 325–342. DOI: 10.1007/s10902-005-8628-3

Lundqvist, A., Liljander, V., Gummerus, J. & van Riel, A. (2012). "The impact of storytelling on the consumer brand experience: The case of a firm-originated story". *Journal of Brand Management,* 20, pp. 283–297 (2013). DOI: 10.1057/bm.2012.15

Lu, W., Jiang, Y., Chen, Z., & Ji, X. (2022). Blockchain adoption in a supply chain system to combat counterfeiting. *Computers & Industrial Engineering, 171*, 108408. DOI: 10.1016/j.cie.2022.108408

LVMH. (2023). *Sephora unveils new flagship Champs-Élysées store.* Retrieved from https://www.lvmh.com/en/news-lvmh/sephora-unveils-new-flagship-champs-elysees-store

Macey, J., & Hamari, J. (2019). eSports, skins and loot boxes: Participants, practices and problematic behaviour associated with emergent forms of gambling. *New Media & Society, 21*(1), 20–41.

Macey, J., Tyrväinen, V., Pirkkalainen, H., & Hamari, J. (2022). Does esports spectating influence game consumption? *Behaviour & Information Technology, 41*(1), 181–197.

Machkovech, S. (2022, April 30). *Tasting Coca-Cola's first "gamer" flavor—and the history of game-and-soda tie-ins. Ars Technica.* https://arstechnica.com/gaming/2022/04/coca-colas-first-gamer-flavor-and-the-history-of-game-and-soda-tie-ins/

Maghan, M., & Madeleine, S. (2024). *The Vogue Business NFT Tracker: Vintage pieces from Prada, Comme des Garcons unveil their stories through NFTs and NFCs*. Vogue Business. https://www.voguebusiness.com/technology/the-vogue-business-nft-tracker

Mago, Z. (2016). Self- and cross-promotion within digital games. In Tănase, M. D. (Ed.), *Proceedings of the International Scientific Conference eLearning and Software for Education* (Vol. 1, pp. 335–340). Carol I National Defense University Publishing House., https://www.researchgate.net/publication/323192329_Self-_and_cross-promotion_within_digital_games

Mallinckrodt, V., & Mizerski, D. (2007). The effects of playing an advergame on young children's perceptions, preferences, and requests. *Journal of Advertising*, *36*(2), 87–100. DOI: 10.2753/JOA0091-3367360206

Mani, R., & Narayanan, V. (2025). *Beauty and the (AI) Beast – The makeover of personalisation, simplicity and trust*. Retrieved from https://www.pwc.com/gx/en/about/pwc-asia-pacific/asia-pacific-blogs/beauty-and-the-ai-beast.html

Mansuroğlu, S. (2002). Akdeniz Üniversitesi öğrencilerinin serbest zaman özellikleri ve dış mekan rekreasyon eğilimlerinin belirlenmesi. *Akdeniz Üniversitesi Ziraat Fakültesi Dergisi*, *15*(2), 53–62.

Marco, M. F., Rumen, P., & Della Irene, S. (2024). Sinergie-SIMA 2024 Management Conference. *Sinergie-SIMA 2024 Conference Management of Sustainability and Well-Being for Individuals and Society*, *1*(1), 267–287. DOI: 10.7433/SRECP.LP.2024.01

Marin-Lopez, X. (2024). *Makeup by Mario launches AR mirror at Sephora Times Square*. Retrieved from https://www.retaildive.com/news/makeup-by-mario-ar-mirror-virtual-try-on-sephora-times-square/718688/

Market.us. (2024). *eSports market size worldwide from 2023 to 2033 (in billion U.S. dollars)*. Statista. Accessed 7 March 2025. https://www.statista.com/statistics/1256162/global-esports-market-size/

Marketing Explainers. (2024). *Sephora's marketing strategy explained*. Retrieved from https://www.marketingexplainers.com/sephoras-marketing-strategy-explained/

Marketing Maverick. (2024). *Sephora is unique because of this and no other brand has ever done it before*. Retrieved from https://marketingmaverick.io/p/marketing-strategies-of-sephora

Martínez-Martínez, I. J., Aguado, J.-M., & Boeykens, Y. (2017). Ethical implications of digital advertising automation: The case of programmatic advertising in Spain. *El Profesional de la Información*, *26*(2), 201–210. DOI: 10.3145/epi.2017.mar.06

Mastercard. (2018, September 18). *Mastercard and League of Legends announce multi-year global partnership* [Press release]. Mastercard Newsroom. https://www.mastercard.com/news/press/digital-press-kits/2018/mastercard-league-of-legends-esports-partnership

Mastercard. (n.d.). *League of Legends e-sports*. Priceless. https://www.priceless.com/celebrity/19286/league-of-legends-e-sports

Masternak, W. (2025). *Sephora's Beauty Insider program: The gold standard in loyalty*. Retrieved from https://www.openloyalty.io/insider/sephora-beauty-insider

Mattan, M. (2024). *How augmented reality storefronts can drive foot traffic*. Retrieved from https://www.brandxr.io/how-augmented-reality-storefronts-can-drive-foot-traffic

Mattan, M. (2025a). *BrandXR research report: How beauty brands are using AR mirrors to increase sales*. Retrieved from https://www.brandxr.io/research-report-how-beauty-brands-are-using-ar-mirrors-to-increase-sales

Mattan, M. (2025b). *Experiences – Blending physical and digital in-store experiences*. Retrieved from https://www.brandxr.io/phygital-retail-experiences-blending-physical-and-digital-in-store-experiences

Mattan, M. (2025c). *AR mirrors vs. traditional retail displays: A conversion rate comparison*. Retrieved from https://www.brandxr.io/ar-mirrors-vs-traditional-retail-displays-a-conversion-rate-comparison

Matt, C., Trenz, M., Cheung, C., & Turel, O. (2019). The digitization of the individual: Conceptual foundations and opportunities for research. *Electronic Markets*, *29*(3), 315–322. DOI: 10.1007/s12525-019-00348-9

Mau, G., Silberer, G., & Constien, C. (2008). Communicating brands playfully: Effects of ingame advertising for familiar and unfamiliar brands. *International Journal of Advertising*, *27*(5), 827–851. DOI: 10.2501/S0265048708080293

McCambley, J. (2013, December). *The First ever banner ad: Why did it work so well?* https://www.theguardian.com/media-network/media-network-blog/2013/dec/12/first-ever-bann er-ad-advertising

McCormack, S., Jones, B., & Elliott, D. (2022). Coaches' assessment of players' physical performance: Subjective and objective measures are needed when profiling players. *European Journal of Sport Science*, *22*(8), 1177–1187. PMID: 34304720

McDermott, R. (2024). "Prospect Theory". *Encyclopedia Britannica*. https://www.britannica.com/topic/prospect-theory

McGonigal, J. (2011). *Reality is broken: Why games make us better and how they can change the world*. The Penguin Press.

McKinsey. (2025a). How beauty players can scale gen. *AI*, *2025*, •••. https://www.mckinsey.com/industries/consumer-packaged-goods/our-insights/how-beauty-players-can-scale-gen-ai-in-2025

McKinsey. (2025b). *The state of fashion: Beauty volume 2*. Retrieved from https://www.mckinsey.com/~/media/mckinsey/industries/consumer%20packaged%20goods/our%20insights/state%20of%20beauty/2025/the-state-of-fashion-beauty-june-2025-f.pdf

McStay, A. (2017). Micro-Moments, Liquidity, Intimacy and Automation: Developments in Programmatic Ad-tech. In Siegert, G., Rimscha, M. B., & Grubenmann, S. (Eds.), *Commercial Communication in the Digital Age* (pp. 143–159). DOI: 10.1515/9783110416794-009

McTear, M., Callejas, Z., & Griol, D. (2016). *The conversational interface: Talking to smart devices*. Springer., DOI: 10.1007/978-3-319-32967-3

Md, R., & Azhar, A. (2017). Article 1 Applying Green Gamification to Support Green Campus Initiatives in Reducing Carbon Emissions. [JCRINN]. *Journal of Computing Research and Innovation*, 2(4), 1–6.

Mehrabian, A., & Russell, J. A. (1976). An approach to environmental psychology. In *The MIT Press*. M.I.T. Press.

Mercedes-Benz. (n.d.). *Esports*. Mercedes-Benz. https://www.mercedes-benz.com/en/art-and-culture/zeitgeist/sports/esports/

Merdin, M. (2023). Dijital oyun reklamlarında oyuncular tarafından üretilen nefret söylemleri. *Selçuk İletişim Dergisi*, *16*(1), 34–62. DOI: 10.18094/josc.1203241

Mestçi, A. (2013). *İnternette Reklamcılık (Internet Advertising)*. Pusula Publications.

Meta. (2025). *What's the difference between AR, VR and MR*? Retrieved from https://forwork.meta.com/gb/blog/difference-between-vr-ar-and-mr/

Mete, M. H. (2021). Programmatic advertising and ethical issues in digital media. *TRT Academy*, *6*(12), 426–449. DOI: 10.37679/trta.876044

Metin, T. C., Kesici, M., & Kodaş, D. (2013). Rekreasyon olgusuna akademisyenlerin yaklaşımları. *Journal of Yasar University*, *30*(8), 5021–5048.

Meyer, J. (2023). *Sephora's stores of the future*. Retrieved from https://www.euroshop-tradefair.com/en/euroshopmag/sephoras-stores-of-the-future-for-an-immersive-shopping-experience

Michaud, L. (2009). In-Game Advertising: Advertising and Video Game, 2009-2013, IDate Consulting and Research. Retrieved from: www.idate-research.com

Miell, S., Gill, S., & Vazquez, D. (2018). Enabling the digital fashion consumer through fit and sizing technology. *Journal of Global Fashion Marketing*, *9*(1), 9–23. DOI: 10.1080/20932685.2017.1399083

Milled. (2022). Win prizes at Sephora spin to win. Retrieved from https://milled.com/sephora-sg/win-prizes-at-sephora-spin-to-win-j1YAMIiL5aUYZQy6

Minecraft (2025). https://www.minecraft.net/tr-tr

Mishra, S., & Malhotra, G. (2020). The gamification of in-game advertising: Examining the role of psychological ownership and advertisement intrusiveness. *International Journal of Information Management*, *61*(3), 1–13. PMID: 33012944

ModiFace. (2025). *We deliver beauty tech solutions to help engage, educate, and empower your consumers*. Retrieved from https://modiface.com/#product

Mohammadabbasi, M., & Değermen, A. (2023). "Dijital Asistanların Müşteri Memnuniyeti Üzerindeki Etkisi: Yapay Zekâ Uygulamaları Türkiye Örneği". *1. Uluslararası Sosyal ve Ekonomik Çalışmalar Dergisi*, *4*(2), 225–248. DOI: 10.62001/gsijses.1371527

Montag, C., Schivinski, B., Kannen, C., & Pontes, H. M. (2022). Investigating gaming disorder and individual differences in gaming motives among professional and non-professional gamers: An empirical study. *Addictive Behaviors*, *134*, 107416. PMID: 35901542

Moore, S., Bulmer, S., & Elms, J. (2022). The social significance of AI in retail on customer experience and shopping practices. *Journal of Retailing and Consumer Services*, *64*, 102755. DOI: 10.1016/j.jretconser.2021.102755

Moor, M., Banerjee, O., Abad, Z. S. H., Krumholz, H. M., Leskovec, J., Topol, E. J., & Rajpurkar, P. (2023). Foundation models for generalist medical artificial intelligence. *Nature*, *616*(7956), 259–265. DOI: 10.1038/s41586-023-05881-4 PMID: 37045921

Morandini, S., Fraboni, F., De Angelis, M., Puzzo, G., Giusino, D., & Pietrantoni, L. (2023). The impact of artificial intelligence on workers' skills: Upskilling and reskilling in organisations. *Informing Science*, *26*, 39–68. DOI: 10.28945/5078

Morgan, J. P. (2024). *Sephora delivers a best-in-class omnichannel experience with J.P. Morgan payments*. Retrieved from https://www.jpmorgan.com/insights/payments/acquiring-and-e-commerce/sephora-omnichannel-experience

Morrison, S., & Crane, F. (2007). Building the service brand by creating and managing an emotional brand experience. *Journal of Brand Management*, *14*(5), 410–421. DOI: 10.1057/palgrave.bm.2550080

Mulcahy, R. F., McAndrew, R., Russell-Bennett, R., & Iacobucci, D. (2021). "Game on!" Pushing consumer buttons to change sustainable behavior: A gamification field study. *European Journal of Marketing*, *55*(10), 2593–2619. Advance online publication. DOI: 10.1108/EJM-05-2020-0341

Munro, B. (2026, January 15). *Interstitial ads: Best practices and examples for publishers*. Publift. https://www.publift.com/blog/interstitial-ads-a-best-practice-guide-for-publishers#Why-Use-an-Interstitial-Ad

Murugan, T. S., & Kumar, C. M. (2024). Unveiling the evolution: Impact of artificial intelligence on consumer buying behaviors in online retail purchase. *Educational Administration: Theory and Practice*, *30*(5), 1072–1078. DOI: 10.53555/kuey.v30i5.3011

Naumovska, L., & Petrusevska, G. (2025). Gamification in Marketing: Analyses of the Impact Beyond Play and Fun. *European Journal of Behavioral Sciences*, *8*(2), 45–57. DOI: 10.33422/ejbs.v8i2.1585

Nelson, M. R. (2002). Recall of brand placements in computer/video games. *Journal of Advertising Research*, *42*(2), 80–92. DOI: 10.2501/jar-42-2-80-92

Nelson, M. R., Keum, H., & Yaros, R. (2004). Advertainment or adcreep? game players' attitudes toward advertising and product placements in computer games. *Journal of Interactive Advertising*, *5*(1), 3–21. DOI: 10.1080/15252019.2004.10722090

Network, C. X. (2023). *How Sephora uses digital channels to deliver on customer centricity*. Retrieved from https://www.cxnetwork.com/cx-experience/articles/how-sephora-uses-digital-channels-to-deliver-on-customer-centricity

Newzoo. (2025). *Newzoo's global games market report 2025*. Newzoo. https://newzoo.com/resources/trend-reports/newzoo-global-games-market-report-2025

Nguyen, H. (2024). *Case study – what does Sephora teach us about digital customer experience?* Retrieved from https://savvycomsoftware.com/blog/sephora-case-study/

Nicovich, S. (2005). The effect of involvement on ad judgment in a video game environment: The mediating role of presence. *Journal of Interactive Advertising*, *6*(1), 29–39. DOI: 10.1080/15252019.2005.10722105

Nikhashemi, S. R., Knight, H. H., Nusair, K., & Liat, C. B. (2021). Augmented reality in smart retailing: A (n) (A) Symmetric Approach to continuous intention to use retail brands' mobile AR apps. *Journal of Retailing and Consumer Services*, *60*, 102464. DOI: 10.1016/j.jretconser.2021.102464

Niknejad, S., Mildner, T., Zargham, N., Putze, S., & Malaka, R. (2024). (Level Up or Game Over: Exploring How Dark Patterns Shape Mobile Games). *In International Conference on Mobile and Ubiquitous Multi- media (MUM '24)*, pp. 1-4. DOI: 10.1145/3701571.3701604

Nimrod, G., & Adoni, H. (2012). Conceptualizing E-leisure. *Loisir et Société. Society and Leisure*, *35*(1), 31–56. DOI: 10.1080/07053436.2012.10707834

Noh, Y., Ryu, Y., & Kim, K. (2025). eSport Consumption and Sponsor Brand Equity: The Mediating Role of Congruence. *Frontiers in Psychology*, *16*, 1594068. PMID: 40678431

Noris, A., Nobile, T. H., Kalbaska, N. & Cantoni, L. (2021). Digital Fashion: A systematic literature review. A perspective on marketing and communication. *Journal of Global Fashion Marketing*. DOI: 10.1080/20932685.2020.1835522

Norum, P. S. (2017). *Towards sustainable clothing disposition: Exploring the consumer choice to use trash as a disposal option*. Sustainability., DOI: 10.3390/su9071187

Obi, A. (2020). *Animal Crossing Fashion: Valentino, Marc Jacobs Get Into the Game*. Wwd.Com. https://wwd.com/fashion-news/sportswear/feature/animal-crossing-new-horizons-nintendo-switch-fashion-world-1203628365/

Odicci. (2025a). *Leading beauty retailer uses always-on gamification to supercharge app acquisition*. Retrieved from https://odicci.com/customer-success-stories/sephora-combining-crm-app/

Odicci. (2025b). *Leading beauty retailer uses Gamification to supercharge their christmas marketing strategy*. Retrieved from https://odicci.com/customer-success-stories/sephora-a-b-testing-calendars/

Oleksandra, B. (2022). *What is Fashion NFT and How Brands are Capitalizing on it?* Techpacker.Com. https://techpacker.com/blog/design/how-fashion-brands-are-taking-advantage-of-nfts/

Önder, B. A. (2021). "Reklam Kampanyalarında Etkileşimli İletişimin Silahı: Oyunlaştırma". *İstanbul Aydın Üniversitesi Sosyal Bilimler Dergisi*, 13(1), pp. 1-40.

Öndeş, A. (2011, August 22). Cadbury: Qwak Smack *Ambalaj üzeri augmented reality oyun*. Retrieved November 2024, from https://bigumigu.com/haber/cadbury-qwak-smack-ambalaj-uzeri-augmented-reality-oyun/

Opena, A. (2025). "Ad Blockers Usage Statistics [2025]: Who's Blocking Ads & Why?". Retrieved from: https://cropink.com/ad-blockers-usage-statistics

Orme, S. (2022). "Just watching": A qualitative analysis of non-players' motivations for video game spectatorship. *New Media & Society*, *24*(10), 2252–2269.

Osborne, M. J., & Rubinstein, A. (1994). *A Course in Game Theory*. The MIT Press.

Owyang, J. (2010, January 26). The New Reality Will Be Augmented. Retrieved November 2024, from https://www.destinationcrm.com/Articles/Columns-Departments/Connect/The-New-Reality-Will-Be-Augmented-60593.aspx

Özdemir, H. (2022). Kullanımlar ve doyumlar yaklaşımı bağlamında tüketicilerin online alışveriş eğilimlerini belirleyen nitel bir araştırma. İletişim ve Toplum Araştırmaları Dergisi, 2(2), 138-153. DOI: 10.29228/itamder.3

Özer, S., & Çolak, A. (2022). Dijital çağın meta-tüketicilerini anlamaya yönelik kavramsal bir değerlendirme. In Uğurhan, Y. Z. (Ed.), *Dijitalleşme Bağlamında Birey, Toplum ve İletişim* (pp. 7–29). Eğitim Yayınevi.

Özkan, Z., & Samur, Y. (2017). Oyunlaştırma Yönteminin Öğrencilerin Motivasyonları Üzerine Etkisi. *Ege Eğitim Dergisi*, *18*(2), 857–886. DOI: 10.12984/egeefd.314801

Öztürk, M. C., & Coşkun, E. (2017). Evaluation of player motivations in terms of advergame applications. *Karaelmas Communication Faculty Electronic Journal*, *4*(13), 48–66. https://dergipark.org.tr/tr/pub/e-kiad/article/629600?issue_id=49304

Ozturkcan, S., & Şengün, S. (2016). Gaining Reward vs. Avoiding Loss. In *Emerging Research and Trends in Gamification* (pp. 48–71). IGI Global., DOI: 10.4018/978-1-4666-8651-9.ch003

Öztürk, M. C., & Coşkun, E. (2017). EVALUATION OF PLAYER MOTIVATIONS IN TERMS OF ADVERGAME APPLICATIONS. *Karadeniz Technical University Communication Research Journal*, *7*(1), 48–64.

Özüölmez, P. (2019). Yeni İletişim Ortamı Olarak Dijital Oyunlarda Deneyim İçerikli Yeni Bir Reklam Uygulaması: Skillful Finger Örneği. *Erciyes İletişim Dergisi, 6*(2), 1383–1404. DOI: 10.17680/erciyesiletisim.484759

Packer, J., Croker, H., Goddings, A. L., Boyland, E. J., Stansfield, C., Russell, S. J., & Viner, R. M. (2022). Advertising and young people's critical reasoning abilities: Systematic review and meta-analysis. *Pediatrics, 150*(6), e2022057780. DOI: 10.1542/peds.2022-057780

Palfreyman, B. M. (2025, March 4). *AI-powered video game advertising: Regulatory and IP challenges.* Harris Beach PLLC. https://www.harrisbeachmurtha.com/insights/ai-powered-video-game-advertising-regulatory-and-ip-challenges/

Pan, H., Chen, M., & Shiau, W.-L. (2022). Exploring post-pandemic struggles and recoveries in the rural tourism based on Chinese situation: A perspective from the IAD framework. *Journal of Hospitality and Tourism Technology, 13*(1), 120–139. DOI: 10.1108/JHTT-11-2020-0300

Pansari, A., & Kumar, V. (2017). Customer engagement: The construct, antecedents, and consequences. *Journal of the Academy of Marketing Science, 45*, 294–311.

Parkin, T. (2023, March 10). *In-game advertising: A marketer's guide.* MarTech. Retrieved from https://martech.org/in-game-advertising-a-marketers-guide/ Accessed on August 31, 2025.

Park, J., & Chun, J. (2023). Evolution of Fashion as Play in the Digital Space. *Fashion Practice, 15*(2), 256–278. DOI: 10.1080/17569370.2022.2149837

Patil, D., Rane, N. L., & Rane, J. (2024). Applications of ChatGPT and generative artificial intelligence in transforming the future of various business sectors. In *The Future Impact of ChatGPT on Several Business Sectors* (ss. 1-47). Deep Science Publishing. DOI: 10.70593/978-81-981367-8-7_1

Patil, D. (2024). Generative artificial intelligence in marketing and advertising: Advancing personalization and optimizing consumer engagement strategies. *Journal of Marketing Analytics, 12*(3), 145–158.

Patov, A. (2024). *How Sephora enhances customer experience (cx) through personalization and digital innovation.* Retrieved from https://www.renascence.io/journal/how-sephora-enhances-customer-experience-cx-through-personalization-and-digital-innovation

Paul, T. (2021). *Fortnite's Metaverse Assembles: The Complete List Of Licensed Skins.* Forbes. https://www.forbes.com/sites/paultassi/2021/02/28/fortnites-metaverse-assembles-the-complete-list-of-licensed-skins/

Pedraza-Ramirez, I., Musculus, L., Raab, M., & Laborde, S. (2020). Setting the scientific stage for esports psychology: A systematic review. *International Review of Sport and Exercise Psychology*, *13*(1), 319–352.

Peker, G. (2017, April 1). Rekreasyonun sınıflandırılması. Retrieved from https://www.rekreasyonist.com/rekreasyonunsiniflandirilmasi/#:~:text=Kapal%C4%B1%20Alan%20Rekreasyon%20Etkinlikleri,bu%20ama%C3%A7larla%20yap%C4%B1lan%20tesislerde%20geli%C5%9Fir

Penezoğlu Yıldırım, D. N., & Ulukol, B. (2022). Dijital Oyunlar ve Şiddet. *TRT Akademi*, *7*(16), 1162–1171.

Peng, K. (2025). The Impact of Loss Aversion on Decision-Making in Marketing and Financial Markets. *Advances in Economics, Management and Political Sciences*, *149*(1), 157–163. DOI: 10.54254/2754-1169/2024.19247

Peng, Q., Dickson, G., Scelles, N., Grix, J., & Brannagan, P. M. (2020). Esports governance: Exploring stakeholder dynamics. *Sustainability*, *12*(19), 8270.

Peng, W., Liu, M., & Mou, Y. (2008). Do aggressive people play violent computer games in a more aggressive way? Individual difference and idiosyncratic game-playing experience. *Cyberpsychology & Behavior*, *11*(2), 157–161. DOI: 10.1089/cpb.2007.0026 PMID: 18422407

Penrose, R. (2023). *Kralın Yeni Aklı, Bilgisayar, Zekâ ve Fizik Yasaları* (T. Dereli, Çev.). Koç Üniversitesi Yayınları. (Orijinal çalışma basım tarihi 1989).

Peters, S., & Leshner, G. (2013). Get in the game: The effects of game product congruity and product placement proximity on game players' processing of brands embedded in advergames. *Journal of Advertising*, *42*(2-3), 113–130. DOI: 10.1080/00913367.2013.774584

Porcu, L., Del Barrio-Garcia, S., & Kitchen, P. J. (2017). Measuring integrated marketing communication by taking a broad organisational approach: The firm-wide IMC scale. *European Journal of Marketing*, *51*(3), 692–718.

Poulus, D. R., Sargeant, J., Zarate, D., Griffiths, M. D., & Stavropoulos, V. (2024). Burnout, resilience, and coping among esports players: A network analysis approach. *Computers in Human Behavior*, *153*, 108139.

Poulus, D. R., Sharpe, B. T., Jackman, P. C., Swann, C., & Bennett, K. J. (2024). Defining elite esports athletes: A scoping review. *International Review of Sport and Exercise Psychology*, 1–36.

Poushneh, A., & Vasquez-Parraga, A. (2017). Discernible impact of augmented reality on retail customer's experience, satisfaction, and willingness to buy. *Journal of Retailing and Consumer Services, 34*(3), 229–234. DOI: 10.1016/j.jretconser.2016.10.005

Power Commerce. (2025). *Sephora and Lyft's innovative partnership: Redefining beauty retail in a digital age.* Retrieved from https://powercommerce.com/blogs/ecommerce-hub/sephora-and-lyfts-innovative-partnership-redefining-beauty-retail-in-a-digital-age

Pradhan, A., Mehta, K., & Findlater, L. (2018). "Accessibility came by accident: Use of voice-controlled intelligent personal assistants by people with disabilities". *Proceedings of the 2018 CHI Conference on Human Factors in Computing Systems*, pp. 1–13. DOI: 10.1145/3173574.3174033

Prendergast, G., Cheung, W. L., & West, D. (2010). Antecedents to advertising avoidance in China. *Journal of Current Issues and Research in Advertising, 32*(2), 87–100. DOI: 10.1080/10641734.2010.10505287

program-ace.com. D. (2024). *Fashion in the Metaverse: Trends, Examples, and More.* Program-Ace.Com. https://program-ace.com/blog/fashion-in-the-metaverse/

Pu, H., Xiao, S., & Kota, R. W. (2022). Virtual games meet physical playground: Exploring and measuring motivations for live esports event attendance. *Sport in Society, 25*(10), 1886–1908.

Purington, A., Taft, J. G., Sannon, S., Bazarova, N. N., & Taylor, S. H. (2017). "Alexa is my new BFF": Social roles, user satisfaction, and personification of the Amazon Echo. Proceedings of the 2017 CHI Conference Extended Abstracts on Human Factors in Computing Systems, pp. 2853–2859. DOI: 10.1145/3027063.3053246

Qian, K., & Xie, Y. (2026). The Power of Star Creators: Evidence from the Live Streaming Industry. *Journal of Marketing Research, 63*(1), 149-166.

Qian, T. Y., Wang, J. J., Zhang, J. J., & Lu, L. Z. (2020). It is in the game: Dimensions of esports online spectator motivation and development of a scale. *European Sport Management Quarterly, 20*(4), 458–479.

Qin, X., & Jiang, Z. (2019). The impact of AI on the advertising process: The Chinese experience. *Journal of Advertising, 48*(4), 338–346. DOI: 10.1080/00913367.2019.1652122

Rane, J., Mallick, S. K., Kaya, O., & Rane, N. L. (2024). Artificial general intelligence in industry 4.0, 5.0, and society 5.0: Applications, opportunities, challenges, and future direction. In *Future Research Opportunities for Artificial Intelligence in Industry 4.0 and 5.0* (ss. 207-235). Deep Science Publishing. DOI: 10.70593/978-81-981271-0-5_6

RapidFire In-Game Advertising. (2015, May 26). *RapidFire and Maxony Media partner to bring in-game advertising to Turkey*. RapidFire. https://web.archive.org/web/20160130150623/https://www.rapidfire.com/blog/dynamic-vs-staticin-game-advertising-a-comparison/ (Accessed: 08.09.2025)

Rebiere, P., & Mavoori, H. (2021), *Sephora: Phygital excellence in beauty tech.* Retrieved from https://hal.science/hal-03138790

Reflectdigital, D. (2025). *A gamified fashion world... | Reflect Digital.* Reflectdigital.Co.Uk. https://www.reflectdigital.co.uk/blog/a-gamified-fashion-world

Rehman, S. U., Gulzar, R., & Aslam, W. (2022). Developing the integrated marketing communication (imc) through social media (sm): The modern marketing communication approach. *SAGE Open*, *12*(2), 21582440221099936.

Rehman, U., Shah, M. U., Abbasi, A. Z., Hlavacs, H., & Iftikhar, R. (2022). Investigating male gamers' behavioral intention to play PUBG: Insights from playful-consumption experiences. *Frontiers in Psychology*, *13*, 909875. PMID: 36059783

Reinold, T., & Tropp, J. (2012). Integrated marketing communications: How can we measure its effectiveness? *Journal of Marketing Communications*, *18*(2), 113–132.

Retail Design, C. A. A. D. (2025). *Gamification in retail: Playful experiences for generations Alpha and Z.* Retrieved from https://caad-design.com/en/gamification-in-retail-playful-experiences-for-generations-alpha-and-z

Reydar. (2021). *Fashion Gamification: Why Brands Are Gaming in 2021 | REYDAR*. Reydar.Com. https://www.reydar.com/fashion-gamification-balenciaga/

Ricci, M., Evangelista, A., Di Roma, A., & Fiorentino, M. (2023). Immersive and desktop virtual reality in virtual fashion stores: A comparison between shopping experiences. *Virtual Reality (Waltham Cross)*, *27*(3), 2281–2296. Advance online publication. DOI: 10.1007/s10055-023-00806-y PMID: 37360805

Rietz, J., & Hallmann, K. (2023). A systematic review on spectator behavior in esports: Why do people watch? *International Journal of Sports Marketing & Sponsorship*, *24*(1), 38–55.

Riot Games. (2022, March 14). *Riot Games announces new equity investment in Arcane animation studio Fortiche Production* [Press release]. https://www.riotgames.com/en/news/riot-games-announces-new-equity-investment-in-arcane-animation-studio-fortiche-production

Riot Games. (2023, June 20). *Mastercard expands global partnership to VALORANT esports.* https://www.riotgames.com/en/news/mastercard-riot-games-global-valorant

Risso, M., & Paesano, A. (2021). Retail and Gamification for a New Customer Experience in Omnichannel Environment. [IJEB]. *International Journal of Economic Behavior, 11*(1), 109–128. https://doi.org/https://doi.org/ 10.14276/2285-0430.3238

Roblox. (2024). Roblox - Roblox Reports First Quarter 2024 Financial Results. In *roblox.com.* https://ir.roblox.com/news/news-details/2024/Roblox-Reports-First-Quarter-2024-Financial-Results/default.aspx

Rodgers, S. (2021). Themed Issue Introduction: Promises and Perils of Artificial Intelligence and Advertising. *Journal of Advertising*, *50*(1), 1–10. DOI: 10.1080/00913367.2020.1868233

Rodgers, W., & Nguyen, T. (2022). Advertising benefits from ethical artificial intelligence algorithmic purchase decision pathways. *Journal of Business Ethics, 178*(4), 1043–1061. DOI: 10.1007/s10551-022-05048-7

Rohr-Sendlmeier, U. A., Gotze, I., & Stichel, R. (2008). Parental education concerning their children's use of modern media: Family rules and motives, extent and effects of using the computer, watching television and playing video games. *Zeitschrift für Familienforschung*, *20*(2), 107–130.

Romero, P. M., Lim, R. E., & Park, H. (2025). Branded virtual worlds in fashion gaming: Examining the role of brand narratives and social presence in consumer engagement. *Computers in Human Behavior, 164*, 108505. DOI: 10.1016/j.chb.2024.108505

Rooney, K. (2022, September 26). *Fortnite x Jordan brand unveil new downtown drop LTM.* https://www.hotnewhiphop.com/219751-fortnite-x-jordan-brand-unveil-new-downtown-drop-ltm-news#google_vignette

Rose, F. (2012). *The art of immersion: How the digital generation is remarking Hollywood, Madison avenue, and the way we tell stories.* W. W. Norton & Company.

Rose, G. (2023). *Visual methodology* (Akgülgil, G., Trans.). İnkılap Kitabevi. DOI: 10.4135/9781036231576

Rosenbaum-Elliott, R., Percy, L., & Pervan, S. (2015). *Strategic brand management*. Oxford University Press.

Roth, A., Kunz, R. E., & Kolo, C. (2023). The players' perspective of value co-creation in esports service ecosystems. *Journal of Media Business Studies*, 1–25.

Rue, P. (2018). Make way, millennials, here comes Gen Z. *About Campus: Enriching the Student Learning Experience*, *23*(3), 5–12.

Rukavina, A. (2025). *What is phygital marketing? 11 examples of phygital experiences*. Retrieved from https://www.infobip.com/blog/what-is-phygital-marketing

Ryan, R. M., & Deci, E. L. (2000). Self-determination theory and the facilitation of intrinsic motivation, social development, and well-being. *The American Psychologist*, *55*(1), 68–78. DOI: 10.1037/0003-066X.55.1.68 PMID: 11392867

Saber Rashid, N., & Zeebaree, R. M., S. (2025). Gamification in digital marketing for e-commerce: A review of strategies to boost engagement and sales. *International Journal of Scientific World*, *11*(1), 95–103. DOI: 10.14419/bfmn7r29

Sailer, M., Hense, J. U., Mayr, S. K., & Mandl, H. (2017). How gamification motivates: An experimental study of the effects of specific game design elements on psychological need satisfaction. *Computers in Human Behavior*, *69*, 371–380. DOI: 10.1016/j.chb.2016.12.033

Salo, M. (2021). Career transitions of eSports athletes: A proposal for a research framework. In *Research anthology on business strategies, health factors, and ethical Implications in sports and eSports* (pp. 478–490). IGI Global.

Sancaklı, P., & Sarı, Ü. (2025). Use of artificial ıntelligence ın digital games and current trends in the example of the 'F.E.A.R' game. *Communicata*, *29*, 87–98. DOI: 10.32952/communicata.1628205

Sandler, E. (2023). *Sephora adds gamified experience to Beauty Insider loyalty program in appeal to Gen Z.* Retrieved from https://www.glossy.co/beauty/sephora-adds-gamified-experience-to-beauty-insider-loyalty-program-in-appeal-to-gen-z/

Santiago, M., Loureiro, S., Langaro, D., & Ali, F. (2024). Adoption of smart technologies in the cruise tourism services: A systematic review and future research agenda. *Journal of Hospitality and Tourism Technology*, *15*(3).

Santos, P., Dias, J., & Bairrada, C. (2024). *Gamification in marketing: Insights on current and future research directions based on a bibliometric and theories, contexts, characteristics and methodologies analysis*. Retrieved from https://www.sciencedirect.com/science/article/pii/S2405844024080782

Say, C. (2024). *50 Soruda Yapay Zekâ*. Bilim ve Gelecek Kitaplığı.

Şaylan, O., Taşkın, E., & Abdulwahid, O. I. A. (2025). Yapay Zekanın Dijital Pazarlama Stratejileri Üzerindeki Etkisi: Kavramsal Bir Çalışma. *Uluslararası Sosyal ve Ekonomik Çalışmalar Dergisi*, *6*(1), 350–367. DOI: 10.62001/gsijses.1687324

Schmitt, B. (1999). *Experiential marketing: How to get customers to sence, feel, think, act, and relate to your company and brands*. The Free Press.

Schmitt, B. (2009). The concept of brand experience. *Journal of Brand Management*, *16*(7), 417–419. DOI: 10.1057/bm.2009.5

Scholz, T. M. (2020). Deciphering the World of eSports. *International Journal on Media Management*, *22*(1), 1–12.

Schultz, D. E., & Block, M. P. (2015). Beyond brand loyalty: Brand sustainability. *Journal of Marketing Communications*, *21*(5), 340–355. DOI: 10.1080/13527266.2013.821227

Schultz, D. E., & Patti, C. H. (2009). The evolution of IMC: IMC in a customer-driven marketplace. *Journal of Marketing Communications*, *15*(2–3), 75–84.

Schultz, D. E., & Schultz, H. F. (1998). Transitioning marketing communication into the twenty-first century. *Journal of Marketing Communications*, *4*(1), 9–26.

Schweidel, D. A., & Moe, W. W. (2019). Listening in on conversations: Speech-based marketing intelligence and consumer privacy. *The Journal of Consumer Research*, *46*(4), 595–622. DOI: 10.1093/jcr/ucz017

Schwilgin, F. A., Arch, B., & Arch, M. (1974). *Town planning guidelines*. Department of Public Works.

Scozzese, G., & Gelli, M. (2023). Lifestyle as a Branding Strategy for the Sustainable Brand. *European Scientific Journal*, *19*(22), 1–26. DOI: 10.19044/esj.2023.v19n22p1

Scratcher. (2024). *Gamification in Fashion: What's Actually Working - Scratcher*. Scratcher.Io. https://scratcher.io/gamification-marketing-in-fashion-industry/

Sebastian, A., Núñez, M., & Muñoz, D. (2016). New business models for advertisers: The video game sector in Spain. Advergaming Vs In-game Advertising. *Icono 14*, *14*(2), 256–279. DOI: 10.7195/ri14.v14i2.964

Self-Determination Theory. (2025). Theory. Retrieved from https://selfdeterminationtheory.org/theory/

Şen, H. (2024). *Mobil oyun reklamlarında reklam çekiciliklerinin kullanımı: Mafia City oyun reklamları örneği* (Unpublished master's thesis). Konya, Turkey.

SendPulse. (n.d.). Cross-promotion – Support glossary. SendPulse. https://sendpulse.com/support/glossary/cross-promotion

Seo, Y. (2016). Professionalized consumption and identity transformations in the field of eSports. *Journal of Business Research*, *69*(1), 264–272.

Sepetçi, T. (2022). Dijital oyun kültürü ve sosyal etkileşim. Ş. Sağıroğlu, Hİ Bülbül, A. Kılıç, M. Küçükali, Ş. Bayzan & Y. Samur (Ed.), *Dijital Oyunlar-1: Araçlar, Metodolojiler, Uygulamalar ve Öneriler* içinde (pp. 111-150). Ankara: Nobel Yayınevi.

Sephora Malaysia. (2025). *Sephora virtual artist.* Retrieved from https://www.sephora.my/pages/virtual-artist

Sephora. (2014). *Sephora Twitter post*. Retrieved from https://x.com/Sephora/status/649252368031346688

Sephora. (2025a). *About Sephora*. Retrieved from https://www.sephora.com/beauty/about-us

Sephora. (2025b). *2024 global impact and progress report*. Retrieved from https://www.inside-sephora.com/sites/default/files/2025-06/SEPHORA_Global%20Impact%20Report%20-%20accessible.pdf

Sephora. (2025c). *Sephora: Buy Makeup & Skincare*. Retrieved from https://play.google.com/store/apps/details?id=com.sephora

Sephora. (2025d). *Website Domian Page*. Retrieved from https://www.sephora.com/

Sephora. (2025e). *Beauty insiders get a free birthday gift set*. Retrieved from https://www.sephora.com/beauty/birthday-gift

Sephora. (2025f). *Sephora Instagram page*. Retrieved from https://www.instagram.com/sephora/?hl=en

Sephora. (2025g). *Sephora - make-up, beauty*. Retrieved from https://play.google.com/store/apps/details?id=fr.sephora.sephorafrance

Sephora. (2025h). *Sephora.* Retrieved from https://sephora.en.aptoide.com/app

Sephoria. (2025). Sephoria webpage. Retrieved from https://sephoria-1f83b.kxcdn.com/storage/thumbnails/data/Postcard/8/1400-_q-90/Manandwomandressedup.webp

Settle, Q. (2018). Introducing communication theory: Analysis and application. *Journal of Applied Communications*, *102*(3), 7.

Shalabi, C. (2024, July 26). *Guide to video game advertising: Trends, tactics, and opportunities for marketers* [Original post March 11, 2024]. eMarketer. Retrieved August 31, 2025, from https://www.emarketer.com/learningcenter/guides/us-gaming-industry-ecosystem/

Shankar, V. (2018). How artificial intelligence (AI) is reshaping retailing. *Journal of Retailing*, *94*(4), vi–xi. DOI: 10.1016/S0022-4359(18)30076-9

Shankar, V., Venkatesh, A., Hofacker, C., & Naik, P. (2010). Mobile marketing in the retailing environment: Current insights and future research avenues. *Journal of Interactive Marketing*, *24*(2), 111–120. DOI: 10.1016/j.intmar.2010.02.006

Shaw, A. (2010). What is video game culture? Cultural studies and game studies. *Games and Culture*, *5*(4), 403–424.

Shemona, S. (2024). *Can blockchain put an end to fakes and ripping-off ideas in fashion? - Just Style*. Just-Style.Com. https://www.just-style.com/news/can-blockchain-put-an-end-to-fakes-and-ripping-off-ideas-in-fashion/

Shimp, A. T. (2008). *Advertising, promotion, and other aspects of integrated marketing communications* (7th ed.). Thomson Higher Education.

Silvia, C. (2024). *Phygital retail: Combining in-store and digital shopping*. Retrieved from https://www.amu.apus.edu/area-of-study/business-administration-and-management/resources/phygital-retail/

Singhal, A. (2024). The role of artificial ıntelligence in enhancing ad personalization: A study on programmatic advertising. [JAIGS]. *Journal of Artificial Intelligence General Science*, *3*(1), 431–445. DOI: 10.60087/jaigs.v3i1.246

Singh, N. (2024a). Building Sustainability in Textile and Apparel Supply Chains. In *Eco-Innovation and Sustainable Development in Industry 5.0* (pp. 198–222). IGI Global., DOI: 10.4018/979-8-3693-2219-2.ch010

Singh, N. (2024b). Circular Economy in Textile and Apparel Supply Chains. In *Innovation and Sustainability Through Circular Economy in Businesses* (1st ed., pp. 25–64). IGI Global., DOI: 10.4018/979-8-3693-4123-0.ch002

Singh, P., & Pandey, M. (2014). Page augmented reality advertising: An impactful platform for new age consumer engagement. *IOSR Journal of Business and Management*, *16*(2), 24–28. DOI: 10.9790/487X-16222428

Sintas, J. L., de Francisco, L. R., & Alvarez, E. G. (2015). The nature of leisure revisited. *Journal of Leisure Research*, *47*(1), 79–101. DOI: 10.1080/00222216.2015.11950352

Sjöblom, M., Törhönen, M., Hamari, J., & Macey, J. (2019). The ingredients of Twitch streaming: Affordances of game streams. *Computers in Human Behavior*, *92*, 20–28.

Smartico. (2025). *How does Sephora's Gamified Beauty Insider Program succeed?* Retrieved from https://www.smartico.ai/blog-post/how-sephora-gamified-beauty-insider-program-succeed

Smith, C. (2024). *Sephora's store of the future locations are immersive.* Retrieved from https://www.trendhunter.com/trends/sephora-store-of-the-future

Smith, M. W., Sun, W., Sutherland, J. ve Mackie, B. (2014). Game advertising: A conceptual framework and exploration of advertising prevalence. *The computer games joumal, 3*(1), pp. 95-124.

Smith, M. W.. (2014). Game Advertising: A Conceptual Framework and Exploration of Advertising Prevalence. *The Computer Games Journal*, *3*(1), 94–123.

Smith, M., Sun, W., Sutherland, J., & Mackie, B. (2014). Game advertising: A conceptual framework and exploration of advertising prevalence. *The Computer Games Journal*, *3*(2), 95–124. DOI: 10.1007/BF03395948

Smith, R., Kelly, B., Yeatman, H., Moore, C., Baur, L., King, L., Boyland, E., Chapman, K., Hughes, C., & Bauman, A. (2020). Advertising placement in digital game design influences children's choices of advertised snacks: A randomized trial. *Journal of the Academy of Nutrition and Dietetics*, *120*(3), 404–413. DOI: 10.1016/j.jand.2019.07.017 PMID: 31892500

Snap Inc. (2025). *Gamified Augmented Reality Lens delivers massive ROI for Sephora.* Retrieved from https://forbusiness.snapchat.com/inspiration/gamified-augmented-reality-lens-delivers-massive-roi-for-sephora

Snipp. (2025). *Gamification in action - 11 examples of gamification for engagement success.* Retrieved from https://www.snipp.com/blog/gamification-examples

Snodgrass, J. G., Dengah, H. F., Lacy, M. G., & Fagan, J. (2013). A formal anthropological view of motivation models of problematic MMO play: Achievement, social, and immersion factors in the context of culture. *Transcultural Psychiatry*, *50*(2), 235–262. PMID: 23690445

Sobhi, N. (2024). *Learn how to retain customers like the world's 14 best beauty loyalty programs.* Retrieved from https://www.gameball.co/blog/best-beauty-loyalty-programs

Somyürek, S. (2014). Öğretim sürecinde Z kuşağının dikkatini çekme: Artırılmış gerçeklik. *Eğitim Teknolojisi Kuram ve Uygulama, 4*(1), 63–80. DOI: 10.17943/etku.88319

Song, T., & Tang, Q. (2015). "Cross-Promotion in Social Media: Choosing the Right Allies", PACIS 2015 Proceedings. Research Collection School Of Information Systems, Retrieved from: https://ink.library.smu.edu.sg/sis_research/2945

Soto, I. (2025). *How beauty influencers are transforming the way we shop online*. Retrieved from https://www.bentley.edu/news/how-beauty-influencers-are-transforming-way-we-shop-online

Speck, P. S., & Elliott, M. T. (1997). Predictors of advertising avoidance in print and broadcast media. *Journal of Advertising, 26*(3), 61–76. DOI: 10.1080/00913367.1997.10673529

Speed, R., & Thompson, P. (2000). Determinants of sports sponsorship response. *Journal of the Academy of Marketing Science, 28*(2), 226–238.

Sreejesh, S., Ghosh, T., & Dwivedi, Y. K. (2021). Moving beyond the content: The role of contextual cues in the effectiveness of gamification of advertising. *Journal of Business Research, 132*, 88–101. DOI: 10.1016/j.jbusres.2021.04.007

stardoll.com. (2025). *Dress Up Games for Girls - Stardoll | English*. Stardoll.Com. https://www.stardoll.com/en/

Statista. (2025). *eSports – worldwide: Market outlook 2025*. Statista Market Insights. https://www.statista.com/outlook/amo/esports/worldwide

Stevens, A., Rau, A., & McIntyre, M. (2016). Integrated campaign planning in a programmatic world. In *Programmatic Advertising* (ss. 193–210). Springer. DOI: 10.1007/978-3-319-25023-6_16

Stewens, J., Schlager, T., Häubl, G., & Herrmann, A. (2016). Gamified information presentation and consumer adoption of product innovations. *Journal of Marketing, 81*(2), 8–24. DOI: 10.1509/jm.15.0396

Subhash, S., & Cudney, E. A. (2018). Gamified learning in higher education: A systematic review of the literature. *Computers in Human Behavior, 87*, 192–206. Advance online publication. DOI: 10.1016/j.chb.2018.05.028

Sucu, A. (2011). Global Markaların Advergame Tasarımı ve Kültür İlişkisi. *ABMYO dergisi*, 24, pp. 32-41.

Suhartanto, D., Brien, A., Primianac, I., Wibisono, N., & Triyuni, N. (2019). Tourist loyalty in creative tourism: The role of experience quality, value, satisfaction, and motivation. *Current Issues in Tourism*, *23*(12), 1–13.

Suits, B. (1978). *The grasshopper: Games, life and utopia*. Broadview Press. DOI: 10.3138/9781487574338

Sundar, S. S., & Limperos, A. M. (2013). Uses and Grats 2.0: New Gratifications for New Media. *Journal of Broadcasting & Electronic Media*, *57*(4), 504–525. DOI: 10.1080/08838151.2013.845827

Sung, E., Kwon, O., & Sohn, K. (2023). NFT luxury brand marketing in the metaverse: Leveraging blockchain-certified NFTs to drive consumer behavior. *Psychology and Marketing*, *40*(11), 2306–2325. Advance online publication. DOI: 10.1002/mar.21854

Super, A. G. I. (2025). *Case studies: How top brands are using AI recommendation engines to boost sales and customer satisfaction in 2025*. Retrieved from https://superagi.com/case-studies-how-top-brands-are-using-ai-recommendation-engines-to-boost-sales-and-customer-satisfaction-in-2025/

Sustainability, D. (2025). *Gamification Sustainable Fashion Consumption Behaviors Scenario*. Prism.Sustainability-Directory.Com. https://prism.sustainability-directory.com/scenario/gamification-sustainable-fashion-consumption-behaviors/

Sweeney, M., & Figas, N. (2024, May 15). *What is in-game advertising and how does it work?* Clearcode. Retrieved August 31, 2025, from https://clearcode.cc/blog/in-game-advertising/

Tandon, U., & Ertz, M. (2024). Modelling gamification, virtual-try-on technology, e-logistics service quality as predictors of online shopping: An empirical investigation. *Current Psychology (New Brunswick, N.J.)*, *43*(16), 14289–14303. DOI: 10.1007/s12144-023-05379-2

Tang, D., Peng, B., Ma, R., & Sum, K. W. R. (2025). Dispelling stigma and enduring bias: Exploring the perception of esports participation among young women. *Humanities & Social Sciences Communications*, *12*(1), 1–13.

Tang, D., Sum, R. K. W., Li, M., Ma, R., Chung, P., & Ho, R. W. K. (2023). What is esports? A systematic scoping review and concept analysis of esports. *Heliyon*, *9*(12). PMID: 38149186

Tang, T., Cooper, R., & Kucek, J. (2021). Gendered Esports: Predicting why men and women play and watch esports games. *Journal of Broadcasting & Electronic Media*, *65*(3), 336–356.

Tate, S. (2023). *Sephora marketing strategy: 6 tactics to makeup a beauty empire.* Retrieved from https://coschedule.com/marketing-strategy/marketing-strategy-examples/sephora-marketing-strategy

Taylor, T. L. (2006). *Play between worlds: Exploring online game culture.* MIT Press. DOI: 10.7551/mitpress/5418.001.0001

Taylor, T. L. (2018). *Watch Me Play: Twitch and the Rise of Game Live-Streaming.* Princeton University Press.

Technavio. (2025). *In-Game Advertising (IGA) Market Analysis North America, APAC, Europe, Middle East and Africa, South America - US, Canada, China, Japan, Germany, India, UK, South Korea, France, Italy - Size and Forecast 2025-2029*. 10 Ağustos 2025 tarihinde https://www.technavio.com/report/in-game-advertising-market-industry-analysis adresinden alındı.

Telyakar, E. (2022). *Yaşam karmaşasının mobil oyun tercihlerine etkisi (The Effect of Life Complexity on Mobile Game Preferences).* Yüksek Lisans Tezi, Sosyal Bilimler Enstitüsü, Yıldız Teknik Üniversitesi.

Teng, C. I. (2021). How can avatar's item customizability impact gamer loyalty? *Telematics and Informatics*, *62*, 101626. Advance online publication. DOI: 10.1016/j.tele.2021.101626

Terlutter, R., & Capella, M. L. (2013). The gamification of advertising: Analysis and research directions of in-game advertising, advergames, and advertising in social network games. *Journal of Advertising*, *42*(2-3), 95–112.

Terlutter, R., & Capella, M. L. (2013). The Gamification of Advertising: Analysis and research Directions of In-Game advertising, Advergames, and advertising in social network games. *Journal of Advertising*, *42*(2–3), 95–112. DOI: 10.1080/00913367.2013.774610

Teskeredzic, E., Paric, M., Sestic, A., Fribert, P., Lukac, A., Hadzic, H., & Lacic, E. (2025, September). Vocalize: Lead Acquisition and User Engagement through Gamified Voice Competitions. In *Proceedings of the 2025 Adjunct Proceedings of the 36th ACM Conference on Hypertext and Social Media* (pp. 35-39).

Thaicharoen, S., Gow, J., & Drachen, A. (2023). An ecosystem framework for the meta in esport games. *Journal of Electronic Gaming and Esports*, *1*(1), 1–14.

Thaler, R. H., & Sunstein, C. R. (2008). *Nudge: Improving decisions about health, wealth, and happiness.* Yale University Press.

Tham, S., Rodgers, S., & Thorson, E. (2017). Trends and opportunities for digital advertising research. In Rodgers, S., & Thorson, E. (Eds.), *Digital Advertising* (pp. 31–44). DOI: 10.4324/9781315623252-3

The Coca-Cola Company. (2023, June 7). *Coca-Cola Ultimate Zero Sugar launches in collaboration with Riot Games' League of Legends* [Press release]. https://www.coca-colacompany.com/media-center/game-on-coca-cola-riot-games-team-up-ultimate-flavor-and-experiences

Theodoropoulos, A., & Antoniou, A. (2022). VR games in cultural heritage: A systematic review of the emerging fields of virtual reality and culture games. *Applied Sciences (Basel, Switzerland), 12*(17), 8476.

Think with Google. (2024a). *How physical stores can benefit from the surge in online*. Retrieved from https://www.thinkwithgoogle.com/future-of-marketing/digital-transformation/buying-online-new-normal/

Think with Google. (2024b). *Trends to inform your 5-year retail strategy*. Retrieved from https://www.thinkwithgoogle.com/intl/en-emea/consumer-insights/consumer-trends/five-year-retail-strategy-trends/

Thomas, D. (2005). Messages and mediums: Learning to teach with videogames. *On the Horizon, 13*(2), 89–94. DOI: 10.1108/10748120510608115

Thorson, E., & Duffy, M. (2012). *Advertising age: The principles of advertising and marketing communication at work*. Nelson Education Ltd., http://ndl.ethernet.edu.et/bitstream/123456789/49236/1/185.pdf

Tian, X. (2024). AI applications in video games and future expectations. *Applied and Computational Engineering, 54*(1), 161–170. DOI: 10.54254/2755-2721/54/20241484

Tleubayev, S. S.. (2017). The game as the essence of culture. *Revista Espacios, 38*(54), 29–41.

Tolunay, A., Alkan, H., & Korkmaz, M. (2004). *Kent ormanlarında rekreasyonel etkinlikler açısından ziyaretçi profilinin belirlenmesi (Determining Visitor Profile in Urban Forests in Terms of Recreational Activities). Türkiye Ormancılar Derneği*. I. Kent Ormancılığı Kongresi.

Topsakal, Y. (2020). Rekreasyon ve dijitalleşme (Recreation and Digitalization). In Y. Yağmur & Ü. Gaberli (Eds.), Rekreasyon: Tarihsel Gelişim, Teoriler, Farklı Alanlarla İlişkiler ve Güncel Gelişmeler (pp. 453-463). Ankara: Nobel Bilimsel Eserler.Torkildsen, G. (2005). Leisure and recreation management. London: Routledge, Taylor and Francis Group.

Tosun, N. (2020). *Marka yönetimi* (4. Baskı). İstanbul: Beta Yayıncılık.

Tosun, N. B. (2010). *İletişim temelli marka yönetimi (Communication-Based Brand Management).* Beta Yayınevi.

Tosun, N. B. (2010). *İletişim temelli marka yönetimi.* Beta Basım Yayım Dağıtım.

Trivedi, J. P., & Trivedi, H. (2018). Investigating the Factors That Make a Fashion App Successful: The Moderating Role of Personalization. *Journal of Internet Commerce, 17*(2), 170–187. DOI: 10.1080/15332861.2018.1433908

Trotter, M. G., Coulter, T. J., Davis, P. A., Poulus, D. R., & Polman, R. (2021). Social support, self-regulation, and psychological skill use in e-athletes. *Frontiers in Psychology, 12*, 722030. PMID: 34858261

Truong, V., Nkhoma, M., & Pansuwong, W. (2019). An Integrated Effectiveness Framework of Mobile In-App Advertising. *AJIS. Australasian Journal of Information Systems, 23*, 1–25. DOI: 10.3127/ajis.v23i0.1971

Turbine, D. (2025). Mobile App Habit Report | Digital Turbine. In *digitalturbine.com*. https://www.digitalturbine.com/insight/mobile-app-habit-report-2022

Türkmen, E., Akgül, B., & Durhan, T. (2024). Dijital okuryazarlığın sanal rekreasyon etkinliklerine katılım sıklığına ve rekreasyon faydaya etkisi. *Tourism and Recreation, 6*(1), 22–29. DOI: 10.53601/tourismandrecreation.1301883

Türksoy, N. (2022). The future of public relations, advertising and journalism: How artificial ıntelligence may transform the communication profession and why society should care? *Türkiye İletişim Araştırmaları Dergisi*, (40), 394–410. DOI: 10.17829/turcom.1050491

Türnüklü, D. A. (2000). Eğitimbilim Araştırmalarında Etkin Olarak Kullanılabilecek Nitel BirAraştırma Tekniği: Görüşme. *Kuram ve Uygulamada Eğitim Yönetimi, 24*(24), 543–559.

Turtiainen, R., Friman, U., & Ruotsalainen, M. (2020). "Not only for a celebration of competitive overwatch but also for national pride": Sportificating the Overwatch World Cup 2016. *Games and Culture, 15*(4), 351–371.

Tütüncü, Ö. (2012). Rekreasyon ve rekreasyon terapisinin yaşam kalitesindeki rolü (The Role of Recreation and Recreation Therapy on Life Quality). Anatolia. *Turizm Araştırmaları Dergisi, 23*(2), 248–252.

Tuyan, B. (2005). İnternette Reklam (Internet Advertising). Retrieved from: https://www.chip.com.tr/haber/internette-reklam_1365.html

Ufford, L. (2023). *6 Examples of retail gamification to boost engagement and sales*. Retrieved from https://www.shopify.com/in/retail/6-examples-of-retail-gamification-to-boost-engagement-and-sales

Uncu, G. (2024). Fijitalizm & metaverse evreninde, markaların pazarlama faaliyetleri (Marketing Activities of Brands in the Fijitalism & Metaverse Universe). *Akademik Sosyal Araştırmalar Dergisi*, *12*(153), 50–70.

UNXD. (2020). *UNXD: Digital Luxury & Culture NFTs*. Unxd.Com. https://unxd.com/drops/collezione-genesi

Uslu, E. G., & Kazaz, A. (2022). The reflection of the concept of consumption on the silver screen: Product placement in cinema, the example of the film *The Island*. In Kazaz, A. (Ed.), *New forms of consumption in the context of the individual, society, and digitalization* (p. 66). Education Publishing House.

Valin, J., & Gregory, A. (2020). Ethics Guide to Artificial Intelligence in PR. Chartered Institute of Public Relations, https://cipr.co.uk/common/Uploaded%20files/Policy/AI/AIinPR_Ethics_Guide_UK.pdf

Valkenburg, P. M., & Piotrowski, J. T. (2017). Digital games. In *Plugged In: How Media Attract and Affect Youth* (pp. 201–223). Yale University Press., DOI: 10.12987/yale/9780300218879.003.0012

van Berlo, Z. M., & Chen, X. (2024). Advergames and consumer brand engagement: Experiential satisfaction as a mediator of gamified advertising effects. *Journal of Interactive Advertising*, *24*(3), 238–246. DOI: 10.1080/15252019.2024.2335398

van Berlo, Z., Reijmersdal, E., & Eisend, M. (2021). The gamification of branded content: A meta-analysis of advergame effects. *Journal of Advertising*, *50*(2), 179–196. DOI: 10.1080/00913367.2020.1858462

Van Reijmersdal, E. A., Rozendaal, E., & Buijzen, M. (2012). Effects of prominence, involvement, and persuasion knowledge on children's cognitive and affective responses to advergames. *Journal of Interactive Marketing*, *26*(1), 33–42. DOI: 10.1016/j.intmar.2011.04.005

Van Rooij, A. J., Meerkerk, G.-J., Schoenmakers, T. M., Griffiths, M., & van de Mheen, D. (2010). Video game addiction and social responsibility. *Addiction Research and Theory*, *18*(5), 489–493. DOI: 10.3109/16066350903168579

Vanderhoef, J. (2013). Casual threats: The feminization of casual video games. *Ada: A Journal of Gender. New Media, and Technology*, *2*(2), 1–28.

Vargo, S. L., & Lusch, R. F. (2017). Service-dominant logic 2025. *International Journal of Research in Marketing*, *34*(1), 46–67.

Vashisht, D., & Chauhan, A. (2017). Effect of game-interactivity and congruence on presence and brand attitude. *Marketing Intelligence & Planning*, *35*(6), 789–804. DOI: 10.1108/MIP-01-2017-0018

Vatsal, R., Mishra, S., Thareja, R., Chakrabarty, M., Sharma, O., & Shukla, J. (2023). (*An Analysis of Physiological and Psychological Responses in Virtual Reality and Flat Screen Gaming*). Communication and Media.

Viant Technology, L. L. C. (2025, March 3). *Why in-game advertising is a game-changer for digital marketing*. Viant. https://www.viantinc.com/insights/blog/in-game-advertising-brand-engagement/

Vox Media. (2025). *This influencer wanted to revamp her skincare routine and discovered the easiest way to do it at Sephora*. Retrieved from https://www.popsugar.com/beauty/sephora-skincare-routine-builder-quiz-first-experience-47643071

Vural, İ., & Öz, M. (2007). "Bir Reklam Mecrası Olarak İnternet" (Internet as a Medium of Advertising) [Journal of Erciyes University Institute of Social Sciences]. *Erciyes Üniversitesi Sosyal Bilimler Enstitüsü Dergisi*, *23*(2), 221–240.

Vyndo. (2025). *Sephora*. Retrieved from https://en.vyndo.io/projects/sephora

Wagner, M. G. (2006, June). On the scientific relevance of eSports. In *International conference on internet computing* (Vol. 6, pp. 437-442).

Wang, C. L. (2021). New frontiers and future directions in interactive marketing: Inaugural Editorial. *Journal of Research in Interactive Marketing*, *15*(1), 1–9. Advance online publication. DOI: 10.1108/JRIM-03-2021-270

Wang, H., & Kosinski, M. (2018). Deep neural networks are more accurate than humans at detecting sexual orientation from facial images. *Journal of Personality and Social Psychology*, *114*(2), 246–257. DOI: 10.1037/pspa0000098 PMID: 29389215

Wang, S. S., & Chou, H. Y. (2019). Effects of Game-Product Congruity on İn-App Interstitial Advertising and the Moderation of Media-Context Factors. *Psychology and Marketing*, *36*(3), 229–246. DOI: 10.1002/mar.21174

Wang, X. (2020). Screening soft information: Evidence from loan officers. *The RAND Journal of Economics*, *51*(4), 1287–1322. DOI: 10.1111/1756-2171.12357

Wang, Y., Su, Z., Zhang, N., Xing, R., Liu, D., Luan, T. H., & Shen, X. (2023). A Survey on Metaverse: Fundamentals, Security, and Privacy. *IEEE Communications Surveys and Tutorials*, *25*(1), 319–352. DOI: 10.1109/COMST.2022.3202047

Watson, M., Smith, D., & Fenton, J. (2022). Introducing esports coaching to sport coaching (not as sport coaching). *Sports Coaching Review*, *14*(1), 1–20.

Watt, T., & Lester, A. (2025), *Phygital service excellence: Reimagining service to create differentiated industry experiences*. Retrieved from https://www.pwc.com/us/en/technology/alliances/salesforce/generative-ai/phygital-service-excellence.html

Waydel-Bendyk, M. (2020). Evaluating Potential of Gamification to Facilitate Sustainable Fashion Consumption. In *Lecture Notes in Computer Science (including subseries Lecture Notes in Artificial Intelligence and Lecture Notes in Bioinformatics): Vol. 12204 LNCS* (pp. 205–215). Springer. DOI: 10.1007/978-3-030-50341-3_16

Wechsler, K., Bickmann, P., Rudolf, K., Tholl, C., Froböse, I., & Grieben, C. (2021). Comparison of multiple object-tracking performance between professional and amateur esports players as well as traditional sportsmen. *International Journal of eSports Research*, *1*(1), 1–17.

Wedel, M., Bigné, E., & Zhang, J. (2020). Virtual and augmented reality: Advancing research in consumer marketing. *International Journal of Research in Marketing*, *37*(3), 443–465. DOI: 10.1016/j.ijresmar.2020.04.004

Wei, R. (2007). Effects of playing violent videogames on Chinese adolescents' pro-violence attitudes, attitudes toward others, and aggressive behavior. *Cyberpsychology & Behavior*, *10*(3), 371–380. DOI: 10.1089/cpb.2006.9942 PMID: 17594261

Welden, R., Hewett, K., Yoo, K., Haenlein, M., Smith, K. M., Pauwels, K., & Hulland, J. (2025). Leveling up retail: How retailers and brands thrive in the video game ecosystem. *Journal of Retailing*.

White, G. R. T., & Samuel, A. (2019). Programmatic Advertising: Forewarning and avoiding hype-cycle failure. *Technological Forecasting and Social Change*, *144*, 157–168. DOI: 10.1016/j.techfore.2019.03.020

Windholz, E. (2020). Governing esports: Public policy, regulation and the law. *Sports Law eJournal*, *1*(1).

Winkler, T., & Buckner, K. (2006). Receptiveness of gamers to embedded brand messages in advergames: Attitudes towards product placement. *Journal of Interactive Advertising*, *7*(1).

Witkowski, E., & Harkin, S. (2025). Esports under sports mega-event conventions: Associational values, inclusivity, and national representation at the Commonwealth Games. *Sport in Society*, *28*(3), 452–472.

Wittgenstein, L. (1953). *Philosophical investigations*. Blackwell Publishing.

Wohlgenannt, I., Simons, A., & Stieglitz, S. (2020). Virtual reality. *Business & Information Systems Engineering*, *62*(5), 455–461. DOI: 10.1007/s12599-020-00658-9

Wohn, D. Y., & Freeman, G. (2020). Live streaming, playing, and money spending behaviors in eSports. *Games and Culture*, *15*(1), 73–88.

Wolf, M. J. P. (2008). *The video game explosion: A history from PONG to PlayStation and beyond*. Bloomsbury Publishing USA.

Wongkitrungrueng, A., & Suprawan, L. (2024). Metaverse Meets Branding: Examining Consumer Responses to Immersive Brand Experiences. *International Journal of Human-Computer Interaction*, *40*(11), 2905–2924. DOI: 10.1080/10447318.2023.2175162

Worldwide Business Research. (2025). *Future stores: Building 'phygital' brand and in-store experiences*. Retrieved from https://etailasia.wbresearch.com/blog/future-stores-building-phygital-brand-and-in-store-experiences

Wu, J., & Holsapple, C. (2014). Imaginal and emotional experiences in pleasure-oriented IT usage: A hedonic consumption perspective. *Information & Management*, *51*(1), 80–92.

Wu, T. (2017). Pokémon Go: Marketing implications for mobile video game. In Tang, J., & Hung, P. (Eds.), *Computing in Smart Toys* (pp. 7–20). Springer Cham. DOI: 10.1007/978-3-319-62072-5_2

Xi, N., & Hamari, J. (2019). Does gamification satisfy needs? A study on the relationship between gamification features and intrinsic need satisfaction. *International Journal of Information Management*, *46*, 210–221. DOI: 10.1016/j.ijinfomgt.2018.12.002

Xu, H. (2025). Applications of artificial ıntelligence in advertising and marketing. *Journal of Fintech and Business Analysis*, *2*(1), 50–54. DOI: 10.54254/3049-5768/2025.21631

Xu, Q., Kim, H., & Billings, A. C. (2022). Let's watch live streaming: How streamer credibility influences brand attitude in esports streamer marketing. *Communication & Sport*, *10*(2), 271–290.

Yamamoto, G. T. (2009). Games, Internet, Advergames, and Mobile Games. *PI Marketing and Communication Culture Journal*, *8*(29), 17–22.

Yang, M., Roskos-Ewoldsen, D. R., Dinu, L., & Arpan, L. M. (2006). The effectiveness of "in-game" advertising: Comparing college students' explicit and implicit memory for brand names. *Journal of Advertising*, *35*(4), 143–152. DOI: 10.2753/JOA0091-3367350410

Yaoyuneyong, G., Foster, J., Johnson, E., & Johnson, D. (2016). Augmented Reality Marketing: Consumer Preferences and Attitudes Toward Hypermedia Print Ads. *Journal of Interactive Advertising*, *16*(1), 16–30. Advance online publication. DOI: 10.1080/15252019.2015.1125316

Yavuzyılmaz, O. (2017). Advertising Games – Advergames. *Academic Social Research Journal*, *5*(62), 588–601. DOI: 10.16992/ASOS.13224

Yee, N. (2006). Motivations for play in online games. *Cyberpsychology & Behavior*, *9*(6), 772–775. PMID: 17201605

Yee, N., Ducheneaut, N., & Nelson, L. (2012, May). Online gaming motivations scale: development and validation. In *Proceedings of the SIGCHI conference on human factors in computing systems* (pp. 2803-2806).

Yengin, D. (2012). *Dijital oyunlarda şiddet*. Beta Yayınları.

Yıldırım, A., & Şimşek, H. (2011). *Sosyal Bilimlerde Nitel Araştırma Yöntemleri*. Seçkin Yayıncılık.

Yıldız, S. Y., & Demir, D. (2023). Oyunlaştırmanın Satın Alma Davranışını Şekillendirmedeki Gücü. *Toplum Ekonomi ve Yönetim Dergisi*, *4*(2), 336–358. DOI: 10.58702/teyd.1350934

Yılmaz, E. A. (2015). *Oyunlaştırma*. Abaküs.

Yoo, S. C., & Eastin, M. S. (2017). Contextual advertising in games: Impacts of game context on a player's memory and evaluation of brands in video games. *Journal of Marketing Communications*, *23*(6), 614–631. DOI: 10.1080/13527266.2016.1155074

Yörük, E. (2024). *Reklamın yeni dünyaları*. İstanbul: Eğitim yayınevi.

Yu, Y. (2021). The role and influence of artificial intelligence on advertising industry. In *Proceedings of the 2021 International Conference on Social Development and Media Communication (SDMC 2021)* (ss. 190–194). Atlantis Press. DOI: 10.2991/assehr.k.220105.037

Yücel, E. (2023). "Pazarlamada Oyunlaştırma Uygulamaları: Türkiye ve Dünya'dan Oyunlaştırma Örnekleri". *İzmir Yönetim Dergisi*, 4(1), pp. 20-30. DOI: 10.56203/iyd.1267187

Yukic, T. S. (1970). *Fundamentals of recreation*. Harper & Row.

Zagni, L. M., & Pera, R. (2024). From immersion to invasion: a netnographic exploration of consumers' responses' to in-game advertising. In *NETNOCON 2024 conference proceedings*.

Zagni, L. M., Baima, G., Nguyen, L. D. X., & Do, B. (2025). Convergence and divergence in digital game-based advertising: A systematic review of advergames and in-game advertising. *Review of Managerial Science*. Advance online publication. https://link.springer.com/article/10.1007/s11846-025-00876-z

Zagni, L. M., Baima, G., Do, B., & Nguyen, L. D. X. (2025). Convergence and divergence in digital game-based advertising: A systematic review of advergames and in game advertising. *Review of Managerial Science*. Advance online publication. DOI: 10.1007/s11846-025-00876-z

Zendle, D., & Cairns, P. (2018). Video game loot boxes are linked to problem gambling: Results of a large-scale survey. *PLoS One*, *13*(11), e0206767. Advance online publication. DOI: 10.1371/journal.pone.0206767 PMID: 30462669

Zeren, D., & Keşlikli, İ. (2019). "Programatik Reklamcılık: Kavram, İşleyiş ve Potansiyeli Açısından Değerlendirmesi", Ç.Ü. *Sosyal Bilimler Enstitüsü Dergisi*, *28*(2), 312–326.

Zervas, K., & Maronitis, K. (2025). Digital bonds: A gamers' perspective on the role of online gaming communities in fostering social interaction and identity. *International Review for the Sociology of Sport*, 1-18.

Zhang, J., Zou, Y., Wang, S., & Xiang, Y. (2025). *Consumer experience and perception in gamification marketing: evidence from the user survey of POPMART*. Retrieved from https://www.frontiersin.org/journals/communication/articles/10.3389/fcomm.2025.1388020/full

Zhang, Y.-S., & Kim, Y.-J. (2023). Exploring the Potential of ChatGPT in Advertising Photography: A Case Study and Validity Research on Elements in Each Production Stage. The journal of the convergence on culture technology, 9(3), 205-211. DOI: 10.17703/JCCT.2023.9.3.205

Zhang, D., Frei, R., Wills, G., Gerding, E., Bayer, S., & Senyo, P. K. (2023). Strategies and practices to reduce the ecological impact of product returns: An environmental sustainability framework for multichannel retail. *Business Strategy and the Environment*, *32*(7), 4636–4661. DOI: 10.1002/bse.3385

Zhao, Y., Baghaei, N., Schnack, A., & Stemmet, L. (2021). Assessing Telepresence, Social Presence and Stress Response in a Virtual Reality Store. *2021 IEEE International Symposium on Mixed and Augmented Reality Adjunct (ISMAR-Adjunct)*, 52–56. DOI: 10.1109/ISMAR-Adjunct54149.2021.00020

Zhou, F., & Li, J. (2020). Current status and prospects of artificial intelligence application in game development. *China Management Informatization*, *23*, 183–185.

Zhu, M. (2025). *Store of the future.* Retrieved from https://www.ideo.com/works/sephora

Zofia, Z. (2023). *Fashion brands evolve NFC tag strategies to provide more value, exclusivity - Glossy*. Glossy.Co. https://www.glossy.co/fashion/why-implementing-nfc-tags-for-fashion-items-isnt-enough/

About the Contributors

M. Nur Erdem was born in 1976. She has been working as an Assoc. Prof. Dr. at Ondokuz Mayis University, Faculty of Communication, Department of Communication and Design since 2015. Erdem studies on digitalization of media and advertising. She has published papers in several journals, conference proceedings, chapters in edited books about digital media and advertising.

Cansu Mayadağlı was born in Samsun in 1988. She completed her master's degree in Media and Communication Management at the Institute of Social Sciences at Yeditepe University in 2018. She then completed her doctoral studies in the Department of Advertising and Promotion at Marmara University's Institute of Social Sciences. Since 2014, she has been working as a research assistant in the Public Relations and Promotion Department of the Faculty of Communication at Ondokuz Mayıs University. Her areas of expertise include brand management, advertising, and marketing management.

***

Meryem Aldağ completed her bachelor's degree in Public Relations and Advertising at the Faculty of Communication, Ondokuz Mayıs University in 2020. In 2021, she graduated from the Master's Program in Media and Communication Sciences at the Institute of Social Sciences at the same university. She concurrently serves as a Project Manager at Markakod Advertising Design and Software Services Agency. Her areas of interest and expertise include new media and digital marketing.

Zihni Can Çamur was born in Istanbul in 1989. He works at Abdi İbrahim Pharmaceuticals. He is pursuing a master's degree at the Department of Radio, Television, and Cinema at Ondokuz Mayıs University. His academic interests include media studies, film theory, and digital culture.

Burak Çeber was born in 1993. He received his bachelor's degree in 2016 from Kocaeli University, Department of Advertising, graduating as the top student of his class. During this period, he gained approximately two years of work experience in the digital media sector. He completed his master's degree in 2018 at Kocaeli University, Institute of Social Sciences, Department of Communication Design. In the same year, he started his academic career as a research assistant at Üsküdar University, Faculty of Communication, Department of Advertising. In 2018, he began his doctoral studies at Marmara University, Institute of Social Sciences, Department of Public Relations, and completed his PhD in 2022 with a dissertation titled "The Use of Artificial Intelligence Applications as a Tool in Public Relations." Dr. Çeber currently continues his academic duties as an Assistant Professor in the Department of Advertising at Üsküdar University, teaching both undergraduate and graduate courses. His research interests include new media technologies, digital advertising, artificial intelligence, and data ethics. He has published numerous national and international articles, conference papers, and book chapters in these areas. Additionally, he is the author of the book Artificial Intelligence and Public Relations and the editor of Artificial Intelligence Ethics and Communication.

Maryam El Oraiby is a Ph.D. candidate and research assistant in Business Administration at Kadir Has University, Istanbul, Türkiye. After she graduated from the School of Information Sciences in Rabat, Morocco, Maryam received a Master's degree in Information Technologies from Kadir Has University in 2016. Her research interest includes the intersection of marketing, data science, and society. She is particularly interested in the research areas of esports marketing and sustainability in marketing. Her published papers in international peer-reviewed Journals include International Journal of Sports Science and Coaching, Telecommunications Policy, Electronic Markets, and Organic Agriculture. Her commitment to positive social change underscores her dedication to making a meaningful societal impact through both theory and practice.

Esma Gökmen, graduated from Ankara Gazi University, Faculty of Communication, Department of Radio, TV and Cinema in 2006. She completed her master's degree at Gazi University, Faculty of Communication, Department of Radio, TV and Cinema between 2006-2008. Since 2016, She is a PhD candidate at Ankara Hacı Bayram Veli University, Faculty of Communication, Department of Radio, TV and Cinema. She worked as a lecturer at Giresun University between 2010-2012. Since 2012, she has been working as a lecturer at Ondokuz Mayıs University Samsun Vocational School. She studied Radio, TV and Cinema in high school, undergraduate, graduate and doctorate. For this reason, she has been working in this field since 1996. Her doctoral thesis is on everyday life and the construction of everyday life in local TV series. She also has a book chapter and published articles about cinema. At Samsun Vocational School, she teach many courses related to the field of communication and media. Photography was also included in her classes and she held exhibitions as part of this course. She continues her work related to cinema, television and media in general.

Biswa Prakash Jena is currently working as Assistant Professor at Alliance University. Dr. Jena has done his PhD from Birla School of Management of Birla Global University, Bhubaneswar. He completed his B. Tech from BPUT Odisha and MBA (HRM) at SOA University. He has also completed FDP (Advanced Certificate Programme in Academic Research and Data Analysis) from Indian Institute of Management Kozhikode. Before joining Alliance University, he worked in various academic and research positions at IIM Bangalore, GIM Goa and IIM Kozhikode. He also has industrial experience (worked at Accenture, Chennai). Prof. Jena has eight years of experience, and his research area is career management. He has published many ABDC and Scopus listed research articles.

Tuğçe Karaca Özdemir graduated from Ondokuz Mayıs University's Media and Communication Department, Vocational School, ranking first in her class. She then graduated from Ondokuz Mayıs University's Faculty of Communication, Department of Radio, Television, and Cinema with a bachelor's degree on January 31, 2022. In 2022, she began her master's degree in the Department of Communication Sciences (Interdisciplinary) at Ondokuz Mayıs University's Graduate Education Institute, and completed her master's degree in 2025 with her thesis titled "Construction of Artificial Intelligence Characters in Science Fiction Cinema." As of 2025, she is currently pursuing her doctorate at Ankara Hacı Bayram Veli University's Radio, Television, and Cinema Department.

Emel Karayel Bilbil completed her secondary education at Istanbul Haydarpaşa High School and obtained her undergraduate degree in Public Relations and Publicity from the Faculty of Communication at Marmara University. Upon graduation, she was appointed as a Research Assistant in the Department of Public Relations. She earned her master's degree in Public Relations at the Institute of Social Sciences, Marmara University. She subsequently pursued doctoral studies in the same field and was awarded a PhD after successfully defending her dissertation entitled "Brand Communication in Terms of Public Relations," under the supervision of Prof. Dr. Alaeddin Asna. Following the completion of her doctoral studies, she continued her academic career as an Assistant Professor at the Faculty of Communication, Marmara University. In 2009, she was awarded the academic title of Associate Professor in Applied Communication by the Interuniversity

Board (UAK). Since 2015, she has been holding the position of Professor in the Department of Public Relations and Publicity at Marmara University. Her scholarly work focuses on Brand and Corporate Communication, Brand Management, Ethics in Communication, Reputation Management, Non-Governmental Organizations, Digital Communication, and Digital Art.

Meltem Kiygi-Calli is an Associate Professor of Marketing at Kadir Has University, Istanbul, Türkiye. She graduated from Marmara University in 1999 with a BSc in Environmental Engineering. She received her MBA from Istanbul Technical University in 2001 and her Ph.D. in Marketing from the University of Antwerp, Belgium, in 2011. Her research particularly covers innovative contributions to advertising research, forecasting, and operations management through the application of hierarchical models to high-frequency data. Her work has been published in top-tier international journals, such as the Journal of Business Research, the International Journal of Research in Marketing, and the International Journal of Forecasting. She has also contributed to book chapters on various marketing-related topics, including corporate social responsibility in packaging considering environmental and social issues, published by Springer.

Tuğçe Şen graduated with honors from the Advertising Department of the Faculty of Communication at Istanbul Aydın University in 2017. Şen began her master's degree at the Department of Public Relations and Publicity at the Institute of Social Sciences at Istanbul Aydın University the same year and completed her master's degree with honors in 2019. She began her doctoral studies at the Department of Public Relations at the Institute of Social Sciences at Marmara University in 2021 and is currently continuing her studies. She currently works as a Research Assistant in the Department of Public Relations and Advertising at the Faculty of Communication at Istanbul Beykent University. Her research interests include public relations, digitalization, new media, consumer culture, brand management, and art.

Indu Sharma is currently working as Assistant Professor at Alliance University. Dr. Sharma received her Ph.D. in Consumer Behaviour from Alliance University, Bangalore. She holds the Executive PGP certification in Digital marketing & Analytics from IIM, and MBA in Marketing from Bangalore University. Dr. Sharma has a rich experience of about one and half decades across industry verticals with companies such as Infosys, Symphony Services, Information Research Incorporation, and British Petroleum in areas such as sales planning, vendor performance management, procurement & order management, business development, media planning, product launch, branding, and market research. Dr. Sharna has worked on various assignments with the Reserve Bank of India, Ministry of Corporate Affairs, Department of Income Tax and Central Board of Indirect Tax and Customs.

Sandeep Shede holds a Doctor of Philosophy (Ph.D.) in African Studies from University of Mumbai. He has a Master of Management Studies (MMS) - Marketing from University of Mumbai (2006) and a Bachelor of Engineering (BE) – Electronics from University of Mumbai (2002). He has also cleared UGC – NET in Management (2013) and Maharashtra SET in Management (2013). Dr. Shede has academic and industry experience of about 22 years. He has over 7 years of B2B Marketing experience in managing innovative advertising, gifting and loyalty products / services. He teaches Marketing, B2B Marketing and Digital Marketing. His core area of interest includes International Marketing, International Business and Strategic Management.

Neetu Singh, Symbiosis International (Deemed) University, Pune, India. The author is a PhD and professor of fashion business at Symbiosis Institute of Design. Her areas of interest are marketing and branding, supply chain, circular economy, retail, and sustainability studies in fashion. Her recent works include chapters on building sustainability in Textile & Apparel supply chains, Consumers' choice behavior towards sustainable fashion based on social media influence, and Circular Economy in Textile and Apparel Supply Chains

Fatma Şişli graduated from Istanbul Bilgi University, Faculty of Communication, Department of Advertising in 2010. In 2017, she completed her master's degree at Istanbul Commerce University, Faculty of Communication, Department of Advertising and Strategic Brand Communication, with her thesis titled "Orientalist and Re-Orientalist Discourse in Advertisements: The Case of Turkish Airlines and Coca-Cola." In 2023, she earned her Ph.D. from Marmara University, Faculty of Communication, Department of Advertising and Publicity, with her dissertation titled "The Reflection of Demarketing Strategy Usage in Advertisements on Consumers' Attitudes Toward Advertising." Şişli continues her academic research in the fields of advertising and branding.

Kıvanç Nazlım Tüzel Uraltaş After completing her undergraduate studies at Marmara University, Faculty of Communication, Department of Public Relations and Publicity, she began working at the same university as a research assistant in the Department of Advertising and Publicity. She earned both her master's and doctoral degrees from Marmara University, Institute of Social Sciences, in the Advertising and Publicity program, specializing in sales promotion directed toward consumers and intermediary businesses. Her research interests include marketing, advertising management, and consumer behavior. She is also involved in topics such as sales promotion, services marketing, electronic retailing, and digital advertising. In addition to her national and international articles published in various academic journals, she has authored numerous books, book chapters, and conference papers. She currently continues her academic career as a faculty member in the Department of Advertising and Publicity at Marmara University, Faculty of Communication.

Yelda Ülker graduated from the Department of Advertising at the Faculty of Communication, Istanbul Bilgi University, in 2010. In 2015, she completed her master's degree in the Department of Advertising and Publicity at Marmara University with her thesis titled "Effect of using masculine image, which reflects attractive and cultural codes on tv commercials whose target audience is women, on brand attitude." She received her Ph.D. degree in 2020 from the Department of Communication at the same university with her dissertation titled "Reflection of store image on icon brand." During her master's and doctoral studies, she worked as a research assistant at Marmara University Faculty of Communication. In 2022, she was awarded the title of Associate Professor in the field of Advertising. In the same year, she joined the Department of Advertising at the Faculty of Economics, Administrative and Social Sciences, Istanbul Gelişim University, where she continues to work. At the undergraduate level, she teaches courses such as Advertising Management, Current Issues in Advertising, Graphic Production in Advertising, and Advertising and Ethics.

Şükrü Yanmaz is a researcher in Communication Sciences. He is studying on artificial intelligence in public relations, marketing and advertising.

Index

A

B

C

D

E

G

www.ingramcontent.com/pod-product-compliance
Lightning Source LLC
LaVergne TN
LVHW080906300926
849162LV00003B/579